Of Dusk and Dawn

The Beautiful Truth
by Ullie Kowcun

First and foremost, to God for allowing me to experience His mercy in my pain - for what are we, if we cannot find beauty in it? To my husband and children who gave me the space and time to write and who nodded and smiled at my poetic ramblings, even when they didn't understand. To all of you, my readers, who believed I had something to say and would say it well. Thank you.

i fumble around for familiarity
feeling the fissures and grooves of fabrics
that have woven their patterns
stiffly around me
but my hands know them still by heart
because i've been here once or twice before
and like a film that's wrapped itself up
into the cuffs of my sleeves
this time i already know the ending
how it all plays out
the dragon is defeated
the music plays
and the girl falls in love
with the night

please understand
that light and darkness
will always exist
sometimes
you will radiate
even from your very pores
like sun seducing the horizon
and sometimes
you will hunt madly
for just a glimmer
yet find yourself
immersed in utter dusk

one day you will realize
that some people were meant for hurt.
they were made for it like salt to the ocean.
you will cry one thousand tears
and only half a dozen will be yours.

how is it
that you knew the flaws
and brokenness
that bruised and scarred me so
and yet
never hesitated
to whisper healing
without minimizing
my journey

even the skies
endure
the darkness
but enlist the stars
to make it beautiful

what's on my mind?
an open field
the bleeding sun
trees endlessly cloned
interrupted only
by an untrodden path
the sea shaking its fists
against the silent sands
mountains that tell me
it's better to have tried and failed
than never to have climbed at all
winds that gently toss my hair
and those that change
everything

you are a puzzle
but not of displaced
words or images
each piece stands
alone
fragility
purpose
masonry
autumn leaves

you
my dear are this
even at every corner
that's claimed and bruised
your skin
palms skyward
your lyrics written into poetry
memorised enough times
to believe it
a house
containing all the remnants
but with the porch light
on

tell me how the water
could have overtaken you
but in mercy
washed you instead

they say that
joy and sorrow sleep
strange lovers on your bed
two bodies curled up
side by side
like smoke
inside your head

all you ever wanted
was to be the sun
at her window
and the very first and last
face she saw
and when the clouds
got too full to hold water
you'd stand over her and
nothing
could put your hands
back in your pockets

she stands there
like an unanswered question
a girl whose words need chapstick
is never quite
enough

her hair grazed her neck
just barely
she was awkward
and clumsy
and had enough quirks
to fill the pages of a book
but she was thunder
when she fought
for the broken
and a steady storm
beside their shoulders

if love were
even remotely close
to being anything at all
about deserving
every one of us would be
unworthy

and here we are again
at the corner
of chesterfield and freedom
one firefly away
from light
and
one streetlight away
from darkness

i want to be
the hand
that takes you back
to your
oasis

you are a vessel
that bends itself around others
wanting dearly
to light your cigarette
and put it out
in the same breath

fix your gaze on that
which turns your head
the stars in the skies
the downtrodden's demise
the wanderer's sighs

your eyes set with the sun
and i waited desperately
for another sunrise.

don't let them tell you
that your tears mean
you are not brave
cry your little heart out
that's how the healing
comes

grace finds you
in between the sheets
at a rundown motel
where you never intended
to rent space

wake up beautiful one.
all the hills and rains
from yesterday
are gone.
daylight awaits and says,
"let's start again".

laundry room confessions:
i'm not here to fold clothes;
the quiet persistent hum
helps me forget.

let's just be clouds
that sit here in
silence for once
absorbing the rays
and the rage
until it is time
to pour

are we all just
misguided sunbeams
waiting for
refraction?

even untruths
nestled perfectly
into the curvature of your spoon
at that pivotal moment
when your soul is depleted
and desperate to be fed -
taste amazing

sometimes loneliness
is not a state of being
but a place
at which you arrive
and sit wondering
how you got there

i've collected a lot of hurt
over the years
but i've also saved up
all of the good things
the kinds of things
that aren't crafted by human hands
that's what gets me through

everyone knew when she walked into the room
but not because she thought she was something
she just had this way of making everyone else
feel like they were
everything

perhaps we were
two broken souls
waiting to catch
the right train
home

if you could trade all your pain in
rewind
undo
turn back the time
and make it disappear
would you
(be as strong as you are)

i live in the tiny subdivision
between
wanting something
and
believing in myself enough
to do it

you are safe here
your tears
your sorrows
your pain
but we don't need to
talk about the things
that haunt you
we can sit in
silence
or contemplate
beautiful things
together

how many storms does it take
to pursue stiller waters
the floods you have endured
overwhelm you with every sunrise and sunset
they crash onto your skin like it was only yesterday
each time taking back another piece of you
that you can't retrieve
your past holds you
not in cradling arms but with clenched fists
good child
you were not created to relive your storm
it was only meant to be
your secret passageway
to hope

oh words
what power you have
to move mountains and carry me through
deepest seas
but sometimes you become
an uncomfortable chair
you twist and turn ugly and jagged
you settle like ashes
underneath all the layers
constantly at the mercy
of being stirred up
even by the gentlest wind

i'll carry your scars
and your sighs
if you'll let me

strip down the outer shell
to the core
and we are all just humans
deeply flawed
yet intricately beautiful
searching for light

somewhere amongst these particles
of dust
these dunes of memories and silence
somewhere deep inside the caverns
of broken dreams
and unfulfilled prophecies
suitcases packed for coming and going
overfilled with misunderstandings
listen
your heart still beats
full and capable of the universe
embrace it my love
you were meant to
live

all these things
the mysteries that haunted us
the pleading against brick walls
and stagnant waters
and the whys
oh the endless whys
they did not fall on deaf ears
after all

running on empty
tires spinning without reprieve
mud splashing recklessly
into the eyes and hearts
of innocent bystanders
don't pour yourself so deeply
that you have nothing left
to give

do we not all stagger a little
in the drunkenness
of our own madness
and crave the same pieces of love
to fill our vacancies?
do we not all come undone
in the throes of weakness
and pray for the same
mercy
to save us?

the greatest tragedy of all
lies within those
who begin to die
while they are yet
living.

hope doesn't always
mend your wings,
sometimes it just
gives you the courage
to fly
half —broken

i'm not a healer
but if i were,
i'd wrap myself
around your wounds
and choreograph
a different
ending.

you're never fractured
beyond repair
sometimes pain just becomes
so familiar
that you forget
how you existed
before it all began

do not tell me that
i wasn't
enough
i took winter
from your eyes
even if it was
just for a season

i guess what it all comes down to
is how we lived despite our aching
and how we loved despite adversity

loneliness has absolutely nothing to do
with numbers
but absolutely everything to do
with the fraction of your heart
that no one is able to touch

life is a concoction
of curveballs and honey
seas without oars
and elixirs of serendipity
strong attempts that end in failure
and frail attempts
that show up at your doorstep
like a garden
love that tries to hang on with broken limbs
and love that comes barrelling in like a train
a seesaw of trying to remember
and begging your head to leave you alone
you will long for your backyard
and lust for the city
words will coil up in your bones
and make their home like an intruder
they will seduce you with wine
and heal you with wisdom
you will bleed a thousand times
on the inside
on the outside
you will break -
but you will mend

don't be afraid to cry
even the oceans wash away
their sadness

there is no glory
in walking with the broken
no applause
for taking a fragment
of their pain upon yourself
there is only wonder
at the grace we all receive
under the same big sky

maybe you can
against the cards you hold cautiously in your hands
shaking furiously like a fist that clenches
and wants to unravel at the same time
your mind a malfunctioning machine
operating on hesitation and what ifs
maybe you can drown in sadness
and feel resurrected at the same time
that moment where roads intersect
like a highway with too many off ramps
free to choose but imprisoned by the fear
to leap -
maybe you can

what about forgiveness
what about a love that runs so deep
it puts oceans to shame

it wasn't the sort of aching
that broke you apart
into a million pieces
but a steady pressing on every limb
that slowly brought you
to consciousness of its rhythm
completing and tethering
everything you already knew

how is it that you knew the flaws
and brokenness
that bruised and scarred me so
and yet never hesitated
to offer healing
without minimising
my journey

even the skies endure the darkness
but enlist the stars
to make it beautiful

you don't need to be complete
embrace your flaws
your brokenness
and the canvas that has
only barely begun
to be painted with colour

close your eyes
listen hard
and i will tell you this
you and i
we're not as different
as the world makes us
out to be

where do you go
when your own body
puts up an eviction notice

i think we're all just a little afraid
that we'll go through this life
unnoticed
unfought for
we want desperately
for touch to become hands
that won't let go
and songs that bring someone back
to dancing with you in the kitchen
we were all taught as children
that a tangled kite climbed for
meant it was worth
the risk
we see sunrises and sunsets
and claim the stars
but what does it all mean
when we're sitting in the living room alone
watching the 6 o'clock news
and dreaming about the liquor store
if a tree falls in the forest
do our words still exist?

when did walking swiftly
stir to life the dead inside your eyes
how is it
that suits and heels
elaborate meals
anything that feels
good
carries you over a mountain of yearning
does it?
your brisk hellos
and faint goodbyes
the rhythmic way you
wake up to the numbers
prearranged beside your bed
every morning
every
single
morning
you live enclosed by
the four walls of your
church downtown
buy another round
forgetting the sound
of children's voices
the rain on the hill
gasping for breath at a blood red sky
stop
unfasten the clothes that give you
relevance
you are still human underneath
you've only just
forgotten

a thousand times
we've come undone
at the seams
at the edges
perforated and punctured
until we were deflated
air withheld and longed for
our own thoughts
yielding inquisitions
that's what a broken spirit does
it subtracts the ounce of courage
from the little that remains
go strong then
do not let them bury you
beneath your own skin
the sailor's masts await you

i was an archway bent backward
to let you catch the light
but more than that
i did not run from all your darkness
and why should i
i have my darkness too

what is freedom if you are
bound from within?

wayward and distraught
in vacant fields
unwelcome amongst
the wildflowers at your feet
what do you seek here
light bends to find you
even where your restless heart
wanders

i walked a pathway strewn with jewels
and i knew you had left your tears
for me to follow

i pound my ribs every morning
to the rhythm of the birds
at my window
scurry now
flee far
fly and find your freedom
but alas they are already free
yet they will come
to perch again
and i'm afraid their refrain sings
stand up
embrace the world
make your peace
but do they know the parts of me
frayed beyond recognition
the words that hunch isolated
in my memory
and serve me breakfast
in bed

i couldn't dismantle her chaos
all at once
so i tried to collect pieces
of her thoughts
the ones that had entangled
her for as long as she could remember
my fingers traced over them
like pebbles and shells derived
from the sea
she was the sea
wild and untameable disguised as
peace
troubled waters dismembered from
glory

a poet thanks their lucky stars
for pain
how else would their words
bleed upon the page?

know what's catastrophic?
waiting your entire life
to realise
you've been
waiting
your
entire
life

for every perfect sonnet
there is someone who is
barely holding on.

if you are asking yourself
if there is more than this
to life,
then chances are,
there is.
search on.
listen hard.
love deep.

and for now
goodnight
may the darkness whisper
only beauty
into your mind

you wear your synthetic cloak
like a shield
that balances fear
against rage
i wish you knew
however
you are not
impermeable

your mind hovers between
brilliance and chaos
the convoluted state
of neither here nor there
the permanence of a
gypsy soul
is this the mess they
speak of?

every day
i wonder at the hands i see
have they folded into each other
skyward
pleading for mercy
have they traced the incapable back roads
that lead to another abrupt ending
numb is a four letter word for heartbreak
turned inside out
a slash that burrows deep
beneath the skin
and begs for surrender
but those same hands
they weave silver
to another's mourning
and paint curiosity like a sunset
unwilling to turn itself
to dusk

i shouldn't have said
don't cry
i should have said
cry
and i will catch your tears

do not tread lightly
on these thorns that encircle you
endure their infliction
feel them prick your tongue
and swim through your bloodstream
they are the makings of a deep
unhindered love

ominous skies
gave way to a storm
that seeped with the tides
through his skin
so swiftly to drench
without pardon it poured
to the clamorous clots
deep within

underneath my clothes
this ribcage holds the fledgling
fighting to be free

it must be exhausting to synchronise
yourself with the pages of a magazine
hunger that sits on your tongue
and waits for the dryer to stop beating
your clothes
the subliminal way your collarbones
are becoming dark comedy
(i'm not laughing)
but neither are you
you are climbing a peakless mountain
with paper limbs
every accomplishment a failure
and every smile a weeping willow
are you thirsty yet
don't you want to take the first cab
back home -
where is home?

i'll give you the benefit of the doubt
you ache
and for every tragedy that has
compiled the map of who you have become
the layers of stone that wrap around
your thighs like anger
for all the times you excused yourself
from the room so that no one could
chase the mascara
running madly down your cheekbones
and when your lips grew shards of glass
to cuss and curdle at the world
you quietly called yourself a coward
i know

let's face it
we're all getting old
grey skies and silver horses
and a myriad of colours that smudge reality
every day we look for lies in the mirror
and truths on our bed sheets
street art vandalised by our own disguises
our liquor laden lips and makeup masterpieces
hidden from the camera
why?
because we're letting ourselves die
before it is time to go

she is biting stale air with her teeth
as though it is all she deserves
(she is wrong)

i am a fossil of what i once was
and what i have become;
beauty and scars
embedded.

why all this drunkenness
on tasteless wine
sipping money
with your emaciated mouths
and stumbling in madness
at things that dissolve
unsweetly into smoke
who stole the light from your eyes
that satiated smile like art
in a gallery of
empty gasoline cans
the days gnaw away
at everything you thought
you'd be
what were your dreams?
you had them
once

i will swallow your sadness
whole.

which parts of you did you untie
to give you wings
with which to fly?

i found you at just the right time
a perfect incongruence that somehow just worked
we didn't know then of all the deep wells and black holes
we would wander
sometimes i led the way and you were frightened
of the places we'd go
but when we came to the ocean you knew my fear of the tides
so without hesitation you carried me through
that's what giving does
no measuring sticks
no tally marks

you don't need permission
to swim against the current
converse in your neologistical way
with words that
stand for
stand against
or just stand alone
hike up your dress and run through
muddy waters
fierce storms
fields of grain
slouch rebelliously in your ripped jeans and sip tea
rage while you crumble and smile while you cry
dream of parallel universes and a place where only the sky tells time
you don't need permission to love with broken arms and cracked ribs
be the antithesis of yourself
because the more you let yourself be
the more you let yourself wander
into the diverse and beautiful lives
of strangers -
who don't need your permission...

a firefly captured
is light contained
and what good is that?

these trees with their crooked spines
ever reaching upward towards light
even in their dying
lending breath -
remind me of you

the troubled sea
with its rhapsodic curse
to feel so deeply
both pain and pleasure

run with limbs untied
to mend the
broken-hearted.

if i could drum up some
imaginary universe
with lilac walls
and horizontal paintings
that lure the eyes
if i could deflect the slivers and cracks
that pierce my body
and tell riddles of pain
that never quite washed away
i would still choose
to live
to feel
with imperfection and brokenness
the life laid out for me

the empty bottle
only makes you forget
for a little while.

she made her own waves
and stayed there to play
until dusk mistook pleasure
for drowning

sometimes beauty and sadness
are strange bedfellows
lovers caught in a labyrinth of
holding on
and
letting go

the four walls around me
were a headache
pounding from every side
memories that made poison
taste like crème brûlée
and thoughts that made glass
go down like whiskey
i was a car broken down
at the side of the road
with passersby that
never
once
stopped
to reel me back in
but it found me
with my teeth clenched
and my hope anorexic
that's the thing about grace

i remember the first time it rained
not the soft drizzly sort of rain
but the kind that makes itself known
by pounding rhythmically
in your chest
not enough to undo you completely
but just enough to make you
aware that it's not subsiding
any time soon

we all end up feeling powerless
and put to shame
at believing for one minute
that life is anything
but a series of twists and turns
that flow softly
at the nape of our necks
and billow wildly through the hollows
of our eyes
to have us laugh carelessly
one moment
and weep tragedy into our bed frames
the very next

from the first gasp
that escaped your lips
to the rolling sea
that scattered you to rest
and all the skies in between
that pulled you
in and out of your bed
the thing we`ve named life
the enormous world
we thought was everything
our hands raised
our tears buried
our laughter caught
our bridges burned
this
was just one single drop
of the ocean yet to come

we are merely souls
dragging around the bodies
that have attached themselves to us
as though they are more than just
our temporary shells

don`t listen to the foolishness
of a world that says
strength begins at the resolve
of tears.

summer never left you,
you just never let it
set you aglow.

i catch stars
like i catch the rain
with my arms open
dysmorphic but strong
and i could find
a thousand reasons
not to
and a thousand more
to reach up
and take the darkness
and dissolve it with light
so i will shovel beauty
down onto your tongue
until you can taste it

perhaps your dark
wasn't dark after all
but a light so dazzling
that you fell to blindness
rather than
letting it carry you through

you walk about
your eyes heavy with
layers of cement
and at 8
you already resemble the soul
of an adult
tears sit seat-belted in
right below the surface
scratching at your throat
to free them
you won`t -
you won`t talk either
because your words are foreign
even to yourself
what is this valley that has you
rocking rhythmically
to silence the pain
who dismantled your
sweet soft soul
and made it asphalt
who?

and none of it mattered
the daggers we threw at ourselves
the beautiful archways we lit up with lanterns
they were as fleeting as the sunset
gone with our exhaling

and more than anything,
i just wanted to know why.
why your voice
had to break me each morning
through the telephone.
and how,
with its barely audible sighs,
it still managed
to sound like screams for help.

i cannot make you happy
that is not within my grasp
and i will never promise
to erase the things in your past
that injured and devoured your heart
to the point where you did not know
if it would ever be unbroken again
i am not your saviour
and i cannot protect you from this world
but when your tears rupture like ink
and your eyes hollow out
like tunnels that do not end
you have to know
i will not hesitate to find my fastest ships
not to save you
but to bring you to me
so that we can gather and hold
your sadness
together

you were never supposed to have it all
you were kind
and loved wildly into everything and everyone
but something broke you
you split open at the seams
and no one was going to thread you back together
instead you wanted it to hurt
you wanted to feel the whiskey burn
vindictively down your throat
and taunted the smoke to evacuate
life from your eyes
but what you are looking for
it is not here
it never was
because you were never supposed to have it all

you will not find me here
in the ashes
where you left me
darkness is fleeting
i made it so

you came carrying a teacup
like i couldn't fill it with the
sea inside of me.

haven't we all missed the mark
just a little
letting loose our canons to the dark
in fierce fight
white caned sight
misguided flight
finding there is no warmth
in the hunt for pain
no pasture
in the claws of clambering men
deep in the canyons of souls
years of pressure
buried and weighted
do not erupt with the sea
that has festered with anger and storm
waves can both injure and carry

i won`t stop
to fill the car with gasoline
and drive you back to the beginning
i`d rather drive you
mad with intention
mad with a streak
of high spirited stubbornness
mad with a sunrise
that refuses to be blotted out
and reduced to a makeshift light
either way
you won't
go tonight
fuel prices are crazy
anyways

and when i feared you knew
too much of my scars,
i grew cliffs
so that you could not
reach me.

"how much land
with this rundown
shell of a house?"
"acres",
she said.

there were clouds and streaks of light,
heartache and hope
like bombs with gloves and ropes;
a showdown of love and loss.

and if we had just
a morsel of time
to conjure up
with our last breath
would we weep out
our painful verses
or in sacredness
make love
to every burning sky
and flickering ember

and even if i leave here
by the skin of my teeth
having spilled my guts
of a thousand words
i hope you will have found me
just a little more than
ordinary

on the table
where yesterday's dishes
still sit like a ghost town
forgotten
is that how you feel?

come with me
i`ll take you to a place
where we can build an ocean
of all the tears
you couldn't cry

i wonder at the heart
that was born
already broken.

she had a beast of a heart
that couldn`t be slain.

scars
beautiful scars
do not disguise
the battle wounds
that have been scratched
onto the skin of your mind
they are not your crucifixion
they are what make you
magnificently
human

sometimes bravery is not defined by
arms and pledges raised in fight and fury
but a still soft voice that whispers,
"carry on".

were we only to walk
bodies tucked inward
or cast to the side
and all that was palpable
with the human heart
was a beauty so raw
that souls need not their eyes
to see

i am a victim
my abuser stands
exactly
eye to eye with me
blue on blue
five foot four
cruel words
and spiralling threats
i`m told i`m not enough
you ask me why i stay
it's because the one
who injures me
`tis i

come softly close
for i am still jagged
at the edges.

you`ve carried a lot
and i keep thinking of all the times you bruised alone
and said you were ok
you don't want to cry
because you are afraid you`ll wash away
the parts of yourself
that have made a home under your skin
and in your skull
i don't want to undo any of who you are
i don`t
but i see you slipping on the very petals
i scattered for you as a path
i want to scream sweetly at you
i`m here
and i`m not going away

if only you knew
of the city inside me
skyscrapers
subways
taxi cabs
and streetlights
that twist about
yet make perfect sense
of each other
but all i leave visible
to your naked eye
is this
my flesh
my oddity

the things that injured you most
the ones that caused you to curl up
on the side of your bed
and weep without tears
into the crevices of your pillow
secrets and ghosts that made you
heavy and undeserving of the sunrise
and became thieves
of everything and everyone you once loved
this is enough
you are not damaged
you are absolutely and beautifully
imperfect
so maybe if we sat down somewhere quiet
and exchanged our broken parts
with each other
we`d find the pieces that fit

i was never lost,
i was just carving my own path.

give her troubled waters
and she will dance in their rhythm
over and under the curves
a concoction of sea and air
in argumentative conversation
laughing at the currents that attempt
to halt her flight
she breathes in freedom
and exhales the rain
should we even wonder
at how she soars?
she sees with different eyes
that's all

perhaps we`re doing it all wrong
lusting after things
that only steal our oxygen
for minutes at a time

"don't leave",
she said,
her eyes burning with salt.
"oh,
i`m not leaving,
sweetheart,
just making my home
in the constellations".

why do we keep telling people
that they are strong
for smiling through it
some of the greatest
soldiers i know
have dropped to their knees
and wept

we built something
her and i
the strangest thing of all
out of deep wells
of sadness
we built laughter
and it became
our mainstay

panic in the street
that sits on my tongue
bullets lodged in my throat
menacing my swallow reflex
like a bully on the playground
my chest is anchored with ropes
that could hold down a ship
it's 7 a.m.
good morning

i wasn't running away from you,
i was running towards
myself.

i find myself praying
into the laundry basket
more often than i can count,
my hands running across
the seams of your shirt;
wondering if you`ll be
ok.

so you feel small against
your world of troubles
come lay yourself down
for awhile
under the archway
of a night sky
those billions of lights
the colossal ceremonies
that flicker and burn
you are greater -
much greater
than all of this

you said i was too soft
as though it was something
i could trade in.
truth is,
my feathers are
the part of me
i love the most;
they let me fly.

her mind was hauntingly beautiful
and dripping with melancholy
and perhaps i thought
i could love away
all the sadness

when you found me
i had mayhem running
from the tips and spines
of my branches
down to the very roots of me
you had this magical way
of weeding through my mind
without taking away from
the wilderness that grew
heartbeats inside of me

i am a lot of things
but i am not alone
maybe a little lost
and a little broken
and a little dishevelled
but not alone

once in a blue moon it sinks in
blessings travel in disguises
and come hell or high water
i should be grateful
life`s not a piece of cake
but we carry chips on our shoulders
like luggage
and rage at the drop of a hat
whoever said `consider the lilies...
hit the nail on the head
so i'll cut to the chase
a bird in the hand is worth two in the bush
and while we`re sitting here crying over spilt milk
calling the kettle black
and worrying more about giving everyone else
a taste of their own medicine
we need to remember that the day will come
when we have to pay the piper
so i'll stop adding fuel to the fire
when you decide
if your cup is half full
or half empty

these days are strange
i can't describe them
any other way
fermented chesterfields
that bake in the sun
and i amongst
the concoction
brewing
waiting
and hoping
something
will come of all this

i will whittle you a box
out of stone
where your heart will be safe
from all the words
you've been told
and every day
as i lay it over the scars
on your hands
i will say
you are loved
you are worthy

i am almost certain
it is not breath
that causes our lungs
to rise and fall with rhythm
it is purpose

when did you realise
you were someone
worth holding onto
that your mistakes never defined you
that mediocrity isn't in your vocabulary
that who you are and what you stand for
rises up from the deepest canyons of your soul
not from the flesh sewn over your bones
when did you realise
you were someone
worth holding onto

how curious these eyes of mine
in streams and dreams
frolicking with my mascara
as though it were this nauseating dance
of happiness and despair
two lovers curled vicariously
underneath the covers
neither going
anywhere

hold on fiercely, madly and with all your might
for even at the very inkling of a loosened grip,
the world becomes a sharpened sword.

don't tell me there isn't good
in your life
you bore black skies
from your hips and an east wind
from your chest
yes and even the thunder cowered at
the rumblings of your pain
but beauty?
it was there all along
the same night
that stole your heartsong
contained the stars
to steal your breath

who told you
to stop dreaming?
who made you a bird
only to clip your wings
at the breast
and confine your oxygen
to the forest of trees
you used to call home?
who reduced your potential
to the symmetry of scars
on your wrists;
ink dipped in veins
to see if you could feel
something,
because hurt felt better
than nothing at all?
who gave you permission
to set yourself neatly aside
so as not to disturb
all the other, more valuable
pulses;
to hush yourself out of the way
with a single stroke of liquid paper,
erased as well as can be?

one day i hope to meet her
with word drenched lips and sorrowing eyes,
deep wells, filled with any emotion at all.
this clark kent of sorts, living uncomfortably
amongst parallel lines that correspond but never intersect.
how much work it must be,
to choreograph two entirely different humans
and train them to cohabitate, to share the same headspace,
the same heartbeat, the same breath;
infusing past participles and future tenses in skies that switch
from blue to black in one single verdict.
how i'd like to meet her; soul unguised and perforated at the seams;
open like a window, fastened down for too many years
to let the light and breeze come in.
i'd tell her, here is freedom.
you are no longer bound to this duality.
perhaps one day, i'll meet her.

i threw all my words from years
spent saving
burying
fermenting
and aimed for your chest
but you just stood there softly
reached out your hands
and caught
every
last
one

our aching was conjoined at the heart
and there was no procedure
that could viably undo that.

it takes a village
because behind the armor is a child
round cheeked and full of inquisitions
in wonderment of why
and when
as though i were asking how big the sky was
or how many stars were painted on
you see most days i am fighting hard
most days i imagine the future
full of lights
and mountains i can grin at
knowing i'll ace the climb
but today
today every ounce of my strength washes down the drain
along with strands of hair
like sandpaper in water
at a farewell party i never wanted to attend
with an after party in some dark and ancient
sewage pipe
today
i am not strong
today my loudest roar
is a whimper barely audible
over the rush of wind in my veins
and arteries
the cavities of my chest
and the crumbling towers in my head
today i am a child
but the green of my eyes
stirs with the seas
the unknown
the hollows yet to come
to play pretend again
and find some beautiful
imaginary land
where i'm ok because some days ok is
more than i could dream of
these locks of mine
will be accounted for
each and every one
as scarce as they may be
he knows my name

she was an artist through and through
her mind burst with colours and shades
frequencies unheard by others
veins throbbed with words
that made pictures and sounds
fall right off their pages
but to separate herself from his pain
to live and love and laugh
without the echo of his tears
pounding fluently in her chest
if there was some sort of art to that
she hadn't mastered it yet

you were always one smile shy
of happiness
like it had planted itself
underneath the surface of your skin
wanting out
but staying in

the wind swept through her branches
and she swayed,
{but she did not break}.

if i see another blister pack
of rainbow coloured morsels
attempting to trade in chemical spills
for some degree of clarity
to carry your sadness at bay
to place your weary head
on your pillow for one hour at a time
to ease the thunder
that resounds in your chest
if i see another piercing look
that begs me for my presence
desperation clinging to sleeves
do not let go
don't leave me
i'm drowning
to undo that embrace
to unwrap my arms from your body
to say goodbye
feels like a sword plunged deep
if i see another cup of coffee
in an isolated room
medium double cream
over words that empty you of life
songs that slowly blend
into the stale white walls
conversation that used to
roll like a train
under undying archways
if i see another table
scattered with life that once was
left like a ghost town
in the dining room
people that came and went
people that loved and were loved
handwritten letters
waiting to be remembered - upturned
if i see another face
unable to let go of the sea inside
because it has emptied itself
given way to a new flood
that courses through brainwaves
and remains lodged

in the cracks and crevices
until it has nowhere left to swim
our family fortune is love
our coins are holding each other
through and over and alongside
wealth in stargazing together
despite every coloured blister pack
that attempts to take us from ourselves
mopping up every chemical spill
framing the photographs
and hanging them on the wall

i am a boy buried in the sanctuary
that bound me fiercely together
through playgrounds
that followed me with inquisitions
and bicycles that clung to my hips
divided amongst fragrant trees
and scissors gnawing recklessly
at my hair
my temple grew silent
disfigured threads
wove their patterns around me
misshapen and awkward
and held me in stagnant waters
adhered to strange ways
and hollow rooms
i built my home
a stone's throw away from myself
the sun aching for my company
lay buried far inside my chest
but sometimes the sky
even when in deepest cavity
plundered
lifts its head slightly and turns
the inquisitions in their place
pouring its life in orchestrated
rainfall
my skin awoke
and i was not calamity
i was freedom
i was not error
i was meadow

dreary and may
sat conflicted
wine in a barrel
and salt on their tongues
a home on a hill
note evicted
forty-two days
in the sun

dreary and may
wore a riddle
silver adorning
the flesh of their skin
corroded like leaves
that are brittle
what is this world
they are in

dreary and may
left unparted
hunger kept bringing
them back there to dine
and dreaming of where
they once started
forever the two
were entwined

dreary and sweet
coriander
could you for once
coexist
where neither the guilt
nor the candor
sever the ties
that insist

whatever you have taught yourself
to believe
in pages
on walls
in words
engraved on your wrist -
you are not
you are not
a statue erect
with motionless limbs
borne to bring to life
everyone but yourself
satiating world hunger
by some fantastically
odd definition of itself
a visual masterpiece
concocted of everything
that means nothing
equal parts
lustre and loathing
you are not
a sonogram
of curves and edges
balancing weight
and weightlessness
martyring self-love
against cordial greetings
and cruel misunderstandings
flowing locks and lips
that quench strangers
at your empty well
equal parts
sorrow and bliss
you
my dear
are this
even at every corner
that has claimed and bruised
your skin
palms skyward
lyrics written into poetry
memorized enough times

to believe it
a house
containing all the remnants
but with the porch light
on

summer comes and blossoms bloom
tales of a time i remember
salt in my eyes has washed the flume
skin scoured soft and limber

oh for the drought that cost my way
naught for a moment is wasted
sweeter the winds that sift and fray
where once the tongue has tasted

wake up and come
where would you be
in the long run
over the hills
with the setting sun
wake up and come
wake up and come

silently this my wordless woe
carries me on to the morning
halting to meet the deepest flow
vanquish the soul of scorning

but in the dawn of passers grim
my breath is skywardly fleeting
bearing it all til flickered and dim
heart in the sail still beating

you were once
you had a name and a soul
and a particular way
you lived obliviously
out of desperation
your stature your gaze
your gait your words
they were imperfect
a beggar in a steeple
unbelonging
you were the wrong shade
the wrong pitch
the wrong religion
the wrong ability
you were a sunset inverted
a pebble at the beach
that never smoothed over
you loved deeply into an ocean
that shouldn't have been yours
you strove to stand against
but everything came out quiet
a mountain built up inside of you
that you could no longer climb
you tore the skin off your own flesh
because you'd rather hurt
than not feel at all
your hands began to curl up
like a stone inside of you
settled
accepted
fragmented into parts
you didn't even recognise
and so you remain
eleven forever

this
i cannot
all my limbs dangling
in cobblestone
so recklessly arched
into the ungreat beyond
surprisingly caught
handcrafted or dark scheme
devised
so hauntingly like slavery
is this the whip
after which we sought?

this
i cannot
medley of bruises
on a platter
the clock synchronized
with the pounding in my flesh
tumultuous clot
dire veins circulating
the truth
deciphering validity
is this the draw
and i won the lot?

this
i cannot
my suit of birthdays
turned inside out
uncensored and scathed
split open to the bare lines
and desperate to blot
hold onto the cold bed frame
find breath
my spirit and Gethsemane
is this the sun
that the giver brought?

you blew in
an umbrella turned backwards
every limb crooked and disheveled
a heap of colour on a road
laden with rainwater
a phantom of what
you wanted to be
and a shell of what
you once were
a crossword puzzle
of missing adjectives
and words without definitions
your arms were a canvas
of misunderstanding
and
maybe one day
but i caught the inside of your sleeve
with my mouth
and saw the pulse
that kept you exhaling
your sweet breath
on everyone else
but yourself
a slow motion re-enactment
of past to present
bedfellows in a strange
love hate relationship
turning off the lights
together
apart
i wasn't your raft
i wasn't the boat that waited
in deep waters
to carry you over
to carry you through
i was only a passerby
caught in a smile
that evacuated every room
of common sense
absorbing every particle
that took you from
your sanctuary of necessity

to let you out to play
feel the sun
for a little while
for a long while
and so
i remain tethered to your side
an umbrella turned backwards
a heap of colour on a road
laden with rainwater

you left with
the flowers
at day break
and took all the books
off the shelf
you stole all the wind
from the back of my sails
and you slept in a rundown
motel

they found you
where lights were
forgotten
high as the day
that you went
cold as the summer
hot as the rain
and as empty as the money
you'd spent

you could have said
your goodbyes
you could have waited
a little while
you could have settled
the storm in my eyes
yeah
you could've waited
awhile

i won't be heart sick
like the paint on my wall
and the colourless shades
in my room
i won't stand to crumble
i won't bend to fall
i'm a girl
i'm a foolish one
too

stones buried
deep on your shoulders
drink like
a belt
on your breath
you framed all your memories
in cognac and smoke
and you ran like the wind
from yourself

and as if the skies were urging me
to make haste
to gather up and find a place
to run in any other direction
that wasn't here
about face
turn around
look for grace - somewhere else
every dark cloud
shook it's fist at me
with cruel ominousity
telling tales that laughed
my bedtime stories
back onto the page
flee from this
hide your rage - somewhere else
but then like summer's morning
on the edge of winter's tail
i saw it clearly moving in
the kind of sun that doesn't pale
despite of where you've been
in sailors' broken masts i found
a painted canopy
so when dark skies surround my eyes
i can still plainly see

i let my eyes run dry
i let the wind blow cold
against my face
i took a shovel and a spade
and i buried every wrong
i ever made

i took it hard that day
i made a deal of stone
beneath the clay
i took a shovel and a spade
and a satchel full of mercy
for my grave

sundown came
and morning woke beside me
loneliness could not dismiss
this flowerbed

i was not scattered 'cross the field
i was not one with waters' rage
today my soul my deepest win
and my loss my sweetest sage

the air that brushes
past my cheek
the artist's paint
has made me weak
i've fallen right down
to my knees
i'm not about to bend
this tree
the river still
runs endlessly

i'm only telling half a lie
it's not your tears
this body cries
and only part of me
has died
it's only half a lie

i can't recall the days
i laid in fields of shimmering grey
and let the haunting meadows sway
and i beneath
the cloudy veil

so every word hangs
from my lips
the wounds that ache
my fingertips
i've crashed through summer's
fragrant kiss
like perfume on
an empty wrist
these photographs
too soon dismissed

i'm only telling half a lie
it's not your tears
this body cries
and only part of me
has died
it's only half a lie

179

something is holding you now
under the crescent that gave you
life that was fragile
and promised to break
they said it was pointless
to save you

darkness rolled in
and attempted to take
but with thunder
accompanies light
over and over
a beaten down soldier
love wins
on this coldest of nights

will you be safe in december
when poetry's lines swept away
and lyrics lie frozen on windshields
silver drops turning to grey
everything dies
just a little inside
we remember the tears
we'd forgotten to cry
will you be safe in december

under the stars we await
this strength to melt into a flood
tides that blow sorrow
in from the sea
and life that is drained
of its blood

we will always mingle
with the roses on the water
winter only holds
the petals in their frame

well this old hotel
is my home
lilacs on paper walls
and roses printed
on the sheets
hello my appropriate rain
hold until you fall
beneath the lamps
that line the streets

don't go to sleep
it's pouring anyways
the furniture is worn
(but surprisingly comfortable)
and if you left
i'm pretty sure even the flowers
would bow their little heads
along with me
so don't go to sleep
don't go to sleep

cars that scurry
headlights fading
an ocean at my door
broken windows
crooked blinds
there must be
a thousand rooms here
deep inside or more
some are smoke filled
some are diamonds

where is the light
where is the power
you thought you had
who picks you up
when there is nothing
left inside
your eyes burned out
with the candle
on the table
a long time ago

so tell me
is this enough
is it worth everything
your broken sails
your tears are falling down
is this enough

what is this love
this strange devotion
that comes and goes
who holds you still
your body trembles
in the cold
your heart moved along
with the soft wind
of an ocean
a thousand years before

so tell me
is this enough
is it worth everything
your broken sails
your tears are falling down
is this
is this enough

even sadness would be glorious
to eyes that cannot
weep.

what is kindness
if we cannot let ourselves
wander a little from comfort and familiarity
make ourselves awkwardly thin and pale
to shine light on another
to water their souls from dying
and ache with their drooping limbs
what is kindness
if we do not reach more than an arm span
to catch storms with our chests
and divert even for one moment
a single fear
sometimes
we soothe and stitch
and sometimes we just let the pieces
fall

she thought she was made of stone
she hung towers and bridges with
her mighty strength
deep and wide
spanning emotion and heartbeats
claiming the waters that met her moat
were tepid and still
free flowing through her veins and bones
but storms
she had mastered them too
for she was best at building walls
and under lock and key
those walls stood
untouched for years
how unfortunate
{or perhaps fortunate}
one day
an east wind blew
just the fragment of a breeze
to reveal her bricks and clay
for the paper that they were

sometimes you find yourself
strange and juxtaposed
liquor in one hand
a bible in the other
drowning in darkness
and praying for light

her dreams were as big as the moon
but she starved them with fear
until they became anorexic slivers
of what they once were

i guess summer wasn't a season
after all,
it was a way of thinking.

i've carried a lot over the years
the wind on my shoulders
bricks on my back
a thousand storms in the pit
of my lungs
and every heartache
that climbed the walls
of everyone else's skin
but when you came along
you carried me
even my heavy
broken bones
and it was the most foreign
most beautiful thing
of all

sometimes we just need to pursue quiet
not to cease the perpetual humming
of the world around us
but to silence the noise inside
we find ourselves merging
with cities and lights
high-rises of wanting more
to fill the same caverns of our souls
solitude does not equal insecurity
introspection does not resemble loneliness
where is power
if it cannot reside in humility
where is strength
if not in the softened vessels
of our veins

my pen helps me quiet
the unrest inside
lives abbreviated too soon
guns in rapid fire
in rapid fire
in rapid fire
hurt turned inside out
to hatred
wars without end
without reason
without change
i tuck myself into my bed
wondering at how this universe
will mend
when will people understand
that love heals
that peace always wins
and that hope does not have to be
an illusion

we cannot be
merely pieces of stardust
floating and colliding in the atmosphere
coursing through time and space
in fractions of ourselves
to make wishes on the unknown twinkle
that happens to
catch our eyes
lover's sighs
great disguise
don't we all want to believe in something much greater than this
that we are more than random pieces
a story not yet complete
but being written
choreographed and
beautifully
orchestrated

i'd give up heartbeats
to see you smile
to watch you feel
to hunger for something
to hunger for anything
just to see a crescent
in the pools of your eyes
some far off light
waiting to dance and mingle
again
to flirt with wonder
and freedom
wild laughter that cinches
at nothing
blue skied days
and nights unharnessed
by dark
what i wouldn't bring
in soft cupped hands
to you

somehow after all this time
i'm still not immune to
fear
the monster i've tried
to suppress
to bury
to shove back into
the glove compartment
of my chest
and all the while i'm wondering
if i am his creator

some leave behind their bravery
with courage like curtains
draped across every inch of their skin
flasks full of fearlessness
shadows that flee from their determination
dying with fists still clasping
great endeavors
and ice cream stains on their cheeks
i leave you words
it's all i have
no valour here
but it's everything
and i hope it is
enough

you became a barcode
because everything you amounted to
was reduced to this
a series of numbers and lines
that felt cold
detached
and separate from worth
but what you didn't know
was that i memorized you
every dash and digit
you adhered to yourself
the rare and remarkable patterns
that made you exactly who you are -
a wonderful unity of bruises
and beauty

how dare we amputate our own souls
for a happiness that is fleeting
and call it martyrdom.

she was a masterpiece of quirks and curiosity
hips that swayed with the pull of the moon
and eyes that stormed like thunder
she never danced to the rhythm of another's song
for the music playing in the corridors of her mind
was much more splendid
they would call her "unusual"
i would call her
magnificent

there are hearts made of petals that cry tears in dewdrops
minds that have used every band-aid
in the box and still remain broken
wide vacant eyes filled with horror films stuck on replay for decades
tiny lives held in the balance of holding on and letting go
to bow my head to these
to beg for sweet release
this comes with greatest ease
but i pray for those who wear hatred like a badge
who gleam and glow in anger and exhale vulgarity like a second voice
i pray for those who laugh in our faces
wreaking of spilled gasoline
setting fires to joy with pyromaniac hands

not all wings were made to fly -
some were meant to shelter.

he reminded me of you,
so i tried to save him too.

the moon and i
we are old friends
light years ago
when i was yet a child
she laughed and cried
at my window pane
and watched me grow
i will never forget the way
she played with the white
of my bedsheets
and pulled me in a little closer
whenever the monsters came

you don't have to cry to feel,
some of us carry entire oceans
inside of us.

i never saw her as broken
because the more of her pieces i knew,
the more i understood,
she was already perfectly whole.

were it absolutely crazy to believe in that
which one cannot see with human eyes,
then let me introduce myself,
hello,
i'm positively ludicrous.

she was not in need of repair,
she was in need of being found
and not forgotten.

you see
we were never supposed to
live perfect lives
it doesn't mean we don't strive
for some sort of becoming
but the failures
the setbacks
the endless amounts of mistakes
and darknesses we travel through
are merely that
a journey towards transformation
not because we aren't
already enough
but because we can always be
a little more

i am letting you go
this world was far too unkind to you
and all these
broken parts
and hearts
endings and starts
they're all too much
good bye
i pray the heavens find you
sooner
rather than
later

i'll carry you
and when i fall
i'll carry you
again

i laid petals
down on his chest
to ease the terror
i tried
dear God
i tried

i want to leave here knowing
i bursted at the seams with love
that i was good enough
even covered in scars
fossilised by years of flaws
i want to leave here having given
more than i received
and ached more for the pain of others
than my own
and i want to leave here breathing in
the very last bleeding sunset
still gasping like i had never laid eyes on one
before

sometimes the big picture is so big
that we cannot see to the edges
and i guess that's kind of the point
to be unknowing of what is to come
but trusting that even in a state
of lostness and disillusionment
there is this unimaginable beauty
woven in
it's just not for us to discover
quite yet

fear is a joy stealer
it has robbed me many times over
preying on my empathy
my beautiful mind
but today i am standing face to face
my lashes the wipers across my eyes
and in my biggest big girl voice
i whisper
go away
and don't ever
come back

i know there is no such thing as perfect
but he was the closest i'd ever seen
and somehow i kept myself
drunk on the notion
that he deserved to be happy
to have at least some small portion
of scattered light
land upon his face

and then again
sometimes i learned the hard way
but i am none the worse for it
i bled some
but don't we all
until we find
our tourniquet?

somehow she loved the flowers most;
with wilted spines and sunken eyes.
for if not her,
then who?

so you think
you're not strong enough?
i've seen whiskey
buckle at the knees,
at the sound of
your name.

we put so much worth
on these shells
we call home
the bodies we carry
along as we go
if only these mirrors
we meet with regret
could replace
our reflections
with souls

she came close to loving herself once
a long time ago before she
portioned herself out
like corner store ice cream
one scoop at a time
dripping
melting
disappearing quickly
into hungry
soul-mouthed paupers
because feeling needed
was a high
and no one
could tell her otherwise
i think she believed that
the more she gave
the less she had to become
she was wrong

when it comes to wrongs
i'm not counting
not because i don't want
to do the math
but because i'm not
keeping score

for what it's worth
i'm sorry
i'm sorry for all the times you cried
and weren't held
for all the words you didn't hear
when you needed to
and all the ones you did hear
that crawled up into your open wounds
and built cities
i'm sorry that your soul and mind
made tombstones
because they could never be worn
like sheer cotton blouses
left to blow freely and proudly
flags waving and growing
from the very root of you
i'm sorry for the whiskey that sits
in your cabinet to this day
to make it all go away
for what it's worth
i'm sorry

i've always marched to the beat of my own drum.
maybe it's the quiet rebel in me but i love "different".
i didn't always love it though. i fought tooth and nail
to fit myself into ice cube trays and jelly moulds;
to be the same; to blend in. but i discovered
that wasn't me at all.
me, meant perched on a limb, ready to fly or fall.
me, meant dancing in the rain, bare feet and messy hair.
me, meant wearing windows on my chest
because if i couldn't let others see into my soul,
then what else was there?

if you have ever seen anguish
if you have ever watched
as hurricanes sweep through the eyes
of another
it is the most tragic thing of all
to stand with hands and heart exposed
unable to silence it

she stuffed her veins full
of colourful nouns
and verbs
and adjectives
so on the days she was pricked
with pain
and disregard
and loneliness
she could bleed out
in words

i'd give torrents of my ocean
just to fill one drop
of your void.

things you find:
seashells
a quaint cafe
your old hoodie
a hair pin
a job
a roommate
matching socks
a new radio station
a penny on the sidewalk
a star to wish upon
yourself
peace
your way back
home

i want to make you less afraid
less afraid of the walls closing in on you
less afraid of standing up for yourself
with your still small voice
less afraid to look up at the great big sky
find a star and make a wish
i want to make you less afraid
of a world that sometimes hates
just for the sake of hating
and tramples over the soft spoken
with steel toed boots
i want to show you that the tender ones
are the strong ones

i wish we could just
silence
each other's chests
for once
not from beating
but from the panic
that makes flowers
feel like a flight
risk

when your body tires of this old world
i will grow wings
not so i can fly you to freedom
but to shelter you beneath them
when you weary of your wanderings
i will knit you into the very fabric
of my bones
so that i may feel every single one of your sorrows
as though they were
my own

we, the ones who feel too much,
who fight endlessly to give love a name;
to give her a voice with which to turn heads
from reason to chaos;
pressing our sweet, soaked lips
to salt rimmed glasses.
it's how we sip the world.
to give with cost
and nothing less.

you were complete
long before you became
complexity
you were whole
by the sum of your divisions
the jigsaw of your mind
intricately woven
with a thousand pieces
of sunrise

i will build you a boat
with my hands
it will hold all your troubles
and tears left uncried
so when you are ready
to wash them away
they can mingle
with ocean and tides

it was his eyes i noticed first
they were broken yet kind
like hollowed out trees
that had spent some years
just as mine
in the darkest of places
but knew how to let the light
in

i always imagined you to be
white horses and fierce disposition
but somehow i came to realize
that the gentle side of you
the way you saw the world
with such softness
was your strongest attribute
of all

today i was not strong
today hope felt like a parody
stretched from one end of the sky
to the other
today even the good songs
did not cause me to move
to find rhythm
to hear beauty in aching violins
and sorrowing cellos
no
today i cried an ocean
and walked on broken limbs
perhaps tomorrow

i've carried a lot over the years
the wind on my shoulders
bricks on my back
a thousand storms in the pit
of my lungs
and every heartache
that climbed the walls
of everyone else's skin
but when you came along
you carried me
and it was the most
foreign
most beautiful thing
of all

i was never empty
even when it felt like
i had given all i had
drenched with fear
made small by the standards
of the world
here i was
a satchel on my back
a heart full of love
and with more than enough
to give again

do you ever wonder if any of this
matters at all
speaking with passerby birds
in languages not yet decoded
standing tall beside these
skyscrapers for trees
and feeling your smallness
against their skin
welcoming the sun back
from its slumber every morning
telling him all about how wonderfully
the moonlight painted your pillow
as it swept through our window
last night
and how you watched wide-eyed
to see the stars
dance and fall
dance and fall
does it matter at all
these words
your words
the dusks and dawns we spill
from the deepest pools
of our souls?

if you ask one thing of this world;
of this life you have been given,
ask that even in the darkest creases
of all the places you are afraid
to uncover,
that you unearth a forgiveness so wonderful
that it looks you straight in the eyes
and stitches you back into love
with yourself

and don't we all breathe the same air
whether flowery and fragrant
or stagnant and stenched
we wander at times with trepidation
and at times we are driven by a swift wind
causing us to stumble forward into opportunity
one day we are lost in breaths of love
and the next we are aching for comfort
we've pricked our fingers enough times
to know red
to know beauty
to know that "same" and "different" are two words
turned inside out
but both just as beautiful as the other
we all time travel at our own velocities
but we are met with
the same speed bumps
the same drum beats in our chests
and the same
amazing skies

sweet turmoil
thank you
thank you for
breaking me down
into all of the
beautiful parts
of myself
i desperately
needed
to find

look at me
do you see the rapids
in my eyes
the currents
that swirl and sweep
with hope and devastation
i know you feel it too
it's in the way
you try to hold it all
together
you don't have to
you never do
it's ok to come
undone

i don't want you to die for me
i want you to live for me
live in a way
that even the stars wonder
where you gathered
your light

tell me the story of the girl
who dreams in colour;
the one who laughs like a river
and feels the earth's sorrows.
does she live just like the others?
do they know she's not
the same?

have you found that one small thing
that makes you stand out from the rest,
the thing that turns your heart with rhythm
and plants gardens in your chest?

she was quiet. she usually walked with her head down; eyes pressed into the tiles of the floor or the pages of a book. you had to build a path to her, slowly, with soft petals and things that made her smile — her smile, it was wild fire to branches and wider than the sea at high tide. you often wondered where she lingered in those years between seconds. did she shut herself off from the world? did she long to be more, have more, live more? did she wonder at how to untame herself or was she a wild horse, silenced by too many sorrows? had i not grown to find love in her heartbeats, over time, over laughter and over words that discomfort sometimes closes, i may still believe she wanted nothing more than to be absorbed by the flowers on the walls. but she didn't. she loved, like everybody else - and she wanted love too.

come to me
as you are
beaten and bruised by the world
confused at hatred
wild eyed
pain singed
and spirit in a heap
i will touch the parts
you've begun to despise
and with soft hands
will simply love them
back to life

because i think
one day
the only thing
we will regret
is not having loved
more fiercely
the ones who lived
so close
but were made far
by our own
self prominence

had i known your chest was heavy
with a thousand howling winds
i would have tread a little softer
on your shoulders
had i known your heart had perished
a thousand quiet deaths
i would have walked a little closer
to your silence
had i known your ears had blistered
at a thousand careless words
i would have made my mouth a garden
for your sorrow
and had i known you longed for beauty
of a thousand bleeding skies
i would have painted every sunset
to your marrow

i'll tell you this
i have made love
to the pangs of
loneliness
as much as i have
to the salve of
beauty

she let the sun and rain
have equal parts of her;
the sun to make her laugh
and the rain to remind her
why.

for all the girls who were told they were pretty
i'm sorry
i'm sorry that you were so greatly misjudged
so vastly underrated
and so terribly misconstrued
i'm sorry that they cut your branches
before you became a tree
because how is "pretty" defined
when there is yet a wild and delicate soul
to discover
when you carry the strength of
ten thousand currents beneath your skin
and when heart stopping lyrics run
through the length of your fingertips
to the hollows of your toes
"pretty" never once made you
beautiful

the rain
never looked
as beautiful
as it did
the night
you let it
fall

how much light do we contain
when we ourselves
reside in thunder
birds within
who long to fly
are chained and fastened in
how much sun in feathered fury
how much left to lend to sorrow
always more for in our
darkness
still enough to give
again

what if i breathed life
back into the cellars
of your eyes
what if they could see
the colours that left and hid
with the light you once had
would you dream again -
would you let me?

i'd like to think
there are angels
killing time
at laundromats
hailing taxi cabs
pulling us out from
muddy waters
and singing beauty
back into
our makeshift
deathbeds

it all comes down to this
when darkness makes a bed in us
we build a fire
we warm our hands
we watch it glow

is love always enough
is it still enough when
hope becomes a perfect stranger
at your doorstep
with flowers limp and broken
when thoughts play shadow puppets
in the eaves troughs of your mind
is it enough when your own bones
rise in anarchy against you
can love undo all that?

some chains grip
beneath your flesh
like vultures
gnawing at the skin
and oh for freedom's
sweet release
to let you fly
again

i'm not afraid of dying.
i'm afraid of living
without having left
a mark.

somewhere a man
is holding up cities
in the cleft
of his ribcage.

i mourn for those
whose lungs are filled with breath
but are far from alive
who see with their eyes
yet fail to have vision
who are free to live
but chained to the very bones
on which they stand

i am weary of this
you and i forgetting what it is
to love
forging our way like we've grown old
shackled by the skin of our own bodies
we should be wanderers
we should remember the shape of the stars
and the way it felt
when they waltzed with the lids of our eyes
we should remember the stories
the ocean laughed into our ears
and how his secrets made us feel
clever and mischievous
what a shame
that we already see the world
with silver eyes
while we have yet
so many blossoms
to grow

i would turn my hands
to ash
to make a fire
that kept you warm
you wear your coat
inside the house
you've felt the cold
for far too long
come now
i'll bring the branches
you lay yourself down

you were so many planets spinning at once.
each one with its own moons and rings and textures.
i wanted to see them all; touch them all;
live through each one of them with you.
but what i saw as a beautiful sky, you felt as pandemonium.
and maybe that's why you never let me in -
why you never let anyone in.
there were just too many galaxies inside.

there are no oceans between us;
only the partitions that we ourselves
have fashioned out of apathy.

and this cathedral is your home -
that's what i wish most for you to know
that you are spirit and stained glass windows
you are the gasp of breath from passersby
in how your steeple dances with the moon
and your eyes catch the glistening sun just so
i wish for you to know that darkness will come
it will haunt your deepest secrets
and it will attempt to leave you in wreckage
no one is immune to bleeding
from that which once cradled them tenderly
but take the road that is less travelled
and if you see a few more weary ones
stop to say hello
i'll be there too

and when i looked closer
i saw that the scars on your wrists
were inkblots of all the things
you hadn't forgiven yourself for

i want to be so naive
that i believe there are tiny buds
and droplets of something pure
in everyone
sanctuaries growing and becoming
vivid and contagious
but the skeptic in me knows
that the world has gone a little mad
inebriated on shots
of narcissism and animosity
and if we are to fix any of this
if we are to assess the mess
we haven't much further to look
than in the very pits of our own
dark hearts

don't let them fool you -
stay soft
this world
will make you think
you need to grow daggers
but the wings you try to push back
into the lapels of your coat
are the same wings
that hold the earth away
from chaos and injustice

sweet one
could you stop for a fraction of time
and gather your breath
even in the mess and the mayhem
you are in
you pack your suitcase full of dreams
and run from place to place
to find yourself
but you are here
right where you are standing now
and everything you are at this very point in time
is the work of a craftsman
fine art worthy enough
to be hung in a gallery
so go find passion
and go find purpose
and go find what makes
your heart beat faster
but do not find yourself -
you are already found

when she said she couldn't remember
his face,
she meant, she wasn't sure
if it looked like a beast gnawing his prey;
claws still embedded,
an uneasy forecast,
that had her running for the cellar
every time she started to feel safe,
or a pilgrimage
to forgiveness.

i wanted nothing to do
with freedom
because freedom meant
finding my way
through murky waters
and no trespassing signs
but what if it came
with the path already cleared
with an open field -
a lantern lit
and all i had to do
was keep my eyes up
my light burning
and follow the man
with the nail marks
in his hands

i often dream of flying
leaving behind
dust and earth
to touch sky with wings
perhaps it's freedom
i have sought for all along
or perhaps i was made
for something more
but oh the liberation
that comes
in leaving the soil
for just a moment
finding air
in a different place
altogether
a place untravelled
a place i have not yet
wept to pieces

each night i tried
to let you in
under the left side
of my chest
away from your
disheveled cot
to sleep soundly there
where i had made a bed
for you

when i die
lay me in and amongst the trees
so that your lungs will always rise and fall
with pieces
of my breath

could you do one thing for me?
forgive yourself of the cliffs
that hang heavily;
draped from your neck;
disguised as pearls.
they are what have placed you
at the very edge
of your eternal falling.

carry me like courage carries a
whisper,
like a breeze carries the songbird's
morning anthem.
make me believe
that my words are a match;
fully capable of fire.

i am a curious girl.
i still wake with wonder stitched to my lids
and question marks riding the brim of my lips.
what a shame that an inquisitive heart
should ever feel they ask too much.

i have always wondered what it would be like
not to feel so much.
but hurting is my greatest strength.
even when it leaves me raw and cold
and breathless -
especially then.

despair is not chosen.
do we not understand this yet?
the grief of a thousand blackbirds
flocking like paparazzi
to the mantle of their shoulders;
hope uninvited.
and yet we tug at their garments
as though we can pull them out
from under it.
at times it is better to sit and mourn,
let ourselves ache quietly alongside
and hold our whispers
over the bruises.
we were not meant to be saviours.

i held onto anything that
looked like hope;
doppelgängers of almosts and empty promises.
even the ocean; tumbling
through the cracks of my fingers
and the pores of my skin,
left just as quickly as she came.
gone.
{without leaving her name}.

there is something you should know.
i try to save every last soul that i fall in love with -
and i will try to save you too.
i will hunt you down like a fever to the sand
and make poetry of your sadness.

one day
i will drink the ocean dry
of its strength.
i will graft my limbs
into the branches
of the biggest tree i can find -
and i will grow there.

they will try to push you away;
the ones who need you most.
but you will stay.
you will be their constant.

i wonder how many hearts loneliness has taken;
how many lives she has abbreviated.
i wonder if she ever wants to raise her voice,
shake the rest of us by the throats and say,
"for heaven's sake, do something!"

when the ground froze over, she did too.
it was like the seasons had changed
beneath her very flesh and bones and held her there.
she counted her fears in nautical miles for she was at sea;
full of unsuspecting glaciers, buried much deeper than they were visible.
ice prowled, like mighty ships, laden with despair and incurabilties.
it tried to take her that day; winter; all of her.
even the hope she had saved in the small gaps of sunlight
in between mornings.
but spring was her beacon.
it came again.
and so did freedom.

i do not visit my mother's grave often.
i go to the places where she lived -
among the cedars and pines,
the pews of her church and the grocery store.
that's where i find her most.
she never breathed her life onto the stone
that holds her now.
she never laid her smile down
on the grasses there.

it takes a lot to anger me.
the quiet side of me rumbles at best,
like thunder that wants to erupt
and trails off into the distance instead.
i have felt it though; the mercury rising in my veins,
the gnawing at my heart to say something;
do something.
but i found my voice in words
that did not repress themselves
back into into the deep of my lungs.
they have fought loudly for the oppressed.
the judged.
the misunderstood.
they have scolded and charred and wept
without restraint.
i have roared wildly now
and i will carry on.

i wish i could have told her
that her eyes would one day
feel betrayal.
that she would wonder at the cruelty
of the world, in a way
that would make her shy away
from reality and curl deeper
into herself.
i wish she would have known
how her curves paved beauty
into the human landscape;
that she was fully permitted
to make mistakes and cry
and crucify her grief to the walls.
and that she would survive it all.

the beautiful part of broken
is not in the brokenness
but in the journey you make
despite of it.

our hands became bird feeders.
we held them out gently
as he nibbled at morsels
of hope.

sometimes i wish i could be a fire
instead of a breeze;
roaring and mesmerizing
everyone and everything around me.
but then i remember that the softest wind
can stir up the wildest flames.

i will always be more alive than dying.
more hopeful than hopeless
and more complete than lacking.

one day you will wake up and feel brittle.
you will wonder how you arrived here;
light-years away from where you once were.
but as you replay your life in silent film
across the screen of your memory,
you will see all the brokenness and the beauty
your heart had to carry.
you will find that at times you were shattered to pieces
and at times you rose from the ashes.
you will hear a still, small voice that says,
"beloved, know this - you have lived life
and you have lived it well".

but a bird anxious for flight
found the wind in its lungs
and drew breath unfrail and steady
corralled only by hope on all sides
punctured but repairing
through and over and away
alas the meadow

your heart was never
shaped like the others.
it was the shape of a house;
with a roof over my head
and windows to let the light in.

i long for the days
when street lights told time
when rocky road
was an ice cream flavour
and bedtime
didn't make me wonder
what tomorrow would
sound like
from the chesterfield
where i stitch myself
together
every morning
waiting to hear
if you are ok

broken
people
are
broken
people.
they are not
shards of glass.
you will not
injure yourself
by letting them
rest
on
your
shoulders.

i have a love/hate relationship
with quiet.
quiet lets me think -
and
quiet lets me think.

before you go,
i want you to know;
i cannot love
the darkness out of you.
but i will wave this light
for as long as it takes -
until my arms grow tired
and even then.
i will rub my bones
to make fire.
i will stay bright
for you.

his eyes reminded me of winter
lingering into may.
a quiet dreariness
that had long overstayed
its welcome.

the way we cause each other
to perish,
simply by setting fire
to these gasoline tongues;
i cannot stand by it.
i have seen it far too often;
how the beautiful ones
grow dark valleys inside
their heads;
how their light
is just snuffed out.
and with mind and soul,
so intimately entangled,
their hearts, too,
become calloused to loving
and being loved.
we've created them;
these wanderers,
without a place to call home,
holding flickers of light
that they've learned
to keep dim.

we are so quick to
diagnose this world
with all its calamities;
all its chaos.
but what if for every ounce
of misadventure,
there was a requisition for
holding on anyways and
a prognosis that made us
question why we ever
doubted in the first
place.

when i asked you
about your past,
it wasn't because
i wanted you to relive
your darkness
all over again.
i wanted to see
if it felt
any different
with someone
beside you.

i only carried the ghosts
with me that kept me humble
enough to remember that i
was never immune to pain
and weak enough to remember
that i was still in need
of forgiveness.

the ones who never cry
for help;
the unwritten ones
who have made their own,
quiet lifeboats and have
us all believing they have
mastered life and tamed
the fires within -
what about them?

this second skin;
your armour,
does it ever get
too heavy?

we could all stand
to lay down for awhile;
collect some peace
along with our
broken vessels for souls.

most people are not angry -
they are wounded.

do you want to know
what hope tastes like?
because it's not what you think.
they say hope sits on your tongue
like a meadow at twilight.
stars disrupting darkness
with incandescent light.
a thousand tiny saviours
that make despair bearable.
this is not my experience at all.
hope does not always
swallow weeds
and bring up bouquets.
sometimes hope goes down
sour and bitter
and wraps caution tape
around your esophagus.
it reeks of fear to let yourself
believe for one more day;
a capsule of
"i can't do this anymore",
disguised with honey
to make it go down.
but it burns with the acid
in your stomach – it burns.
and some days
it gets the better of you;
the nauseating idea
to keep swallowing,
keep overdosing,
keep praying it's not a
placebo.
that's what hope tastes like.
i can't sugar-coat it.
it's not always delicious.
not always palatable.
but it is hope.
and if anything, it is something.
because something
is always better
than nothing at all.

311

do not tell me
that your heart does not feel.
do not tell me
that i have dreamed up
your gentleness with my
utopian mind.
i know you hurt.
but i also know you love.
and i know you do both -
deeply.

i cannot tell you exactly
what i saw.
there were bursts of
colours and light;
a small miracle perhaps.
but it was more of a feeling
that wrapped blankets
over my disbelief,
than something i could
lay my eyes upon.
i think she heard music again.
i think her mouth and hands
drank from its healing.
and i think she moved with it,
just as gracefully
as she had before.

sometimes you will become
your own comforter.
sometimes you will hold yourself
against the troubles of this world
and say,
"rest here, i will not leave your side".

even the misplanted parts of you
can grow.
the dry, chapped lips that spoke
too many words to unlistening ears.
the wide flung heart that danced
delicious freedom,
only to be forgotten;
deprived of appetite.
you can still grow here.
in desert soil.
this is where love holds you fast.
this is where hope resides.

she was broken
but not one part of her
was missing.
even when her heart
shattered into tiny pieces,
it was fully capable
of beating and loving.
a million times,
her soul crumbled
and yet it was as whole
as the harvest moon.
she gave every part
of herself away;
her hands,
her mind,
her tears,
and there she was,
as complete as the day
she started.

some days i am just
a lamb of a soul.
i hold my sword
by my fingertips;
profusely shaking,
unsteady - but ready.
those are the days
i consider myself
the strongest;
the ones where
i have nothing left,
but refuse to go down
without a fight.

sometimes things got so quiet
that i thought you had forgotten
me altogether.
but you were there.
you were silently making garments
of all my tattered shreds.

it's ok to be happy.
don't let misery
get a two for one deal.

- empathy

i simply sat there and realized
i had finally found myself.
and in the strangest of places;
in the tunnel they speak of,
where lights shine -
just out of reach.
on the brink of my madness,
i stumbled on a beautiful thing;
some truths are found
only in darkness.
and sometimes wisdom comes
in the shape of broken eyes
and sleepless nights,
to bring you back home;
back to yourself.
and i wasn't even looking.

i nailed them to my past;
the thoughts that said
i wasn't worthy.
one day, one limb of nonsense
at a time.
i crucified them.

i always knew
words would not
trample me.
i always knew
i would find love
in their wings;
that they would
carry me to
and from home.
but i did not know
that one day
they would save me too;
like a mother
leaping into
wild waters
to claim her
drowning child.

i wept into her clothes
they still lived there
on crocheted hangers
like yesterday's roses
vibrant with scent
longing for remembrance
and somehow i couldn't
let go

i told you we
would find home.
here in this
imperfect place
between heaven
and grief.
here where the
birds fly free
and the flowers
wither and grow
wither and grow.
it's all we could
ask for.

i will stand by you.
but when your legs give out
beneath the weight
and you are face down
to the floor,
i won't stand by you
anymore.
i will lay by you.
my body next to yours.
i will pound my fists and tears
into the ground.

i would rather walk barefoot,
even if that means i
will feel every prick
and puncture to my feet.
even if i bruise and bleed
from time to time.
i cannot live to tread
lightly.
i will not wish away
the pain.

we sit here
holding the earth
like tuesday's trash
hap-hazardous waste
a schoolgirl
with butterfly eyes
a crash course of
cruel wild ways
made to drink the venom
of adult hands
wings cut
she's seen too much
and we wonder at the
sanctity of life
where freedom hides -
oh God the children

we do not understand pain.
we want to turn our eyes from it;
shelter our hearts and bones
from becoming its feast.
and yet, here we are.
the very bodies that
pushed it away;
that begged for mercy,
somehow a little stronger
for it.

strength is not in how much
you can lift
but in how many
you have carried.

bravery?
i know bravery.
but perhaps not the same way
as the universe sees it.
i have fallen more times
than i can count.
i have wept and mourned
and thrown my tears into the bed.
i have stood silent
when i should have spoken
and i have
drowned others with words
that had no right to leave
my lips.
i am not strong.
no.
but i am enduring.

for it was in the darkest places
that my greatest petals
grew.

there will come a day when
you feel desperate loss.
you will fall into a thousand hopeless pieces,
you will hurt
and you will question why.
the wonder of the world that once lived
burrowed comfortably in your chest,
will rumble.
you will be stirred from familiarity.
this is where hurt and growth will merge;
the breaking point of what you were
and what you will become;
the backbone of all you are able to carry.
and yes you will fall beneath its weight,
you will weep,
and you will rupture.
but the day will not be over.
the sun will not set on your sorrow.
you will find it;
the thing that makes you rise up
one more time
and one more time again.
and it will be your saving grace.

and so, my little songbirds, be free.
fly softly then into the wooded groves
of unknown dusk,
knowing you will always find your way
back to the dawn.

Savage Owl Press

Of Dusk and Dawn by Ullie Kowcun
@fierceword on instagram

Published by Savage Owl Press
Dallas, TX
SavageOwlPress.com

Made in the USA
Middletown, DE
15 November 2018

Figures of the Future

Latino Civil Rights and the Politics of Demographic Change

Michael Rodríguez-Muñiz

PRINCETON UNIVERSITY PRESS

PRINCETON AND OXFORD

Requests for permission to reproduce material from this work should be sent to permissions@press.princeton.edu

Published by Princeton University Press
41 William Street, Princeton, New Jersey 08540
6 Oxford Street, Woodstock, Oxfordshire OX20 1TR

press.princeton.edu

All Rights Reserved

ISBN 978-0-691-19946-7
ISBN (e-book) 978-0-691-20590-8

British Library Cataloging-in-Publication Data is available

Editorial: Meagan Levinson and Jacqueline Delaney
Production Editorial: Brigitte Pelner
Production: Erin Suydam
Publicity: Kate Hensley (US) and Kathryn Stevens (UK)
Copyeditor: Anita O'Brien

Jacket Credit: Shutterstock

This book has been composed in Adobe Text and Gotham

Printed on acid-free paper ∞

Printed in the United States of America

10 9 8 7 6 5 4 3 2 1

In honor and in memory of my mother—Nellie B. Muñiz—my first and fiercest teacher

There is no human science of the future. There is only faith in the future; and among the forces which combine to bring this future into being, the faith in its coming is one of the most effective.

—HENDRIK DE MAN

CONTENTS

ILLUSTRATIONS

ABBREVIATIONS

CCC   Center for Community Change

CHCI   Congressional Hispanic Caucus Institute

LCLAA   Labor Council for Latin American Advancement

LULAC   League of United Latin American Citizens

MALDEF   Mexican American Legal Defense and Educational Fund

MFV   Mi Familia Vota

NALEO-EF   National Association of Latino Elected and Appointed Officials Educational Fund

NCLR   National Council of La Raza

NHLA   National Hispanic Leadership Agenda

NILP   National Institute for Latino Policy

NLIRH   National Latina Institute for Reproductive Health

SEIU   Service Employees International Union

PREFACE

Ages ago, in 2001, long before I began writing this book, and well before I came to see population *as* politics, I wrote this sentence: "Latinos make up 31 percent of the total school population." I was in my early twenties, a first-generation Puerto Rican undergraduate at Northeastern Illinois University. By the time I had enrolled, this former teaching college on Chicago's north side was a "Hispanic-serving institution." No doubt, this federal designation was a legacy of the Puerto Rican/Mexican/Latinx student and community activism that opened up its doors. Yet much to my dismay, while Northeastern reaped financial gain from this status, it stubbornly resisted making its source a priority: there was no Latino cultural center on campus, the Latino Studies program—then called Mexican/Caribbean Studies—was on life support, Latino faculty members were few and far between, and Latino students rarely crossed the stage at graduation.

Alongside other frustrated students, I helped launch what became known as the "Status of Latinos" campaign. We searched for demographic statistics to help us prove the existence of a large but underserved student population. By juxtaposing the size of the Latino student population with the minuscule number of Latino faculty, graduates, courses, and services, we believed we could shame university administrators and catalyze students into action. We all but plastered the campus with flyers exclaiming our 31 percent figure, our proof that Latino students constituted one-third—and an increasingly growing portion—of the student body.

Those days are long gone, but writing this book has forced me to return to those past efforts and make sense of them in a new light. I don't think my comrades and I ever discussed the tactical decision to moor our arguments to demographic data. In retrospect, our use of numbers was, at least for us, a somewhat odd choice. We did not invoke demographic data to demand freedom for Puerto Rican political prisoners or an end to the U.S. bombing of the island of Vieques, the stock in trade of anticolonial Puerto Rican activists at the time. Nor were we leveraging numbers to speak about the conditions and contributions of undocumented people or advocate for the expungement of criminal records. Yet from another angle, our turn to demographic statistics was not all that unexpected. Like our contemporaries at the time, we inhabited a political and cultural horizon in which statistical "facts" were trusted and valued, and in which talk of "Latinos" was ubiquitous. We heard from all corners that the Latino population was on the verge of becoming the country's largest "minority" group. Journalists and pundits variously celebrated and fretted about the "Hispanicization" and "Latinization" of "American" cities, music, cuisine, and politics. With its national and local inflections, all this talk drew on a parade of figures from the census in 2000. In some form or another, we absorbed this demographic conversation, in the process encountering the categories and claims-making tactics we ourselves came to adopt. As I later contemplated, an earlier generation of student activists fought, even risked expulsion, for a campus center named after the Latin American revolutionaries Emilio Zapata and Pedro Albizu Campos. Our group, instead, earnestly requested a "Latino" cultural center. Something had transpired over the decades that placed such distance between otherwise similar demands.

For me, at the time, the proliferation of data and discourse about Latino demographics and my own contingent embrace of "Latino" as a meaningful political identity prompted no reflection. That would come later, in 2006, when historic marches shook cities across the country to successfully oppose a repressive anti-immigrant congressional bill, the Border Protection, Anti-terrorism, and Illegal Immigration Control Act (H.R. 4437). Often referred to simply by the name of its chief sponsor, Representative James Sensenbrenner (R-WI), the bill sought to criminalize undocumented immigration and charge any individual or organization convicted of assisting undocumented immigrants with a felony. The upheaval took place as I was settling into life as a graduate student at the University of Illinois-Chicago. Two of my mentors, Nilda Flores-González and Amalia Pallares, invited me to join an interdisciplinary research project on the sources of these unexpectedly massive local mobilizations. I chose to explore why Puerto Rican elected officials and community activists—with access to U.S. citizenship—were actively involved in immigrant rights. Seeing how this solidarity was bonded to desires to build a "Latino Agenda," I wondered: How have heterogeneous Latin American–origin groups come to be imagined—and to some extent imagine themselves—as part of a "panethnic" whole? What forces have been at play and what have been the consequences?

Reading soon led me to realize that a major part of the answer to my questions was contained in the very categories of "Hispanic" and "Latino." Their proliferation and uptake across community, political, economic, and academic sites made possible and intelligible phrases such as "Latino Agenda," "Latino vote," and "Latino student population." Only later did I come to recognize that these phrases—and the projects tethered to them—helped create and constitute the very entities they presume to describe. This process opened up new possibilities for subjecthood and solidarity but at the same time, and unavoidably so, constrained, if not closed, other possibilities. The fact remains that appeals to and articulations of *Latinidad* (or Latino-ness)—as with other ethnoracial categories—do not arise out of nowhere. They stem from, and are marked by, complex, shifting, and stratified colonial relations that have systematically centered particular raced, gendered, classed, and sexual experiences and systematically marginalized others. The more I listened and reflected, the clearer it became that I couldn't afford to take for granted this formation.

Ironically though, this newfound desire to interrogate the category "Latino/Hispanic" did little to dislodge the ease with which I still dispensed data and claims about the "Latino population." It was almost as if the categories were complicated and complicit, but the statistics were self-evident, neutral even. I hadn't yet connected how statistics and projections, like the ones I regularly consumed and communicated, had also naturalized and normalized ideas about this apparent population—its purported characteristics, proclivities, and affinities. In short, the politics of numbers still escaped me. That awareness, serendipitously enough, came with the 2010 census.

That census took place during my first year as a doctoral student at Brown University. Looking initially to satisfy a class research assignment, I immersed myself in census promotional campaigns in Providence and Central Falls, Rhode Island. In interviews, Latina and Latino educators, politicians, cultural workers, and activists narrated why they had chosen to promote the census. Census data, they said, gave them "proof" about the size and growth of the Latino community—evidence they planned to use to influence local and state policy. But as I continued to listen to them and observe them encourage participation in the census, I came to see that this data was not only a bargaining chip or simply a method to demonstrate disparities. It was also being used as an instrument to assert presence and power. This was far from abstract. Demography, as demonstrated by the census, informed not only the content of their words but also *how* they said them. Raising his voice with pride, a Puerto Rican immigration attorney sat confidently upright to recount how the 2000 census had made Latinos a "legitimate group." Now, thinking about the 2010 census, he said, "The numbers are there, and we are going to be a political giant." A Mexican American leader and amateur historian beamed, "The whole idea of doubling numbers was an exciting thing. . . . The more Latinos, the more political power." The sense of *progress* felt palpable.

But this was not all. These same leaders also worried out loud that further proof of Latino demographic growth was likely to trigger white backlash. Anti-immigrant and anti-Latino politicians, they anticipated, would seize and negatively spin the results of the census. Seemingly on the precipice of political grandeur, these actors contemplated how to convince relevant public and political elites to interpret the numbers in the ways they did, as positive and promising.

What these local leaders were describing to me was what I call *population politics*. Whatever value they might have wanted to glean from census statistics demanded they work to shape how Latino demographic growth and its relation to the future were locally perceived and understood. This entailed supplying answers to what are preeminently political and yet deeply existential questions: *What does Latino population growth mean? Is it something to embrace or fear? Is this future close or distant, inevitable or uncertain?* And, as their own worries registered, these actors were not alone in answering these questions.

Population politics is not new. It has long been used, in the United States and elsewhere, to legitimate projects of population control and management, such as restrictive immigration policies and sterilization campaigns. Yet, as comments from the Rhode Island leaders I interviewed suggest, population politics aren't always narrowly or neatly conducted in the service of what scholars have labeled "demographic engineering." They can serve, and have served, other political aims and aspirations (not to mention economic and intellectual ones). Indeed, for some advocates and activists from minoritized groups, population politics have become a means, however constrained and conflicted, to pursue political recognition and empowerment in ostensibly democratic polities.

Figures of the Future tells a story, or a set of stories, about such a project of population politics. It is a story with many characters but organized around the intertwined relationship between two sets of protagonists: *political figures* and *demographic figures*. The political figures at the heart of this story are national Latino civil rights organizations and coalitions, such as the League of United Latin American Citizens (LULAC), the National Association of Latino Elected and Appointed Officials Educational Fund (NALEO-EF), Voto Latino, UnidosUS (formerly the National Council of La Raza), and the National Hispanic Leadership Agenda (NHLA). These organizations have engaged in population politics for decades, advancing particular ideas and images about the "Latino population" and the country's ethnoracial future.

The second, and no less important, set of protagonists are demographic figures, literally statistics and projections. Data about the "Hispanic" or "Latino/a" or, as of late, "Latinx" population has grown exponentially since the 1980 census, which not coincidentally debuted the category "Hispanic." This knowledge has been implicated, interrogated, and imitated in current struggles over the meaning of ethnoracial demographic change—struggles in which national Latino advocates are intimately involved.

This book describes and analyzes how national Latino civil rights organizations and advocates have actively *forecasted, foreshadowed*, and *forewarned* of Latino demographic futures in dogged attempts to turn population into power. It is based on seven years of sociological research that allowed me to peer into a far-reaching but understudied political network. For this, I observed and participated in, among other events, voter registration drives in Orlando, conventions and conferences in Las Vegas and Chicago, and congressional visits and public forums in Washington, DC. My understanding of this network and its population politics was further deepened through conversations with eighty leaders, consultants, activists, public relations specialists, volunteers, and elected officials with direct knowledge of contemporary Latino civil rights and demography-related issues. And throughout, I amassed a large collection of primary materials—print and multimedia—that offered additional insight into how Latino demographic figures were being made and marshalled for political ends.

Yet, this is not only a book about the population politics of contemporary national Latino civil rights advocacy. The account it offers tells us much more than that. The efforts of Latino advocates, as we shall see, are part of a much longer history inseparable from the population politics of state agencies, political parties, social movements, think tanks, and the media. Focused on a period that spanned the administrations of both Barack Obama and Donald Trump, it traverses the severe economic downturns, resurgent white supremacist movements, and intensifying partisan polarization that have characterized those years and our shared present. As such, this book provides a window into concrete and consequential struggles about how ethnoracial population trends should be understood and acted on. Although these struggles have generated diverse and contradictory visions and emotions about the country's ethnoracial future, they have also inspired strong belief that a momentous transformation is underway.

Given this reality, my intention is not to add another prognostication about the future or to further entrench the sense of inevitability and destiny that pervades demographic discourse. Rather, I strive to encourage critical reflection on the politics and pitfalls of our contemporary demographic imagination. My concern thus extends beyond the "Latino demographic," which is often and incorrectly seen as uniquely problematic or manufactured. No ethnoracial population is natural, and none of our views or reactions about population trends are ever automatic or unavoidable consequences of said trends. As a result of population politics, we often fail to see that it is politics—not demography—that governs what we think and feel about ethnoracial demographic change. As such, what we are confronting, therefore, is a political rather than a demographic phenomenon—one that demands ethical vigilance, not simply better data.

Only now, decades later, do I see there was much more than I could have imagined or foreseen in the banal sentence, "Latinos make up 31 percent of the total school population."

FIGURES OF THE FUTURE

Introduction

Propelled by an enthusiastic introduction, Janet Murguía walked across the stage to a standing ovation. Born and raised in Kansas City to Mexican immigrants, Murguía was set to deliver her annual presidential address as the figurehead of the National Council of La Raza (today known as UnidosUS), a leading national Latino civil rights organization. This former deputy assistant to President Clinton took the podium before hundreds of affiliates, corporate sponsors, and political operatives attending the organization's annual conference.

When Murguía delivered her speech in July 2011, the country was still reeling from the Great Recession, the Democratic Party had lost control of the House of Representatives, Tea Party insurgencies were erupting throughout the country, and Republican state governments were aggressively pursuing draconian immigration laws. President Barack Obama, who had spoken to a mix of cheers and boos at the conference the day before, had not only failed to secure comprehensive immigration reform in his first term but also had overseen an unprecedented spike in deportations.

Murguía did not shy away from discussing these and other challenges in her speech. Yet her remarks exuded much optimism about the future:

> I know as sure as I am standing before you today that the future of the Latino community is bright. I know that as a community we will be stronger and that our voices will be heard and that our potential will be realized. I know that one day soon, we will be treated as full American citizens, our presence in communities will be welcomed, and our

1

contributions to this great country at every level of society will be acknowledged.

With idealized allusions to "American history," Murguía claimed, without elaboration, that this soon-to-come future was rooted in the U.S. Declaration of Independence and Constitution. But more than in the past, it was reflected in the then newly released results of the 2010 census. Slowing her pace to emphasize each word, she continued: "One—out—of—every—six—Americans—is—Latino." Then, just as pointedly, she continued, "Put simply, we—are—America's—future." The assertion, she added, was "not a brag; it's a fact."

Latinos, she voiced with confidence, did not have to—and could not afford to—passively wait for that bright future to dawn. Rather, they had to assert their capacity to *accelerate* its arrival. "How that future unfolds, how quickly it is realized, is in a large way up to us. We can no longer look to politicians in either party to produce it for us." Applause rumbled through the ballroom as she raised her voice: "It is ours to achieve!" Murguía drove the point further. "It's our work to finish. I don't know about you, but I don't want to wait two or three generations to see that future. I don't want to wait for the *inevitable* demographic tide to bring our community to shore. I want to embrace that future now."

Murguía cautioned that some opposed the future foretold by the census. Needing little specificity for this audience, she spoke of "those" who instead wanted "to turn the clock back" to "when Latinos weren't so numerous, a time when we didn't speak out and we didn't matter." This advocate was adamant that she had no intention of going backward. She was determined instead to go forward:

> I want to turn the clock *ahead* to a time when every Latino eligible to vote, votes. I want to turn the clock ahead to a time when Latino and Latina senators, judges, police chiefs, mayors, governors, and school board members are the rule and not the exception. I want to turn the clock ahead to a time when all Americans understand and appreciate the contributions Latinos make and the role we play in this great nation.

But how could the proverbial "clock" be turned ahead? What would accelerate the arrival of this projected, or prophesized, future? If Murguía's speech was a guide, voter participation was paramount. Her words were meant to energize the organization's affiliates to invest in voter registration and outreach for the upcoming 2012 presidential election. Awakening the so-called sleeping giant, she and her colleagues claimed, would transform the political landscape. But that was not all. The speech also exercised—yet did not name—another potential catalyst. Interfacing temporal metaphors and statistical figures, she encouraged those in attendance to envision an idyllic Latino-propelled demographic future. This future was, at once, monumental, inevitable, and auspicious. Far from unique, the basic contours of her utopian forecast have been commonplace among national Latino civil rights organizations and leaders for decades. It is part of a longstanding tradition of *population politics*. Far from being a sidebar, this tradition and its tactical repertoire are present in all major aspects of its advocacy, including its public relations, voter operations, and legislative campaigns. And yet we know little about how these civil rights advocates have wielded demographic numbers and narratives to affect political change and how this relates to, and is shaped by, wider contention about ethnoracial demographic change.[1]

Figures of the Future examines the contemporary population politics of national Latino civil rights advocacy. Like their predecessors, advocates hold an organizing conviction that is rarely stated outright: achieving or least approximating the political power that tomorrow seemingly promises rests, to a great extent, on how the "Latino demographic" and its growth are publicly perceived and received. To this end, I argue, they have employed a set of temporal tactics to accelerate the *when* of Latino political power. This effort must be understood against the backdrop of public discourses that have framed this population as a population of the future, one perpetually on the rise.

Focused primarily on the second decade of the new century, across the politically polarized Obama and Trump presidencies, I followed these figures as they sought, and struggled, to render the "second largest" ethnoracial population both politically potent *and* socially palatable in the public imagination. This has meant contesting entrenched tropes of Latino threat and passivity, which in practice has often seen such tropes replaced with sanitized, no less essentialist, representations. Based on several years of qualitative and ethnographic fieldwork, I further show how, among these actors, projected demographic futures operate, variously and viscerally, as objects of aspiration, sources of frustration, and weapons for struggle. This book ultimately finds that imagining a bright Latino future is much easier than accelerating it.

Whereas scholars have been largely concerned with the causes and potential consequences of ethnoracial population trends, this book centers on the meanings ascribed to these trends and the political struggles in which they are being wielded. Moreover, it goes beyond the almost exclusive focus on the population politics of white—typically white supremacist—political projects. Without question, such analyses are important, and increasingly so. But these are not the only agents of population politics. Political actors from minoritized groups are also bringing ethnoracial futures to bear on the present, in the process shaping contemporary politics and identities. It is important to take stock of how these projects and movements have also envisioned, mobilized, and pursued ethnoracial futures. Without doing so, we compromise our ability to fully understand the political present here and elsewhere.

The Flood

The United States is in the midst of a demographic data downpour. It began decades ago and will likely continue beyond the year 2050. This is not the first time that numbers and narratives about ethnoracial population trends have *flooded* U.S. public life.[2] The current rains have been, above all, about the purported growth of "nonwhite" populations and the decline of the "white" population, what has been popularly, albeit inexactly, labeled the "browning of America." National Latino civil rights organizations are but one source of precipitation among many. The Census Bureau is another—if not the major—source. Not only does it supply much of the "raw" data and official taxonomies others use to produce population projections, it also generates its own authoritative but by no means uncontested demographic forecasts. In its latest projections, census officials claim that the country is becoming "more racially and ethnically pluralistic."[3] Such phrasing softens the sharper language it has employed in previous announcements about a coming "majority-minority" future.[4] Downstream from this leading agent of population politics, we find a diverse collection of entities that have advanced their own interpretations about demographic change.[5]

The news media plays an influential role, as both a contributor to and conduit of population politics. As scholars have shown, the press actively thematizes rather than passively reports on population dynamics.[6] Headlines such as "U.S. Steps Closer to a Future Where Minorities Are the Majority," "Fewer Births than Deaths among Whites in Majority of U.S. States," and "Hispanic Population Reaches New High of Nearly 60 Million" regularly shout from newspaper pages.[7] New technologies online have transformed static maps and charts into sites where individuals can intimately and interactively engage with demographic trends.[8] Together, this stream

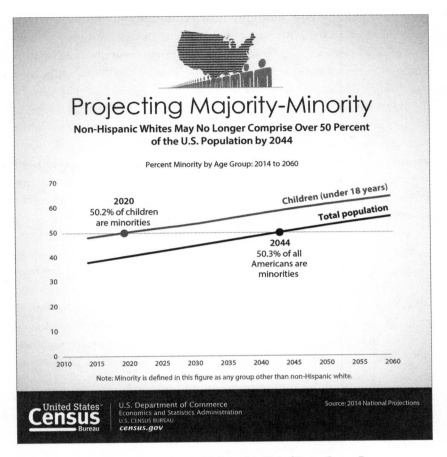

FIGURE 0.1. "Projecting Majority-Minority" infographic. United States Census Bureau, March 2015.

of texts, photographs, and data visualizations renders demographic change "newsworthy."[9]

In debates over ethnoracial demographics, academic scholars and researchers are not mere bystanders who at most produce disinterested, scientific knowledge. Instead, in offering interpretations of demographic trends and their potential societal impacts, they contribute to the inundation. Along with academic-based work, think tanks, "fact tanks," and policy institutes have had much to say about how demographic dynamics should be understood. These include the Brookings Institution, Center for Immigration Studies, Cato Institute, Pew Research Center, and Center for American Progress, among others.

Finally, political, civic, and movement leaders from across the ideological spectrum have further saturated public life with demographic statistics and stories. Take, for example, former Republican representative Steve King's white supremacist tweet in 2017 stating that "culture and demographics are our destiny. We can't restore our civilization with somebody else's babies."[10] With less anxiety and more ambivalence, then president Barack Obama, in his farewell address, described "demographic change" as both one of the factors testing the country's security, prosperity, and democracy and "something to embrace" rather than fear. Social movement leaders and activists have also engaged in population politics. As progressive groups have made celebratory proclamations of an emerging "new majority," white supremacist groups have decried "white genocide" and used it to justify violence.

National Latino civil rights groups swim in these turbulent waters. But, as Murguía's speech illustrates, they have also contributed to this deluge of demographic data and discourse—a deluge that has made it difficult, perhaps impossible, for any of us to remain unconcerned, untouched, or unnerved by ethnoracial population trends. Indeed, there is widespread consensus that—for better or worse—the United States will *look* and *feel* dramatically different in the decades to come. At the same time, and not at all coincidentally, there is also widespread disagreement and division about what this all means and how this projected future should be met.

Contrary to the undertow of contemporary population discourse, neither consensus nor dissensus about the country's ethnoracial future arises outright from the "demographics" in question. These demographics do not dictate which population trends matter, which deserve our attention, and how we should respond to them. Nor do they determine how populations are classified and how trends are studied. Yet these are precisely the powers that are often ascribed to demography. However, this pervasive misattribution is one of the most potent outcomes of population politics. Thus to investigate these waters, as this book endeavors, demands considerable vigilance, lest we be unwittingly overtaken by its waves and currents.

Demographic Naturalism

When writing about the "state," the preeminent French sociologist Pierre Bourdieu once professed, "If it is so easy to say easy things about this object, that is precisely because we are in a certain sense penetrated by the very thing we have to study."[11] Bourdieu could have just as well been referring to demography. To study population politics, whether of national Latino civil rights organizations or of some other political project, we must confront demographic naturalism, the dominant attitude toward demography.[12] We must also, and with equal fervor, confront racial essentialism, with which demographic thinking is often closely linked. Only doing so will prepare us to examine—rather than to parrot—the political struggles through which ethnoracial demographics are constituted and contested.

Demographic naturalism holds three major assumptions. First, it views populations as "real," natural, and actually existing entities. In politics, populations are regularly conflated with peoples and attributed collective agency and coherence. Second, it conceives of population trends as akin to natural forces with the potential to affect social and political life unmediated by modes of perception. For instance, demographic anxieties and fears are regularly depicted as automatic, seemingly unavoidable, outcomes of population dynamics rather than as sentiments of political cultivation. Third, it believes that demographic knowledge—as a product of science—more or less reflects or approximates said demographic realities.

I depart from each of these assumptions. Demographic populations are not what they seem, at least in a straightforward sense. They do not exist "out there," as basic and obvious features of the social world. As the sociologist Bruce Curtis writes, "Population is not an observable object but a way of organizing social observations."[13] Similarly, population trends cannot be studied, known, or managed apart from the political relations, social imaginaries, and statistical techniques and conventions through which we constitute populations. Additionally, the apparent power of demographic trends rests to a great extent on interpretation—and it must be stressed that interpretations do not grow naturally from trends. Furthermore, demographic knowledge is a "political science."[14] This should not be taken to mean that demographic statistics are necessarily and reducibly partisan, corrupt, or ideological. Rather, it is to recognize, as William Alonso and Paul Starr wrote long ago, that "political judgements are implicit in the choice of what to measure, how to measure it, how often to measure it, and how to present and interpret the results."[15]

Naturalistic assumptions pervade public discussions about ethnoracial population change. Claims are routinely made about "racial" populations that presume their actual existence and treat racial statistics as plainly objective. But such claims not only express naturalized assumptions about demography, they also rest on and further reify assumptions about race. Accordingly, it is not enough to problematize demographic naturalism without also addressing its relationship to racial conceptualization.

Sociologist Ann Morning defines "racial conceptualization" as "working models of what race is, how it operates, and why it matters."[16] Despite the social constructionist critique, racial essentialism remains prevalent.[17] "Racial groups" are often seen as different on putatively biological and cultural grounds.[18] This is evident in demographic discourse, where it is common to encounter expressions that attribute, subtly or not, particular traits and interests to specific populations. As Susanne Schultz writes, "Demographic rationalities tend to 'essentialize' social relations by ascribing fixed characteristics or properties to specific population groups and by introducing reductionist and reifying forms of analysis."[19] For example, the Asian American population has often been characterized as almost innately intelligent and respectful to elders. The Latino population has been regularly described as almost inescapably passive and religious. Such stereotypes are relational; for some to be seen as family oriented or prone to crime, others must be seen as not, at least implicitly.

Yet even when population-specific attributions are absent, a deeper assumption about the nature of race itself is often present. What makes a population a *racial* population, as opposed to another type of population, say, an "ethnic" one? This question is rarely asked in public discourse because the answer is seen as self-evident. Left unquestioned, it is often presumed that the racialness of a population inheres in the population itself, that is, it is a racial population because its constituent members purportedly belong to a race. This tautology does not necessarily whither when challenges to specific essentialist claims are raised. What must be asserted vigorously is that there is nothing inherent about individuals, peoples, or groups that makes them "racial" or be seen as "racial" by others. Race does not rest in "the eye of the beholder or on the body of the objectified."[20]

Building on the contributions of political theorist Barnor Hesse and others, I instead conceive of race as a modern colonial practice of classification and constitution anchored in the ideological and material division between Europeanness and non-Europeanness.[21] It is, above all, a political relation, one that "registers the state of colonial hostilities" at a given time and space.[22] The concept of population has been one of the prime idioms through which colonially constituted notions of race have been naturalized and normalized. Indeed, demographic knowledge emerged, in part, as a form of racial knowledge. As such, this knowledge exhibits what the philosopher David Theo Goldberg has described as a "dual movement." On the one hand, it has "parasitically" appropriated the assumptions, techniques, and credibility of scientific knowledge; and on the other, race has been a foundational object and motivation for the development of scientific fields, including demography.[23] Moreover, the concept of race has survived critique on the back of the seemingly benign, impartial, and objective notion of population. Thus we must account for rather than take for granted the preeminently political processes and practices through which peoples are variously racialized or ethnicized *as* populations.

At this point, it is necessary to note that the problem of essentialism and naturalism cannot be exclusively charged to "public demography," or what has been more dismissively labeled "garbled demography."[24] Academic researchers are no less liable for ignoring or taking for granted the political conditions and imaginative scaffolds on which demographic knowledge rests.[25] Further, as demographers and other social scientists have historically pioneered and partaken in population politics, the line between "public" and "academic" demography can be quite blurred. Although this book focuses on the former, the challenge is the same: to examine the struggles, conventions, and histories implicated in the construction and communication of demographic knowledge.

Population Politics

Many scholars have explored the relationship between politics and demography.[26] Writing in 1971, the political scientist Myron Weiner laid out three components for the study of what he termed "political demography."[27] The first component focused on the "study of the size, composition, and distribution of population in relation to both government and politics." Said more plainly, this research sought to understand how demographic processes affect political systems.[28] The second component addressed what Weiner described as the "political determinants of population change," or how governments have shaped population dynamics. Research on what scholars have called "demographic engineering" has contributed to this line of inquiry.[29] The third component concerned "knowledge and attitudes that people and their governments have toward population issues." Research in this vein has endeavored to study how demography is publicly perceived and to what effect. Examples include work on "innumeracy" and experimental research on views of ethnoracial demographic change.[30]

Of the three components, the last one is the closest to the line of inquiry taken here. However, perceptions about demographic trends, and what emotions they inspire, are neither an inevitable response to demography nor entirely explainable based on individual characteristics, such as socioeconomic status, racial identification, or geographic location. For this we need an account of efforts undertaken—successfully or not—to construct populations and cultivate how they should be publicly understood and engaged.

Drawing on past scholarship, we can distinguish between two phases of population politics. The first phase pertains to efforts to influence the production of demographic knowledge. Spurred in large part by Foucault's writings on governmentality and biopolitics, scholars have excavated the origins of demographic knowledge and the field of demography.[31] More directly, for present purposes, has been work on the creation of demographic statistics through national censuses. This scholarship has shown that population politics occurs most visibly, and often most intensely, over the categories used to construct "official" populations.[32] There are countless examples of actors lobbying for specific categories: white U.S. census officials calling for the removal of any categorical distinctions among any individuals with "black blood" in the early twentieth century; members of the "Other Backward Classes" demanding full caste enumeration in the 2011 Indian census; and French scholars and activists petitioning for the inclusion of racial categories in its national census, to name a few.[33] Such population politics do more than determine what populations exist and do not exist; they also define them, at least for official purposes. The U.S. government designates "Hispanic" as an ethnic category. In Brazil, *pardo* is officially defined as different from the category *preto*. Again, there is nothing inherent about the individuals and peoples said to belong to these categories that justifies these or any other conceptions. Both are the result of histories of population politics. All these decisions influence population counts.[34] For example, as Richard Alba has argued, the choice of the U.S. Census Bureau to count individuals that report "multiracial" parentage as nonwhite decreases the overall size of the "White" population and accelerates the projected arrival of a "majority-minority" future.[35] Although made in the heat of past negotiations and contestations, decisions tend to cool over time, increasingly appearing neutral and necessary.[36] Yet this neither erases the impact of these decisions nor how it sets the stage for the second phase.[37]

Once demographic knowledge is produced, actors—who may or may not have been involved with the earlier phase—begin to wield population statistics. At this point, such knowledge may become objects of struggles over how populations and population trends are to be interpreted and projected to relevant publics. What does it mean that a given population is growing or decreasing? How should we prepare for the future apparently disclosed in the data? Who will benefit from demographic change, and who will suffer? Although comparatively less documented, past scholarship offers numerous examples of this phase: mid-twentieth-century Israeli demographers mobilizing projections of Palestinian population growth to urge Zionist officials to adopt policies to increase Jewish reproduction; Latin American elites using demographic projections to communicate "national progress" to their international counterparts in the nineteenth century; white supremacists citing population statistics as proof of "white replacement" in the early twenty-first century.[38] Despite their differences, such projects often contribute— sometimes by intention—to what scholars have termed "demographization," or how "social conflicts and problems" become "interpreted as demographic conflicts or problems and within which demographic or population policies are highlighted as solutions."[39] In racialized social systems, this typically entails the racialization of demography, whereby demographic processes (e.g., birth, mortality, and migration) come to be imagined, and engaged as "racial" phenomena.

This scholarship provides a foundation on which I build an analytic scaffold to further study and theorize population politics. It has three intersecting elements that I will detail below, in turn. Readers anxious to get to the case of national Latino civil rights advocacy may skip ahead.

Analytic Scaffold

TEMPORALITY

Actors conduct population politics with the expressed aim to shape how demographic time and temporalities are experienced and perceived. It is therefore necessary to consult works that have examined and theorized the temporal dimensions of social and political life. Informed by this work, I recognize that our representations and embodied sense of time are neither universal nor constant. Although individuals may, through practices of "timework," manage and modulate for themselves the duration, sequencing, and allocation of time, among other things, I am concerned with the *temporal tactics* employed by political projects.[40]

In the scholarly record, I find two major types of temporal tactics. The first targets *temporal experience*. E. P. Thompson's classic essay "Time, Work-Discipline, and Industrial Capitalism" addresses this type. In it, Thompson describes how British capitalists, employing incentives, coercive measures, and technical devices, especially clocks, not only rendered workers compliant but also transformed their phenomenological sense of time. In his "tempography" of an Argentinian welfare office, Javier Auyero shows that street-level bureaucrats exercised power over citizens through imposed and arbitrary waiting.[41] Such "durational time" operates at different scales, from the time it takes to receive social services to the timeframes that regulate when citizens can vote or immigrants can naturalize.[42] In racialized societies, such as the United States, durational time often closely intersects with "racial time."[43] Disproportionately monitored and policed in public spaces, Rahsaan Mahadeo writes, Black and Native American youth rarely have time to feel at peace.[44] In their own ways, these and other works confirm that temporal experience is not only a social phenomenon but a political one, shaped through particular exercises of and resistances to power.[45]

The second type of temporal tactic targets instead *temporal imaginaries*. Past scholarship suggests a number of ways. Foundationally, political actors and institutions can designate what counts as the "past," "present," and "future." They can also delineate the temporal boundaries of particular events, influencing, for example, what people take as the birth of the nation or the end of a military conflict. Moreover, political actors may draw connections across time. In her examination of French commemorations of the abolition of slavery, Crystal Fleming shows that some social movements deliberately sought to link the transatlantic slave trade to current racial inequality.[46] On the contrary, narratives of racial progress communicate, more or less starkly, a disjuncture between a racist past and post-racial presents and futures.[47] Recent research on nationalist projects and "invented traditions" suggests that such temporal tactics have often depended on material culture and objects.[48]

Key for population politics is futurity, which has received far less attention than the past within sociology.[49] Elaborating a contemporary "sociology of the future," a growing body of work breaks with the tendency to treat imagined futures as a domain of speculation rather than as a topic of theoretical and empirical investigation.[50] This work coincides with work on expectation, anticipation, preparedness, and temporal multiplicity in science and technology studies.[51] These works have produced a number of conceptual tools to assist the analysis of imagined demographic futures. Ann Mische, for example, has outlined several dimensions of what she calls "projectivity."[52] These dimensions encourage researchers to answer a range of questions about the "future" under analysis, such as, does it extend into the short, medium, or long term? Is it fixed or flexible? Detailed or vague? To what extent does human action (or inaction) determine the future? Mike Michael proposes other dimensions, including what he labels "speed," whether the movement toward the future is seen as fast or slow, or what he terms "valency," whether the future is imagined as positive or negative, utopian or dystopian.[53] These and other dimensions will prove valuable as we proceed.

QUANTIFICATION

Demographic futures are often anchored in population statistics and statistical projections.[54] To deepen what we know about population politics requires adopting an unconventional attitude toward statistics, one that recognizes that statistics—like the populations they help construct—do not objectively reflect or approximate reality.[55] This does not mean, however, that "realist" attitudes should be dismissed. To the contrary, they should be taken seriously, and their formation and consequences examined. A number of scholars have done precisely this, uncovering some of the historical, organizational, and cultural factors that have generated widespread "trust in numbers."[56] While important, this line of inquiry is not enough for the task at hand: to understand the sociopolitical and cultural life of demographic statistics as tools of population politics. As such, the objective is neither to prove nor disprove the factness of demographic data, nor to adjudicate "good" from "bad data."[57] Over the past few decades a vibrant and growing disciplinary and interdisciplinary body of research on quantification has generated useful insights for this enterprise.[58]

First, scholars have foregrounded the politics of quantification, specifically in relation to modern statecraft. Given the centrality of censuses to contemporary population politics, this move is vital. From this vantage point, statistics are understood as "an inherently political and administrative knowledge."[59] Michel Foucault, for instance, argued that this new political science enabled what he described as the "governmentalization of the state," a mode of power oriented, above all, to the control, management, and welfare of "populations."[60] Statistics—in the words of James Scott—endowed elites and bureaucrats to "see like a state." Through censuses and other knowledge-gathering techniques (e.g., cadastral maps, civil registries, and passports), heterogeneous people, places, and things were simplified, homogenized, and ultimately rendered "legible."[61] Official racial classification and quantification represents one of the ways that peoples were made legible for rule. The history of "racial legibility," especially since the mid-twentieth century, reveals that statistics have been used not only as instruments of control but also as weapons of critique and contestation.[62]

Second, recent works have focused on not only the politics of quantification but also its powers. Several terms have been used to express a foundational provocation: statistics and numbers are world-making rather than world-representing instruments. Labels such as *performativity* and *reactivity* offer resonant ways to capture how numerical data can shape social life and even create new forms of sociality. In the words of the philosopher of science Ian Hacking, "The systematic collection of data about people has . . . profoundly transformed what we choose to do, who we try to be, and what we think of ourselves."[63] Empirical cases abound. Opinion polls helped create an "American public" and normalize particular, and often essentialist and restrictive, notions of Americanness.[64] Censuses and other quantifying techniques have fomented the formation of new collectivities and the transformation of old ones.[65] Statistics have influenced prevailing conceptions of democracy and democratic citizenship.[66] Such statistical effects, however, elevate the need to reflect on the ethics of quantification, the potentials, limits, and excesses that working with numbers entails.[67]

Third and finally, I draw on scholars who have explored the meaning and emotive potency of numbers. This work approaches statistics as multivalent rather than singular. The same statistic may be taken to mean, depending on context and perspective, that a population is strong or weak. Numbers may be seen as insignificant or as emblematic, collective representations, what Martin de Santos has labeled "fact-totems."[68] Take, for example, the power of the stylized figure of the 1 percent, as a symbol of the hyperconcentration of wealth.[69] A major part of the politics of numbers is efforts to charge and impose them with meaning. This extends from the process of production to the process of circulation. But, as this scholarship suggests, this is a fraught process as actors cannot control outright the interpretations and meanings given by others.

EMOTIONS

As we will see, population politics cannot be properly studied without an eye to emotions and affects.[70] Demographic numbers, for instance, can inspire hope and anxiety, excitement and boredom.[71] Among U.S. Jewish leaders, anthropologist Michal Kravel-Tovi has found that numbers and practices of counting the Jewish population have elicited a wide range of "affective positions," including ambivalence and hostility.[72] Traditionally, however, political sociologists and students of social movements have narrowly conceived of politics as a cognitive enterprise. This stems at least in part as a response to early behavioralist accounts that framed social movements as irrational.[73] But this has begun to change.

Importantly, some recent scholarship has emphasized the role of emotions in politics. These extend far beyond anger and fear. For example, Deborah Gould intimately narrates how activists from the radical AIDS activist group Act Up expressed and managed feelings of sadness, pain, and pleasure.[74] Writing about imagined futures, Arjun Appadurai comments that our visions about tomorrow are "shot through with affect and with sensation," capable of producing "awe, vertigo, excitement, disorientation."[75] These accounts urge us to consider actors engaged in population politics as embodied and emotionally complex agents, who are led not only by "instrumental" goals. Furthermore, it helps us recognize that goals such as political power and recognition are themselves affectively charged.

Some works have provided means to move beyond individualist or internalist accounts of emotions. In her influential work, Sara Ahmed has proposed the notion of "affective economies." Instead of conceptualizing emotions as "psychological dispositions," Ahmed argues for the "need to consider how they work, in concrete and particular ways, to mediate the relationship between the psychic and the social, and between the individual and the collective."[76] Said differently, she trains our attention on what emotions do. Building on this conception, it is necessary to attend to the ways that political projects—often intentionally—seek to transform affective economies. This point is important, as population politics are in the business of "sticking" particular emotions to particular populations and trends. Indeed, without attending to emotions, we cannot understand what scholars have called *demographobia*.[77] Political projects may thus be both objects and orchestrators of affective economies. Consider, for example, sociologist Hiro Saito's analysis of national commemorations of Hiroshima. Saito argues that these commemorations were not meant to simply present facts about the U.S. nuclear bombing of Japan and its effects. Instead, they were designed to generate a collective sense of trauma, one meant to generate "sympathy and solidarity" with the victims of the atomic bombing.[78] In the case of population politics, we must further consider how political projects *racialize* emotional economies.[79] Ahmed has, for instance, examined how hate and fear circulate through narratives about immigrants and mixed-race couples. In all cases, however, political actors cannot entirely determine or constrain what emotions are unleashed by particular discourses or representations, or even how political actors themselves are emotionally moved in the process.

National Latino Civil Rights Advocacy

Equipped with conceptual tools and sensibilities harvested from the literatures discussed above, I turn my attention to the case of population politics at the center of this book. National Latino civil rights advocacy organizations are part of the broader landscape of contemporary Latino/a/x politics. One aspect that distinguishes national advocates from most elements of this landscape is their explicit desire, untenable as it may be, to advocate for the "Latino community" as a whole. No matter the location of their headquarters or the majority of their staff, they are preeminently focused on the "national" political scene. In this scene, they interface, in some cases regularly and in others episodically, with state agencies, elected officials, courts, think tanks, academics, media, philanthropy, corporations, social movements, and other advocacy organizations. With a few exceptions, the vast majority of national Latino civil rights organizations were born during or after the period that sociologist John Skrentny has dubbed the "Minority Rights' Revolution" and as such are part of the "explosion" of advocacy organizations that has occurred since the 1960s.[80]

In 1991 the major national Latino civil rights organizations and leaders established the National Hispanic Leadership Agenda (NHLA).[81] Its mission calls for "unity among Latinos around the country to provide the Hispanic community with greater visibility and a clearer, stronger influence in our country's affairs. NHLA brings together Hispanic leaders to establish policy priorities that address, and raise public awareness of, the major issues affecting the Latino community and the nation as a whole." Building on increased collaboration for the 2008 election and the 2010 census, plus an influx of new leadership, the coalition has expanded its influence and membership to over forty-five organizations. Although these organizations still compete at times for resources and recognition, there has been a concerted—even if sometimes inconsistent—effort to build a united front.

Herein I largely focus on NHLA's most visible and arguably most influential members. These include the League of United Latin American Citizens (LULAC), UnidosUS (formerly known as the National Council of La Raza), the National Association of Latino Elected and Appointed Officials Educational Fund (NALEO-EF), the Mexican American Legal Defense and Educational Fund (MALDEF), Mi Familia Vota (MFV), and Voto Latino. LULAC, UnidosUS/NCLR, NALEO-EF, and MALDEF are "legacy" organizations that have anchored national Latino advocacy for decades. Mi Familia Vota and Voto Latino—as their names indicate—emerged as civic engagement and voter mobilization projects in the 2000s. They are among the newest members of the coalition.

National Latino civil rights organizations are "professionalized" and officially nonpartisan organizations.[82] In an influential essay, John McCarthy and Mayer Zald distinguished "professional social movements" from classic models based on several features: the former were led by full-time leaders, largely externally funded, generally possessed a "paper membership," assumed the role of spokesperson for a given constituency, and sought to influence policy for the benefit of that constituency.[83] Each of these characteristics applies to the majority of the above organizations.[84] They are led and mostly staffed by full-time advocates. Their work rests on government, philanthropic, and corporate funds. They are, as a result, comparatively better funded than their grassroots counterparts (although most have comparatively smaller budgets than many business or professional lobby groups).[85] With the exception of LULAC and NALEO, most are nonmembership advocacy organizations.[86] Furthermore, all speak on behalf of the "Latino community" and advocate for policies that will improve the welfare and status of this constituency.

Latino advocacy groups have influenced U.S. public policy and politics. For example, they played a major role in the inclusion of a language amendment to the Voting Rights Act in 1975. Central to the story I tell, these political groups were also instrumental to the development of the statistical category "Hispanic" and its eventual integration into the official ethnic and racial classification system of the United States. They have carried out successful naturalization campaigns and challenged gerrymandered districts, voter suppression tactics, and anti-immigrant laws. Most recently, MALDEF, for example, was part of a successful lawsuit against the Donald Trump administration's proposed inclusion of a citizenship question on the 2020 census. Yet these organizations and their efforts have not gone without critique. They have been labeled "reformist" and "accommodationist" and criticized for being out of touch with everyday struggles and social movements. Serious concerns have been raised about the influence of philanthropic and corporate funding on their policy agendas, a process that political scientist Megan Ming Francis had termed "movement capture."[87] As discussed later on, advocates themselves have expressed—sometimes publicly—similar reservations and concerns about the state of national Latino civil rights.

The scholarly record on these organizations and NHLA, as a whole, is rather sparse. What research exists has almost entirely attended to the origins of these entities and their activity during the Civil Rights era.[88] With the exceptions of works such as Deirdre Martinez's *Who Speaks for Hispanics* and David Rodríguez's *Latino National Political Coalitions*, we have limited knowledge of the actual workings and composition of national Latino civil rights today.[89] Like advocacy groups generally, it is difficult to define and demarcate these organizations and their efforts. This is the case because these entities not only mediate relations between different constituencies and governmental and nongovernmental institutions but also are multifaceted.[90] Their efforts, on the whole, involve legislative and legal advocacy, public relations, civic engagement, and research and analysis.

But what concerns me most is a particular aspect of their tactical repertoire. Accordingly, this book does not offer—nor aim to offer—an exhaustive portrait of this political network. Rather, it focuses specifically on how these agents of population politics have constructed, communicated, and contested ideas about the ethnoracial population positioned at the eye of the demographic storm.

The Latino Demographic

A nonstop torrent of knowledge production over the past forty years has helped make the "Latino demographic" a major figure in the contemporary U.S. ethnoracial imaginary. Before this period, this figure did not exist. As noted earlier and expanded in the next chapter, national Latino civil rights groups are partially responsible for the emergence of this population in public life. The predecessors of today's advocates pressured the federal government to produce knowledge about what would become, through chance and compromise, the "Hispanic" population. The current attention placed on this population cannot be disentangled from the broader demographic deluge of which it is part.

Public discourse and representations have, above all, emphasized the *future* impact of the Latino population, routinely described as one of the "fastest-growing" populations. The future anchors what anthropologists Leo Chávez and Arlene Dávila have called, respectively, "Latino threat" and "Latino spin."[91] On the one hand, the Latino population has been narrated as a serious danger to the future of the country. On the other hand, some have claimed that it promises to strengthen the country and revive its ethos. However inflected, the future animates both claims about the population. Every general election cycle as of late has been inundated with talk about the "Latino vote," a constituency some say holds the fate of the major parties in its giant hands. Report after report of market research has announced

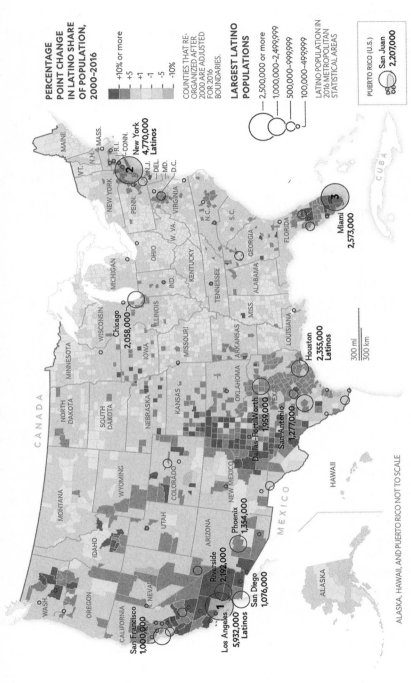

PERCENTAGE POINT CHANGE IN LATINO SHARE OF POPULATION, 2000–2016

+10% or more
+5
+1
-1
-5
-10%

COUNTIES THAT RE-ORGANIZED AFTER 2000 ARE ADJUSTED FOR 2016 BOUNDARIES.

LARGEST LATINO POPULATIONS

2,500,000 or more
1,000,000–2,499,999
500,000–999,999
100,000–499,999

LATINO POPULATION IN 2016 METROPOLITAN STATISTICAL AREAS

PUERTO RICO (U.S.)

San Juan 2,207,000

This U.S. territory is 99% Latino. All people born in Puerto Rico are U.S. citizens.

ALASKA, HAWAII, AND PUERTO RICO NOT TO SCALE

New York 4,770,000 Latinos

Miami 2,573,000

Chicago 2,058,000

Houston 2,355,000

Dallas-Fort Worth 1,959,000

San Antonio 1,277,000

Phoenix 1,354,000

Riverside 2,192,000

San Diego 1,076,000

San Francisco 1,000,000

Los Angeles 5,932,000 Latinos

300 mi
300 km

① Los Angeles is 45% Latino and has the largest Latino population of all U.S. cities. People of Mexican descent make up 78% of L.A.'s Latinos.

② New York's metropolitan area is 24% Latino. Puerto Ricans and Dominicans make up 27% and 21% of the Latino population, respectively.

③ Miami is 43% Latino; nearly half are of Cuban origin, and many arrived as political refugees.

RILEY D. CHAMPINE, NGM STAFF
SOURCES: PEW RESEARCH CENTER; U.S. CENSUS BUREAU; INTEGRATED PUBLIC USE MICRODATA SERIES, NATIONAL HISTORICAL GEO-GRAPHIC INFORMATION SYSTEM, UNIVERSITY OF MINNESOTA

FIGURE 0.2. "Expanding Latinidad" infographic. *National Geographic*, July 2018. Used by permission of National Geographic Society.

the arrival of an ever-growing consumer base with an annual buying power far into the trillions. Comedic routines and pieces of satire have delivered demographic punchlines about the "Hispanic" future. Journalists and scholars have written about how this population will transform schools, churches, cities, and rural communities. Old ideas of race will buckle, some have said, under the immense weight of this demographic multitude. By midcentury, we hear incessantly, the face of the country as well as its tongue and culture will be dramatically different. A new normal, population politics has told us, is on the horizon (fig. 0.2).

National Latino civil rights organizations and leaders have not passively consumed narratives about the Latino population and its future impact. On the contrary, they have crafted and communicated their own narratives to rally supporters, entice funders, challenge opponents, and insert themselves onto the national stage. Although they tend to traffic in inevitabilities, their efforts suggest a recognition that capitalizing on demography cannot be left to demography alone. Indeed, as they are quick to criticize, Latino political power has not run apace with Latino demographic growth. Underlining this frustration is the sense that demographic and political influence are intertwined, or at least should be. This is not their naiveté; it is one of the conceits of liberal democracy.[92] Thus woven into their advocacy, population politics have come to be seen as a way to speed up the rate of progress. In the wake of the 2010 census, as later chapters describe, they have worked to project tomorrow's power onto today's political landscape. Indeed, as Janet Murguía told her audience in the speech discussed at the onset, "we don't have to wait ten to fifteen years to have our future realized."

Following the Figures

This book is the culmination of research carried out between 2012 and 2019. The research I conducted is known as ethnography, one of the three major methods used by sociologists (and other social scientists). Ethnographic studies can take different forms but tend to share a commitment to learning through some degree of immersion in the lives and worlds of others. It therefore represents a deeply embodied and experiential mode of research.[93] Given its substantive concerns, this work joins a recent wave of political ethnographies.[94]

Across the country, I tracked the population politics of national Latino advocates in civic engagement campaigns, legislative lobbying, and a range of public-facing activities. But this research was not only interested in political figures but also in demographic figures. As such, this book is "peopled" with human beings and population statistics, among other objects.[95] Attentive to both, I pursued three major sources of data, each based on a different technique: participant observation, interviewing, and the collection of primary material (print and multimedia). Below I will provide details about each. Some chapters draw more on certain data sources than others, but the book in its entirety integrates each to tell a set of nested stories.

No matter the wealth of data I collected and analyzed, the ethnographic account I provide cannot be understood as definitive. Like all forms of knowledge, it is situated and incomplete. The conclusions I draw are as much shaped by the social world I examined as by the interpretative, political, and biographic features I brought to it. The result comes from an uneven encounter between these two "landscapes of meaning."[96] While this encounter cannot produce the lofty generalizations of other methods, this fact need not be seen as a weakness but as a strength.[97] Ultimately, the reader will decide whether this project was a success.

PARTICIPANT OBSERVATION

In April 2012 I boarded a plane to Los Angeles to attend Voto Latino's first "Power Summit." This research trip, the first of many, began my effort to observe and participate, as closely as possible, in the world of national Latino advocacy. Within a matter of months I made visits to Washington, DC, Las Vegas, and Orlando to attend conferences and conventions organized by leading organizations. At these events I took notes, photographs, and videos as I heard presentations and leaders dispense demographic statistics and narratives about the Latino demographic. These experiences gave me a glimpse into what I later designated as population politics.

In late September of that year I returned to Orlando for an extended stay, curious to learn about the role of demographic rhetoric in civic engagement efforts. I could have chosen a number of locations, but I was drawn to central Florida. Part of my motivation was personal: as a Puerto Rican, I have long been interested in Puerto Rican Orlando, the site of the largest migration of Puerto Ricans—from across the diaspora and the archipelago—over the past three decades.[98] The more direct reason was the fact that most of the major national Latino advocacy groups were invested in Latino "civic engagement" efforts throughout the state and particularly in central Florida in anticipation of the 2012 presidential election. There I connected with the voter campaigns of Mi Familia Vota, Voto Latino, the National Council of La Raza, and a joint campaign of the League of United Latin American Citizens, the Labor Council for Latin American Advancement, and the Hispanic Federation. Fieldwork entailed volunteering in their respective campaigns, through which I registered voters outside of local groceries and community centers, canvassed neighborhoods, phone banked, and attended local community events and organizational meetings. These activities took place primarily in Orange County, mostly within Orlando proper, though trips to Tampa and Miami helped me learn about operations outside of central Florida.

In January 2013 I moved to the Washington, DC, area, where I spent a year observing—and, in some sense, participating in—Latino advocacy. Like Orlando, I entered DC with few contacts and worked to gain access to an unfamiliar city and political world. My only previous experiences there were limited to attending protests and lobbying for Puerto Rican human rights issues. Thankfully, some of my contacts opened doors and I began to attend postelection forums and lobbying efforts in the capital. For nearly four months, LULAC opened its doors to me, generously giving me a workspace, access to its staff meetings, and the ability to follow its advocacy for comprehensive immigration reform. As a very minor compensation, I proofread documents, designed posters and flyers, reached out to potential speakers for immigration town halls, and provided logistical support where possible. One of the highlights of this work was taking part in legislative visits on Capitol Hill with LULAC council members from across the country. I also participated in similar efforts organized by Voto Latino and the National Council of La Raza.

My time in Washington was also punctuated by public events organized by leading Latino lobbyists, major think tanks and research institutes, and Latino advocacy groups and their collaborators. I moved away in early 2015 to complete my doctorate but returned for regular visits—between two and four each year—until 2019. This more "episodic fieldwork" not only updated my research but deepened my understandings of national Latino civil rights and their population politics.[99]

INTERVIEWING

Participant observation gave me insight into the ways that these political actors and their contemporaries have wielded data and projections. To learn more about their perspectives, aspirations, and frustrations, I conducted interviews. Gaining access to advocates often proved difficult and frustrating. I was not a familiar face and had no history with any of the organizations.

In Washington, initial reactions to me ranged from suspicion to annoyance to mild interest. It became clear to me that some leaders and organizations were much more open to researchers than others. Even after the better part of a decade trying, I was unable to speak to some advocates, and thus they appear here only through their public pronouncements. Several, however, generously made time to speak with me and put me in contact with their colleagues.

In total, I interviewed eighty individuals. These respondents included organizational leaders, public relations specialists, policy analysts, researchers, canvassers, federal appointees, partisan lobbyists, consultants, and staff members of national Latino groups. These interviews were typically conducted in English, the primary language used by these advocates in their professional and, in most cases, personal lives. Interviews typically lasted an hour but on several occasions exceeded two and a half hours. I interviewed some individuals repeated times. While most interviews were semistructured, I did use a more structured interview protocol in select cases where I was interested in capturing some of the variance between similarly positioned actors. Adapting certain techniques of the "focused interview," I used prompts and objects, including newspaper articles, promotional materials, and infographics, to elicit specific reflections on current events. I found infographics containing graphs and other visualizations of statistical data especially helpful in discussing ideas and assumptions about demographic trends.[100] In what follows, I use pseudonyms for all respondents except organizational leaders who are regularly in the press.

COLLECTION OF PRIMARY MATERIALS

Along with ethnographic and interview data, I built a large cache of primary materials, both documents and multimedia products. These included hundreds of newspaper articles, commentaries, and visualizations (e.g., infographics, photographs, and cartoons), and reports and documents produced by national Latino advocacy organizations and other organizations within the broader Washington, DC, political-policy field. These reports covered a wide range of substantive issues, including immigration, electoral outcomes, demographic trends, and voting rights. The multimedia products I collected included public service announcements made by national Latino organizations and video shorts produced by media outlets, as well as recordings of webinars on the latest polling data on Latinos, immigration reform, and the results of the 2012 and 2016 elections.

In sum, *Figures of the Future* marshals a wealth of qualitative and ethnographic data collected across multiple sites, both physical and virtual. I integrate ethnographic observations, interview data, and primary materials throughout this book to understand the population politics of national Latino advocacy within a context of growing anxieties about the country's ethnoracial future.

Chapter Overview

The remainder of *Figures of the Future* is divided into six chapters and a conclusion. The chapters are roughly chronological. The first two set the stage for the analysis of contemporary population politics and together comprise the section of the "Past." Chapter 1 situates the book in a distant but living past. Drawing on primary and secondary materials, it begins with an account of the earliest expressions and episodes of racialized population politics in the United States. Throughout this history, white political projects and movements have cast ethnoracial demographic futures as a racial problem or threat to white domination. Moving closer to the present, I discuss the mid-twentieth-century reemergence of discourses about overpopulation and how this "problem" came to be linked to Mexican and Latin American immigration in the 1970s. Finally, I show how this episode of population politics was coincident with another development: the Civil Rights era creation of the "Latino demographic." As the book demonstrates, these layered histories powerfully structure how and in what ways Latino advocates engage in population politics.

Chapter 2 tells a more recent story. It returns to the early years of the Obama presidency, when the 2010 U.S. census was on the horizon. As in prior decades, national Latino organizations and leaders made that decennial census a top priority. To ensure a "complete count" of the Latino population, advocates pressured the Census Bureau and legislators and launched community campaigns to promote participation and confront obstacles to census enumeration. Looking closely at tropes of "strength in numbers," this chapter details how advocates have contributed to the statistical construction of the "Latino population" and its projected future.

The content of the second set of chapters takes place after the 2010 census. Each chapter foregrounds a different temporal tactic of population politics used to accelerate Latino political power. For this reason I have labeled this section the "Future." Chapter 3 takes off as census data became public. Flooded with newly available census data, journalists, pundits, scholars, and activists immediately began to articulate various, sometimes explicitly, competing interpretations and narratives. I describe how, within this discursive context, advocates *forecast* Latino demographic futures as a benefit to the country's future. This account was a deliberately calibrated response to expressions of—and worries about—white demographobia. Seeking to assuage white fear over demographic change and to rebut racist stereotypes, Latino advocates advanced deracialized demo-utopias.

As the 2012 presidential election approached, Latino advocates also sought to *foreshadow* the future in the present. Chapter 4 analyzes this enactment. Coupled with voter registration and mobilization campaigns, these political actors produced and mobilized statistical knowledge to convince onlookers that the future had, in a sense, arrived. I focus on how two key figures—the projection that 12.2 million Latino voters would cast a ballot and the estimate that 50,000 Latino citizens turn eighteen every month—entered into circulation, came to be treated as "facts," and eventually validated the idea that the Latino "sleeping giant" awoke in the 2012 election and offered a glimpse into the future.

Confident that the election opened a new day in Latino politics, advocates immediately sought to seize the postelection moment and translate demographic futures (and electoral results) into concrete political gains. Zeroing in on beltway politics, chapter 5 analyzes attempts to *forewarn* that the failure to pass comprehensive immigration reform would seal the fates of political leaders and their parties. Although expectations were high, advocates quickly encountered serious challenges to their agenda. They could not control internal shifts within the Republican Party nor how swiftly the future foreshadowed in the election was forgotten.

The final chapter takes us up to the near present and is part of its own section. The election of Donald Trump in 2016 ushered in an unexpected, even unthinkable, present. Chapter 6 explores how, during the first two years of the Trump presidency, advocacy organizations and leaders responded to an intensification of anti-Latino and anti-immigrant rhetoric and policy. Among other things, the chapter discusses the fate of population politics in unsettled times. This context has brought to light longstanding internal and external frustrations about the political tactics and orientations of the major national Latino organizations, as well as a growing demand for new ideas and strategies for the realization of "Latino" power.

In the conclusion, I return to the major themes and tensions that mark the population politics of national Latino civil rights organizations. But more than this, I restate and broaden the central argument of this book—that the so-called browning of America owes more to politico-cultural dynamics than to the complexion of emergent populations. Calling for greater demographic reflexivity, it challenges naturalistic and essentialist accounts of ethnoracial demographic change.

A Word on Labels

Decisions about what labels or categories to use should not be taken lightly. Much is in a name. I therefore want to say a few words about one that appears throughout this book: "Latino." Like other ethnoracial categories, its meaning is not self-evident or universal. It is historical, political, and situational.

For decades scholars and activists have grappled with this label. In the 1980s intense debates raged about whether it was at all beneficial or legitimate to group heterogeneous persons and peoples under a single, encompassing "panethnic" label. Those who endorsed this practice won that debate, but it led to others. What specific term should be used? Hispanic or Latino? The former was viewed, simplistically, as a government imposition, and the latter, no less simplistically, as a bottom-up, community-born alternative. Not long after, Latino itself came under criticism. The masculinist Latino, it was charged, erased and subordinated the identities and realities of "Latinas." Not without resistance, new alternatives were put forth, such as "Latina/o" and "Latin@." These gained some currency in the 1990s and 2000s.

More recently, these alternatives have themselves been critiqued for preserving gender binaries and erasing and subordinating gender-fluid and nonbinary peoples. In response, several newer alternatives have been proposed, including Latinx and Latine. Others have challenged the historical erasure of Blackness and Indigeneity from dominant representations and conceptions of "Latinidad" (or Latino-ness). Identities and constituencies have begun to form around labels, such as "Afro-Latinx." Still others have voiced calls for the abandonment of Latinidad, writ large. This appeal in some sense revives older debates about the utility of pan-Latino labels. Overlapping and intersecting with many of these debates is contention about the meaning of these labels. The most controversial of these surrounds whether "Latino/Hispanic" designates a "race," "ethnicity," or "panethnicity." Together, these are only some of the struggles that have been and are being had over these names, to say nothing of those that may come in the future.

Bearing this history in mind, which I have only sketched here, I thought long and hard about what term to use in this book. No decision can fully appreciate and acknowledge the complexity of these labels and their contingent relations to peoples and projects. That said, I have chosen to primarily use the now somewhat archaic "Latino." This choice might influence how the book is received and what assumptions are made about it. Perhaps this is unavoidable. But more important for me was remaining close to the labels and categories used by national Latino civil rights organizations. While this political network has recently, and modestly, begun to integrate "Latinx," I worried that my adoption of this label in the text would overstate its prevalence among these groups. Moreover, using Latinx or any other alternative could cloud rather than clarify the meanings that civil rights advocates have ascribed to Latinidad. And these meanings, as will become evident, are quite important to the story I tell.

In using the term "Latino," however, I want to make clear that I do not assume a correspondence between this category (or any sociopolitical category) and those categorized as such. That correspondence, if and when it exists, is contingent and conditional rather than autonomic and necessary. My approach follows political theorist Cristina Beltrán in viewing Latinidad as a verb, something that must be done or enacted, and not as a noun that signifies something that someone *is*.[101] Rather than dismiss or embrace these labels uncritically, the question for this book becomes how, in what contexts, for what ends, and with what consequences these labels have been invoked, quantified, and temporalized.

Past

1

Demographic Futures Past

Imagined futures have pasts. Demographic imagined futures are no different. How previous political projects have envisioned demographic tomorrows—the ways these imaginings expressed and entrenched particular raced, gendered, classed, and national ideologies—remain alive in the present, in both obvious and occluded ways. Understanding contemporary population politics thus demands an account of demographic "futures past."[1]

To capture this layered and living history, I draw inspiration from the German historian and theorist Reinhart Koselleck. In a recently translated collection of essays, Koselleck critiques both linear and cyclical time for failing to capture and appreciate the "different temporal levels upon which people move and events unfold."[2] Considering historical time multiple and overlapping, he proposed the geological metaphor of "sediments" as an alternative conception of historical time.[3]

I will use this notion of sediments to set the stage for the chapters to come. Specifically, this chapter traces three historical layers of population politics. The first and oldest layer roughly spans the inception of the U.S. settler colonial project to the end of the Second World War. Throughout this period, white supremacist political projects and intellectuals cast putatively nonwhite demographic futures as a racial problem and threat to white domination. In key respects, its various episodes of racialized population politics set the "racial scripts" that subsequent actors would conjure or contest.[4]

The second sedimentary layer is more recent. This layer encompasses the mid-twentieth-century emergence and circulation of racialized discourses about non-Western "overpopulation" and its domestic U.S. permutation. By the mid-1970s leading proponents of zero population growth began to articulate, that is, link national overpopulation to Mexican (and Latin American) immigration, which was already being depicted as a political and economic problem in policy and media circles. Although there were some antecedents, it was during this period that these populations were cast in the public imagination as a biopolitical and cultural threat to the future of the United States.

The third layer emerged in the heat of the civil rights era and is the most directly related to national Latino advocacy. Here, a set of Mexican American and, soon after, Puerto Rican and Cuban American advocates aspiring for national political significance helped usher into existence the category "Hispanic." In time, these actors would turn to statistical data not only to reveal socioeconomic disparities but also to forecast Hispanic futures. Demography came to be seen as a means to political recognition, a belief still held by their political descendants—the primary subjects of this book. Due to its importance, I devote the most space to this layer.

The objective of this chapter, therefore, is not to provide an exhaustive account of these sediments of history. Rather, it is to mark out the political and intellectual terrain, or what the anthropologist David Scott calls "problem-space," that informs and impinges on the population politics of national Latino civil rights advocacy and those of their contemporaries.[5]

The First Layer: White Demodystopias

The long history of U.S. population politics is a story of "demodystopias."[6] With or without population statistics, political actors have articulated visions of negative, troublesome, even cataclysmic demographic futures. Defying notions of progress, such narratives have been articulated to instill demographic fear, or demographobia. The vast majority of these have been propelled by fantastical renderings of "nonwhite" populations as threats to perpetual white dominance.

An apt starting point is Benjamin Franklin. In 1751 Franklin penned an essay that would become an "influential precursor" of Thomas Robert Malthus's *Essay on the Principle of Population*.[7] Read across the thirteen colonies and Europe decades after its initial publication, Franklin's "Concerning the Increase of Mankind, Peopling of Countries, Etc." presents twenty-four brief observations on a wide range of demographic issues. The last third of these observations reveal his reservations, if not anxiety, about the growth of "foreigners." Franklin had particular foreigners in mind: Germans. He worried that Germans in Pennsylvania—a colony, he reminded, established by the English (or Anglo-Saxons)—"will shortly be so numerous as to Germanize us instead of our Anglifying them." For Franklin, there was no reason to expect that Germans would "adopt our Language or Customs any more than they can acquire our Complexion." (For today's readers, this racial conceptualization rings strange; for Franklin, Germans were neither "white" by culture nor by color.) His fears, however, extended beyond his beloved Pennsylvania. The scale of the problem, he tells his compatriots, is global. In this final observation, Franklin remarks:

> The Number of purely white People in the World is proportionably very small. All of Africa is black or tawny. Asia chiefly tawny. America (exclusive of the new Comers) wholly so. And in Europe, the Spaniards, Italians, French, Russians and Swedes, are generally of what we call a swarthy Complexion; as are the Germans also, the Saxons only excepted, who with the English, make the principal Body of White People on the Face of the Earth.

He continues, "I could wish their Numbers were increased." Calling for restrictions on German immigration and the importation of enslaved Africans, Franklin puts forth what may have been the "first proposal for a policy to shape world population."[8] His comments about Germans, as historian Erika Lee writes, "established a template of anti-immigrant attitudes, prejudice, and rhetoric that would be repeated and refashioned for later immigrant groups."[9] Moreover, and more broadly, they would serve as an influential model for racialized population politics.

Franklin did not, of course, pioneer such politics. By the time he made these observations, many of the thirteen colonies had prohibited sexual relations between those classified as "white" and "black."[10] The historian Rickie Solinger writes, "Early laws governing sex and pregnancy show that founding fathers and leaders of subsequent generations believed that regulated reproduction was crucial to building and keeping the United States a 'white country.'"[11] Laws and rhetoric about the dangers of miscegenation (or race mixture) continued after the War of Independence, increasingly supported with race science. For example, proponents of polygenesis—the idea that racial groups emerged from distinct rather than shared origins—pursued the inclusion of the category "mulatto" in the census of 1850 to prove that miscegenation led to degeneracy.[12]

Miscegenation was hardly the only subject of anti-Black population politics in the nineteenth century. In northern states, free Black people were widely depicted as a "depraved population." In 1821 the Massachusetts legislature, as historian George Fredrickson writes, "appointed a committee to look into the possibility of restricting Negro immigration, on the grounds that blacks constituted a 'species of population' that could 'become both injurious and burdensome.'"[13] These racist depictions powered white support for the relocation of African Americans to Africa. Southern planters and their political representatives publicly stoked fears about the growth of enslaved Black people and the prospects of rebellion. The Haitian revolution intensified these anxieties and their pronouncement for political ends, specifically the expansion of slavery to western territories.[14] For instance, in 1849 the Alabama Democratic Party predicted: "The negroes will become insupportable when they shall have doubled and trebled the white population South. The sequel may be easily discerned. We have an illustration in point in St. Domingo."[15] In the decades after the Civil War, white supremacist officials and scientists debated whether the Black population was destined for extinction or "alarming" growth. These positions increasingly drew on statistics, particularly census data, as proof. Through decontextualized data about crime, disease, and the Black population, "white Americans," Fredrickson argues, "could make their crimes against humanity appear as contributions to the inevitable unfolding of biological destiny"[16]

In the final quarter of the nineteenth century, social Darwinists and nativists rallied against Chinese immigration, cast as a present and future threat. Reminiscent of the ways Franklin thought of Germans, Chinese people within the United States were depicted by their vilifiers as a racially unfit and unassimilable population. "A foreign race has invaded California. It comes not to assist, but to destroy the hopes and aspirations of free labor. The descendants of the brave pioneers are unable to cope with a race that 'produces, but does not consume,'" stated one article in the *San Francisco Chronicle*.[17] To stem this "unarmed invasion," the U.S. Congress passed what contemporaries called the Chinese Restriction Act of 1882 and the Chinese Exclusion Act of 1888.[18] In the decades to come, anti-Chinese sentiment and policy would be generalized, serving as the blueprint for how other Asian populations would be imagined and targeted.[19] Senator James D. Phelan (D-CA), marshalling newly available—yet questionable—statistical projections, warned that "in ninety years there will be more Japanese in California than whites if the present birth rate continues."[20] Such expressions were not merely xenophobic but demographobic; that is, they articulated a fear not just of foreigners but of their numbers.

By this period, eugenics had become a major scholarly and political force in the United States. Often employing biological analogies, eugenicists spoke about the need to restrict immigration from the "unfit." In 1919, for instance, Prescott F. Hall, the influential founder of the U.S. Immigration Restriction League, advised:

> Just as we isolate bacterial invasions, and starve out the bacteria by limiting the area and amount of their food supply, so we can compel an inferior race to remain in its native habitat, where its own multiplication in a limited area will, as with all organisms, eventually limit its numbers and therefore its influence. On the other hand, the superior races, more self-limiting than the others, with the benefits of more space and nourishment will tend to still higher levels.[21]

Hall and other eugenicists narrated demodystopias that figured Southern and Eastern European immigration as threats to "Anglo-Saxon" survival. These pronouncements also echoed Benjamin Franklin, but by this time Germans and other continental Europeans were viewed as racially white, although on a hierarchical scale.[22] Thinkers like Madison Grant advanced theories of "Nordic" supremacy. In *The Passing of the Great Race*, published in 1916, Grant expressed little concern about indigenous peoples, whose "Indian blood" he believed would have no future impact on the country (save for a few isolated places), and Black people, who he claimed were innately subservient. He was, however, deeply concerned about those he described as "a large and increasing number of the weak, the broke, and the mentally crippled of all races drawn from the lowest stratum of the Mediterranean basin and the Balkans, together with hordes of the wretched, submerged populations of the Polish Ghettos."[23] Following an argument made decades earlier by Francis Amasa Walker, a prominent social scientist and census official, Grant charged that because of their willingness to work for lower pay, these immigrants depressed the economic prospects for "native" Americans (i.e., "Nordic" whites). This, in turn, was causing them to decrease their birth rates.[24] Writings and speeches about this looming "race suicide" animated movements to curtail immigration from Southern and Eastern Europe. These movements, and the political pressure they exerted, culminated in the Johnson-Reed Act of 1924, which introduced, among other things, national quotas on European immigration.[25]

Other white supremacists and eugenicists directed their fury at non-Europeans. One influential example was Lothrop Stoddard, who authored the popular tome *The Rising Tide of Color against White World Supremacy*. The book featured an introduction from his mentor Madison Grant and contained a map of the racial composition of the inhabited continents. Stoddard was a historian, born and raised in Massachusetts, where he received his PhD degree from Harvard in 1914. In his book's preface, he quoted words he had penned before the start of the First World War, convinced they had only become truer: "The world-wide struggle between the primary races of mankind—the 'conflict of color,' as it has been happily termed—bids fair to be the fundamental problem of the twentieth century, and great communities like the United States of America, the South African Confederation, and Australasia regard the 'color question' as perhaps the gravest problem of the future."[26] Stoddard projected a future race war in language that, albeit twisted, calls to mind the words of his fellow Harvard alumnus, W.E.B. Du Bois (who would later demolish Stoddard in debate).[27] In *The Souls of Black Folk*, Du Bois famously wrote, "The problem of the twentieth century is the problem of the color line—the relation of the darker to the lighter races of men in Asia and Africa, in America and the islands of the sea."[28] But where Du Bois sought to dismantle the colonial-racial order in the name of human equality and fraternity, Stoddard saw a movement to end what he considered the apex of human civilization, "white supremacy."

The tropes and narratives about floods, swarms, and invasions developed and deployed throughout this long history of white supremacist population politics did not fade into oblivion. Repurposed and recalibrated countless times since, they remain, in the words of Koselleck, "simultaneously present and effective."[29]

The Second Layer: The Origins of Latino Threat

THE DOMESTICATION OF OVERPOPULATION

The second sediment of history took place in the aftermath of the Second World War and the Nazi genocide of Jews, Romani, and other "inferior" populations. Even though the Holocaust led to a retreat from (though by no means a complete repudiation of) eugenics, population politics would continue to justify projects of demographic engineering.[30] In particular, the postwar period saw the revival of Malthusian concerns with overpopulation. Legitimated by the demographic methods and theories, Western officials, philanthropists, and social scientists problematized "population growth" in what later became known as the "global South."[31]

As the U.S. government began to invest in family planning and the use of contraceptives overseas and in its territorial possessions (e.g., Puerto Rico), several prominent figures and government officials questioned the absence of similar policies and projects in the United States. In 1965 John D. Rockefeller, III, founder and trustee of the Population Council, warned that overpopulation was not "somebody else's problem" but a domestic problem—a "crisis" even—and that "only government can attack it on the scale required."[32] Pressure from government agencies, foundations, and academics led President Lyndon Johnson to broaden his demographic purview. As he told attendees at the United Nations' twenty-fifth anniversary celebration in San Francisco in 1965: "Let us in all our lands—including this land—face forthrightly the multiplying problems of our multiplying populations."[33]

The next U.S. president, Richard M. Nixon, continued the domestication of overpopulation rhetoric. One year after the publication of Paul R. and Anne Ehrlich's vastly influential *The Population Bomb* in 1968, Nixon delivered a speech on population. In it, he claimed that global population growth was "one of the most serious challenges to human destiny in the last third of this century."[34] Though global in reach, his speech focused on domestic growth and the problems that it posed for the country and its future inhabitants. He urged Congress to establish a Commission on Population Growth and the American Future.

Congress agreed, and Nixon—with his aide, later senator Patrick Moynihan, behind the scenes—eventually tapped Rockefeller as the commission's chair.[35] With a membership that one observer described as "conservative by college student standards" and "liberal by national and White House standards," the commission completed its report in 1972.[36] Titled *Population and the American Future*, it contained fifteen chapters, as well as specific comments from a subset of its members. The report's opening paragraph rejected the assumption that "progress and 'the good life' are connected with population growth." Instead, the commission claimed its research had found the opposite to be true. The final sentence of its opening paragraph read, "We have concluded that no substantial benefits would result from continued growth of the nation's population."[37]

The report thus framed domestic population increase as a potential national problem. Yet, as with demographic discourse before and after its publication, racialized populations were not far afield from the commission's concerns. For some time, African American reproduction, in particular, had been viewed as a cause and exacerbator of a host of social pathologies. The fixation on Black fertility persisted even as fertility rates of poor, nonwhite people saw the greatest declines in the late 1960s.[38] Contrary to this position, the report claimed it a "myth" that population growth was primarily fueled by minorities and the poor "having lots of babies." It nonetheless viewed the higher fertility of "socially and economically disadvantaged racial and ethnic minorities" as precipitating a crisis. Although admitting that structural conditions, such as poverty and unemployment, were more significant, the commission noted that their combination with population growth was "a demographic recipe for more turmoil" in inner cities.[39] As one scholar at the time observed, the report "opens the gates to a primrose path which can divert attention from the true causes of social ills, blame the plight of the poor and minorities on their family size, and lead to the conclusion that fertility control will in some way improve our moral, social, and economic condition."[40] The vice-chair of the commission, attorney and civil rights advocate Grace Olivárez, issued a similar and scathing critique:

> Many of us have experienced the sting of being "unwanted" by certain segments of our society. Blacks were "wanted" when they could be kept in slavery. When that ceased, blacks became "unwanted"—in white suburbia, in white schools, in employment. Mexican-American (Chicano) farm laborers were "wanted" when they could be exploited by agri-business. Chicanos who fight for their constitutional rights are "unwanted" people. One usually wants objects and if they turn out to be unsatisfactory, they are returnable. How often have ethnic minorities heard the statement: "If you don't like it here, why don't you go back to where you came from"? Human beings are not returnable items. Every individual has his/her rights, not the least of which is the right to life, whether born or unborn.

Olivárez continued, arguing that "the 'wanted' and the 'unwanted' child smacks too much of bigotry and prejudice." She added, "Those with power in our society cannot be allowed to 'want' and 'unwant' people at will."[41]

Eventually, and after "acrimonious debates" within the commission, it submitted a final report to Nixon in May 1972.[42] After several months of silence, the president—to the surprise of many—chose not to endorse the report and explicitly rejected its antinatalist recommendations, particularly with respect to abortion. Charles Westoff, who was tasked by the American

Sociological Association with contemporaneously analyzing the commission, attributed Nixon's decision to a number of factors: Catholic opposition, a lower national population rate, less public concern over environmental issues, and, most of all, the fact that it was an election year.[43] But beyond these issues, historian Derek Hoff argues that the report was "stillborn" long before its publication. The real problem for Nixon was geographic concentration, not overpopulation.[44] Moreover, libertarian conservatives and pro-growth economists influenced the president's opposition to zero population growth.[45] Yet even though the report was dead on arrival, it contributed to a major ideological and policy shift in one population-related domain.

The commission's report devoted a chapter to immigration. That chapter, one of the shortest in the report, called for immigration policy to consider demographic issues. While it invoked the "nation of immigrants" trope and celebrated the contributions that immigrants have made throughout U.S. history, the chapter expressed strong reservations about the idea that immigration, as an engine of population growth, was necessarily beneficial. Leaving out the history of eugenics and race science, it benignly asserted that a changing demographic "situation" in the early twentieth century "became reflected in new immigration policies." Accordingly, the report suggested that the population situation at the time necessitated it "review the role of immigration."[46]

The chapter contained a few noteworthy elements. It described the entry of "illegal immigrants" as a "major and growing problem" with potentially negative economic implications, especially for members of the working class and U.S. citizen minorities. Notably, concerns were not limited only to undocumented immigration. Legal immigration, too, "could have a negative impact if not regulated carefully." Suggesting a concern with race, the chapter also detailed of the geographic-ethnoracial composition of current immigrants:

> Because of past restrictions, backlogs of demand, and the 1965 change in policy, there has been a dramatic shift in the geographic origins of our immigrants. From 1945 to 1965, 43 percent of immigrants came from Europe. But, from 1966 to 1970, only one-third of the immigrants were European, while one-third were Canadian and Latin American, and the remaining third were West Indian, Asian, and African. This geographic change has also affected the racial composition of immigrants, increasing the number of nonwhites.

It further pointed out that undocumented immigration was notably less heterogeneous: "Eight out of 10 illegal aliens found are Mexicans." Still, the commission urged policy makers to "take special care not to infringe upon the civil rights of Mexicans, Mexican-Americans, and others who are legally residing here and working or seeking work."[47]

In its concluding paragraphs, the report noted that there was a "division of opinion" about immigration policy within the commission. The most critical tension was between the "humanitarian" value of immigration and desires for national "population stabilization." As far as recommendations, the commission proposed that no increases to legal immigration should be made without a prior review of projected impacts on rates of population growth. It also recommended taking aggressive measures to stop or slow undocumented immigration, including through border control and employer sanctions. Although Nixon did not endorse any of the recommendations, some of these proposals have had a long afterlife. As sociologist Elena Gutiérrez has argued, the report helped relink immigration and overpopulation in the American imagination.[48] This shift, as we shall see, would color the remainder of the 1970s and shade policy for decades to come.

MEXICAN IMMIGRATION AS A DEMOGRAPHIC PROBLEM

In 1970s the "problem" of overpopulation became increasingly couched as a problem of "illegal" immigration from Mexico and other parts of Latin America.[49] Such was the central argument of the Ehrlichs' follow-up to the *Population Bomb*. Published in 1979, *The Golden Door* shifted from global overpopulation to overpopulation in one country—Mexico:

> Across the southern border of the United States are 67 million Mexicans. They are poor and Americans are rich. They speak Spanish and we speak English. They are brown and we are white. They want it and we've got it: jobs, prosperity, the Ladies Home Journal–Playboy lifestyle. As a result we are being invaded by a horde of illegal immigrants from Mexico. . . . The furor has attracted the attention of bigots and bureaucrats as well as concerned citizens who ask: If we are limiting our family sizes so that our children can inherit a better nation, why should we throw open our doors to over-reproducers?[50]

The Golden Door, as this quote illustrates, drew a stark line between Mexico and the United States, one that was at once demographic, economic, linguistic, and racial. The central preoccupation was the worry that successful efforts to decrease population growth in the United States were being subverted by "over-reproducers" coming into the country. Even as the Ehrlichs inveighed against "myths about Mexicans" and "outright fear of an invasion"—which were diagnosed as symptoms of ignorance—the book, anthropologist Leo Chavez contends, "reaffirmed already-taken-for-granted assumptions about the family values and fertility rates of Mexican women."[51]

While Paul Ehrlich and his collaborators further popularized the theme of Mexican immigration as a source of overpopulation, it was John Tanton who gave this position organizational muscle. The Michigan-born ophthalmologist with eugenicist leanings sat on the board of directors of the national group Zero Population Growth (ZPG) and was at the time the national chair of the Sierra Club population committee.[52] Well-respected, Tanton spoke at public hearings held by the Commission on Population Growth and the American Future. By at least 1971, he began urging the ZPG to take on immigration control, a stance that members cautioned as too controversial.[53] Within the environmental conservation movement, he also began to problematize Mexican immigration. However, worries about being perceived as racist led established environmental groups to largely reject his pleas.[54] Unable to gain sufficient traction, Tanton set out to build his own immigration-focused organizations. In 1979 he founded the Federation for American Immigration Reform (FAIR) and later the Center of Immigration Studies (CIS). He also influenced the creation of Numbers USA and other anti-immigration organizations espousing a Malthusian-laden vision laced with racial eugenics. This was plainly evident in Tanton's Social Contract Press decision to republish a translated version of Jean Raspail's inflammatory treatise The Camp of the Saints.[55] And according to many political observers, Tanton and the organizational network he helped establish in Washington, DC, have both influenced public discourse and helped block several key pieces of immigration reform legislation.

In the 1980s Tanton hosted retreats called Witan, an old Anglo-Saxon term for a council of wise men. Attended by Tanton's colleagues and staff, the retreats offered a space to strategize on the best ways to intervene in the public debate about immigration and overpopulation. In leaked memos written for these retreats, Tanton made explicit reference to the demographic and political implications of Mexican and Latin American migration on white U.S. society. Although he long denied any racist motivations, the memos suggested otherwise. In one, he posed the incendiary question: "As Whites see their power and control over their lives declining, will they simply go quietly into the night?"[56] He further questioned, "Will the present majority peaceably hand over its political power to a group that is simply more fertile?" Tanton also quipped, "Perhaps this is the first instance in which those with their pants up are going to get caught by those with their pants down!" As political scientist Alfonso Gonzales has rightly noted, "Tanton assumes that Latinos and the Euro-American majority could never peacefully coexist and live under the same political community."[57]

The centerpiece of Tanton and his collaborators' population politics is the idea of Mexican "hyperfertility." As Elena Gutiérrez details, "John Tanton's advancement of an immigration control platform focusing on the fertility of Mexican-immigrant women clearly shows how policymakers and population activists constructed and manipulated a racialized demographics aimed to incite fear in the general public for the advancement of an immigration control agenda."[58] In 1980 FAIR, for instance, issued vastly inflated projections that the country might be home to upward of sixty million "illegal immigrants" by the year 2000.[59]

Tanton's efforts coincided with—and contributed to—growing public discourse about the "problem" of Mexican immigration. Rekindling old racial scripts, Mexican immigration and reproduction were depicted as an "invasion."[60] Leo Chavez has shown that this depiction became prevalent in the mid-1970s, in part fueled by a series of U.S. News and World Report articles that drew a comparison between the U.S. Southwest and the Canadian province of Québec. What Chavez describes as the "Québec Model" was the assertion that Mexicans were unwilling to assimilate into white American society and would eventually constitute a threat from within, similar to Québécois separatists. By the early 1980s the idea that Mexican and Latin American immigration in general was a demographic threat was a fixture in U.S. public discourse.[61] The effects of these population politics would continue well into the twenty-first century.

Growing domestic concerns about overpopulation and Mexican immigration coincided chronologically—but did not initially, at least, intersect substantively—with the emergence of national Latino civil rights advocacy during the Civil Rights era. The political struggles of the period added important layers to the history of U.S. racialized population politics. As I will narrate next, the predecessors of current national Latino advocates went, in a matter of years, from being largely unconcerned with population trends and futures to being deeply engaged in population politics. In fact, while demographic numbers and narratives saturate many expressions of Latino politics, activism, and advocacy in the early twenty-first century, this was not always the case. When LULAC was founded in the late 1920s, population politics were not a major part—if at all—of its repertoire. Nor were they for the farmworkers movement decades later or for the Young Lords or the Brown Berets. That would change in the 1960s and 1970s, in no small part due to political shifts in the meaning and value of ethnoracial statistics and the creation of the panethnic statistical category "Hispanic." This category, in particular, would change the terms and targets of population politics, far beyond nascent Latino civil rights advocacy.

The Third Layer: The Birth of "Hispanic" Civil Rights

THE PROBLEM OF INVISIBILITY

During the apex of the Civil Rights era, the Mexican American predecessors of today's national Latino advocacy were frustrated with the "invisibility" of Mexican Americans in policy making and public discourse. They believed that this condition hindered their ability to call attention to the social, economic, and political needs of their population. These leaders felt ignored and absent from the national conversation.[62] Politicians and journalists, they asserted, treated Mexican Americans as a local or regional concern, one that led public officials "to shrug [this population] off as a quaint accident without consequence," as the authors of the influential book *The Mexican-American People: The Nation's Second Largest Minority* (1968) concluded.[63] Mexican American leaders also felt eclipsed by the Black Civil Rights Movement. Prominent Mexican American activist Herman Gallegos, for example, once commented, "Every time we walk out in Albuquerque, we're clouted by something happening in Selma or Montgomery. . . . We are invisible to the eyes of public officials in this country." Although Gallegos and his colleagues recognized the historical marginalization of African Americans and were inspired by the fight for Black civil rights, they believed they needed "new ways to attract national attention to their issues."[64]

For Mexican American leaders, this sense of invisibility and unimportance was regularly confirmed by national policy makers and leaders. One prominent example was President Johnson's refusal to invite Mexican American leaders to the White House Conference on Civil Rights in 1966. Johnson agreed only to host a Mexican American–specific conference at a future date.[65] Organizations like the Mexican American Political Association, LULAC, and others also criticized the Equal Employment Opportunity Commission for its inattention to work discrimination against Mexican Americans, leading to a dramatic walkout of one of its meetings in spring 1966. LULAC leader Alfred J. Hernández declared, "In spite of our number we are America's invisible minority. Because we have not demonstrated, because we have not cried out when we have been abused and exploited, we have been ignored."[66]

These pronouncements did not go unheard. In 1966 the country's leading teachers' union, the National Educational Association, elected to title its report in support of bilingual education for Spanish-speaking students *The Invisible Minority*.[67] A 1968 U.S. Commission on Civil Rights paper on the Mexican American population conveyed a similar sentiment. It claimed that a "lack of Anglo understanding and of attention" to the social conditions of Mexican Americans "has been extensive, not only at the national level, where it is virtually complete, but in the Southwest itself." This ignorance, the paper argued, was related to the "astonishing lack of 'hard data' on this population."[68] Journalist Helen Rowan, who authored the commission's report, wrote a condensed version for the *Atlantic Monthly*, poignantly titled "A Minority Nobody Knows."

Within this context, Julian Samora, a young Mexican American sociologist at the University of Notre Dame, elected to name his edited volume in 1966 *La Raza: Forgotten Americans*. Samora, one of the cofounders of the National Council of La Raza, emphasized the need for more research on Mexican Americans: "Not many scholars have concerned themselves with the Spanish-speaking people. During the last twenty-five years only a few books have been written on them, and most of these have been on specialized topics. . . . It is no surprise that the professionals in private and public agencies have a limited knowledge and understanding of these people whom they would serve."[69] In this and other works published at the time, the apparent invisibility of "Spanish-speaking people" was framed to a large extent as a problem of ignorance and knowledge. As Congressman Edward Roybal (D-CA), a towering figure in Latino civil rights, later remarked, "Statistical visibility is policy visibility."[70]

STATISTICS AS A CIVIL RIGHT

The absence of statistics on Spanish-speaking populations became a major political problem for Latino advocates just as ethnoracial statistics were undergoing a dramatic transformation. Up until the Civil Rights era, racial statistics—as the earlier discussion of racialized population politics illustrates—had been wielded, almost without exception, as instruments of white domination.[71] This history, and specifically the still-living reality of Jim Crow, had encouraged Black civil rights leaders at the time to adopt a color-blind position. When challenges to the implementation of newly passed legislation, such as the Civil Rights Act of 1964 and the Voting Rights Act of 1965, led to discussion about the use of race-based record keeping, leaders like the famed NAACP lobbyist Clarence Mitchell voiced strong opposition: "The history of the reason why we do not include this is sadly and surely proven, that the minute you put race on a civil service form, the minute you put a picture on an application form, you have opened the door to discrimination and, if you say that isn't true, I regret to say I feel you haven't been exposed to all of the problems that exist in this country." As the historian Hugh Davis Graham noted, a decade before Mitchell made this statement, he had influenced President Eisenhower's decision to end race-based records in federal employment. Mitchell passionately argued that the reintroduction of racial statistics (and classifications) to track discrimination would "put us back 50 years and nullify all the work we have been doing to correct this thing."[72] However, not long after, albeit with much contention, racial statistics came to be seen as useful, even necessary, to civil rights protections. As a consequence, ethnoracial statistics soon gained new uses and new values. Numbers once used to legitimate relations of domination were leveraged to expose those very relations. For political scientist Deborah Thompson, this new political and intellectual change "provided minority groups with more incentives for being officially counted, raising the stakes of racial enumeration."[73]

Attempting to seize and deepen this shift, Mexican American and later Puerto Rican and Cuban American advocates began to make public demands for data. They argued that the production of statistical information about the Spanish-speaking population would both elevate the needs of the population and help them tap into new federal protections and resources. But statistical knowledge was not only a means to an end; it was also seen itself as a civil right.

The conception of ethnoracial statistics as a civil right was most clearly and extensively elaborated in the National Council of La Raza's nearly hundred-page report, *Impact of Limited Federal Statistical Data/Information on Hispanic Americans*, in 1974. In its preface, NCLR's acting director Alex Zermeno wrote, "For too long, the Hispanic American has been buried in the anonymity of statistics and semantics which neither apply to them nor characterize them." The author, Roberto Olivas, a Los Angeles–born World War II veteran, stressed that the problem was not categorical or terminological; rather it was a failure of the entire information system that resulted in "de facto exclusionary policies, patterns and practices which work against the Hispanic Americans." Olivas asserted: "The public has a right to quality information. Public institutions have an obligation to provide sound information, not misinformation; useful information, not statistical atrocities!"[74] The report further accused the federal government of having a "biracial"—that is, black/white—information infrastructure that mischaracterized and thus underrepresented the country's multiethnic population.

Urging an overhaul of the federal information system, the report made clear that the decennial census was only part of a much broader issue. However, NCLR and other organizations saw the Census Bureau and how it categorized and counted Mexican Americans and other "Spanish-speaking" groups as a vital starting point. To cease being invisible, they began to make demands to become "legible" in this constitutionally mandated exercise.[75]

TARGETING THE CENSUS

In 1968, as the Census Bureau prepared for the 1970 decennial census, the U.S. Interagency Committee on Mexican-American Affairs, which was established by President Johnson, issued a recommendation regarding the inclusion of a question to count Mexican Americans.[76] The request stemmed from local activists' demands for data. The Census Bureau, however, resisted the recommendation, responding that it had already printed all the forms. Still, pressure from the new Nixon administration resulted in the addition of a question on "Spanish heritage" to the long forms, which were distributed to a sample of the national population.[77]

The inclusion of this new question was a major departure in classificatory practice. Following the Treaty of Guadalupe that brought the Mexican-American War to a close in 1848, Mexicans settled in now U.S. territory were classified as "white" unless "visibly" nonwhite (i.e., Indian). Similarly, Puerto Ricans, who became colonial subjects in 1898 after the Spanish-American War, were categorized "white" unless visibly Black or mulatto. Notwithstanding official ascription, Mexicans and Puerto Ricans were largely considered and treated as racially mixed and inferior.[78]

For the 1930 census, the official classification of Mexicans was changed. It was the first and only time "Mexican" appeared on the census as a racial category. The rationale was that the government needed to more effectively track the demographic size and growth of the Mexican population. The category initially provoked little to no opposition. That would change in 1936, when it began to be used for coding vital statistics.[79] Mexican American elites, such as the newly formed League of United Latin American Citizens, as well as the Mexican state rejected the disaggregation of Mexicans from the white category. Exemplifying a "defensive" embrace of whiteness, this opposition viewed incorporation into the "colored" category, along with African Americans, as both a racial affront and a threat to their access to U.S. citizenship.[80] This response led the Census Bureau to drop the "Mexican" race category in subsequent censuses.

Instead, the bureau spent the midcentury period relying on a series of "objective" measures, such as birthplace, surname, and language, to track these populations. In the 1950 and 1960 censuses, for instance, Mexicans in the Southwest were primarily counted through surnames. With the assistance of the Immigration and Naturalization Service, the Census Bureau compiled over seven thousand Spanish-sounding surnames and taught enumerators to distinguish these names from ones derived from other romance languages.[81] It applied specific measures by region and nativity to capture the growth of the Puerto Rican and Cuban populations in the Northeast.[82]

In the 1960s Mexican American advocates charged that each of the so-called objective measures failed to adequately count Mexican Americans and other Latin American descent groups.[83] They questioned the logic of using surnames, a practice that reduced the overall count of the community because it undercounted individuals who did not have Spanish-sounding names (including because of intermarriage). Spanish language was also called into question as a measure. Just as leaders today insist that not all Latinos speak Spanish, Mexican American advocates in the 1960s pointed out that many in the younger generations were not fluent in Spanish and would be left uncounted by this measure.[84] Moreover, classifying this population as racially white, they insisted, continued the practice of rendering invisible the specific conditions and needs of the Mexican American and Spanish-speaking population.[85]

However, the addition of a "Spanish heritage" question on the long form in 1970 did not quell the conflict. Mexican American groups remained critical of the data produced from the Census Bureau's population surveys. For instance, in 1971 the Mexican American Legal Defense and Educational Fund filed a class-action lawsuit in California to bar the Census Bureau's use of data on the Mexican American population, citing a large undercount and potential loss of federal resources.[86] The suit received the support of the U.S Commission on Civil Rights, which in April 1974 issued a report titled *Counting the Forgotten*. To the displeasure of census officials, the report charged that the Census Bureau's "procedures have been insensitive to the Spanish speaking background population."[87] It identified several problems, including the lack of a uniform measure of the population, inadequate assistance for Spanish-speaking households, and insufficient bilingual enumerators. Although Census Bureau officials contested the conclusions drawn by the commission, political and legal challenges from Mexican American groups had already forced it to revise its figures for the Spanish-origin population, adding 1.5 million to the 1970 total.[88]

Political advocacy about undercounts coincided with and in some ways furthered calls for a standardization of ethnic and racial categories. In 1973 a subcommittee of the Federal Interagency Committee on Education (FICE) released a report titled *Higher Education for Chicano, Puerto Ricans and American Indians*. One of the report's major recommendations was that "uniform, compatible, and nonduplicative racial/ethnic categories be developed for use across federal agencies."[89] The following year FICE established the Ad Hoc Committee on Racial and Ethnic Definitions. After much deliberation, the committee created a racial classification system based on a continental conception of race. It also introduced "Hispanic" as an ethnic rather than racial designation, noting in its final report in 1975 that the "term 'Hispanic' was selected because it was thought to be descriptive of and generally acceptable to the group to which it is intended to apply." Specifically, the committee defined "Hispanic" as "a person of Mexican, Puerto Rican, Cuban, Central or South American, or other Spanish culture or origin, regardless of race."[90]

It is important to note that Mexican, Puerto Rican, and Cuban advocates had not initially called for an encompassing term, nor was it even obvious to the parties involved that they should be lumped together. As scholars have shown, the willingness of early civil rights leaders to come together under a shared categorical umbrella was not straightforward or preordained.[91] And neither was the decision to define Hispanic as a special *ethnic* category.[92] Research suggests that this definition had less to do with the nature of the groups in question and more to do with placating competing political and methodological interests. Given that much of the "Spanish-speaking" population had been traditionally counted as white, census officials were concerned that making it a racial category would make it difficult to compare census data over time. They were also worried about the impact that such a designation would have on the counts of other racialized "minorities." At a time when groups were politicizing census undercounts, the prospects of lower numbers for the African American, Native American, and Asian American populations was a situation that the Census Bureau also sought to avoid. For them and other actors, the ethnic definition of Hispanic, and the two-question data collection format it necessitated, came to be seen as the best method to render Latin American descent statistically legible with the least amount of institutional change and political commotion.[93] In 1977 the Office of Management and Budget (OMB) issued Directive 15, stating the federal government's official racial and ethnic categories, and the Census Bureau debuted the "ethnic" category Hispanic in the 1980 census. These struggles over how the government classified people by race and ethnicity shaped the production of statistical data and enabled the creation of the "Hispanic population" (and its curious opposite, the "non-Hispanic population").

As discussions and negotiations over classifications were taking place, the Albuquerque-born Congressman Roybal was spearheading—with the support of civic leaders—a legislative push to mandate the collection of data on the soon-to-be designated "Hispanic" population. After several attempts, Congress passed Public Law 94–311 "Americans of Spanish Origin—Social Statistics" in 1976. As one scholar noted, "it remains the only law in the country's history that mandates the collection, analysis, and publication of data for a specific ethnic group, and it goes on to define the population to be enumerated."[94] At the hearings, Mexican American, Puerto Rican, and Cuban American leaders testified in support of the bill. In a 1974 hearing, the former general counsel of MALDEF Manuel Obledo, the president of LULAC Joe Benitez, and the president of Raza Association of Spanish Sur-named Americans jointly issued a statement and addressed representatives on the need for statistics on the Spanish-speaking poplation.

As sociologist Cristina Mora and others have shown, these advocates—in collaboration, and at times in conflict, with census officials and media entrepreneurs—were deeply involved in the development of the category Hispanic and its subsequent popularization.[95] Setting the foundations for practices that continue to the present, these actors began to deploy this category and data produced with it in their reports, testimonies, and public pronouncements. Equipped with this new knowledge, the predecessors of contemporary Latino civil rights advocacy not only highlighted disparities in the present; they began to project into the future.

FROM DISPARITY TO DEMOGRAPHY

Spurred by civil rights legislation and federal grants-in-aid, advocates challenged the Census Bureau to address "undercounts" in order to make disparities and discrimination visible. The NCLR report in 1974 stated: "An accurate count of the Hispanic American does not by itself lead to improvements in national policies—it merely indicates that the problems may be larger than have previously been recognized."[96] This data was supposed to inform how government resources (e.g., federal grants) were being allocated and help track whether interventions were actually working.

Using available data, however incomplete, advocates stressed the socioeconomic challenges faced by the "Spanish-speaking" population. In 1970 a publication of the Cabinet Committee on Opportunities for Spanish-Speaking People (CCOSP), the successor to the Inter-Agency Committee on Mexican Affairs, presented a litany of figures on educational attainment, college enrollment and completion, employment, poverty, law enforcement, political representation, and casualty rates in Vietnam. The report noted that, although the federal government had "focused its attention on domestic unrest more than 10 years ago with a host of educational, anti-poverty, and economic development programs," the "Spanish-speaking minority" was provided "only token participation."[97] The report depicted the committee as a means to correct that state of affairs. But like its predecessor, it was saddled with limited funds and had few enforcement powers and little autonomy amid partisan wrangling.[98] Although both committees were rendered largely ineffectual, they each prioritized and promoted the production of data.

Originally sought to document ethnic and racial discrimination and socioeconomic disparities, by the second half of the 1970s, data production was also being increasingly used by Latinos to give temporal heft to their arguments and claims for political recognition. Demographic knowledge offered a novel type of ammunition—ammunition they would grow accustomed to using.

This shift was visible in NCLR's magazine *Agenda*. The magazine published sixty issues between 1972 and 1981. At its peak it had a circulation of nearly thirty thousand. As its mouthpiece, *Agenda* focused on domestic U.S. issues and, like the organization, increasingly embraced a panethnic rather than Mexican-specific orientation.[99] An issue in 1976 began with a short but impassioned essay that opened: "Over the past decade, La Raza in this country has moved from being the invisible minority to being a group with knowledge that within the next ten years—and most certainly by 1990—the Spanish-speaking of the United States will constitute the nation's largest minority."[100] The following year, Reynaldo F. Macías, then a linguistic graduate student, published an article about demographic projections in *Agenda*'s May–June issue. In between an article on the radical theater group El Teatro Campesino and one on the thorny semantics of affirmative action,

Macías's article noted that Latino leaders had begun projecting that "by the year 2000 Latinos will be the largest racial ethnic group, after the Anglos in the United States." The article further reported that "Hispanic Americans number approximately sixteen million in the United States with a growth rate of over half a million per year."[101] Demographic statistics and projections like these gave advocates a method to bolster arguments that the Spanish-speaking population was now a national and not merely a regional population confined to the U.S. Southwest, Northeast, and southern Florida. This made possible claims of political significance distinct from declarations of inequality. Other articles in the magazine would also broach the topic of demographics in the years that followed. For instance, the cover of the first issue of 1980 featured a photo of sunlight beaming through a pair of interlocked hands and the words "Our Time in the Sun." The issue featured a reprinted editorial from NCLR's president, Raúl Yzaguirre, in which he predicted, "If the 1960s was the decade of our Black brothers, surely the 1980s will be the decade for Hispanics."[102] Yzaguirre attributed his firm belief that the "immediate future will be our 'Golden Age'" to four reasons. The first and "most obvious" reason was numbers. These numbers showed not only a population that was national and not merely regional but also "that we are, or shortly will be, the nation's largest minority." Yzaguirre expressed confidence that, as a result, "we can no longer be ignored."[103]

None of this is to suggest that advocates had not previously made use of demographic knowledge. For some time, advocates had described "Mexican Americans" and the Spanish-speaking population as the "second largest minority." Indeed, this claim was made on the opening page of the 1970 CCOSP report discussed earlier.[104] But such claims increased in frequency over this decade. More important, there was a change in how such claims were made. Earlier demographic claims tended to be more informational and descriptive. As time passed, they became more rhetorical and projective.

HISPANIC FUTURE, LATINO THREAT

By the end of the 1970s we see a noticeable uptick in talk of the future—a burgeoning Hispanic future. Latino activists and leaders were beginning to express a demographic consciousness. Reminiscent of today's population rhetoric, one California leader predicted political empowerment through population growth: "Change is inevitable because of the growing population." Another claimed, "The Anglos know we're becoming the majority in the Southwest. They're afraid of the sleeping giant that might be waking up." Both individuals were quoted in a 1978 article in the *Washington Post*, which was part of a series entitled "MexAmerica."[105] NCLR's Yzaguirre wrote a letter to the editor commending the *Post* for recognizing that the "Latino community" was a "national entity deserving of national coverage and concern." He further noted that his organization had long sought to "call national attention to the rapid growth and potential impact of Hispanic Americans on the nation's future."[106] Within a matter of years, articulations from Latino advocates and elected officials such as the following would become commonplace: "The Census Bureau says there are approximately 14.5 million Hispanics in this country. The actual number may be as high as 20 million. This is more than a 50 percent increase over the 1970 official figure, representing a real potential for political power."[107]

Journalists also began to write about the growth and future of Latino demographics. Initially, much of this coverage was about local and regional growth. In 1973, for instance, the *Los Angeles Times* ran an article on projections for the Mexican population in Los Angeles County and cited a finding from the Mexican-American Population Commission of California: "Spanish-surnamed residents will constitute at least one-fourth of the population of Los Angeles City and County."[108] Increasingly, however, the stories adopted a national perspective. An article in the *New York Times* entitled "Hispanics Lead U.S. Minorities in Growth Rate" appeared in 1979.[109] It characterized the "Hispanic people" as the "nation's fastest-growing minority" and noted that the population is expected to "overtake" the Black population before 1985. Not only was the Hispanic population framed as a sizable minority group, as had been reported for well over a decade, but the article forecast that someday soon they would be the country's largest minority group.

Media reporting on Hispanic demographics did not only list a series of statistics and projections. It painted a picture about this population and the implications of its population trends. Take, for example, the cover of the October 16, 1978, issue of *TIME* magazine. It featured a collage of multichromatic and multigenerational faces of men and women, boys and girls, casually and professionally dressed.[110] Diagonally across the image read the words "Hispanic Americans Soon: The Biggest Minority." The issue's cover story was titled with a quote from California governor Jerry Brown, "It's Your Turn in the Sun," which the *Agenda* issue cited earlier also invoked. The subtitle was more direct: "Now 19 million, and growing fast, Hispanics are becoming a power." Written by *TIME* associate editor George Russell and based on research from four correspondents stationed in the Southwest,

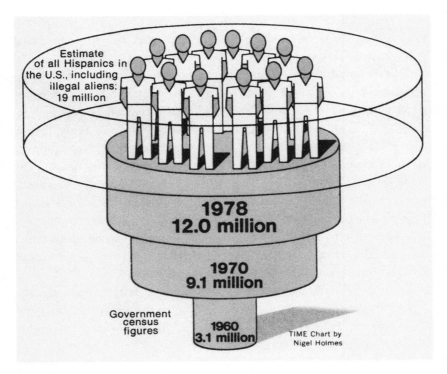

Estimate of all Hispanics in the U.S., including illegal aliens: 19 million

1978
12.0 million

1970
9.1 million

Government census figures

1960
3.1 million

TIME Chart by Nigel Holmes

FIGURE 1.1. "It's Your Turn in the Sun" infographic. *TIME* magazine, October 16, 1978. Used by permission of Nigel Holmes.

Chicago, Miami, and New York City, the article mused, "American melting pot is bubbling once again. The source of the ferment: American residents of Spanish origin, whose official numbers have increased by 14.3% in the past five years alone."[111] This growth was prominently depicted and projected in a visual graph of layered circles on which stand a mass of red-clay-colored figurines. The graphic (fig. 1.1) notes that population estimates "include illegal aliens."

The article depicted Hispanic population growth as inextricably linked to growing political influence: "The Hispanics' very numbers guarantee that they will play an increasingly important role in shaping the nation's politics and policies."[112] More or less, such claims paralleled or parroted arguments that Latino advocates were beginning to make during this period. Projections of future power, however, sat uncomfortably next to characterizations of the population as both internally heterogeneous and prone to division, as well as its overall assessment that Latino population trends were a mixed bag for the country. Serving as a primer for U.S. whites, it professed racially laden ambivalence: "Most intangibly, latinos offer the U.S. an amalgam of buoyancy, sensuousness and flair that many northern peoples find tantalizing or mysterious—and sometimes irritating or threatening."[113]

That the language of threat appeared in the article is no surprise given the layers of history discussed earlier. Growing attention to the Latino demographic took place during the same decade that witnessed the formation of what Leo Chavez has labeled the "Latino Threat Narrative."[114] This "threat" was, as we've seen, closely linked to immigration, particularly undocumented immigration. Like a slew of other contemporaneous articles, the *TIME* article devoted space to "illegal aliens," described as "the most shadowy portion of the Hispanic community."[115] Even though it acknowledged there were no precise numbers on this population, it concluded that "there is little doubt that the tide of undocumented Hispanic immigrants has reached flood stage." In the past and still today, immigration has been used as a proxy for concerns about ethnoracial demographic change.

In the decades that have followed, we have only seen an intensification of discourse about the Latino demographic growth and the country's ethnoracial future. For instance, in 2004 Harvard political scientist Samuel P. Huntington controversially expressed:

> The persistent inflow of Hispanic immigrants threatens to divide the United States into two peoples, two cultures, and two languages. Unlike past immigrant groups, Mexicans and other Latinos have not assimilated into mainstream U.S. culture, forming instead their own political and linguistic enclaves—from Los Angeles to Miami—and rejecting the Anglo-Protestant values that built the American dream. The United States ignores this challenge at its peril.[116]

Huntington did not restrict his concern to Mexican immigration but expressed unease, too, with Latin American immigration and the descendants of Latin American peoples writ large. His article was titled, after all, "Hispanic Challenge." Huntington and other "threat" narrators publicly fretted that as long as Mexicans and other Latin Americans were allowed to immigrate, maintain their cultural identity and language, avoid assimilation, and exhibit fertility rates far above white Americans', the national and racial survival of the United States was at risk. As we have seen, this rhetorical positioning of the Latino population is part of an older "discursive tradition," one that has deep roots in the racialized population politics of this country.[117] Yet, it is not the only tradition at play. Advocates, as we have seen and will see throughout, have projected their own demographic accounts. Although these traditions did not arise together in any straightforward sense, they eventually clashed."[117] Indeed, just as Latino activists and leaders in the late 1970s were beginning to mobilize demographic statistics and futures to advance their agendas, the population for whom they advocated was being cast as an imminent threat to the racial, economic, cultural, and linguistic integrity of the country. As we shall see, this conundrum remains unresolved and continues to haunt and frustrate national Latino civil rights advocacy.

———

Contemporary population politics stands on uneven and unsettled historical sediment. Its layers have imparted and imprinted many of the major tropes and tensions that persist into the present. Indeed, these demographic "futures past" continue to resurface and reverberate.[118] Demodystopias also circulate and shape popular imaginaries about ethnoracial demographic change. Latino advocates, in particular, continued to confront and attempt to counterattack those stoking fear about Latino demographics. At the same time, they have used population politics to grow political influence. No different from their political ancestors, today's advocates remain ever vigilant about the official production of demographic knowledge. Thus, three decades after the 1980 census, they once again aggressively invested in the production of census data about the "Latino population," that figure of the future.

2

Strength in Numbers

In September 2008, two months before the historic presidential election that brought Barack Obama to the White House, the chief executive officer of the National Association of Latino Elected and Appointed Officials Educational Fund addressed a subcommittee of the U.S. Senate Homeland Security and Government Affairs Committee. Arturo Vargas was invited to offer his assessment of the Census Bureau's proposed plans for the upcoming 2010 census. Early into his testimony, this proud Californian and Stanford graduate affirmed the broad significance of the census:

> Mr. Chairman, we need the 2010 census to produce the most accurate count of our nation's population as possible. Census data are the fundamental building blocks of our representative democracy; census data are the basis for reapportionment and redistricting. Policy makers at all levels of government also rely on census data to make important decisions that affect the lives of all Americans. These data help make such determinations as the number of teachers that are needed in classrooms, the best places to build roads and highways, and the best way to provide health and public safety services to our neighborhoods and communities. The accuracy of census data is also critical for the effective allocation of government funding for schools, hospitals and other vital social programs.

Vargas claimed the decennial census as vital to "democracy." He gave two reasons: political representation and federal resources. Both were expected.

Census Bureau officials have long cited them as universal justifications for the census.[1] But this was not mere rhetoric for Latino advocates. As we have seen, they have long leveraged census data to increase resources and political representation. One of the particular means through which they have done so, I contend, has been through tactics of population politics. Further into his testimony, Vargas demonstrated this fact:

> To secure an accurate count of the nation's population, an accurate count of the 45.5 million Latinos who are now the nation's second-largest and fastest-growing population group is imperative. An undercount of such a large segment of the U.S. population means a failed census. An accurate count of the Latino community is necessary if we are to make sound policies for the economic, social and political well-being of the entire country.

The population Vargas references is a statistical artifact. His ability to speak about its size and its rate of growth is inseparable from the ongoing practice of population making. The census, these actors know too well, is one of the most powerful makers. But it takes a great deal of work to create and assemble populations; the Latino one is no different. This is not labor that advocates are willing to forgo or to trust others to carry out alone—not the Census Bureau or the federal government. Too much rests on it for them, and for the people on whose behalf they advocate. Thus in the lead-up to the 2010 census—as they have done for four decades—advocates engaged in both census advocacy and promotion to remake the Latino population.[2] As Vargas's quote illustrates, not only do population politics rest on the making of populations, but the making of populations rests on population politics. For these actors, as the messages they convey to the public attest, this process is all about "respect–future–power."

Critique and Collaboration

For most U.S. residents, the decennial census comes and goes. Any public awareness or concern with it peaks with the enumeration and soon after recedes until the next count, a decade later.[3] Not so, for national Latino advocacy groups. The census, for them, demands ongoing vigilance. They closely observe and regularly intervene in the decade-long planning process that culminates in the census enumeration. This was no different for the 2010 census.

A subset of organizations and individuals led census advocacy. Among them was NALEO-EF and its leader Arturo Vargas. In 1994 Vargas came to the organization with experience with the census gained at the Mexican American Legal Defense and Educational Fund. Another cornerstone was Angelo Falcón, a trained political scientist born in Puerto Rico but raised in New York. He founded and led the National Institute for Latino Policy (NiLP), which is also a member of the National Hispanic Leadership Agenda.[4] Prior to his passing in 2018, Falcón fought aggressively for decades to decrease census undercounts and improve Latino representation in the Census Bureau.

Both Falcón and Vargas were members of numerous census-related committees and working groups. In 2008 Falcón was appointed to the Census Advisory Committee on the Hispanic Population, one of the Census Bureau's Race and Ethnic Advisory Committees (REAC).[5] By the 2010 census he had become the committee's chair, as well as chair of the steering committee of the Census Information Centers program.[6] When Vargas addressed the Senate subcommittee in 2008, he was serving on the secretary of commerce's Census Advisory Committee and the Joint Advisory Advertising Review Panel. Vargas was also cochair of the census task force of the Leadership Conference on Civil and Human Rights, a major coalition of civil rights groups based in Washington, DC. Together, Falcón and Vargas were cochairs of NHLA's census working group.

These advocates and their colleagues were determined to ensure a successful enumeration of the Latino population in 2010. To this end, they made numerous requests and demands to census and congressional officials. Most of their demands had been made on previous occasions. Once again, they pressed for bilingual English/Spanish census forms, arguing that monolingual English forms contributed to an undercount of Spanish speakers. Unlike past censuses, the Census Bureau warmed to the idea for the 2010 count. Advocates applauded the move but questioned the decision to distribute the bilingual form only in areas with a known high density of Spanish speakers. This meant that many Spanish-speakers elsewhere would only receive the traditional English form.

Employment was another issue. For years advocates have criticized the Census Bureau for its abysmally small number of permanent Latino employees, especially in leadership positions.[7] As a NALEO press release reiterated in July 2009: "The Census Bureau must also ensure that its Census 2010 workforce reflects the diversity of the nation's population, from its highest managerial positions to its field enumerators."[8] In other words, only a diverse workforce could enumerate a diverse society. Concerns were also raised about how race and ethnicity were counted in the census. Vargas told

congressional officials that "confusion or concern" with "the race and His-
panic origin questions persists."[9] Voto Latino's leader Maria Teresa Kumar,
a Colombian American raised in California, charged that the Census Bureau
failed to recognize "how layered the Latino self-identity is." Unlike other
political projects, however, these advocates did not for the most part make
explicit demands for changes to the Hispanic origin or race questions nor
mount campaigns to encourage individuals to identify in specific ways.[10]

Such critiques notwithstanding, advocates ardently supported and defended
the census. In the lead-up to 2010, NALEO and its counterparts called on
Congress to adequately fund the Census Bureau and its decennial operation.
Insufficient funds, it was argued, would adversely affect participation rates,
most severely among "hard-to-count" populations. Leaders also urged Con-
gress and President Obama to fill empty leadership positions at the Census
Bureau. When the University of Michigan sociologist Robert Groves was
nominated to become the bureau's director, NALEO sent an endorsement
to the Senate. It called for "swift confirmation" of this "skilled professional
who understands the science and substance of the Census, who understands
the Bureau and who is fully committed to a process that counts everyone."[11]

The relationship between Latino civil rights groups and the Census
Bureau thus involves both collaboration and critique. While some tensions
remain, they are far less intense than those described by Harvey Choldin in
the 1970s.[12] Nonetheless, many found census officials too hesitant. Reflect-
ing on the struggle for bilingual forms, one leader wondered aloud whether
census officials were "politically naïve or supercautious." In his mind, their
long-term objection rested on fear of being perceived as giving some groups
preferential treatment: "Oh, you're playing favorites with the Hispanics or
you're playing favorites with this group or that group." Census officials, for
their part, have obsessively maintained that they represent a "scientific"
rather than a political enterprise. This organizational presentation of self
was a source of humor for some advocates. In April 2010, as I looked on, a
census official's repetition of this claim was met with open laughter among
members of the Race and Ethnic Advisory Committees. The census, for
these individuals, was political. How could it be otherwise when it produces
politically valuable data tied to resources and representation? But it was not
and should not be partisan. Thus advocates were always ready to defend
the idea that the census was merely a head count, disassociated from the
other aspects of statecraft. One can certainly contest this position, as some
scholars and activists have, but for these actors there was no contradiction.
For many others, however, things are not that simple.

Fear and ICE

For many U.S. residents, the idea that the decennial census is just a head count requires a leap of faith and trust. Fear of participation represents a major obstacle to a successful enumeration.[13] Among immigrant communities, fear stems from the actions of immigration authorities and the suspicion that, as government entities, the Census Bureau and Immigration and Customs Enforcement (ICE) work together.[14] In 2010 Latino advocates, as we will see, devoted much energy to assuring Latino immigrants that the census was safe, confidential, and disconnected from ICE. But this was not the extent of their efforts.

Advocates also fought to have ICE cease activity during the enumeration. In 2007 LULAC president Rosa Rosales pleaded with members of Congress to recognize the serious challenges that ICE and the broader politics of immigration would create for the 2010 census. A longtime activist hailing from San Antonio, Texas, and never without her signature wide-brimmed hats, Rosales told a subcommittee of the House of Representatives Committee on Oversight and Government Reform: "I fear that the anti-immigrant rhetoric, large-scale raids and local targeted legislation that have been taking place in the last year have created an additional challenge that the Bureau must take into account. Unfortunately, tens of thousands of migrant families have been broken apart and millions more continue to live every day as if it might be their last day in the United States." Rosales used a hearing on census workforce diversity to make this statement. Shifting from the national to the local, she described how state-level immigration ordinances were denying undocumented immigrants health care, educational services, and library access.[15] Her comment was prescient. Three years later, during the 2010 census, Arizona passed the controversial Senate Bill (S.B.) 1070, at the time the country's most expansive and rigid statute targeting undocumented persons.[16] Along with depressing census participation, such laws, Rosales predicted, would "inevitably lead to more discrimination against Latino citizens and undocumented populations."

Rosales left representatives with recommendations. The Census Bureau should invest more in outreach and form stronger partnerships with community organizations, and census officials should "negotiate" with ICE to "halt its enforcement raids throughout the census process." She was quick to remind the subcommittee members that immigration raids had been temporarily stopped in previous censuses. Rosales's pleas and recommendations, along with those of other advocates and elected officials, went largely unheeded. In a response to an inquiry from Representative Nydia Velázquez (D-NY) in May 2010, Secretary of Homeland Security Janet Napolitano stated: "As the Commerce Department has made clear, neither the Commerce Department nor the Census Bureau will ask ICE to refrain from exercising its lawful authority."

Unable to achieve a temporary reprieve, advocates urged ICE to at least exercise greater discretion in its activities. ICE's director, John Morton, in response to a letter from Arturo Vargas in April 2010, claimed he was "sensitive" to Vargas's concerns. He offered three assurances. First, Morton said he notified its agents that "enforcement operations should be conducted in a manner that avoids even the appearance that census employees are sharing information or providing assistance to ICE." Second, ICE field offices had been "mandated" to communicate with regional census officials to "ensure that enforcement operations do not inadvertently interfere with census activity." Third, the ICE Office of Public Affairs had been tasked with providing public information disassociating the census from ICE. None of these assurances, however, were backed up with substantive details or means of accountability. Ultimately, ICE fueled challenges to enumeration, heightening, among other things, the need for effective messaging.

Reaching a "Diverse America"

Aware of public apprehension, advocates closely monitored the Census Bureau's communication strategy. As members of its advisory committees, Arturo Vargas and Angelo Falcón were given an opportunity to weigh in on the first round of designs and marketing materials for the 2010 census. The materials were produced by the major advertisement agency, DraftFCB, which in 2007 was awarded a multimillion dollar contract for the Census Bureau's "integrated communications" campaign. The campaign was its latest attempt to increase mail-in participation and minimize the costly use of door-to-door enumerators. It built on the successes of the bureau's Partnership and Marketing Program for the census in 2000.

Messaging and marketing were the linchpin of the integrated communications campaign. The Census Bureau and DraftFCB lauded their use of a quantitative and qualitative research-based approach to both test and tailor messages.[17] The campaign adopted a segmented rather than a universal approach to outreach. The decision was justified in part on the basis of demographic trends. As stated in its 347-page plan document, "While the Integrated Communications campaign must reach everybody, given the nation's growing diversity, a one-size-fits-all approach will not move the masses of people that need to participate to make the 2010 Census an unprecedented and overwhelming success."[18] Broadly, the campaign was divided between two large sets of "audience" plans. The first, and anchoring, plan was labeled "Diverse America." Its audience was all English speakers in the country, irrespective of ethnic or racial identification, who were subdivided into eight socioeconomic and cultural "clusters."[19] The second set of audience plans were for specific ethnoracial and language populations: Hispanic, Asian, Black, American Indian/Alaska Native, Emerging (Arab-Speaking), Native Hawaiian/Other Pacific Islander, and Puerto Rico. These populations were understood to be unevenly distributed across the "Diverse America" clusters.

Even as census officials and ad agency designers stated that a universal campaign would be ineffectual, census promotions were organized around a "unifying idea": "Only YOU can make the Census OURS." The campaign emphasized individual agency and claimed that "universal participation" would make the census "an embodiment of the people, not an instrument of government."[20] The Census Bureau's official slogan for the 2010 census distilled this message: "It's in Our Hands."

While the unifying idea was generally resonant with national Latino civil rights groups, they were displeased with its execution in promotional materials. This was no trivial issue. Through television commercials, radio announcements, billboards, newspaper ads, posters, and flyers, the Census Bureau hoped to reach the entire country and especially those it considered difficult to count. Vargas was astonished by the disconnect between the upbeat designs and the harsh realities confronting much of the country. Reflecting on the matter years after, he shared with me, "We told them, 'Look, [your] campaign is tone-deaf; it's obsolete. You've designed a campaign for a feel-good census. We just had [Hurricane] Katrina, people are going through the Great Recession and losing their houses. There's a lot of anxiety in the American public right now." In testimony before a subcommittee of the House of Representatives Oversight and Government Reform Committee in 2009, he urged the Census Bureau to "implement a communications and outreach plan that takes into account the current economic and social realities confronting residents of our nation." A chief preoccupation for Vargas and his colleagues was the need to vigorously reassure the public that participation in the census was safe, confidential, and unrelated to immigration enforcement.

Vargas's concerns were widely shared by other members of the Joint Advisory Advertising Review Panel and REAC. Both entities recorded votes of no confidence against DraftFCB and the Census Bureau. The affair did not attract much media attention, but it did trigger a meeting between these advisory bodies and the newly appointed census director Robert Groves and other top census officials. Advocates restated their apprehensions with the initial marketing materials and gave a number of recommendations. After the meeting, Falcón wrote that the "meeting effectively restored confidence in the direction of the planning of the media strategy and overall in the new team that was at place now at the Census Bureau."

There remained some reservations, however. In 2009 Vargas testified that while NALEO was "heartened" that the advisory committees' recommendations had been "taken into consideration," he believed that the "retooled" messaging required "further testing and refinement." Addressing representatives, he questioned the Census Bureau's assumption that English-speaking Latinos could be reached through general rather than population-specific messaging: "The Census Bureau will fail to reach a large segment of the 'hard-to-count' population if it believes that its strategy for reaching all of the nation's Latinos can be achieved by exclusively relying on Spanish-language advertising." Vargas was challenging the stereotypical view—also seen in political campaigns—that the Spanish language is the essential vehicle to reach this population. This stereotype represents an example of what linguistic anthropologist Jonathan Rosa has described as "raciolinguistic enregisterment"—the process by which "particular linguistic forms are constructed as emblematic of particular racial categories, and vice versa."[21]

Reservations about messaging and the communications plan aside, advocates did not waiver on their support for the census. The data were too valuable for them to abstain. As in the past, but in more ambitious ways, they partnered with the Census Bureau to promote the enumeration of the Latino population.

National Latino Promotional Campaigns

By the time census schedules began to arrive at homes across the country in March 2010, national Latino civil rights groups were deep into census promotion. They were among a sea of census partners, reportedly comprising more than 250,000 civic leaders and community organizations. Far exceeding their advocacy, census promotion was arguably the biggest contribution they made to the production of data on the Latino population. Through several ambitious national campaigns, activists encouraged census participation from border towns to rural communities to urban neighborhoods. Elsewhere I have theorized census promotions as a form of consent building by which state and nonstate actors work to gain the cooperation or trust of the governed for state projects.[22] National civil rights groups were not, in this work, doing the bidding of the federal government; they were advancing their own agendas and equipping themselves with the "informational capital" their efforts require.[23]

The largest and most expansive of the promotional campaigns developed by national Latino advocacy groups was the ¡HAGASE CONTAR! (Make Yourself Count) campaign. It was the third phase of the broader campaign known as *ya es hora* (now's the time), which was launched in 2007 to "incorporate Latinos as full participants in the American political process."[24] Building on its two other phases—CIUDADANÍA and ¡VE-Y-VOTA! (Go and Vote)—¡HAGASE CONTAR! counted on the leadership and experience of several national civil rights groups and media conglomerates. Spearheaded by NALEO-EF, the census campaign also included the League of United Latin American Citizens, Mi Familia Vota, National Council of La Raza and Service Employees International Union, Univision Communications, Entravision Communications, and impreMedia.

The campaign, as one coordinator put it, had both an air and a ground game. It organized community-based educational forums about the census, produced its own branded promotional materials, hosted webinars, and distributed a CD-equipped toolkit to assist local leaders. The campaign also launched a website and a census assistance hotline, said to have received nearly fourteen thousand calls. Media partners produced public service announcements (PSAs), including a Univision special on the census. It was a coordinated campaign of saturation. As SEIU leader Eliseo Medina told the *Wall Street Journal*, "People will be hearing about the census on their way to work, at church and at union meetings. . . . We are going to get the word out until people are sick and tired of hearing about the census."[25]

Other Latino advocacy organizations developed their own campaigns. Voto Latino established the BE COUNTED campaign, which, like the organization, focused primarily on young adult Latinos, who tend to participate at lower rates than the national average. Like ¡HAGASE CONTAR!, Voto Latino's efforts built on the organizational capacity it had grown in its civic engagement work during the 2008 electoral season. Savvy about the internet and social media, it made extensive use of Facebook and Twitter, sent text messages about the census, and even worked with iTunes to create an eclectic, free playlist featuring artists like Pitbull, Los Tigres del Norte, and Mos Def.[26] On the campaign, Voto Latino collaborated with other Latino civil rights groups, such as LULAC and MALDEF. MALDEF also launched its own campaign, ¡*Cuéntate . . . Porque Tú Vales*! (Get Counted . . . Because You Count!), in December 2009 focused on the Los Angeles region.

In many respects, the promotional messages of Latino civil rights groups and their campaigns were similar to, and overlapped with, those of the Census Bureau. Given that advocates helped shape the bureau's messaging through their involvement in census advisory committees, this resonance is unsurprising. Messaging about the role of the census in the distribution of federal funds illustrates how official census promotions and those of advocacy groups were often indistinguishable. Take, for instance, the following statement made by Voto Latino's Maria Teresa Kumar during an appearance on the NBC-Telemundo cable station Mun2:

> The 2010 census is perhaps the most important civic action that you can do this year. Why? Because the 2010 census is not only going to ensure you'll get counted for political representation, but it also ensures that 400 billion in federal funding is allocated appropriately to your community. So for every person that is counted, it's $10,000 that we're talking about that goes to your local community, in the form of funding for classrooms, roads, and clinics. So you know that pothole that you really hate. That 10,000 will go back to fix that pothole or that overcrowded classroom you're always worried about; that helps again address classroom size. Help Voto Latino ensure you don't leave money on the table. We're talking about ten grand!

Kumar's message, delivered to the cable channel's target audience of young English-dominant Latino viewers, posited a straightforward distribution of federal funds based on census data. Luis Coronado, the ¡HAGASE CONTAR! campaign coordinator, instructed his staff and local community partners to "personalize" the census and its effects. Thus when he visited *colonias* on the U.S.-Mexico border, Luis communicated to local leaders that "because of the fact that they were underrepresented in the last census, their school system has fifty of their kids . . . [but is] only receiving dollars for twenty." His message was precisely what the Census Bureau wanted. It encouraged "trusted voices" to develop outreach plans and messages that "target the unique characteristics of their community."[27] In collaboration with the bureau, promoters tailored their messaging not simply to the population at hand but to the political themes that the organizers thought were meaningful.

Campaign promotions often framed participation in the census as a measure of belonging and integration. Kumar, for example, said, "I think for too long people keep looking at Latinos as foreign. I think what the census is going to demonstrate is that we are not foreign. We are Americans that happen to be Latino and we are proud to be able to participate." In a similar vein, a NALEO press release quoted Arturo Vargas: "As a community we need to understand that American life also requires standing up and being counted." Indeed, the *ya es hora* campaign was explicitly about integrating Latinos into U.S. civic life. The census was understood as a key component of this project. Curiously, even as Latino advocates advised the Census Bureau that the Latino population was predominantly English speaking and mostly composed of U.S. citizens, for some sufficient signs of integration, their rhetorical emphasis on civic integration suggested otherwise. The claims above were a riff on the more universal appeal to participate in the census as a "civic" responsibility.

Another major and distinct theme found in advocacy promotions was power and strength. For example, MALDEF's informational packet for census partners made use of the word "power" several times. The subtitle for a page on the importance of the census read "*Opportunity and Power!*" (italics in original). The examples given, however, were not explicit about the nature of said power. Another page, offering a list of ten "census talking points," made the connection more directly: "This is the chance to make sure your voice is heard next year. This is the time to bring economic opportunity to our struggling neighborhoods. Participating in the census will send a powerful message to policymakers that our Latino community is strong, vibrant and willing to partake in our democratic system." Another set of talking points, this one from the ¡HAGASE CONTAR! campaign, was even more forthright. Its first point read: "Ensuring All Communities Are Counted in the 2010 U.S. Census is Critical to Recognizing the Nation's Full Diversity and to Building Future Political Strength." This and its other points linked Latino demographics, as documented by the census, to particular outcomes for the Latino population. For example, it noted that an "accurate count" of the Latino population could result in "an additional 100 million in federal funds for their communities." Thus, rather than claims about the national distribution of $400 million, the two-page document articulated an unambiguous relationship between "Latino" futures and census participation. In some cases, demographic data was used to convey such points. One ¡HAGASE CONTAR! presentation opened with a slide with four bullet points, each highlighting a different statistic. The first stated: "U.S. Latinos are now the second largest population group, comprising 14% of the total U.S. population."

The most explicit discussions of power in census promotions like these were directed at local community organizations. Latino campaigns wanted to enroll these local groups in promotions, and that would start, they believed, with educating them on the importance of census data. The theme was also present, albeit more subtle, in public-facing promotions, which drew on but also creatively departed from official Census Bureau messaging.

"Respect–Future–Power"

The ¡HAGASE CONTAR! campaign produced numerous promotional items. One in particular was a glossy, double-sided bilingual flyer (fig. 2.1). The front featured a full-color photo of a smiling young girl holding a colorful, hand-drawn sign: "*¡Hazme Contar!*" (Make Me Count!). The message was directed at parents, who were responsible for enumerating the children in their household. Additionally, at the top of the flyer were three capitalized words: *RESPETO–FUTURO–PODER* (Respect–Future–Power). Connected by dashes rather than commas, the formatting tied these concepts together.

On the back of the flyer, readers were given visual and textual details about what these interlinked words meant. *Respeto* was accompanied by a photo of an older woman and two bullet points: "senior centers" and "better access to healthcare clinics." *Futuro*, with another picture of the young girl, had "daycares" and "schools bulleted." *Poder* was visualized through a photo of a slender young man, whose list included "access to better jobs," "a stronger voice for our community," and "better political representation." The flyer implied that Latino participation in the census would improve all these issues. Toward the bottom, Spanish and English information indicated that an incomplete count in the 2000 census made the Latino "community" lose millions of dollars. As with other resource-based messaging, the flyer drew a straight line between census participation and federal resources. Distributed in the middle of the Great Recession, such messages sought to entice residents to participate in the census to access federal dollars for community needs. And finally, as with most promotional items, the flyer also noted that the census was "100% confidential," and that, by law, not even the president could access the data. That coda was clearly added to reassure undocumented immigrants and their families that their responses were vital and safe.

Undeniably, this flyer can be read as a standard census promotion. But there is more. The flyer conveyed and sought to tap into a specific ethnoracial sense of "we-ness." Indeed, it assumed that there is an "us." And though there

RESPETO-FUTURO-PODER

CENSO 2010

ya es hora
¡HAGASE CONTAR!

Para más información:
For more information:
www.yaeshora.info

1-877-EL-CENSO
(1-877-352-3676)

Textea **censo** al 62571
Text **census** to 62571*

*ya es hora no cobra por los mensajes, pero la tarifa de
su proveedor puede aplicar.
ya es hora does not charge for text alerts but standard
message and data rates may apply.

 impreMedia

FIGURE 2.1. "Respeto-Futuro-Poder" Censo 2010 flier, circa 2009. Used by permission of the National Association for Latino Elected and Appointed Officials Educational Fund.

CENSO 2010

¿QUE ESTA EN JUEGO?

El Censo decide la distribución de más de $440 mil millones de dólares anuales a gobiernos estatales y locales.

WHAT IS AT STAKE?

The Census decides the distribution of more than $440 billion dollars annually to state and local governments.

RESPETO-FUTURO-PODER

- ▶ mejor acceso a servicios de salud
- ▶ centros para personas de edad

- ▶ escuelas nuevas
- ▶ centros de cuidado infantil

- ▶ acceso a mejores trabajos
- ▶ mayor voz para nuestra comunidad
- ▶ mejor representación política

RESPECT
- ▶ better access to health clinics
- ▶ senior centers

FUTURE
- ▶ new schools
- ▶ daycare centers

POWER
- ▶ access to better jobs
- ▶ a stronger voice for our community
- ▶ better political representation

El conteo incompleto de los Latinos en el Censo del 2000 nos hizo perder miles de millones de dólares en fondos para nuestras comunidades.
NO PODEMOS PERMITIR QUE ESTO SUCEDA EN EL 2010.

- ▶ Su cuestionario del Censo del 2010 es 100% confidencial y está protegido bajo la ley, ni el Presidente de los Estados Unidos tendrá acceso a sus respuestas.
- ▶ Su cuestionario del Censo llegará por correo a partir del 15 de marzo y se le recomienda regresarlo antes del 1° de abril.
- ▶ Para obtener su cuestionario en español, llame al 1-866-928-2010

The undercount of the Latino community in the 2000 Census cost billions of dollars in lost funding for our communities.
WE CANNOT AFFORD TO LET THAT HAPPEN IN 2010!

- ▶ Your Census 2010 questionnaire is 100 % confidential and protected under the law; not even the President of the United States can see your answers
- ▶ Your Census form will arrive by mail beginning March 15, and we recommend you return it by April 1.

FIGURE 2.1. (*Continued*)

are many ways one could frame the types of benefits the census purportedly makes possible, the choice to add the themes of respect and power to the theme of the future when targeting Latino populations is notable. This suggests that not all populations were seen as *needing* respect or power in ways that could serve as motivation to participate in the census. ¡HAGASE CONTAR! organizers deliberately chose these three semiotically laden words. Perhaps, just as they aspired for the Latino population, they hoped that together these words would mean more than the sum of their parts.

¡Cuéntate . . . Porque Tú Vales!

One of the distinctive promotional products MALDEF produced was a twenty-page color comic, *Fuertes with the 2010 Census.* A collaboration with the syndicated Chicano cartoonist Lalo Alcaraz, the comic (figs. 2.2 and 2.3) saw over 100,000 print copies distributed nationally in English and Spanish.

The comic tells the story of the working-class Fuerte family, who lives in "a modest little house in a neighborhood you might know." Over breakfast, the mother, Anita, a slender woman in a white bathrobe, asks her husband, Frankie, a bald, stocky mechanic, to fill out the census. Hesitant, he responds, "I pay my taxes, I follow all the rules! Why does the government want to snoop in my life? I thought this was a free country!" His precocious daughter, Yasmin, listens with a look of disapproval. Having recently learned about the census in school, she reassures him, "Papi, the government isn't snooping in our lives. They just need to know some information about us." Yasmin shares what she has learned: the country's first census took place in 1790, at a time when, as she tells it, the population of the country could have fit into present-day Los Angeles. She continues, "The data compiled from the census will actually be used to help our community." Yasmin lists familiar benefits, like funding apportionment for schools, hospitals, roads— all pictured in the comic as idyllic, spacious, verdant, and orderly. Combined with the narrative, it is unclear if what was being depicted was the present, or if it was showing what the future could look like thanks to participation.

Hoping to further convince her parents, and especially her father, Yasmin tells them that the census only asks "10 simple questions," which are drawn in the comic's centerfold. Her mother inquires, "But then what happens?" "All the collected information is kept confidential and the census workers are sworn to secrecy," confident Yasmin replies. Comically, the theme of confidentiality is represented by the brother, Panchito, wearing a suit with his hand over his chest inside a figurative "cone of silence." Frankie remains unconvinced,

FIGURE 2.2. "Fuertes with the 2010 Census." Mexican American Legal Defense and Educational Fund, circa 2010. Used by permission of Lalo Alcaraz.

worrying aloud about the information being shared with the police and FBI. Maybe they will track him down for unpaid parking tickets! Mother Anita reinforces her daughter's message. As Frankie notices a parking ticket on his van, she reassures him. "They'll never ask for social security numbers, credit cards, immigration documents, home titles, leasing agreements, back

FIGURE 2.3. "Fuertes with the 2010 Census." Mexican American Legal Defense and Educational Fund, circa 2010. Used by permission of Lalo Alcaraz.

documents, or certain parking ticket information." In the text bubble, the word "never" is bolded for emphasis.

At work, a coworker sees Frankie looking at the census form. The coworker believes that only citizens fill out the census and doesn't plan to participate because he is undocumented. "We all count in the census, paisa. You don't need to have papers, the census doesn't care about your visa or your residency status, and the census does not ask about your status. Your information is protected by law!" The exchange captures Frankie's transformation from census skeptic to census promoter. In a scene that would make her transformed father proud, the story ends with Yasmin giving a presentation about the census at school. She is seen wearing a pink T-shirt that reads *El miedo no cuenta* (fear does not count) as she proclaims, mouth wide open, "Let's all be counted in the 2010 census—for a fuerte future."

Like most Census Bureau promotions, the comic communicated major talking points. However, it had a specific population or audience in mind. This is seen in the Spanish surname of the family; the brownish complexion of all the characters; the mention of Los Angeles, so tied to Mexicans and Latinos in the public imagination; and the problem of legal status. But the comic was not only directed at Latinos, it went beyond general messages to communicate a particular one—a message, like the ¡HAGASE CONTAR! flyer, of strength and power.

It conveyed power, however, not in terms of political representation, which it made no note of. Instead, and rather creatively, the theme was camouflaged in the surname of the family—Fuerte—which means *strong* in Spanish. This connotation explicitly emerged only in the final panel, where Yasmin completes her presentation predicting a "fuerte future" if "we" participate in the census. It is also telling that the phrase is bilingual. The theme of strength also appeared, even if obliquely, on the back page of the comic, which featured a large drawing—seemingly not drawn by Alcaraz—of a boy hoisting a red, white, and blue flag or banner carrying the same slogan on Yasmin's shirt. Although he is young, the boy's stance and facial expression evoke optimism and strength. The sentiment is underscored by small print underneath the image: *Vence el miedo y conquista un mejor futuro* (Overcome the fear and conquer a better future).

Be Counted!

Celebrities play a big role in Voto Latino campaigns. Building on its 2008 get-out-the-vote efforts, the organization produced a star-studded, three-part PSA about the census.[28] The cast included actors Rosario Dawson, Wilmer Valderrama, and Luis Guzman along with singer Demi Lovato and other celebrities.

Set in a large, mansion-like home, the video centers on a debate about the census that erupts during a birthday party. As the well-dressed cast alternately sits and paces around the living room, the characters bring up numerous themes about the census. The debate was sparked by the character played by Valderrama (Voto Latino's most active celebrity, second only to Dawson, who is a cofounder of the organization). A young but cynical guy with no intention of filling out the census, his character is the chief antagonist. The census, he says, "is exactly how the government gets the information to get your ass." His girlfriend, played by Dawson, is appalled and frustrated that he would choose this setting to start a debate. As the conversation unfolds, Guzman's character, the uncle, surprises the partygoers by sharing that his pastor asked parishioners to boycott the census unless immigration reform was passed. "If the majority doesn't want us here, why should they get money from our numbers?" The statement was a callout to an actual group of Latino clergy who called for a boycott, which I will discuss shortly. Other partygoers retort that most religious leaders, even in the Catholic Church, are urging Latinos *not* to boycott the census. Back and forth, characters list the pros and cons they associate with the census. There is talk about the census helping improve the quality and representativeness of elected officials. One character suggests their participation might lead to immigration reform. Another questions whether the census form even asks about legal status. Dawson's character replies that it does not, but several remain unconvinced. She insists: "If you can't vote in the election, you count in the census. That's real power."

Soon after, Demi Lovato's character, a college student, adds her own pro-census take: "Before 1980, Latinos weren't even considered a separate ethnic group on the census form, this is an opportunity for us to assert ourselves, to define ourselves. We can't pass that up!" Her mother and aunt express pride at the girl's blossoming civic awareness, and her words move another character, initially ambivalent about the census, to agree to participate. Throughout, Valderrama's character remains steadfast in his opposition. As the sentiment in the room shifts, however, he begins to soften his stance. Admitting he might have been wrong, he says, "Maybe the census could help our *gente* (our people), maybe . . . being counted would help us get some right representation, you know, and help fix some of these problems." Again, though, he quickly retracts, revealing that he is undocumented. The rest of the characters express empathy and reassure him that census data cannot be shared—participation is no threat to him. Dawson's character sits down next to him and states, "This is a constitutional right and it's an imperative that we all have to fill out this form. It is not something they can take away from us. And we can use it to create more rights." After this, her friends joke that she should run for office. Referring to Justice Sonia Sotomayor, who only months prior had been appointed to the Supreme Court, Lovato's character says they already have some Latinos on the bench, so Dawson's character should run for president. With everyone on board, ready to be counted, they return to the festivities.

Like the previous promotional items, the Voto Latino PSA communicated major promotional messages. Thanks to its medium, it was able to offer greater elaboration on the various talking points, even offering responses to some of the thorniest issues some might wrestle with come census time. As with the other promotional products, the theme of "Latino" strength and power was also broached. Participation was explicitly described as a means to achieve "real power" and assert presences. It also linked census participation to the prospects of legislative change, implicitly related to immigration reform. In these ways, it articulated the census with Latino identity, recognition, and empowerment.

Who Counts?

The campaigns of national Latino civil rights groups and their local collaborators were, as we have seen, intent to increase and maximize Latino participation in the census. They believe the messaging: census data will inform apportionment, redistricting, and the distribution of federal funds. It also matters, I argue, for population politics. But not everyone is keen on the enumeration of this population or subsets of it. Some projects emerged that sought Latino exclusion or abstention rather than participation.

In October 2009 Republican senators David Vitter and Robert Bennett put forth an amendment to an appropriations bill in the U.S. Senate meant to fund the census. Vitter and Bennett proposed that the census ask a question on legal status. As Vitter told the press, "It obviously won't help us identify all illegal aliens, but it's a step in the right direction. Illegal aliens should not be included for the purposes of determining representation in Congress, and that's the bottom line here."[29] The senators' contention was, in essence, that states with larger numbers of undocumented immigrants were robbing other states of political representation.

National Latino advocates saw the amendment as a tactic of intimidation and exclusion and immediately condemned it. NALEO described the amendment as an "unconstitutional effort to suppress Latino participation in the decennial Census."[30] LULAC, among others, sent out action alerts and lobbied to prevent the passing of the amendment. Ultimately, much to their relief, the amendment failed to gain sufficient support in the then Democratic-majority Senate. In a public statement issued after the Senate vote, LULAC president Rosa Rosales wrote, "The community won an important battle today in the fight for a fair and accurate 2010 census that counts every person in the United States as required by the U.S. Constitution."[31]

Debate about the so-called Vitter-Bennett amendment coincided with another—albeit differently motivated—effort to minimize Latino and immigrant participation in the census. In April 2009 the National Coalition of Latino Clergy and Churches (CONLAMIC), based in Washington, DC, issued a national call to boycott the census. Its chairman, Reverend Miguel Rivera, justified the boycott as a response to the treatment of undocumented immigrants. In a widely circulated press release, Rivera maintained, "Our church leaders have witnessed misuse of otherwise benign Census population data by state and local public officials in their efforts to pass and enact laws that assist in the perpetration of civil rights violations and abuses against undocumented workers and families."[32] CONLAMIC and its local representatives demanded the legalization of the country's estimated eleven million undocumented immigrants prior to enumeration. As its slogan expressed, *"Antes de contar, nos tienen que legalizar"* (Before you count, you have to legalize us).

For its part, the Census Bureau remained largely silent about the proposed boycott. It relied instead on national and local groups to respond. This in turn frustrated Latino advocates. One leader remarked to me, "They weren't hitting back hard. Their response was like 'Oh, no. We encourage everybody to be counted.' They just stayed on the message."

Nonetheless, national Latino organizations and leaders immediately denounced the boycott—publicly and persistently. They widely characterized it as "irresponsible." A Voto Latino deputy director said in the press, "It's very misguided logic to boycott the census," and asked rhetorically, "if we don't know how many immigrants there are in this country how can you ever advocate for immigration reform?"[33] NALEO-EF developed a detailed, six-page document rebutting the boycott's talking points. Invoking the future in both general and group-specific ways, the document opened with the following sentences in bold letters: "Ensuring all communities are counted in the 2010 U.S. Census is critical to our nation's prosperity and well-being. For Latinos, an accurate Census count is key to further building our political strength, and ensuring our communities have the resources they need."[34]

To confront the boycott and prevent its success, these actors and their partners took to writing op-eds, debating on the radio, and, perhaps most important, organizing religious support for the census. In November 2009 the leaders of the ¡HAGASE CONTAR! campaign met with a group of prominent Christian ministers, resulting in a press release that quoted several religious leaders. One quote, from Dr. Jesse Miranda, CEO of the National Hispanic

Association of Evangelicals of the National Hispanic Christian Leadership Conference, said, "Participating will help us secure a better future. The Census results will be the catalyst for financial and community development opportunities that can lift our community into social and economic prosperity."[35]

The same press release unveiled a promotional poster specifically designed to counteract the boycott (fig. 2.4). Purple-hued, it recalled the biblical story of Jesus's birth, specifically Mary and Joseph's travel to Bethlehem to take part in a Roman census. Just weeks before Christmas, about seven thousand copies of the poster were circulated to churches across the country. Luis Coronado, the lead coordinator of ¡HAGASE CONTAR! and one of the individuals behind the poster, recounted its story with pride. Raised in a religious Puerto Rican family, he shared, "It hung in my church. All of my friends who are pastors, we sent it out to all of them. They were hanging it in their church. They loved it. They said, 'this is beautiful, this is a beautiful message.'" For Luis, the poster was a huge success. "It did exactly what I wanted it to do." It "created a foothold within the churches" and "awareness." He further lauded the national media coverage the poster drew, including a front-page article in the *New York Times*.[36]

In response, CONLAMIC's leader, declared the poster blasphemous, and the press seized on that, too.[36] Rivera described the poster's distribution as "an anti-Christian and despicable act."[37] He also claimed that it violated the separation of church and state, a charge that forced the reticent Census Bureau to issue a statement: "We work with people from all walks of life to get an accurate count, but we do not provide funding to partner organizations and play no role in the creation of material by private community groups."[38] In an interview, Arturo Vargas acknowledged the pushback. "We got some harsh criticism from some people, people who were like it's historically inaccurate or the reason the census was going on at the time of Jesus' birth was a way to control people and oppress them." He also pointed out the enormous support they received for the poster from their extensive network of religious leaders, who publicly testified to its message. In the end, by most accounts, the census boycott was largely ineffectual, and only a handful of leaders outside of the leadership of CONLAMIC openly endorsed it.

———

For the fourth time in as many decades, national Latino civil rights organizations dedicated time and energy to the decennial census. This investment,

FIGURE 2.4. "This is how Jesus was Born" poster, circa 2009. Used by permission of the National Association for Latino Elected and Appointed Officials Educational Fund.

as we saw in the previous chapter, has deep roots. Numerous motivations animate their efforts. But none is more powerful than one expressed to me, years after the 2010 census, in an overcrowded and noisy Starbucks in Washington, DC. As he charged his phone and kept track of time for his next meeting, Ben Monterroso, then head of Mi Familia Vota, shared this with me:

It was earlier on that we realized that if you want to be part of the picture, you have to be in the picture or else you don't count. You know how those family pictures are when you get everybody together, and if you are not part of the picture then the picture is going to go on the wall, and you were not there. . . . So the way that I—the way that we—saw this is like if our community is not being seen in the picture, they are not going to pay attention to us.

Monterroso described the census as a family photo, a fitting metaphor as the census is often described as a "national portrait." He brought out two meanings in the phrase "to count": one is to count numerically; the other is to matter, to be taken into account. His comment, read alongside the promotional messages he and his collaborators deployed, suggested that these two meanings were more than linked. He indicated a causal direction. The presence and strength of the Latino community rests, to great extent, on numbers, in what the figures state.

Although separated by many years, one can still hear in Monterroso's words the echo of the first generation of Latino advocates who went to Washington, DC: statistics as a means of visibility. With this in mind, it is not difficult to understand why the census is so central to this political project. This point cannot be overstated. Even though advocates have challenged the Census Bureau regarding its lack of employee diversity and hesitance on other issues, they also have publicly and vigorously defended its mission against those who would defund it or tarnish its overall legitimacy. With rhetoric that overlaps and exceeds generic talk of resources and representation, these political actors actively worked to enroll Latino communities in the census project around the idea that to count, one must be counted and together fashioned into a population that can assert its demographic strength and political value. And yet this is only the beginning: what is done to data after it is produced and made public is another question for population politics altogether.

Future

3

A New American Reality

As the lights dim, silence quickly comes over the Mandalay Bay convention hall. I sit among hundreds of attendees at the National Council of La Raza's 2012 annual conference. Insulated from the blistering Las Vegas sun, we have directed our attention at a massive projection screen. Univision's video, "The New American Reality," has begun to play.

Its opening seconds fill the hall with a warm blue light and soothing Flamenco guitar. The puzzle piece, symbolizing the Latino population, sits beneath two words that unfold into a bold sentence: "Without me America would not GROW as fast or be as STRONG."

The assertion is as definitive as it is familiar.

Even so, the video—judging from the room's silence—is engrossing. Developed as a marketing tool, the video is seductive, from its smooth animation and vivid colors to the simplicity of its narrative. It serves up a stylized and carefully curated story about the Latino population, anchored by demography.

> "Without me playgrounds in TEXAS, NEW YORK, FLORIDA, CALIFORNIA would be HALF EMPTY."
> "I am 1 out of 4 babies born each year."
> "I will account for 95% of the TEEN population growth THROUGH 2020."

The statistics are accompanied by line graphs and images, but the video is far more than an animated infographic. One slide poses the existential question, "Do you know who I am?" Answers followed in a series of claims:

"I am NOT the MELTING POT."

"I am the new American reality."

"I live at the intersection of my TWO CULTURES."

"I am reggaeton and rock 'n roll."

"I am TAMALES and CHEESEBURGERS."

The list goes on, but the message is clear: the Latino population is bilingual and bicultural, at once and wholly Latino and wholly American. There is no hint of internal tension or external threat. I am reminded of W.E.B. Du Bois.[1]

In its final seconds, three simple words appear: "I am here." All those seated at my table and across the convention hall burst into applause.

On cue, journalist Maria Elena Salinas, the luncheon's master of ceremonies, returns to the podium. Facing out to a hungry audience, the co-anchor of Noticiero Univision, the country's most watched Spanish-language news show, states: "I love that video. I've seen it a couple of times, and each and every time, it makes me feel so proud to be a Mexican American in this country."[2]

As I begin to contemplate from my seat how an explicitly panethnic message nonetheless incited ethnic pride, Salinas invites to the podium Univision's senior vice president to speak on behalf of the conference's lead media sponsor.[3] Ivelisse Estrada approaches and asks, "Are we or are we not the new American reality?" Without allowing for a second of reflection, Estrada leans into the microphone, lightly clutches it in her right hand, and declares, "Yes we are!"[4] Applause, once again, fills the room.

———

Two years after the 2010 census, NCLR's conference was awash in figures and tales about the Latino population. Time and time again, invited speakers and corporate sponsors described this population as large, growing, youthful, and primed for economic advancement and educational success. The storylines of NCLR leaders were similar but focused on politics and power. In that year's presidential address, Janet Murguía once again claimed that young Latinos were "America's future" and that "inevitable" demographic shifts were remaking electoral landscapes. "We are a community of fifty million people and it is long past time we start acting like it," she told her affiliates.

All these expressions were acts of a particular—I argue foundational—tactic of population politics: *forecasting*. This tactic encouraged, even recruited, audience members to imagine the future in certain ways. To this end, they were offered emotive visions of a demographic tomorrow. Fore-casting tells a story about the future, what it means and how one should feel about it. It is akin to what Dutch sociologist Fred Polak theorized as "images of the future."[5]

What I have in mind is therefore not mere statistical projection. Yet the specific forecasts that national Latino groups have developed and deployed are inseparable from data—census data above all. It is often said that numbers speak for themselves, as if their meaning were self-evident and uncontest-able. But this is, of course, not the case. Data does not convey bare truth. Rather, they are like a ventriloquist dummy; they must be *made* to speak. Forecasting is one of the ways that advocates have done so.

Forecasting requires considerable cultural-political work. This chapter highlights three interlinked practices by which Latino advocates (and their colleagues and opponents) have forecast demographic futures in the wake of the 2010 census. These practices are curation, qualification, and narra-tion. *Curation* refers to choices about emphasis and selection—whether, for instance, to "lump" or "split" statistical populations or to place particular fig-ures in the foreground or background.[6] *Qualification* refers to the ways that statistics are charged with meaning. In other words, how a quantity is made a quality.[7] And *narration* involves how numbers and their ascribed meanings are temporally plotted.[8] Analysis of these narratives reveals their reliance on what the linguist Mikhail Bakhtin called "chronotopes."[9] Chronotopes, literally time-space, are the narrative structures that make "narrative events concrete, make them take on flesh, causes blood to flow in their veins."[10]

The demographic forecasting of Latino advocates does not emerge within a political or discursive vacuum; other groups are working to forecast different visions. Census data, they are well aware, can be filled with meanings that post-pone rather than accelerate Latinos' acquisition of political power. The Census Bureau, the mainstream press, and diverse political and intellectual entities work to impose their own conceptions of the demographic tomorrow as well. Some similarly frame demographic trends optimistically, while others advance more pessimistic, even dystopian narratives from demographic futures past. Amid colleagues and collaborators, opponents and antagonists, Latino civil rights groups have articulated a largely utopian forecast that seeks to commu-nicate that the Latino population is strong yet simultaneously non-threatening. The former aspect grows out of a desire to increase political recognition, while the latter aims to manage white demographobia and counteract conservative and far-right depictions of invasion. Sustaining these seemingly opposed posi-tions is, as we shall see, a difficult and delicate dance.

Census Data Goes Public

Once the Census Bureau completes the census, preparations begin for the rollout of data. Before the end of the calendar year in which the enumeration took place, census officials are to deliver apportionment counts to the president, who then sends them to Congress to determine the state distribution of seats in the House of Representatives. Coinciding with this, they also begin to make data accessible to the press, researchers, and the general public. But the Census Bureau is no mere distributor of ethnoracial statistics. It also powerfully shapes discussion and debate about ethnoracial demographic change. In part, it does so through its own forecasting.

On March 24, 2011, reporters hungry for sound bites gathered at the National Press Club in Washington, DC, to hear from census officials. Census director Robert Groves discussed the quality of 2010 census data and announced the new geographic center of the population. Marc Perry, chief of the Population Distribution Branch, spoke on the growth, decline, and geographic distribution of the overall national population. But as questions from journalists (and the press coverage that followed) revealed, the major story was ethnoracial demographic change. At the press briefing, that story would be told by Nicholas Jones, the then chief of the bureau's Racial Statistics Branch.[11]

Jones began his career at the Census Bureau in 2000. Presentations like the one he gave at the National Press Club were routine affairs. Affable and accessible, Jones seems to relish opportunities to engage academics and members of the public on the bureau's work of tracking ethnic and racial demographic trends. Speaking about the census of 2010, he told journalists: "These data provide insights to our nation's changing racial and ethnic diversity and illustrate the new portrait of America." The content of his presentation, as he noted, was also to be found in his coauthored census brief, "Overview of Race and Hispanic Origin: 2010," which was included in press packets and posted online.

Before he dove into the data, Jones provided some history and definitions about how the Census Bureau classified and counted by race and ethnicity. This is a routine part of such presentations. He reminded the press that the bureau follows what he described as the "guidance" of the Office of Management and Budget—the government agency that sets the "standards for federal data collection on race and ethnicity."[12] OMB, not the Census Bureau, he clarified, determines the "official categories" and their official meanings. This included the conceptualization of race and Hispanic origin as "separate and distinct concepts."[13] Yet these categories, Jones's own presentation revealed, were regularly treated as roughly commensurate by the Census Bureau and other political actors.[14]

Jones divided his presentation into three parts. The first focused on the new data from the 2010 census. He presented data in the order of the census schedule, beginning with the results of the "Hispanic origin" question: "In 2000, the Hispanic population numbered 35.3 million, and Hispanics made up 13 percent of the total United States population. The Hispanic population crossed the 50 million mark in 2010. And people of Hispanic origin now clearly represent the second largest group in the country, with 16 percent of the total U.S. population." He then outlined the findings from the "race" question. The White population, he noted, was the largest, accounting for over 72.4 percent of the U.S. population, while the Black, Asian, American Indian and Alaska Native, and Native Hawaiian and Other Pacific Islander populations, respectively, accounted for 12.6, 4.8, 0.9, and 0.2 percent of the total population in 2010. Another 6.2 percent of census-takers selected "some other race." Jones explained that percentage primarily reflected "people who reported their ethnicity in response to the race question as Hispanic." Those who self-identified as being more than one race, the multiracial population, stood at 2.9 percent. Although left unmentioned, all these "race" statistics included those who identified as "Hispanic" in the previous question. Had Jones removed those individuals, as is sometimes done, the percentages, particularly for the White population would have decreased.

The decision to include self-identifying "Hispanics" in the overall "race" tabulations was, however, only one of many curatorial choices expressed during the presentation. At other points, Jones aggregated "Hispanics" and all non-Hispanic Whites into a broader "minority" category or disaggregated them to highlight particular age cohorts. Together, his words and their accompanying slides painted a cross-sectional portrait of the country's *present* ethnoracial composition. This portrait, however, lacked temporal depth.

Jones used the second portion of his presentation to add this depth. He accomplished this by discussing the demographic rates of change between 2000 and 2010: "Over the decade, two groups, the Hispanic population and the non-Hispanic Asian population, experienced the fastest growth rates, at about 43 percent. Of the 27.3 million people added to the U.S. population over the last ten years, 25.1 million were minorities, and more than half of the growth, 15.2 million people, came from increases in the Hispanic population. Non-Hispanic Asians had the next largest increase, with 4.3 million people." In terms of raw numbers, every major population had grown over the decade, but their growth rates were wildly different. These differences, he claimed, were "even more striking" in younger cohorts. Non-Hispanic Whites, Blacks, and American Indian and Alaska Native children saw percentage declines. In contrast, the 2010 census revealed "tremendous growth in non-Hispanic Asian and Hispanic children, and especially in children ascribed more than one race." Even though Jones offered no projections, this section of the presentation directed attention toward the future.

In the third and final part of his presentation, Jones focused on the spatial scope of ethnic and racial demographic change: "Across the country, the proportion of the total population that reported that it was minority ranged from 22.2 percent in the Midwest to 31.3 percent in the Northeast, 40 percent in the South, and 47.2 percent in the West." Along with these "national trends," he presented a series of county-level maps. One map showed which counties were at least half "minority." Some 348 counties (out of more than 3,000) met this criteria and were shaded dark blue. Other maps depicted the regional concentration of the minority population and the percent of change since the previous census. In these ways, his demographic portrait was chronotopic, showing change not only over time but also across space.

Jones and other officials understand themselves as supplying, more or less, "raw" data for public consumption. But, as his presentation shows, they go beyond providing data. Census officials also curate, qualify, and narrate them. In other words, they engage in forecasting and thus also engage in population politics. They make choices about how and what data to present. For instance, there is nothing in the data itself that necessitates the aggregation of all non-Hispanic Whites into a "minority" category. These and other curatorial choices enable certain accounts of demographic change and constrain others. Data is not only curated, it is also qualified. One clear example from Jones's presentation came when he described the "Hispanic population." Not only did he provide more data than given for other groups during that portion of the presentation, he also used qualifying phrases, such as "crossed the fifty million mark"—a phrase that suggests a significant threshold has been surpassed. Again, the data alone cannot tell us why crossing this "mark" is meaningful. Finally, census data was used to plot a narrative. Several times Jones stated that figures from the 2010 census provided insight into the future, or as he said with regard to youth trends, "what the future may bring in future generations." In a similar vein, Director Robert Groves at the press briefing concluded: "Our country is becoming racially and ethnically more diverse over time, as is clear in the growth rates of the minority populations. Geographically, there are a lot of areas of the country growing in number that have large minority proportions. And we expect this to continue."

The Census Bureau therefore not only made its ethnoracial statistics public at the briefing, it put forth its own forecasts. In this the bureau is arguably uniquely influential. Via the OMB, it sets the categorical landscape that others travel over to construct their own forecasts. But this is not all. Through its presentations and reports, as Jones's presentation illustrates, the bureau also renders its data publicly meaningful in particular ways.[15] Yet, influential as it is, it is only one agent of population politics.

Fast-Forward

The release of 2010 census data reignited population politics about ethnoracial demographic futures. Soon after, the public sphere was flooded with diverse and divergent forecasts. Informed by different assumptions and motivations, these forecasts recruited audiences and constituencies to perceive population trends in particular ways. As with those of the Census Bureau, all of them rested on practices of data qualification, curation, and narration. These forecasts almost exclusively depicted ethnoracial population shifts as nearly, if not completely, inevitable.

Within hours of the briefing, the first wave of media coverage appeared and took the latest census data far beyond the confines of the Census Bureau. The wave designated ethnoracial demographic change as the biggest story of the 2010 census. This was foreshadowed during its question-and-answer session at the National Press Club. Although race and ethnic population issues occupied just a third of the briefing, most of the questions sought clarifications, additional details, and extrapolations about the growth of "minority" populations, in particular the Latino population.

The initial national coverage forecast a momentous and rapidly approaching future. Headlines proclaimed, "Census Offers New Proof That Hispanic, Asian Growth Skyrocketed in the Past Decade" (*Washington Post*); "Census Data Presents Rise in Multiracial Population of Youths" (*New York Times*); "Census: A New Face of America" (*USA Today*); and "U.S. Hispanic Population Tops 50 million" (*Los Angeles Times*).[16] *Washington Post* reporters Carol Morello and Dan Keating wrote: "The nation's racial and ethnic mix shifted sharply over the past decade, driven by soaring numbers of young Hispanics and Asians and an aging white population that was essentially stagnant.

The census statistics released Thursday from the 2010 count underscore the country's rush toward a day, barely three decades from now, when non-Hispanic whites will be a minority."[17] Similarly, in the *Atlantic Monthly*, Ron Brownstein marveled at the speed of demographic change and its implications for partisan politics. "The next America is arriving ahead of schedule. And it could rattle assumptions about the coming presidential election." Describing the results of the census as a "postcard from the future," he remarked that the U.S. was on "fast-forward."[18]

Echoing the Census Bureau, the Associated Press's first article characterized Latinos as having "crossed a new census milestone: 50 million, or 1 in 6 Americans."[19] CNN journalists Michael Martínez, who attended the Census Bureau briefing, and David Ariosto described Latino population growth as the "most significant trend" revealed by the 2010 census. They further qualified the trends as a "massive expansion."[20]

Ethnoracial demographic change was not only communicated via text; it was communicated via images. The day after the briefing, the front page of the *Wall Street Journal* featured a panel sandwiched between articles about NATO confrontations with Libyan rebels and dropout rates in Europe. Titled "Los U.S.A.: Latino Population Grows Faster, Spreads Wider," the panel featured four maps, each corresponding to a different ethnoracial population and its demographic change between 2000 and 2010 (fig. 3.1).[21]

In this and other media products, ethnoracial population sizes and growth rates were juxtaposed against each other. Unlike national press coverage after the 2000 census, this time the primary comparison drawn was between the "Latino" and "White" populations rather than the "Latino" and "Black" populations.[22] For example, *US News* published a handy list of seven takeaways from the 2010 census. The fourth, with the subheading "Becoming More Diverse (. . . and Particularly, More Hispanic)," read:

> The white, non-Hispanic segment of the population is steadily shrinking, and has dropped from 69.1 percent in 2000 to 63.7 percent in 2010. The Census Bureau predicts that, by 2050, white people will only make up 46.3 percent of the population. The burgeoning Hispanic population is one major reason for this projected shift—the Hispanic populace grew a staggering 43.1 percent from 2000 into 2010, and is expected to make up 30 percent of the population in 2050, up from its current share of 16 percent.[23]

In another *Wall Street Journal* article, journalist Conor Dougherty adopted a tone of lament and loss as he described the abandonment of the

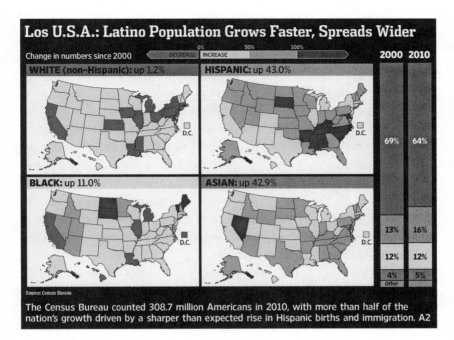

Los U.S.A.: Latino Population Grows Faster, Spreads Wider

FIGURE 3.1. "Los U.S.A." infographic. *Wall Street Journal*, March 25, 2011. Used by permission of Dow Jones and Company, Inc.

"nation's heartland" for cities. "The white population is older on average, so more whites are dying, and fewer are in their prime child-bearing years," he explained. By contrast, Hispanics were described as the "nation's demographic driving force." The article featured a photograph that deepened the narrative's racially coded geography. The photo showed an older white couple from a small Kansas town that, the caption stated, had lost more than 15 percent of its population since 2000. This loss was racialized and presented in chronotopic terms, related to both space and time.[24]

Media reporting on white demographic decline only intensified with time. In 2012, for example, the press seized on a Census Bureau report on birth rates.[25] The opening line of a *New York Times* article on white population loss read, "After years of speculation, estimates and projections, the Census Bureau has made it official: White births are no longer a majority in the United States." The author, journalist Sabrina Tavernise, continued: "Such a turn has been long expected, but no one was certain when the moment would arrive—signaling a milestone for a nation whose government was founded by white Europeans and has wrestled mightily with issues of race, from the days of slavery, through a civil war, bitter civil rights battles and, most recently, highly charged debates over efforts to restrict immigration." None of this apparent gravity and history were signaled by its matter-of-fact headline: "Whites Account for Under Half of Births in U.S."

In subtle and less than subtle ways, media coverage generally depicted ethnoracial demographic trends speeding toward an inevitable future in which whites were no longer the "majority." As elsewhere, this narrative and its accompanying qualifications rested on a particular curation of the data, most significantly the aggregation of all putatively "nonwhite" populations into one large "minority" category and the removal of individuals that identified ethnically as Hispanic/Latino and racially as white from the overall white population. Along with these choices, journalistic renderings narrated ethnoracial population change in more or less pessimistic, optimistic, or ambivalent terms. In all these ways, media outlets went beyond reporting the data; they actively forecast the future.

Along with the Census Bureau and the media, other actors and entities have advanced their own forecasts. As with others, these forecasts take for granted the existence of the ethnoracial populations they depict and frame the demographic future as more or less inevitable. There are marked differences, however, in the valences ascribed to these apparent shifts, ranging from alarmist to ambivalent to affirmative.[26]

On the far right, we find the most explicit articulations of alarmist forecasts. Summoning old tropes and metaphors, the post-2010 census period has seen racialist and racist demodystopias. In 2011 Patrick Buchanan, a paleoconservative author and former senior advisor to Presidents Nixon, Ford, and Reagan, published *Suicide of a Superpower*. The controversial book was his latest in a series of monographs and essays that projected the decline and demise of the United States and the West. In this particular book, Buchanan mourned the passing of the imagined white, heteronormative, patriarchal, Christian Protestant America of his youth and blamed its passing on usual targets including globalization, culture wars, and atheism. Most significantly, Buchanan was horrified at the "problem" of ethnoracial demographic change. Writing unabashedly to "Americans"—that is, white Americans—he wrote that "the 2010 census confirmed it: the end of white America comes in thirty years." Like early twentieth-century demodystopian prognosticators, Buchanan saw this as a harbinger of the defeat of Western civilization: "Peoples of European descent are not only in a relative but a real decline. They are aging, dying, disappearing. This is the existential crisis of the West."[27] As noted earlier, considerable media coverage was dedicated to reports of white population stagnation and loss. While he ended with a call to action—a "last chance" to avert catastrophe—Buchanan remained largely fatalistic.

Racial demographic threat also loomed heavily in Ann Coulter's *New York Times* best seller *¡Adios America!* (2015). Characteristically inflammatory, Coulter argued that the "Left"—basically, the Democratic Party—has used "Third World" immigration to seize political power. Seeking to drum up anger and anxiety, she cynically mobilized selective and sometimes false statistics and stories to paint nonwhite immigrants as harshly as possible. She depicted Mexicans as rapists with a proclivity to ruin, among other things, national parks; claimed Arab immigrants are prone to "honor killings"; and accused Hmong residents of child sex trafficking. Like Buchanan, Coulter wrote that America's future is being robbed from the *real Americans*: "America is not a nation of immigrants. It's a nation of British and Dutch settlers."[28] Authors like Coulter and Buchanan mediate between the general public and the far and extreme right, where immigration restrictionists and white supremacists of every stripe have long sought to stoke white demographobia. Census statistics and projections of ethnoracial demographic growth have been cited as proof of "white genocide" or "white replacement." What these alarmist forecasts seem to generate among some white people is less what Kathleen Woodward calls "statistical panic" and more a racialized sense of *statistical terror*. The difference is not merely intensity but the fact that statistical panic is a condition linked to risk and probabilities rather than certainty and inevitability.[29]

Ambivalent forecasts are those that envision ethnoracial futures as both *potentially* promising and problematic. One example is Progress 2050, a project of the liberal Center for American Progress, launched in fall 2011. In the project's inaugural report, *Progress 2050: New Ideas for a Diverse America*, demographic trends are qualified as "dramatic," "remarkable," and "profound." It informs the reader that by "the year 2050 there will be no clear racial or ethnic majority in the United States." This curation both refuses the language "majority-minority" and rejects the idea that the country is essentially a white nation, as in the writings of Coulter and Buchanan. The tone of the report is neither alarmist nor celebratory. On the one hand, population growth is described as a benefit. Unlike countries experiencing population decline, "our country will be in a strong position of global competitive advantage because of its growing labor force." On the other hand, harnessing that benefit will require substantial planning and investment. "If we close the economic and social gaps facing different racial and ethnic communities of color, then there is every reason to believe we will be better off as a nation in the year 2050."[30] The potential problems posed by demographic trends, as this quote states, are the consequence of social inequality and not anything inherent to these populations. The report, in a sense, offers two forecasts, two scenarios, for the future. It claims that Progress 2050 and the Center for American Progress can serve as a vehicle to fulfill the more promising of the two.

A similar though subtler ambivalence runs through William Frey's influential book *Diversity Explosion: How New Racial Demographics are Remaking America*. Frey is a lead demographer at the Brookings Institution who has published extensively on population issues and garnered considerable media attention. Initially published in 2014 and updated in 2018, *Diversity Explosion* offers a detailed and data-rich account of ethnic and racial population trends. In the revised second edition preface, Frey writes, "the phrase 'demography is destiny' is increasingly relevant for understanding the nation's future." Overall, Frey urges readers to view demographic trends as a "good-news story" that holds "the potential for continually reinvigorating the country's demography and economy." Despite this, the book mobilizes metaphors that suggest otherwise. The title itself uses a familiar combustible metaphor, one that has been used to project population threat, most famously *The Population Bomb*. Frey further describes current U.S. society as undergoing "the most demographically turbulent period in the country's recent history." Turbulence, Frey assures readers, does not mean conflict. It "offers the vibrancy, hope, and promise associated with young generations of new minorities from a variety of backgrounds interacting with older minorities and white Americans in their pursuit of opportunities in a country that is in dire need of more youth."[31] Intentions aside, such passages suggest—or at the very least can be interpreted as signs of—future tension and turmoil. Although the overall forecast is positive, it can be read to convey ambivalence.

Among the affirmative forecasts were those developed by Democratic Party operatives and liberal political scientists. Ethnoracial demographic trends were believed to ensure a bright future for the Democratic Party. The 2010 census revived a thesis popularized almost two decades ago in John B. Judis and Ruy Teixeira's influential book *The Emerging Democratic Majority*. In his 2016 *New York Times* and *Washington Post* best seller, *Brown Is the New White*, Steve Phillips lays out a "road map" for the Democratic Party to capitalize on the country's "new American majority," an electoral bloc composed of African Americans, Asian Americans, Latinos, and progressive whites. Focused on the Latino population, Matt Barreto and Gary M. Segura, political scientists and founders of the polling agency Latino Decisions, argue in

Latino America that Latino demographic growth will transform the country's political landscape, likely pushing social policy and politics to the left. These forecasts are almost polar opposites of Republican prognostications that ethnoracial demographic trends constitute an electoral threat—a topic I will return to later.[32]

Demographic forecasts thus are not developed in isolation. They are relational, produced in response—directly or not—to other forecasts, other claims about population dynamics. I have treated the examples above as ideal types of "alarmist," "ambivalent," and "affirmative" forecasting. A closer reading would, for most, reveal greater tonal complexity and contradiction. Within some celebratory accounts, degrees of ambivalence remain. Ambivalent accounts can lean, more or less, in pessimistic or optimistic directions. Even alarmist forecasts might, at least in their inconsistencies, reveal less dystopian possibilities.

Employing particular qualifications, curations, and narrations, numerous actors and projects—far more than presented here—advanced competing forecasts following the release of the 2010 census data. Together these entities and their forecasts set the broader field of population politics. National Latino civil rights organizations and leaders know the contours of this field very well and have not settled for the conclusions drawn by others. Instead, as the remainder of the chapter illustrates, they have produced their own forecasts about the Latino demographic and its role in the country's future.

Initial Reactions

Upon the release of the census results, national Latino civil rights organizations and leaders immediately began to harvest new data from the question on "Hispanic origin." As with others engaged in population politics, these actors took these statistics as facts, as if they represented reality quantified. In this manner, they exhibited what Alain Desrosières described as the "statistical realism" of data users.[33] Unlike statisticians, the attitude of realism of data users rests on the "consistency and plausibility of the results obtained." The results of the 2010 census were consistent with their expectations and, initially at least, raised no red flags.[34] Vanessa Aguirre, a NALEO staff member, told me, "I can't say I was surprised. I think that we've seen the numbers growing." Clarissa Martinez of NCLR put it this way: "Obviously, if you're a Latino organization you live that every day. So, in many ways, we didn't think necessarily it was big news because we've seen that every day."

Advocates, however, did recall, often with considerable delight, the surprise and shock of their political contemporaries. SEIU leader Eliseo

Medina, for instance, described to me how members of Congress reacted. On Capitol Hill, he shared, "people were saying, 'Holy Moly, this is the future!'" He wasn't surprised by their reaction, considering what the census revealed. "You're talking about fifty and a half million people. That's a significant number of people. And then when you look that it's a young community, it tells you and gives you a glimpse of what the future America is going to look like." These types of responses validated the long-held conviction that statistical visibility was linked to political recognition.

The responses of journalists intrigued these advocates, too. Ingrid Ramos, NCLR's director of research, recalled how the press went "crazy" when the Census Bureau announced that more nonwhite children than white children were born in 2011.[35] Ramos viewed the development as a "significant" sign of change but thought the media had exaggerated it into a "watershed moment." Anyone who had been following demographic trends, she noted, should have seen this coming: "Maybe there still are a lot of people that need to be woken up about this change." This language of waking up implies that ethnoracial demographic change is not a dream but an objective reality. The work of Ramos and her colleagues, however, suggests something more complicated. Forecasting is a practice of world making, one made possible by analytically distinguishable practices of qualification, curation, and narration.

Fifty Million Strong

National Latino civil rights organizations and leaders are not passive consumers of census data. As the previous chapter detailed, they have actively invested in the production of said knowledge. But more than this, once figures about the Latino demographic are produced and made public, they are worked into their forecasts. A key aspect of this is the process of qualification. Numbers, whether census statistics or otherwise, are quantitative entities that must be qualified or charged with meaning. NALEO-EF, for example, issued a series of press releases that variously characterized Latino demographic growth as "key," "pivotal," "exceptional," and "significant."[36] The day after the Census Bureau press briefing described earlier, the headline of the NALEO-EF press release read: "Latinos Play Major Role in Nation's Growth." Its opening paragraphs were a cascade of statistics: the percentage of overall population growth accounted for by the Latino demographic (59 percent), the rate of Latino growth since the 2000 census (43 percent), the size of the population in 2010 (50.5 million), and the Latino percentage of the total population (16 percent). Taking stock, NALEO president Sylvia García was quoted as saying: "The growth of the Latino community offers a great opportunity to strengthen our nation . . . these numbers show we are and will be an integral part of this great nation."[37] NALEO-EF and its counterparts would extensively use each of the figures noted above, but none more so than the figure of 50.5 million, the number of self-identified "Latino" persons counted in the census. This figure came to anchor their population politics.

Through its public invocation, the 50.5 million figure became what sociologist Martin de Santos calls a "fact-totem," or a statistic rendered as an emotively charged, collective representation.[38] Ubiquitous in speeches, presentations, reports, and op-eds, this figure was used to project demographic strength.[39] But this meaning was not inherent to the number; strength was ascribed to it. In an op-ed in March 2011, Arturo Vargas asserted, "Latinos are now more than 50 million strong and represent one in 6 Americans. We accounted for more than half of the U.S. population increase since 2000, and we exceeded estimates in some states. We are the fastest-growing segment of the nation's population and already the second largest."[40] The abstract of a LULAC panel on Latino consumers, sponsored by Nielsen, stated: "Come learn more about how your company can better target this ever growing consumer base; with more than 52 million strong and representing the majority of population growth over the next five years, Latinos have become prominent in all aspects of American life." In each of these examples, the word "strong" qualified the figure and gave it meaning. It instructed readers and audiences to interpret the figure as a sign of strength.

Amplifying this effect, the figure was made into a slogan. I first encountered it in April 2012 as I made my way into Voto Latino's first "Power Summit." Walking past registration tables at the University of Southern California in Los Angeles, I and the hundred or so other participants were greeted by tall, colorful banners proclaiming: "We are 50 Million Strong." The slogan was very much alive across the summit's two days of workshops and speeches from the likes of actress and Voto Latino cofounder Rosario Dawson, actor Wilmer Valderrama, and labor and civil rights legend Dolores Huerta.

Years later I spoke with Voto Latino's graphic designer Jeff Perez, a graduate of the Art Institute of Los Angeles, who told me he immediately "fell in love" with the organization when he met the organization's executive director and cofounder, Maria Teresa Kumar. Its focus on getting Latino millennials—his own demographic—civically engaged resonated with him. Just before the presidential election in 2008, he moved to Washington, DC, as Voto Latino's first hire to manage its social media accounts.

Jeff was inspired by the growing popularity of infographics. The inspiration was evident in his designs—business cards, banners, and online graphics were populated with demographic information. Major advertisement agencies, he recalled, were "creating beautiful stuff based on data."[41] "Why can't I take some of this information . . . but do it for civic engagement, for good?" he pondered. I asked what motivated his extensive use of the 50 million number. "We had the number," Jeff responded. "It was after the census. We knew that number was—it was a big number. I was like, 'Wow, that's powerful.' Again, us here in DC thinking, 'oh, my god.' We think into the future a lot, and we forget that everyone else doesn't think that way." At the time, he strongly believed that numbers presented in an aesthetically captivating manner could help mobilize millennial Latinos. Although now less enthused with number-based designs, which were insufficiently peopled, his earlier belief wasn't totally far-fetched.

At the 2012 Power Summit's closing plenary, Kumar gave a rousing speech to invigorate the largely college-age participants. Assisted by a snazzy presentation Jeff had designed, she spoke about the awesome political potential that Latino millennials possessed and could collectively realize. Midway through her slides, the figure 50.5 million appeared on the screen. Even though the figure was prominently placed at the event, many of the students sitting near me seemed surprised by it. Some people whispered about the number, while other participants jotted it down in their notebooks. Articulated verbally and visually, surprise transformed into awe and then into pride. The figure ceased to be—at least in that moment—a mere factoid: it became an ethnoracial emblem. As such, it blurred the lines between "numbers that mark" and "numbers that commensurate."[42] Shifting my attention from Kumar to the audience, I noticed that the response of students seemed to evidence what the sociologist Wendy Espeland has described as an "emotional attachment" to numbers. As Espeland argues, such attachments—from revulsion to excitement—are not automatic. Rather, they are conditional on context.[43] Part of this context, I argue, was the practice of qualification, of designating a number as a mark of strength and potential.

Panethnic Curation

Forecasting not only entails qualification; it also entails curation. Whereas the former transforms quantitative data into a quality, the latter connotes the choices made about what data to highlight, whether and how to aggregate or disaggregate statistics. We have already seen curation at play in the decision to focus on 50 million. Here, I am concerned with the decision to almost exclusively present "Hispanic/Latino" data in publications and other public-facing media.[44]

National Latino civil rights groups after the 2010 census have had comparatively little to say about national subgroups (e.g., Cuban Americans, Mexicans). This is not because the data was not disaggregated; it was, in various ways. The NALEO-EF's press releases discussed earlier presented statistics about the Latino population by state. NHLA launched the Latinas Represent campaign to increase Latina elected officials. The campaign, along with several organizations, made extensive use of demographic and electoral data about Latinas. Census statistics were frequently disaggregated by age. This move provided the statistical scaffold for claims about Latino children and millennials. So in these and other ways, these actors chose to disaggregate in particular ways. Notably, data on ethnic subgroups (e.g., Mexican American, Dominican American) were rarely extrapolated.

NCLR reports and briefings provide a useful object of comparison. Since the 2010 census, the organization's publications have data presented almost exclusively panethnic.[45] This differs from earlier publications. The 2001 document, *Beyond the Census: Hispanics and an American Agenda*, for example, painted both a panethnic and an ethnic portrait. It noted, among other things, that the percentage of the Mexican population relative to the total Latino population had decreased, yet it remained the "principal source of growth" of the overall Latino birth rate. An NCLR factsheet in 2003 opened with the pronouncement that the "Hispanic population" was "now the largest racial and ethnic minority in the United States." Yet it used a large pie chart to visualize the claim that this population was "characterized by a wide diversity of ethnic subgroups." Two years later the organization produced population fact sheets for the country and for each state. Along with overall demographics, each featured a trio of pie charts: the first presented the population's age distribution; the second, its "ethnic subgroup" distribution; and the third, the population's legal status distribution.[46] These examples indicate a choice to include subgroup rather than only panethnic information.

When asked about the de-emphasis on subnational groups, most advocates seemed not to have noticed a shift at all. Upon reflection, the shift didn't appear troubling. NALEO civic engagement director Alonso Padre saw the change as a positive development: "I think it's becoming—and this is a good thing—more along the lines of how we divide up the rest of the country. It's other demographic variables. There's income, education, age, and immigration status." He also suspected that subgroup differentiation was, in general, becoming less salient as anti-immigrant and anti-Latino sentiments rose. Essentially, racists weren't too worried about the details of which *kind* of Latino they were denigrating, and advocates were understandably concerned with taking a big-tent approach that would consolidate and amplify panethnic Latino power. Within this context, he concluded that "[these categories] are going to increasingly become less of a factor, politically speaking, definitely."

The curatorial preference for panethnic data was expressed largely through a categorical preference for "Latino" over "Hispanic." This leaning exhibits the often close relationship between curation and qualification. While this preference precedes the 2010 census, it has continued to grow. NCLR documents, for example, typically use Latino two times more often than Hispanic. Op-eds reveal a similar pattern. NALEO's Vargas did not use Hispanic in either his commentary prior to the census's release or his communications immediately after it came out. Janet Murguía's first postcensus op-ed included Hispanic in the title but more frequently used Latino.[47] Language in interviews was also strongly skewed toward Latino, suggesting a personal preference. Until about the mid-2000s, Hispanic was the principal term, although its frequency had begun to decrease in the 1990s. It is difficult to gauge the significance of this shift, as these organizations have historically refused to police these categories (instead considering ambiguity productive).[48] In documents, they claim that these terms are interchangeable and refer "to persons of Mexican, Puerto Rican, Cuban, Central and South American, Dominican, Spanish, and other Hispanic descent," to quote a standard line in NCLR reports.

Along with the emphasis on panethnicity and the preference for the label Latino, national Latino advocates today favor a particular way of curating ethnographical demographic futures. In speeches and publications, change is principally, and often nearly exclusively, framed as a singularly Latino affair. An example comes in Arturo Vargas's *Huffington Post* commentary in 2011, in which he claimed: "New Census data confirms what we've been seeing for some time now: America has a new face."[49] That new face, like the Univision video described at the start of the chapter, is *Latino*. The same year, the Labor Council for Latin American Advancement (LCLAA) released a report on the state of Latino workers. Like other documents of this period, it began with a statement on Latino demographics. "Latinos represent an ever-increasing share of our population, workforce and electorate." Then, with numbers from the 2010 census and the latest figures

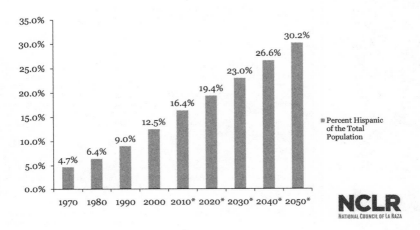

Historical and Projected Latino Share of the U.S. Population, 1970-2050

FIGURE 3.2. "Let's Put Numbers to Use" powerpoint, Projection of Latino Population, 2011. Used by permission of UnidosUS (formerly National Council of La Raza).

on Latino purchasing power, the report went on to claim that the Latino population was "an economic and political force to be reckoned with."[50]

That these organizations focus on Latino demographics is expected. But even so, this focus does reveal certain curational choices, particularly as their politico-cultural milieu offers numerous ways to talk about and present demographics. Some groups have framed population trends as the emergence of a "new majority," composed of the country's "minority" populations. Others have used phrases like "majority-minority." For reasons that will become clearer shortly, national Latino leaders have opted not to use these terms (nor any language that connotes that the country is "browning"). Talk of diversity did appear, but typically in service of a narrative about Latinos as the primary drivers of diversification. For instance, NCLR produced a presentation titled "Latinos and the 2010 Census: Let's Put Those Numbers to Use."[51] In it, one slide gives the "historical and projected" percentage of the U.S. population of the Latino population from 1970 to 2060 (fig. 3.2). Such a graph is possible only through a series of curational choices, which, as sociologist Mara Loveman has argued in her research on Latin American censuses can be "read for clues that reveal the assumptions and aspirations of their creators."[52]

NATIONWIDE GROWTH IN THE LATINO POPULATION IS A BOON FOR THE COUNTRY

Latinos* have been part of the American fabric since the birth of the country and will play an essential role in the progress of the nation.† Newly released 2010 Census national data show that in the past decade, the Latino population has grown remarkably in most regions of the country and is characterized in large part by its youthfulness. Given the aging of our overall population and the growing number of baby boomers approaching retirement, the increase in the Latino population is good news. The expansion of this vibrant population in major cities, suburbs, and rural areas is a boon, as Hispanics increasingly contribute in essential ways to the economic, social, and political life of the country and to its future well-being.

Currently, one in four American children is Latino, nearly three in four Hispanics are U.S. citizens, and more than nine in ten Latino children are U.S. citizens. Latino workers are fueling U.S. industries that are key to the nation's economic growth: more than one in five American agricultural, construction, and food manufacturing workers are Hispanic. Through hard work and entrepreneurship, social and civic contributions, and a determination to see their children become productive Americans, Latinos are strengthening communities throughout the country.

1. Between 2000 and 2010, the Hispanic population in the United States grew from 35.3 million to 50.5 million, accounting for more than half of the overall national growth rate during that period.

   • The growth rate for the Latino population was 43%, compared to 5% for all non-Hispanics, 6% for non-Hispanic Whites, 12% for non-Hispanic Blacks, and 43% for Asians.[1]

   • One out of every six people in America is Latino, with Latinos currently representing 16% of the overall American population; 23% of American children under age 18 are Hispanic.[2]

   • The highest rates of growth in the Latino population can be seen in children and youth under the age of 18; the growth rate for Latinos under age 18 was 39%, while the rate of change in the same period for non-Hispanic youth decreased by 5%.[3]

2. The Latino population has grown in most areas of the country and has been particularly strong in the Southeast and West. In several states, the Hispanic population has more than doubled (see Map 1).[4]

   • The states with the highest numbers of Hispanics are California, Texas, Florida, New York, Arizona, Illinois, New Jersey, Colorado, New Mexico, and Georgia.

   • The states with highest percentage of Latinos are New Mexico (46%), Texas (38%), California (38%), Arizona (30%), Nevada (27%), Florida (23%), and Colorado (21%) (see Table 1).

   • Between 2000 and 2010, the Latino population more than doubled in South Carolina, Alabama, Tennessee, Kentucky, Arkansas, North Carolina, Maryland, Mississippi, and South Dakota (see Table 2).

---

* The terms "Hispanic" and "Latino" are used interchangeably by the U.S. Census Bureau and throughout this document to refer to persons of Mexican, Puerto Rican, Cuban, Central and South American, Dominican, Spanish, and other Hispanic descent; they may be of any race. These data do not include the 3.7 million residents of Puerto Rico.

† This fact sheet was prepared by Patricia Foxen, Associate Director of Research, National Council of La Raza (NCLR), and Sara Benítez, Research Analyst, NCLR. Clarissa Martínez De Castro, Director of Immigration and National Campaigns, provided substantial oversight and input. Kari Nye, Senior Development Editor, and Kelly Isaac, Production Assistant and Graphic Designer, prepared this document for publication.

FIGURE 3.3. Fact sheet "Hispanics in the U.S.," 2011. Used by permission of UnidosUS (formerly National Council of La Raza).

There are, however, exceptions to this emphasis on "Latino" data. Take, for example, NCLR's teaching guide for its 2013 "Latino Kids Data Explorer." Unlike LCLAA's report, this guide began with a statement that situated Latino demographics within a broader story: "It has become clear in recent years that broad-scale demographic change is considerably transforming the social landscape of America. Today's racial and ethnic minority groups are growing far more rapidly than the White population, and in 2012 the Census Bureau reported that minority children under age one now make up over 50% of all American babies."[53] No matter the differences, the organization's literature makes it clear that the country's future is unmistakably Latino.

Latino Boon

The forecast of national Latino civil rights groups was based not only on particular qualifications and curations of census data but also on particular narrations. While numbers and narratives are often treated as distinct, this "binary division of numbers and stories does not capture their complex interplay, the way numbers sometimes evoke a narrative, and vice versa."[54] Statistical figures and even projections need to be narrated to become meaningful.

Contending with and contesting other forecasts, advocates put forth their narrative of the future. That narrative was affirmative, perhaps even utopian. In a *Huffington Post* commentary, NALEO's Vargas wrote: "Many ponder what it all means. It means that Latinos are an integral part of America's future; we are and will continue to make vital contributions to our country's economic and civic life. It means that this growth of the Latino population presents a great opportunity for our nation."[55] Vargas was not alone in narrating Latino demographics as an "opportunity" or "benefit" for the country at large.

NCLR's first postcensus fact sheet carried this same message, as captured in its title, "Nationwide Growth in the Latino Population Is a Boon for the Country" (fig. 3.3). The fact sheet opened:

> Latinos have been part of the American fabric since the birth of the country and will play an essential role in the progress of the nation. Newly released 2010 Census national data show that in the past decade, the Latino population has grown remarkably in most regions of the country and is characterized in large part by its youthfulness. Given the aging of our overall population and the growing number of baby boomers approaching retirement, the increase in the Latino population is good

news. The expansion of this vibrant population in major cities, suburbs, and rural areas is a boon, as Hispanics increasingly contribute in essential ways to the economic, social, and political life of the country and to its future well-being.[56]

Although only a few pages long, the document—as this quote illustrates—was not short on narrative. It told readers that Latino population growth was positive and beneficial; in short, a boon for the country. The underlying narrative has a few points of interest. While definitely pointing to the future, it also looked to the past, claiming Latinos as "part of the American fabric" since the beginning. This contested the idea that this is a "new" or "foreign" population. In addition, the narrative was spatial as much as it was temporal. Latino growth was geographically far-reaching, a point that these organizations have been making since the 1970s. The text also marshalled a number of positive qualifications (e.g., "vibrant" and "essential") and showed clear curational preference for "Latino" data.

The fact sheet deepened its forecast (and its constitutive elements) through four major points, each weighted with textual and graphical presentations of data. The first point was plainly demographic, focused on the overall size and growth of the Latino population (and its under-eighteen population) as compared to other populations. The second point added a geographic component that emphasized growth in the Southeast and West.

The remaining two points each communicated something about the value and character of the Latino population. Building on the opening narrative, the third point claimed, "Latino population growth continues to bolster the country's economic strength and troop readiness, and will increasingly do so in the future."[57] This claim was bolstered by data from the Census Bureau on labor force participation, Latino-owned businesses, and population projections, as well as data from the Office of the Secretary of Defense. The data was used to claim that, among other things, "the growing Hispanic population will provide substantial contributions to Social Security coffers in a nation whose aging population increasingly depends on this program." This population was thus becoming a major, vital even, contributor to the national economy and security. This characterization was further elaborated in the fourth and final point: "Trends over the past two decades show that Latinos are active participants in civic life and have a positive outlook toward the future."[58] As with the other claims, this one was reinforced with data: "In the past decade, nearly six million Latinos became eligible to vote"; "Hispanics exhibit the highest growth rates of voter registration and participation"; "nearly three in four Latinos (74%) are U.S. citizens, and more than nine in ten Latinos under the age of 18 (93%) are U.S. citizens"; and "the majority of Hispanics (76%) speak English, and 52% speak both English and Spanish; of the latter, 40% are fluent in both English and Spanish." In addition, the fact sheet claimed that the population was largely optimistic about the future, based on polling data. Ultimately, the fact sheet anchored its bright forecast on the ways it characterized the population at hand as committed to work, civic engagement, patriotism, and hope. It answered without asking, what could there be to fear? What it didn't answer was what explained these characteristics. Without such explanations, it implied that they were intrinsic to the population, as if it possessed, for example, inherent optimism.

Other advocacy groups and spokespersons expressed narratives similar to the one in the fact sheet. In August 2011 Voto Latino's Kumar gave a TEDx Talk in Washington Heights, New York. In it she proclaimed that Latinos "exemplify the true America." Standing to the left of a large screen, she accompanied her remarks by a series of graphs and maps—tools to help the audience visualize her image of the Latino population. Kumar described Latinos as young, hardworking, and entrepreneurial. More important, she said, they still believed in America:

> We have a lot of people right now, a lot of naysayers that America is on the decline. I actually say that the Latino community is the silver lining of where we are going in the future. Because we're young, we're workaholics, and we believe in America when everybody else doesn't. Despite our economic difficulties and educational needs, we profoundly believe in what America is and the possibility, that immigrant belief. It is because of that, that America's best days actually lie ahead.

Kumar's statement depicted Latinos as *essentially* positive and *quintessentially* "American." It is an aspirational vision.

These accounts and narratives of Latinos as patriotic, entrepreneurial, and religious are examples of what the anthropologist Arlene Dávila has referred to as "Latino Spin." Dávila argues that the emphasis on seemingly positive stereotypes of Latinos emerged within a neoliberal horizon that demands minoritized ethnoracial groups "prove their value as political constituencies and consumers if they are to be welcomed to the national political table."[59] These characterizations often rest on essentialisms—for example, the idea that this population is almost by nature hardworking. This view omits and obfuscates conditions of precarity and exploitation that undergird much Latino labor.

Narratives of Latinos as hyper Americans position Latino population growth to biologically and culturally rejuvenate the country rather than radically transform it. As such, these demographic trends, projected decades into the future, are presented as a national and universal, as opposed to merely a population-specific, good. In this manner, these actors posit, strangely enough, both change and continuity, suggesting some ambivalence as to whether Latino demographic growth represents a transformation of the country into something different altogether or a hyper version of itself. From this vantage point, it remains unclear whether Latino population growth actually signals a "new" American reality.

Demographic Linked Fate

The forecast of Latino civil rights groups also expressed that the future of the country was tied to the future of the Latino population. A popular refrain among these organizations was "as Latinos go, so goes the country." What this conveyed was a kind of linked fate. But this linked fate is quite different from what political scientist Michael Dawson has theorized. Dawson developed the term to understand political homogeneity among African Americans. He argued that historical and present-day discrimination and oppression led Black people to perceive their individual futures as linked to the fate of the Black population as a whole.[60] Linked fate, therefore, was an outcome of sociohistorical conditions and present-day circumstances that confronted the Black community. Sociologist Jennifer Jones argues that Latinos and African Americans are forming a sense of "minority-linked fate" in parts of the South. This formation, she shows, is ripest in places where these groups occupy a similar racial status (vis-à-vis whites) but dissimilar position in the labor market.[61] In contrast, the kind of linked fate espoused by Latino advocates is rooted not in shared social, economic, or racialized conditions but in the future determining power of Latino demographics.

This demographic linked fate has been most clearly spelled out by Henry Cisneros, a former mayor of San Antonio who served in the Clinton administration as the secretary of housing and urban development. Cisneros was also one of the founders of NHLA. In a series of commentaries, he has creatively appropriated the statistical postulate of the "Law of Large Numbers" to forecast the impact of Latino demographics on the country. In April 2009 he wrote:

I offer here a bold assertion—that the concept of the "Law of Large Numbers," as it applies to the Latino population of the United States, must and will result in extraordinary changes in our society as a whole. Simply put, the Law of Large Numbers means that quantitative changes inevitably bring forth qualitative changes. . . . Latinos will move the national averages in almost every measurable category of American life—economic, social indicators and educational attainment.[62]

Cisneros elaborated on his thesis in an edited volume published the same year, carrying the title *Latinos and the Nation's Future*. The book featured a forward from Janet Murguía, who wrote, "The fate of the country and that of Hispanics is inextricably linked."

The argument being made is twofold: demographic change is inevitable and will result in dramatic societal change. This transformation thereby links the future of the country and the Latino population together. Articulations of it can be found throughout the publications and pronouncements of Latino advocates. For example, just prior to the Democratic and Republican national conventions in 2012, NHLA released its *2012 Hispanic Public Policy Agenda*. Nearly forty pages long, the report details the coalition's major legislative priorities, such as economic development, health, civil rights, and immigration. The document's opening message, written by then chair Hector Sánchez Barba, stated:

> The Latino population consists of over 50 million individuals spanning the United States, Puerto Rico, and other territories. In the last ten years, Latinos represented more than half of the total population growth. This explosive demographic change signals a shift in community attitudes, political representation, and electoral power. Indeed, the Census estimates that by 2050 Latinos will comprise nearly one third of the entire nation's population.

Similarly, a 2011 white paper of the Congressional Hispanic Caucus Institute (CHCI), a member of NHLA, linked Latinos to the country's scientific and technological advancement: "As the fastest growing ethnic group, the U.S. scientific and technological competitiveness will be largely influenced by the achievements of the Latino community."[63] At public events sponsored by advocacy organizations, honored speakers and corporate sponsors vocalized the demographic linked fate. During the NCLR conference in 2011, President Obama told the audience, "Your country needs you. Our American family will only be as strong as our growing Latino community." Unlike his words on immigration reform, these pronouncements were greeted with strong applause.[64] At that same conference, mogul Arianna Huffington told attendees, "50 million Hispanic Americans are a central part of moving us towards a more perfect union." Both claims, not by accident, were made only months after 2010 census data entered public circulation.

Now, most national Latino leaders are careful to explicitly avoid the idea that demography is destiny. Articulations of demographic linked fate often stress the need to invest in the Latino population. Cisneros, for example, notes that "the Hispanic population is becoming so large that the future of the country will in many important areas be significantly determined by how Latinos progress."[65] Similar to the ambivalence seen in Progress 2050's founding document, Cisneros and others believe that realizing the "good" of Latino population growth will require investment in the present, particularly in education and employment. In this manner, the Latino population is projected as having inevitable impacts, even as the *nature* of those impacts is conditional on the actions and interventions taken in the present. Even so, the major thrust of their forecasts was what we might label demo-utopian. Its emotional tenor was assuring and hopeful, projecting a bright future not only for the Latino population but for the country as a whole.

Managing White Demographobia

Efforts to build hopeful anticipation about the future cannot be understood apart from fears about pessimistic or dystopian reactions to demographic change. As NHLA member Angelo Falcón told the press in January 2011: "With a more conservative Congress in place, this next census announcement will reignite the next generation of the immigration debate, with all the anti-Latino rhetoric it brings with it."[66] Ironically, perhaps, the census—a tool so vital to Latinos' political work and agenda—was expected to intensify "anti-Latino rhetoric."

Unwilling to wait for a backlash, organizations prepared and promulgated messages to manage demographobia, that is, anxiety or fear about demographic trends. Months before census data was released, Ingrid Ramos, NCLR's associate director of research, spearheaded the preparations. When hired in 2009, Ramos had little experience working with census data. A trained anthropologist, she had to quickly acclimate to a political landscape that privileged quantitative knowledge. However, her qualitative and ethnographic sensibilities proved useful. Using "message maps," she assembled leading staff members to create positive narratives about "who we are as

Latinos." She feared that, in the absence of a coordinated public relations strategy, people would read the new census data and conclude, "Oh my god, there's such a huge Latino population. It's terrible; the country is going to fall apart." She believed that NCLR could "assuage the fears that people have around changing race and ethnicity issues" and viewed the construction of a counternarrative as a defensive move against long-standing stereotypes and representations. But she recognized, along with her colleagues, that this narrative had to be equipped with "data to back it up."

Her collaborator, Jackie Montalvo, was tasked with securing this information. Raised in a nearly all-white community in southeastern Idaho—for a time represented by the rabid anti-immigrant member of Congress Tom Tancredo—Montalvo was familiar with expressions of demographic anxiety. In ninth grade she debated a white classmate on California's controversial Proposition 187. To prepare for the debate, she hit the library to find facts that showed positive contributions made by undocumented immigrants. Years later, in her mid-twenties, she would find herself doing similar research, albeit with a broader platform.

Montalvo identified various kinds of "positive" data for use in reframing Latino population growth: figures on military service, employment, attitudinal optimism, and citizenship. Of these, numbers and percentages on Latino citizens were regarded as most important. Montalvo told me she was personally conflicted about the emphasis on legal status, but the data provided evidence to challenge stereotypes of illegality. As Miguel Molina, NCLR's director of communications, shared with me: "These fifty million aren't undocumented immigrants. They aren't going to turn this country Spanish speaking. They aren't going to do all these things they're accused of. And we took that data . . . and create[d] messages that, you know, 70 percent of Latinos are U.S. citizens." That percentage was even larger for Latinos under eighteen years old. As Ingrid Ramos told me, "93 percent of all Latinos under eighteen are born in the United States" and thus are citizens by birth. These statistically supported claims were meant to persuade the public and the media that Latinos were an essentially domestic rather than foreign population—in other words, that they were part of, not separate from, the United States. Equally important, the emphasis on citizenship was not only meant to tell a story about the present population. It was intended tell about the future—a *documented* Latino future composed primarily of U.S. citizens.

These numbers and narratives were assurances made to those anxious about demographic change, those for whom Latino population growth did not yet seem beneficial. Although demographic change was posited as real, the nature of this change was forecast as rejuvenating more than transforma-tive. This forecast stood distinct from white supremacist discourses, which instead conveyed a chronotope of "crisis."[67]

NCLR advocates were under no illusions about the limits of the strategy they had adopted. Some people would remain unconvinced—those Ramos said had animosity toward Latinos rather than anxiety about their growth. Anxiety, though, was an "emotion that people want to resolve," she said. Her group probably couldn't erase all the animosity, but it could assuage anxiety. Clarissa Martinez was blunter: "Nobody here is trying to win over nativ-ists, alright!" Nativists, or those who peddled anti-immigrant, anti-Latino, pro-white rhetoric, she argued, were not the "majority of Americans." But they did have an outsized influence on public discourse on immigration and population change. Anti-Latino activists and leaders needed to be chal-lenged, but also those merely anxious needed to be engaged.

Even as they were well aware of the likes of John Tanton and Ann Coul-ter, as well as many lesser-known nativists and white nationalists, advocates almost universally depicted demographic fear as a *natural* response to popu-lation change. As such, these opponents were framed as bad actors tapping into "our worst instincts" rather than fomenters of anxiety. As Martinez stated, "it's okay to feel anxious about change; we all do. It's a human thing." The organization's leader Janet Murguía has publicly expressed this point on numerous occasions. For instance, in a *Wall Street Journal* op-ed in April 2011 titled "Hispanic Values Are American Values," she framed demographobia as a "natural human anxiety." Pointing to past moments of demographic change, Murguía wrote: "Like others who brought demographic change to America, our presence has stirred anxiety among some of our fellow Ameri-cans. A century ago, people expressed the same concerns about waves of immigrants from Italy, Ireland and Eastern Europe. It was understandable—but it also turned out to be unfounded." She continued: "As the number of Latinos grows, our fellow Americans need to overcome the natural human anxiety that accompanies change and look for common ground." This con-ception naturalizes rather than politicizes demographobia, and reflects natu-ralized assumptions about populations and population change.

A Delicate Dance

In the years since the 2010 census, national Latino advocates have fore-cast a future propelled by Latino demographics. They have drawn on cen-sus statistics, investing them with particular cultural meanings. However effective—and only time will tell—these efforts have involved qualifying and curating census data and putting forth their own narratives of what this data tells about the future.

Their image of the future differs from the affective valence ascribed to population dynamics by other political projects. Most sharply, they diverge and dispute—by implication, if not intention—the racial dystopias espoused by the intellectual spokespersons of "white reaction."[68] Their account can read, for instance, as a counterpoint to the doomsday prognostications of Buchanan, Coulter, and others on the far right. National Latino advocates have tried to articulate a more hopeful story. Embracing Latino Spin tropes, they cast the Latino population as essentially American and "inextricably linked" to the country's future. As Arlene Dávila rightly warns, however, tropes of hard work, patriotism, and traditional values simultaneously stake claims on "Americanness" and narrow its definition.[69]

The narratives crafted by national Latino advocates resonate with many who seek to project a positive and inspiring account of Latino demographic growth in the United States. Take, for instance, the words of the syndicated columnist, Ruben Navarrette:

> Where some Americans look at changing population figures and see calamity, I only see opportunity. This country continues to draw to its shores the determined and the daring, who come here—to the land of second chances—to reinvent themselves and, in the process, wind up remaking and revitalizing the country. That's not a threat to America. Quite the contrary. It's the very essence of America. Bring on the change.[70]

Sam Fulwood, a senior fellow at Center for American Progress and contributor to its Progress 2050 project, told me much the same: "Diversity makes us stronger and we should embrace it rather than trying to reverse it. We cannot stop the demographic forces that are let loose on this country. What we want to do is understand it, keep people from being afraid, and then develop policies that work to the advantage of everybody." These utopian articulations, right alongside pessimistic and dystopian ones, are part of a broader cultural-political field. This field, as shown, is populated with competing—and occasionally coalitional—entities engaged in population politics. Some are more influential, more powerful than others. Some push against dominant interpretations and others defend them. Regardless, these are relational narratives.

Demographobia hovers over national Latino advocacy. Concerns over enflaming white fears and the energies expended attempting to manage them have led to a set of parameters, the rules of engagement when it comes to describing Latino population growth in the public sphere. Many actors struggled, particularly in the wake of the 2010 census, to even name those most anxious and afraid of ethnoracial demographic change. In her commentary, Murguía speaks vaguely about "fellow Americans" and implies that anxiety is universally distributed rather than more pronounced among certain populations.[71] Just as Latino advocates resist any language or images that can be construed as projecting a demographic takeover or reconquest, they have often avoided directly naming white demographobia.

I take this as a pressing political predicament. John Williams, one of NCLR's most senior leaders, reflected: "In terms of a broad strategy, it's a matter of how to navigate the line of being sufficiently respected so that you have the space to, at least, have a fair shot at policy and practice that's going to equitably serve the community, but at the same time resisting and avoiding being perceived or exacerbating the existing perception [of] this community." How NCLR and its fellow Latino organizations engage in population politics—how they forecast Latino demographic futures—is inseparable from, and entangled in, this delicate dance. Somehow, they have tried to minimize anxiety while proclaiming demographic strength. While they feel themselves unable to stop the dance, for if not how can they keep the alarmists at bay, they express frustration over the sluggishness of progress. This condition has invited them to adopt other tactics to accelerate the arrival of the future.

4

Awakening a Giant

Making my way through the satellite campus of Ana G. Méndez University, I arrive at a narrow classroom filled with ten or so rows of chairs arranged auditorium style. About twenty some people are present, waiting for the press conference to begin. They include community leaders, elected officials, reporters, and representatives from the state's Board of Elections. The election of 2012 is about a month away, and the leadership of El Movimiento Hispano is here to announce their get-out-the-vote operation in the Orlando metropolitan area. El Movimiento Hispano is a collaborative project of the League of United Latin American Citizens, the Labor Council for Latin American Advancement, and the Hispanic Federation.

The press conference commences with opening remarks from José Calderón, president of the Hispanic Federation. Calderón, a Dominican American in his mid-thirties, is seeking to build a national profile for the New York-based organization. He proclaims: "We have fifty-two million Latinos across this nation. You hear about Latinos everywhere you go. People are very excited. We are a young, dynamic, and growing community. It is a community that will continue to grow." Cracking a smile, he adds, "We are very fertile. We like babies, and that is a good, good story." Several in the room chuckle.

Taking a more serious tone, Calderón continues, "One of the things that is critically important, as you are hearing about the Latino movement and growth, [is that] none of that matters, none of it matters, if we don't exercise our right to vote." Depicting raw demographics as politically insufficient, he calls for robust Latino electoral participation. Other speakers reiterate the message, but none as compelling as the first public service announcement shown at the press conference.

The PSA is the product of a collaboration between El Movimiento Hispano and Lin-Manuel Miranda, the Nuyorican playwright and musician, best known for his Tony award-winning Broadway musical *Hamilton.* Fittingly titled "Found in Translation," the one-minute-long video makes an impassioned, creatively bilingual pitch for Latinos to vote. Dressed in all black— from button-up shirt to scally cap—Miranda raps, a cappella, directly into the camera for the duration. At the onset he poses a demographic question in search of an answer:

> When is a minority no longer a minority?
> When those in power make our issues a priority?
> Well here's the lead story America, there's already 50 million
>   Latinos here and counting.
> Hi Majority!

As Miranda deftly interweaves numbers and narratives, you can sense frustration. There's invisibility. There's others making decisions for Latinos. There's the conflation of Latino and immigrant. But all this seems besides the point. The main source is Latinos themselves. This is conveyed most clearly in the subtitles, which are entirely in Spanish—in contrast to the mostly English-language performance—and are also not direct translations. The subtitles, as linguistic anthropologist Jonathan Rosa argues, "offer an in-group message that doubles down on and amplifies the critiques offered in English."[1] It is here that Miranda chooses to express his frustration:

> Pero tenemos que votar, y todavía
> No entiendo por qué no votamos como si fuéramos la mayoría
> Nuestra gente representa el 12% del ejército
> Somos 50 millones y creciendo
> ¿Pero sólo votamos el 7%?[2]

Latinos, in other words, are abdicating their power at the ballot box. Resonant with the comments of José Calderón at the press conference, Miranda argues that demographics are not enough.

Whether intentionally or not, the narrative closely shadowed the longstanding characterization of the Latino population as a "sleeping giant." This metaphor simultaneously signals size, cohesion, and an ironic (or perhaps tragic) inability to act. Sleeping giants have *potential* but unrealized power.

The video, as well as the voter operation that commissioned it, tries to awaken this giant, this electorate, to affect not just the upcoming election but how the very future is imagined. At the press conference, LULAC executive director Brent Wilkes sketched this temporal arc: "We want to make sure that the turnout of Latino voters in this election cycle is a historic turnout." A massive Latino vote, he affirmed, would both affect the election and make a statement about "every election from here on out." As Wilkes and his collaborators and counterparts put it, all hinged on voter mobilization. This, however, was only one ingredient needed to foreshadow the future.

———

Ever in pursuit of greater political influence, national Latino civil rights organizations and leaders saw the 2012 election—the first after the 2010 census—as an opportunity for acceleration. As always, population politics are never far away. To seize this opportunity, more than forecasting was needed. They needed to shape not only how Latino population trends and ethnoracial futures were envisioned (e.g., beneficial, positive) but also that the future was not far away. It was already, even if in an embryonic form, in the present. For this, another temporal tactic was in order—what I call *foreshadowing*. In the context of population politics, foreshadowing is a proleptic technique to convince that the demographic tomorrow is in the here-and-now.

Advocates therefore approached the election as a means to stage a public *demonstration* of the future. Science studies scholars have long been interested in the ways demonstrations and experiments have generated scientific "facts." But they are not limited to scientific pursuits, as they are equally vital to political life—and in fact serve as a bridge between the two. Above all, demonstrations are tools and technologies of persuasion.[3] They are meant to convince audiences that can serve as witnesses of what has been shown.[4]

In this chapter I explore the population politics of foreshadowing. For Latino advocates during the 2012 presidential election season, this meant two major kinds of mobilization. The first, as noted previously, was the mobilization of Latino voters. For this, these organizations launched independent and collaborative voter registration and get-out-the-vote campaigns across the country. The second aspect, closely intersecting with the first, entailed the mobilization of data—demographic and electoral. I focus on the rhetorical deployment of two influential statistical figures: a projection and an estimate. The projection, produced by one of the national organizations, held that 12.2 million Latino voters would participate in the 2012 election. The estimate maintained that fifty thousand Latino citizens were turning eighteen every month—thus becoming eligible to vote—in a trend that would continue long into the future. In the process, these interlinked and mutually dependent mobilizations met with numerous obstacles, including efforts to suppress the Latino vote, persistent and vexing questions about the apparent political dormancy of Latino voters, and doubts about whether there was even *such a thing as* a "Latino vote" to begin with. Despite these and other challenges, this mobilization of bodies and figures together helped lead many observers to conclude, at least for a time, that the 2012 election offered a definitive glimpse into a Latino accented political future. This contributed to transforming the election into what the sociologist Ann Mische has called a "site of hyperprojectivity" or an arena "of heightened, future-oriented public debate about contending futures."[5]

Introductions

Electioneering was in full swing by the time I arrived in Orlando in late September 2012. Both the Obama and Romney presidential campaigns had their operations in place, as did a number of local races. The "civic engagement" campaigns of interest to me were also in full effect. These campaigns are examples of what political scientist Ricardo Ramírez has characterized as "proactive mobilization"—"elite-sponsored activities targeting barriers to Latino civic and political incorporation."[6] To this end, they invested in phone banking, mailers, promotional events, and direct voter contact—the most expensive but most successful method of engagement.[7]

National Latino civil rights groups—sometimes to the chagrin of local leaders—saw Orlando and central Florida as impossible to ignore. Their chief target was the region's growing Latino population—particularly its Puerto Rican population—in the counties of Orange, Osceola, and Seminole. For the presidential campaigns, this demographic shift threatened to unsettle, if not unseat, the Republican-Cuban stronghold in southern Florida. As a result, the area became, as one advocate put it, "the battleground of battlegrounds."

I came to the region with few contacts. Luckily, I knew Juan Robles, the national field director for Mi Familia Vota (MFV), for more than a decade. Before he made his way to Washington, DC, in the early 2000s, he worked as a high school teacher and community activist in Chicago's Puerto Rican community. Juan offered to connect me with the Orlando MFV operation. At his invitation, I visited the headquarters, located just a couple of miles from the city's downtown. Juan greeted me with a hug and walked me over to meet the operation's coordinator, Carolina Diego. We entered a small room with walls covered by handwritten sheets of voter registration tallies, posters, and other campaign paraphernalia. Carolina seemed up to her neck in work, and her eyes were fixated on her computer screen. Juan got her attention, but to my relief she didn't seem bothered by the interruption. She quickly stood up and extended her hand, welcoming me to the operation.

Carolina expressed interest in my research topic, asking me a series of questions. She was particularly curious about whether the work of MFV would appear in an eventual book. As we were speaking, some canvassers entered the room. Carolina looked to one team leader, who I later learned was named Glenda, and kindly asked her to give me a crash course in voter outreach. Glenda was in her thirties, with Spanish I recognized from Puerto Rico. She directed my attention to a tangle of phones, about twenty or so, charging against a wall. Every canvasser was assigned a phone when out in the field talking to voters. On the phone, she showed me, was a voter application that contained the names, addresses, contact info, and other identifying data of voters. It also contained a bilingual script that canvassers were asked to memorize for their exchanges with potential voters. Canvassers were responsible for updating voter information after every visit. Did anyone answer? Were they unavailable or unwilling to communicate? Were they deceased or had they moved? The app also contained a short survey on social issues, such as education, the economy, and immigration. During their visits, canvassers, she added, were asked to encourage voters to pledge to vote come Election Day. Glenda then set the phone to recharge and pointed to one of the walls. It was papered with large sheets that logged how many houses her team had visited and how many voters they had spoken with since the operation began.

By the time the tutorial ended, several other canvassers had arrived for work. Carolina, perhaps noticing my introversion, made a few introductions. One was Manuel, a middle-aged Chilean man who, before moving to Orlando, had lived in Puerto Rico for nearly seventeen years. As I responded to his questions about my research, Manuel lodged a complaint: Latinos are big talkers, *hablan en la calle* (they talk in the streets), but when it comes to taking action—like voting—they were at home drinking. It surprised me a bit to hear this familiar trope about Latino political passivity from a canvasser.

I later learned that Miguel was rather opinionated and often made statements at odds with those of his fellow workers.

Shortly after my conversation with Miguel and a few other canvassers, Juan and Carolina instructed us to form a circle in the main room and introduce ourselves to a visitor, a leader from SEIU, the parent of MFV. As we went about introductions, it caught my attention that nearly every team member stated their national origin. It was a reminder that even within "Latino" projects, national identities may be quite meaningful and not at all mutually exclusive. One young canvasser stated he was from New York and Puerto Rico. Another shared being from Puerto Rico and a newcomer to Orlando. The next canvasser identified as Venezuelan, followed by a Cuban and a Dominican. Several more were from Puerto Rico. Although most introductions were brief, a few volunteered that they enjoyed and had learned a lot from working in this outreach campaign. Carolina, one of the last to speak, told the group that she was a proud Venezuelan. Later I would learn that she had a promising political career in Venezuela but left after becoming disaffected with the Hugo Chávez regime. She framed the 2012 U.S. election as a matter of respect, saying in her accented English, "This minority is going to make a change."

Carolina's comments, which drew nods from some canvassers, echoed arguments that national Latino civil rights leaders were making about the election: the election was going to be transformative. The agent of transformation was not any candidate; it was the "Latino community." Janet Murguía, for instance, told the *Los Angeles Times*, "We will be voting for ourselves. . . . We will be enhancing our own ability to create the power and the clout that will ultimately turn the policies we want to see change."[8] Similarly, but with a demographic twist, an El Movimiento Hispano pamphlet read: "Do your research on both candidates and both party sides. What matters is that we let our voice be heard. We fought for the right to vote so we need to take advantage of it now, not later, NOW. We are 50 million strong and we can be a deciding factor in this election and in the future."

Although canvassers I met and worked with in Orlando had their preferences, they consistently framed their efforts as broader than those of partisan campaigns. To be sure, this distinction was not made for purely ideological reasons; their operation demanded—by law—they not blur matters between nonpartisan and partisan electoral work.[9] But this was not the whole story. Many felt that their livelihoods, not just as individuals but as members of a marginalized population, rested not so much on whom Latinos voted for but on whether they voted at all.

National Latino Civic Engagement Table

Mi Familia Vota was the first operation I made contact with in Orlando. In time I connected and participated with the local operations of Voto Latino, the National Council of La Raza, and El Movimiento Hispano (League of United Latin American Citizens, the Labor Council for Latin American Advancement, and the Hispanic Federation). I learned that each operation had its own "turf," or area of work. Some were larger and better funded. Some concentrated on phone-banking and public events, while others sent out teams of paid canvassers several times a week. It wasn't obvious, at least to me, that these different operations were actually part of a nationally coordinated campaign to mobilize Latino voters.

Historically, national Latino civil rights groups have pursued their "civic engagement" more or less independently. This has meant struggles over turf, access, and resources. The 2012 election, however, saw unprecedented collaboration. No doubt, partnership to promote the census, such as the *ya es hora* ¡HÁGASE CONTAR! campaign, set some organizational infrastructure. Interviews with advocates hinted at some other reasons. Leaders admitted that the task at hand was logistically impossible for a single coalition, let alone a single organization. There were, after all, many voters in that 50.5 million population. Then there was the political economy of voter engagement. Leaders complained that a lion's share of available resources were being allocated to white-led organizations. This frustration has only grown over time. They knew that whatever they managed to raise individually from foundations and corporations was woefully insufficient to influence Latino voter participation. Collaboration raised opportunities to pool resources.

Perhaps more instrumental was the recognition that foundations and political parties were not genuinely interested in building long-term Latino political empowerment. As one respected Democratic strategist and former advisor to Bill Clinton put it, "Political operatives and consultants care only about winning the next election, and so they don't spend much energy on building true infrastructure that goes from cycle to cycle." She added, "If in fact Latino civic engagement power is to be realized it is going to require the commitment of organizations that care about the long-term strength and vitality and influence of the Hispanic organizations." The absence of this commitment made it more difficult to push back against anti-Latino and anti-immigration politics and policies. Ironically, this predicament helped fuel a sense that these organizations and the population as a whole were "under siege." Another leader expressed to me, "Whenever you're under attack and you're in the foxhole together, you build relationships that are strong. It makes organizations set aside [egos] for the good of the overall vision."

It was within this context that a group of leaders took part in a series of conversations with Latino leaders in the spring of 2011. These fruitful discussions led to the creation of the National Latino Civic Engagement Table. The Table, as it is often called, began with Mi Familia Vota, the National Council of La Raza, Voto Latino, the National Association of Latino Elected and Appointed Officials Educational Fund, and the Center for Community Change (CCC), an immigrant rights organization. Eventually LULAC, LCLAA, and the Hispanic Federation joined the Table as well.

The Table capitalized on—and extended—the infrastructure developed to promote the 2010 census. SEIU and foundations, such as the Ford Foundation, provided funding, and national Latino groups began to coordinate logistics and resources. A key objective, expressed by several organizers, was to avoid repetition or mismatches between goals and organizational capacities, so they made attempts to tap into the strengths and expertise of specific organizations. Voto Latino, for example, was seen as particularly effective at leveraging social media and celebrities, while NCLR had extensive experience with field operations. The SEIU-funded Mi Familia Vota had a strong reputation for coordinating an effective voter registration network in Florida, Arizona, Nevada, and Colorado. And, as in past elections, NALEO coordinated a national voter support hotline and conducted small, localized get-out-the-vote operations in several states. Combining efforts, LCLAA, LULAC, and the Hispanic Federation jointly coordinated civic engagement campaigns, hosted public forums, and produced public service announcements. The Table carried out an unprecedented effort to mobilize Latino voters amid a wave of Republican- spearheaded laws and policies that made it more difficult to register voters and created obstacles to voting.

Data was a major part of these civic engagement operations. As I immediately learned, the organizations were employing what scholars have described as "technology-intensive campaigning."[10] Although primarily used by partisan campaigns, this mode of electoral work involves a deep reliance on data and data analytics. Voter data was actively mined to inform what houses to visit and what areas to concentrate on. During visits, canvassers also collected and updated available voter data. In these ways, data was a key part of the logistical infrastructure of these operations.

At the same time, data—specifically figures about the Latino electorate—was also central to their rhetoric, mobilized to motivate voters and shape public discussions about the "Latino vote." These rhetorical uses of data were in the service of population politics. But, as we will see, statistical invocations were not meant to forecast a distant future or assuage white fears about population change. Rather, they were specifically and strategically deployed to foreshadow the future through the election. To this end, they did not rely exclusively on data about the present size of the Latino population or electorate but also drew on and circulated figures that could project both short- and long-term political impact.

12.2 Million

Nearly eighteen months before the election, NALEO-EF released projections for national Latino voter participation at a breakfast plenary during its annual conference. The date was June 23, 2011, and the location was San Antonio—home to the Democratic twin dynamos the Castro brothers, Julián and Joaquín, who had just entered the national political spotlight.[11] Over a hundred Latina and Latino elected officials were in attendance for the day's opening session, sponsored by BP America and Walmart. Held months after the release of the results of the 2010 census, the session was dubbed "Latino Political Power—Turning Numbers into Clout."[12]

Moderator Monica Lozano, the chief executive officer of ImpreMedia (which owns several major Spanish-language newspapers), began with remarks centered on the census. Specifically, she applauded NALEO and other Latino media and advocacy groups for achieving "historically high" Latino participation rates. Lozano enthused that the size and growth of the "Latino demographic" was being "heralded by virtually every media outlet in America":

> The *Wall Street Journal*'s front page captured the sentiment with the headline "Latinos Fuel Growth in Decade." And if any of you saw that front page, there was a map and over the map the headline "Los United States." And as we all know, it wasn't just in the traditional urban centers like Los Angeles and Houston and New York; it was all across America and in communities like Akron, Nashville, and Indianapolis. Latinos are changing the face of America.

Lozano spoke in a way that felt familiar: national spokespersons and media commentators had, in the months since the census release, narrated a demographic dispersal of the U.S. Latino population that was almost as astonishing (and celebrated) as the numeric size and rate of growth. In the course of my research, I was frequently told that the 2010 census, perhaps for the first time, had revealed a *national* population (though everyone acknowledged that the vast majority of this panethnic population remained concentrated in just ten states). But this demographic profile just prefaced the conversation; the question on all these leaders' minds was how to *translate* Latino demographic growth into greater political (and economic) influence—hence the title of NALEO's opening plenary. For these political actors, the answer to this question was mass electoral participation. The prospect of Latino voters flooding the ballot box was the subject of the event's main presenter, NALEO-EF leader Arturo Vargas.

Vargas began his presentation with an excited reminder of the "impact of Latino voters" in the previous two national elections and primaries. The audience, composed of the organization's membership base—Latino elected and appointed officials—clapped at the news that NALEO-EF's projection for the 2010 midterm elections had been off by just 100,000 voters. Latino voter turnout had helped the Democratic Party maintain control of the Senate. The razor-thin reelection of Nevada senator Harry Reid was cited as proof. Vargas also mentioned the increase in the number of Latino politicians, including Republicans Marco Rubio (R-FL) and Susana Martinez, the first Latina governor elected in the country.

On his seventh slide, Vargas arrived at the heart of his presentation. Past victories and impact had nothing on what was to come in 2012 and beyond. "Nationally, we anticipate that 12.2 million Latinos will go to the polls next November; that's a 25 percent increase in voters from 2008, and we will become 8.7 percent of the national share of all voters." The magnitude of the projection was given meaning in relation to the percentage of growth in voter turnout. On the screen were also state-specific projections for the Latino vote in Arizona, California, Colorado, Florida, New Jersey, New Mexico, New York, and Texas, where the Latino vote was projected to increase between 14 and 38 percent. The focus, however, remained on the national figure.

As intended, the NALEO-EF voter turnout projection was quickly picked up by the media and became a fixture in public debate about the "Latino vote."[13] The following day, Fox Latino and CNN ran the respective headlines "Record Number of Latinos Expected to Vote in 2012" and "Latino Officials See Big Hispanic Vote in 2012."[14] Sometimes media outlets credited the projection to NALEO, but most often, as Vargas readily admitted to me, it was repeated enough to become "conventional wisdom" or even "fact." Indeed, science studies have noted that the production of facts rests on their circulation and uptake, a process of movement that "black boxes" or strips away the contextual and contested origins of such data.[15]

The voter projection was circulated and consumed throughout civic engagement operations. While conducting fieldwork in Orlando, I encountered the figure on numerous occasions. One especially poignant example occurred weeks before the election. On a cloudy Saturday morning, the canvassers of MFV and the Florida New Majority, another SEIU voter project, staged a small rally in the parking lot of a public library. The library was located in an area densely populated by Puerto Ricans, just miles from the Orlando airport. At this time, it doubled, as did others throughout the state, as an "early voting" polling station.

Several hundred feet from the library and a major thoroughfare crowded with partisan campaign signs and workers holding large posters, Nilda Escobar, whom I had met during my first visit to MFV's operation, convened the canvassers. Escobar was most passionate about environmental issues, but that day she spoke as MFV's voter registration coordinator. Although she admitted not having much prior experience speaking at public events, she wielded the bullhorn with confidence. Into it, she shouted, "We're going to make history, right?" Her exhortation was met with spirited endorsement, as bodies drew closer and hands clapped. She continued, elaborating the kind of history (or future) that was to be made: "12.2 million Latinos! We are going to show the world, because everybody is looking at us today. The I-4 Corridor . . . [we are] the determining factor of the presidential election. We're going to mobilize our people. We're going to go and vote. . . . We're not going to let these people tell us who we are and what we're going to do! No, we're going to take action!" Escobar voiced the projection as a certainty. While the figure was national, she localized it, claiming that central Florida (the I-4 Corridor) would determine the election. Implied but not stated outright in her speech was the confrontation with local officials bent on suppressing the vote. Energized by her words, the canvassers soon after set out to encourage voters to take advantage of early voting.

The 12.2 million projection also found its way into the civic engagement literature produced by the organizations. Just days before the election, MVF produced a colorful, bilingual comic, *Todos a Votar*, for distribution in Arizona, California, Colorado, Nevada, Texas, and Florida (fig. 4.1). Similar to the MALDEF comic produced to encourage participation in the census, the MFV comic centered around a two-parent, working-class Latino family. It

FIGURE 4.1. "Todos a Votar" comic, circa 2012. Used by permission of Mi Familia Vota.

addressed several of the issues that advocates were confronting, such as voter apathy and suppression, while invoking community empowerment and an awakening giant. Without attribution, NALEO's voter projection was integrated into its message. At one point in the story, the wife in the comic remarked to her husband: *"¡Yo siempre he votado desde que me mudé de Puerto Rico a los Estados Unidos, y ahora vamos a poder ir juntos gordito! Se espera que más de 12 millones de Latinos salgamos a votar en estas elecciones"* (I have always voted since I moved from Puerto Rico to the United States, and now we are going to be able to go together! It is expected that more than 12 million of us Latinos will vote in these elections). In the end, the entire family, even the initially cynical youngest son, participated in the election.

National Latino advocacy groups leveraged the 12.2 million voter projection to tout the power of the "Latino vote." It helped them secure funding and attract greater media attention. But it also raised pressure and expectations about actual voter participation. As scholars have shown, numbers, particularly in circulation, are "reactive." They can change how people act and generate new expectations. Indeed, whether intended or not, the figure became the public metric by which partisan and nonpartisan observers alike would determine whether the so-called Latino sleeping giant actually arose in the 2012 election.

A Sleeping Giant?

NALEO-EF's projection gave a concrete numerical figure to ideas already in circulation about the potential impact of the "Latino vote." Indeed, after the 2010 census, political pundits, campaign strategists, and the media had begun to actively discuss Latino voters, describing them not only as the "fastest-growing" segment of the electorate but, perhaps equally important, as the key "swing vote" in the 2012 national election. Long before a single ballot was cast, the "Latino vote" was deemed "decisive" for the presidential election. *TIME* magazine's front cover on March 5, 2012, most firmly, if controversially, stated this point.[16] For the first time in its history, the cover featured text in Spanish. The issue title read: "Yo Decido. Why Latinos Will Pick the Next President." *TIME*'s managing editor, Richard Stengel, described Latino voters as "America's New Decisionmakers":[17]

> *Nosotros vamos a decidir.* We will decide. That has been the presidential-election mantra of Latinos all across the U.S. And it's hard to argue with

the premise. The numbers alone tell an amazing story. Nearly 10% of all voters in 2012 will be Hispanic, up 26% from four years ago. One of four newborns in America is Latino, and those births now account for more than half of U.S. population growth. Hispanics make up 16% of the population today and will account for close to a third of all Americans in 2050.

As told by Stengel, the decisiveness of the Latino vote was rooted in the population's demographic growth—growth that he reminded readers would make up nearly 30 percent of the country by midcentury. Bold as the statement was for a magazine to make, the Yo Decido! issue reflected some of the consensus at the time. Political pundits and consultants from both major parties also argued that victory would elude Republican presidential candidate Mitt Romney if he failed to capture a substantially larger percentage of the Latino vote than John McCain had garnered in 2008. Just weeks before the election, incumbent president Barack Obama confidently (but, he believed, off the record) told an Iowa newspaper: "A big reason I will win a second term is because the Republican nominee and the Republican Party have so alienated the fastest-growing demographic group in the country, the Latino community."[18] The Obama campaign drove this message home with a T-shirt that quoted *TIME* magazine's cover line.

Yet not everyone was convinced. More than a hint of uncertainty remained about where the "Latino vote" would materialize. For years, this constituency has been described as a "sleeping giant." Its failure to realize its political potential was a running theme—a joke, even—in U.S. politics. As Cristina Beltrán rhetorically asked: "What are we to make of this Latino Leviathan, this narcoleptic colossus that seems to periodically stir only to fall back into civic obscurity?"[19] In posing this question, Beltrán sought to interrogate the conceptual and historical underpinnings of this trope.

Advocates were haunted by the specter of the sleeping giant. Many openly detested the characterization. They acknowledged that about half of all eligible Latino voters were unlikely to participate in the election but attributed this to a number of structural issues, including the fact that partisan operations ignored Latino voters with their emphasis on "likely voters." Often stripped of context, the sleeping giant metaphor was commonplace in media coverage and pundit discourse. As the 2012 election drew closer, the depressed voting rates of Latinos were regularly compared to other ethnoracial constituencies. Moreover, frequent charges were made that the Latino voter was inconsistent and unreliable. As the *National Journal* staff writer Janell Ross surmised, "The strategy will boost Latino voter turnout in swing states, but won't likely expand Latino political power or engage more Hispanic voters." The "sleeping giant," she insisted, would not wake in November 2012.[20]

The National Latino Civil Engagement Table and its respective operations did not take failure as a fait accompli. They believed that they could reach what Vargas and his colleagues called the "great unengaged." It was not that these voters were sleeping or apathetic. Rather, they were ignored—ignored by the major political parties, ignored if they lived outside the "swing states," and ignored by most of the major funders of civic engagement. Advocates hoped to change this state of affairs and realize the projection of twelve million Latino voters. If successful, perhaps, not only would it shake off, once and for all, the pejorative characterization of this heterogeneous constituency as a sleeping giant but also provide uncontestable proof of the *future* in the present.

Fifty Thousand

The 12.2 million voter projection made claims about the near future. In a sense, it shadowed the outcome that advocates were working to achieve. But the advocacy groups did not want only to influence the immediate election; their goal was to make a statement about what was to come in the long run. For this, these entities relied on another statistical figure that claimed the "power" of the Latino vote into the foreseeable future. That figure was the estimate that, every month, fifty thousand Latino citizens turn eighteen and thus become eligible to vote. During the 2012 election season and beyond, only this figure came close to rivaling the 50.5 figure in terms of frequency.

The figure of fifty thousand was invoked in a variety of ways. As with the 12.2 million figure, it was used to reach Latino voters and attract attention to their efforts. Voto Latino, for example, included it in a series of graphics displaying "facts" about the Latino electorate (fig. 4.2). The graphics were circulated through the organization's social media platforms.

In ground operations, the figure also made appearances. In Miami, Camila Burgos, the statewide coordinator of NCLR's Florida operations, shared with me—without being prompted—that she cited that figure to motivate her canvassers: "[When] I would talk to my team this year . . . I would also [mention] how every month fifty thousand Latinos turn eighteen and, from here on until 2050 or something like that, and that these are eligible voters." Data once again was more than logistical support; this knowledge was seen as rhetorically useful. Of course, as Camila and other

FIGURE 4.2. "50,000 Latinos Turn 18 Every Month in the United States" infographic, circa 2012. Used by permission of Voto Latino.

field coordinators expressed, the figure (as well as other ones) was one of several motivating tools. Due to the quick pace of canvassing, where every second counts and canvassers are evaluated on the number of doors they knock on and conversations they held, they preferred to stick to "bread-and-butter" issues, such as public services and employment opportunities.

For national leaders and spokespersons, the figure appeared ubiquitously in press conferences and their publications. NCLR produced a fact sheet about the growth of the Latino electorate titled "Latino Children Will Add Nearly 15.8 Million Potential Voters to the Electorate."[21] Drawing on American Community Survey and census data, the fact sheet asserted that almost a fourth of all U.S. children were Latino and that an "overwhelming majority"— some 93 percent—are U.S. citizens. Tracking the number of Latino children at every age and in what year they would turn eighteen, NCLR analysts concluded that "between 2011 and 2028, an average of 878,000 Latino citizen children will turn 18 each year, and by 2024 that number will reach one million annually." This fact sheet elaborated on the fifty thousand per month figure and projected the number of each new cohort of eighteen-year-old Latino voters. The substantive import of this electoral growth went unstated, but the message was clear: the "Latino vote" was powerful and would be for decades to come.

Other documents, from NCLR and others, used this statistic in narratives and normative discussions about the "Latino demographic." For example, an NCLR blog post dated May 23, 2012, read: "If you're a Latino in America, the future appears to be a grim one, but being the resilient and optimistic people that we are, it's important to remember that we have the power to do something about it. We have the power of the vote. And with 50,000 Latinos turning 18 every year for the next 20 years, those votes have awesome potential to translate into power." These sentences appeared after an opening paragraph describing the impact of the foreclosure and economic crises and the emergence of anti-immigrant legislation and practices on U.S. Latinos. It urged that, if Latinos wanted to address these and other issues, the vote was the primary, and perhaps only, mechanism that would allow them to convert future demographic "potential" into present political "power."

No Giant at All?

The figures that Latino advocacy organizations rhetorically mobilized during the election presume, at a foundational level, that the "Latino vote" is not a mere statistical artifact. That it represents an actual, even if heterogeneous, constituency or community. This assumption undergirds what Cristina Beltrán has theorized as "civic Latinidad," the vision of Latino politics held by Latino political elites, including most Latino civil rights advocates.[22]

But what if most of those said to compose the "Latino vote" do not identify or understand themselves to be "Latino"? Maybe the giant doesn't even exist? These were precisely some of the questions that erupted after the publication of the Pew Hispanic Center report, *When Labels Don't Fit: Hispanics and Their Views of Identity*.[23] The episode revealed that the ontological status of the "Latino vote" (and Latino population by extension) can—and does—get called into question.

The Pew Hispanic report appeared in April 2012, just as civic engagement operations were being launched. It found that "nearly four decades after the United States government mandated the use of the terms 'Hispanic' or

'Latino' to categorize Americans who trace their roots to Spanish-speaking countries, a new nationwide survey of Hispanic adults finds that these terms still haven't been fully embraced by Hispanics themselves." For scholars of Latino panethnic identification, the findings were not all that remarkable. Research has long found a strong preference for national designations over panethnic labels but also that for many individuals panethnic and national labels are not mutually exclusive. Context very often determines what identity label is chosen.[24]

Media coverage and commentary raised critical questions about the assumed "groupness" of Latinos.[25] For example, *Los Angeles Times* journalist Paloma Esquivel reported: "Only one-quarter of those polled used the terms Hispanic or Latino most often, while about 21% said they predominantly use the term American. Most of those polled did not see a shared common culture among Latinos—as sometimes is assumed by politicians courting a voting bloc." Instead of one cohesive group, the article explained, Latinos represented "dozens of nationalities."[26] Univision anchor and journalist Jorge Ramos wrote a commentary prompted by the study titled "The Nameless Many." Ramos wondered whether the panethnic labels currently in fashion have lost their utility. The author of *The Latino Wave* seemed to think so. Calling for greater specificity, he concluded: "No, 'Hispanic' is not enough. As the Pew study rightly concludes, the current labels are virtually useless. But another 40 years may have to pass before we can come up with an adequate solution."[27] Notably, being "nameless" did not invalidate the idea of there being "many" for Ramos. The Pew findings and the public discussion they generated raised questions—and rebuttals—about the "precondition" for civic Latinidad: Latino panethnicity.[28] Projections about the Latino vote seem to demand at least some modicum of groupness and identification.

Latino advocates were not about to allow such doubt to trouble their foreshadowing. The Latino population, they asserted, was more than a mere "methodological construction."[29] It is precisely this argument that Arturo Vargas and Janet Murguía made in response to the report. Pew invited them and other civic leaders, academics, and writers to "share their views" on Latino identity. In their own ways, Vargas and Murguía took the opportunity to stress the existence of this panethnic community, even if some of its purported members distanced themselves from the category.

The thrust of Vargas's position was captured in his commentary's title, "Labels Aside, Latinos Share Common Values." He wrote:

I fully respect the individuality and self-identification they express, yet I have come to understand that what brings these people together is not a religion, a language or even a culture. In each community, I have observed common values: love of family and community, and optimism in life. I also have come to understand that what often binds diverse Latino national origins in this country is how they are treated and regarded by the non-Latino majority; this often serves to bring Latinos together in common cause.

Vargas departed from dominant characterizations of Latinos as bonded by language and culture. Instead, he offered two alternative bonding agents. First, he claimed that Latinos—notwithstanding their personal identities—shared a set of "values." He identified three: love of family, love of community, and optimism about life. Vargas did not identify the source of these values. Are they intrinsic or unique to this population? As you may recall, a persistent thread in the rhetoric of advocates is the characterization of this population as hopeful and optimistic. Latinos, it would seem, were the consummate believers in "America." The second bonding agent was less mystical and more sociologically grounded: anti-Latino sentiment served as a unifying factor. As Beltrán writes, the notion of the civic Latinidad has often rested on the belief that "Latino subjects are marked and constituted by historical circumstance."[30] Ultimately, while Vargas acknowledged internal diversity, he was unwilling to conclude that this negated the existence of a Latino community.

In her response, Murguía directly challenged the results of the Pew poll. She noted that the report showed that people were now more comfortable with panethnic labels than in the past. She also questioned the idea that ambivalence toward such labels precluded community building and solidarity, as witnessed on the issue of immigration:

> On paper, immigration is not an issue that affects Puerto Ricans or Cuban Americans much. But are there any stronger voices for immigrants than Rep. Luis Gutiérrez, a Puerto Rican congressman from Chicago, and Sen. Bob Menendez, a Cuban American senator from New Jersey? And isn't it a Cuban American U.S. Senator, Marco Rubio, who is trying to save the Republican Party from themselves on this issue?[31]

The case of immigration demonstrated "the reality is that there is a connection among the 50 million-plus Hispanics." Not only did she imply universal support for immigration reform—which was and is not the case—it also implied that Latino commonality and community was already a fact. Yet there was ambiguity here. Murguía ended her essay with a normative appeal to unity. "We should want, and we should work, to be connected. Because in our unity lies the power to make the policy changes necessary to advance our community and our country forward." This call for unity suggested a reality of disunity or separation. It would seem, then, that any existing commonality has not been enough to foster unity outright. In this manner, this commentary indexed a lingering tension over whether civic Latinidad is "less found than forged."[32]

Ultimately, Murguía and Vargas—both in their assertions as well as in their silences—argued that *something* holds together the "Latino community," ethnic identity preferences aside. Long proponents of panethnic identification and knowledge production, these advocates reaffirmed the ontological "reality" of Latinidad and its transformative political potential. While they could not escape foundational questions about the existence and future of the "Latino vote," these leaders wagered that the election would foreshadow a definitive answer.

Final Push

After months of voter registration and door-to-door canvassing, the presidential election was now about a week away. In Orlando and elsewhere, canvassers were the linchpin of the operations of national Latino civil rights groups. These individuals, mostly working class, were far removed from the press conferences and strategy sessions of the national Table. The rarefied air of Washington, DC, and other political hubs was foreign to most of them, many of whom—at least where I observed—were recent migrants and in some cases noncitizens. Their responsibility was to mobilize local Latino voters as the leadership mobilized resources and rhetoric in support. With much at stake, coordinators worked to motivate their canvassers for a final push.

One Friday afternoon I made my way to MFV's office. It was alive with activity. In the "war room," I found Carolina, as usual, fielding a barrage of questions, all the while typing away on her laptop. Within minutes, a Puerto Rican canvasser in his early twenties came in and proudly told Carolina he had taken advantage of early voting. She hugged him and we clapped as he told us he had seen other voters carrying MFV literature at the polling station. Carolina shared with me that she was waiting for the arrival of MFV's national leadership, including SEIU leader Eliseo Medina, MFV executive director Ben Monterroso, and several SEIU representatives. They had come to Orlando to assess the local field operation. Not long after, I recall, the group arrived.

After a round of introductions, I noticed Eliseo Medina standing alone, inspecting a large map of Florida's Orange County. Although hesitant to disturb him, I took the opportunity to start a conversation with this life-long labor organizer. While more than able to deliver a rousing speech, he has a calm and humble demeanor. Unlike my experiences with some national leaders, Medina wasn't guarded. He shared with me his delight in the "enthusiasm" and "spirit" he found among the Orlando canvassers. Motivated by more than a paycheck, they exhibited a personal commitment, he concluded. Having spent time with these canvassers, I couldn't disagree. Such commitment was vital. The stakes of the 2012 election, he narrated, were incredibly high. In his words, it wasn't "about a person or parties, but our future." As we continued, I realized the future he was referring to wasn't the faraway demographic future I had been tracking. On his mind instead was the future to come after the election, and above all the prospects of immigration reform. Shaking his head in frustration, he mouthed, Congress has "smoke in their heads." He wanted to give them a wake-up call and was confident the election would do just that. But high hopes had been dashed in the past. "What will make this election any different from past presidential elections?" I asked. His answer was not as direct as I had hoped, but he offered a prediction. The election would empower him and his colleagues to make political demands rather than "moral" appeals. Both political parties would learn that their "political futures" hung in the balance.

Later that afternoon, all the canvassers were led into the office's small lobby. Standing tightly, shoulder to shoulder, some twenty-five of us received inspiring remarks from our guest. Rocio Sáenz, the leader of SEIU's successful Janitors for Justice campaign and future international executive vice president for the union, addressed us first. With labor experience that stretches from coast to coast, Sáenz declared that MFV was *"creando un movimiento"* (creating a movement). Every door we knocked on *"¡nos va dar poder, ese futuro!"* (will give us power, that future). Our efforts were making history. Moved by her remarks, the young canvasser who earlier announced that he had voted belted out a cheer.

Medina was next to speak. Now sporting an MFV T-shirt over his dress shirt, he told the canvassers that their work was based on a *"compromiso con nuestra comunidad"* (a commitment to our community) and that, because of it, *"vamos hacer la historia"* (we are going to make history). He reminded them of his earlier visit to Orlando and acknowledged the *calorcito* (heat) and *los perritos* (the dogs) that they had endured for months. Hearing this, a canvasser near me giggled. *"El cambio es difícil,"* he told us. Change is difficult. But with struggle, *"vamos a ganar"* (we will win). *"No hay un gigante dormido. . . . Ellos lo despertaron"* (There is no sleeping giant . . . they have awoken it). Nodding heads indicated there was no need to specify who "they" were. The "giant," he added, was not only composed of immigrants or one type of Latino nationality—it was all Latinos, who together have been told, "you don't belong." Medina ended his speech recalling his relationship with Cesar Chávez, the famous Mexican American labor leader. Calling us "authors of change," he modified Chávez's famous slogan, which had been appropriated by the Obama campaign in 2008. Medina urged us to transform *"¡Sí se puede!"* into *"¡Sí se pudo!"* on Election Day. The statement stimulated a vigorous round of applause that spilled out of the lobby. Invigorated canvassers, joined by Medina and the other leaders, then headed out for another session of door knocking.

On the afternoon before polls would open, the leader of NCLR's Orlando operation also set out to motivate her canvassers for a last push. Born and raised in Puerto Rico, Angela Olmeda had left her Caribbean homeland to make a life in Florida. Although younger than many of the canvassers, there was something maternal about her relationship with them. It was immediately obvious that she had gained their respect and affection. Before she began her customary daily meeting, Angela told the group that the national office wanted canvassers to videotape each other on their phones reflecting on their experiences as canvassers. The request fit the introspective mood in this cramped second-floor office. Like their counterparts at other operations, these canvassers had become a tight-knit group. It was routine to hear them make jokes and converse about kids and health as they busily gathered their election literature, clipboards, pens, water, and, most important, their assigned phones. But today was different. The video reflections, while filled with fond memories and a sense of accomplishment, triggered feelings of sadness. Their time together was ending, and few would remain in the employ of NCLR after the election.

I think Angela sensed this. She stepped out of her office with a big smile and greeted the teams. The twenty or so canvassers, split among four team leaders, formed a jagged circle for the meeting. Angela's election eve message warned against being *negativo*. Acknowledging their hard work, she nonetheless demanded a final push. *"No es tiempo de chiste"* (It is not time for jokes). Making direct eye contact with the canvassers, she urged them to remember *la supresión del voto* (voter suppression) and focus on their objective to *sacar el voto* (turn out the vote). She then asked for volunteers to "adopt a precinct" when the polls closed. Expecting long lines, she pleaded with us to do everything in our power to keep voters in line—even if that meant dressing up as "George Washington, a clown, or Barney." She lamented that the volunteers would not be paid for work done after the polls closed, but stressed *"que vale la pena"* (that it matters). She didn't elaborate much more. The past few months had been more than enough instruction. And if not, there were reminders all around the office. One in particular stood out to me. A handwritten poster—nestled between a drawing of U.S. Supreme Court Justice Sonia Sotomayor and a poster of Orlando's official Hispanic Heritage Month 2011 celebration—read: *"50 Millones de Hispanos, Solo Somos Fuertes Si Votamos. En 2012 los hispanos representan el 10% del voto electoral"* (50 million Hispanics, we are only strong if we vote. In 2012, Hispanics represent 10% of the electorate).

A Giant Awakens

Election Day began before 6 a.m. All day I was teamed up with Jesus and Pablo, with whom I had worked in the past. Most of our time was occupied with placing vote reminders on doorknobs and occasional visits to polling places to make sure they were operating properly. We were tired and hungry but when we returned to MFV's office that evening we were struck by the air of accomplishment.

The main room had been given an Election Day makeover. Red, white, and blue streamers were everywhere, and miniature American flags decorated a food table closely orbited by famished canvassers. Carolina was beaming with an ear-to-ear smile. Huddled with three of her team leaders, they exchanged Election Day tales. The night was young, especially in Florida, where election nights can seem to stretch forever. The presidency was far from decided, but the mood was festive. In one way or another, every canvasser I spoke to told me with confidence that they had made "history" and triumphed over apathy, misinformation, and voter suppression. Without the support of a single exit poll, they were convinced that Orlando's Latino voters had responded positively to their message and exercised their right to vote. In fact, for the time being, no greater validation was needed than the sight of hundreds of voters waiting in lines, long after polls were to have closed.

As the evening's celebration progressed, we received statistical confirmation of our ethnographic observations. Crowded around a large flat-screen television rented for the occasion, we intently watched the postelection coverage (fig. 4.3). Cheers and applause erupted as journalists and political pundits discussed the impact of the "Latino vote" locally and nationally. Exit

FIGURE 4.3. Election Day 2012 at Mi Familia Vota Orlando, November 2012.
Photo by author.

poll data now confirmed that Latino voters participated in higher numbers
than in previous elections and had given President Obama a three-to-one
edge over his Republican challenger, Mitt Romney.

Eliseo Medina was in Las Vegas, another major MFV outpost, on election
night. Two months of visiting operations across the country—interacting
both with canvassers and voters—had filled him with confidence about
Latino voters' impact. Watching from his hotel, he noticed that, in contrast
to Obama, Romney's biggest victories were coming from states without "a
huge Latino population." But as he would tell me months later, the impact
of the Latino vote only became "crystal clear" for him after doing several
television and radio interviews. "That night people discovered Latinos as a
political force." Just as he said this, he revised it: that night English-speaking
media discovered Latinos as a political force. The Spanish-language media
had expected this and did not need to ask: "Where did this come from?" *Yo
decido* apparently became *yo decidí.*

By the following morning, as MFV's Orlando operation began a day-
long debriefing, a cascade of articles and opinion pieces would begin to
congeal exit poll data into a narrative: the country's (then) fastest-growing

population and electorate had played an important, if not the *most* important, role in the reelection of President Barack Obama. Headlines told the story: "Growing Share of Hispanic Voters Helped Push Obama to Victory" (*Washington Post*), "Latino Voters in Election 2012 Help Sweep Obama to Reelection" (*Huffington Post*), "Election 2012: Obama Wins Re-election, Clinches Latino Vote" (Fox News), and "Latino Vote Key to Obama's Re-election" (CNN).[33] Latino voters were the first ethnoracial constituency named in the *New York Times*'s lead article on election results: "Hispanics made up an important part of Mr. Obama's winning coalition, preliminary exit poll data showed."[34] This sentiment was echoed in the Spanish-language press. For instance, *La Opinión* stated, *"Por si quedaba alguna duda sobre el impacto del voto latino, basta ver en detalle la victoria del presidente Obama. Sin la intensidad de este electorado el mandatario no habría sido reelecto. Así de simple"* (If any doubt remains about the impact of the Latino vote, you only need to see in detail the victory of President Obama. Without this intensity, this official would not have been reelected. It's that simple).[35]

Simple *now*. But just weeks before, there had been considerable uncertainty and fierce debate over whether the Latino vote would actually materialize, partisan affiliation notwithstanding. The election settled this debate, at least temporarily. Fox News proclaimed "Obama Victory Proof That the Sleeping Latino Giant Is Wide Awake."[36] The Pew Hispanic Center similarly titled its postelection report "An Awakened Giant: The Hispanic Electorate Is Likely to Double by 2030," noting that while Latino voters "still punch below their weight," they are an "ascendant ethnic voting bloc that is likely to double in size within a generation."[37]

Media discourse and political punditry about the Latino electorate and the wider coalition that reelected Obama were refracted through post-census demographic discourse. In the words of an Associated Press article in the *San Diego Union-Tribune*, "It's not just the economy, stupid. It's the demographics—the changing face of America."[38] CNN journalist Josh Levs wrote, "America woke up Wednesday, looked into a giant mirror made up of millions of votes and saw how it has been changing for decades."[39] Conflating white demographic decline with white political decline, conservative commentator Bill O'Reilly cried before Fox viewers: "It's a changing country, the demographics are changing. . . . The white establishment is now the minority." His tears spoke to white demographobia.

Discussions about an awakened Latino electorate were anchored statistically and representationally in another figure: 10 percent. The day after the election, Univision's Jorge Ramos stated, "Barack Obama was elected president, in large measure due to the support of millions of Latino voters. Ten percent of all voters were Hispanic."[40] Another article proclaimed, "The sleeping giant has awoken: Latinos not only helped Obama win in key battleground states, but they made up 10 percent of the electorate for the first time."[41] The figure and its historicity would be repeated widely in the press and among national Latino leaders. For example, Presente.org, a Web-based Latino advocacy group, produced and circulated a colorful infographic after the election. Among other statistics, it included, "LATINOS were 10% of ALL VOTERS in 2012, up from 8% in 2004." Before the election, the number had been just a corollary to NALEO-EF's voter projection. Afterward, 10 percent would stand in as proof of a new day in U.S. ethnoracial politics.

Emboldened by the turnout, Latino civil rights leaders immediately claimed the power of the Latino vote. Eliseo Medina, speaking to the press, said with some levity, "The sleeping Latino giant is wide-awake and it's cranky."[42] NCLR's director of civic engagement, Clarissa Martínez, told the press, "It's unequivocally clear now that the road to the White House goes through Hispanic neighborhoods."[43] The fall 2012 front cover of LULAC's quarterly magazine did not mince words: "Historic Latino Vote Determines Election" (fig. 4.4). In its postelection press release, the organization stated, "Before the election, LULAC and our partners had predicted that a record 12 million Latino voters would cast their ballots in the 2012 Presidential race and, based upon exit polling, our prediction has been validated." Brent Wilkes, LULAC executive director, further commented: "We knew there could be two stories out of this election. One could be the Latino vote fizzled and didn't live up to its promise and another story could be the Latino vote surprised and again was a record historic vote and that it in fact was influential in battleground states. And that is the story that came out. Because of that, we are now in the [political] position to be able to achieve victory on a lot of other issues."

In an op-ed in the *Huffington Post*, Janet Murguía signaled that the election represented a "new normal":[44]

> Since election night, one topic of immense interest to me has dominated the news cycle: the impact of the Latino vote on the 2012 election. After years of being treated as one of the best-kept secrets in politics, the need to reach out to Latino voters has suddenly become the hot topic of conversation for people on both sides of the aisle—even Sean Hannity. It has all the makings of not only a political phenomenon but a cultural phenomenon as well. In fact, if this were a sitcom, it would be called "The New Normal."

LULACnews

Fall 2012

Historic Latino Vote
Determines Election

LULAC Voter Protection Call Center

INSIDE:
Latino Voters Center Stage
Meet the Challenge!
Latinos Living Healthy
Hispanic Corporate Leadership

FIGURE 4.4. "Historic Latino Vote Determines Election." LULAC News, Fall 2012. Used by permission of the League of United Latin American Citizens.

Murguía claimed that "this 'New Normal' is not just about 2012; for several key reasons, our community's clout is only going to grow in every election from here on out." Like her colleagues, Murguía framed the election as not only historic but also indicative of the future. The country's political landscape was never going to be the same.

In a similar fashion, Arturo Vargas's postelection commentary opened: "Less than four weeks ago, Latinos reshaped the nation's political map and exercised the strength of their political power, both as voters and candidates." Vargas devoted the majority of his commentary to naming Latinos elected to state and federal offices, and their presence near the highest levels of the two major parties. While he said there was much work to be done, he was pleased "that Latino representation at the state and congressional levels is beginning to mirror the demographics of our country." Like his counterparts, he assured readers that 2012 was no aberration; "there is much more to come from the nation's second largest and fastest growing population group."[45]

As the year came to a close, advocates began to leverage their newfound political clout to secure "comprehensive immigration reform." It seemed like this was the moment to finally bring millions "out of the shadows" and end the legalized exclusion and marginality of the undocumented population.

5

Dreams Deferred

The reelection of Barack Obama in 2012 was widely interpreted as a sign of a long-projected future—one of a more diverse, inclusive, and progressive United States. The election, it seemed to many, had accelerated—decisively and irreversibly—the arrival of that future. Demographic naturalism would lead us to conclude that this interpretation, with its accompanying feelings of excitement or dread, was an obvious consequence of the ethnoracial composition of voters and those elected. But this was not the case. It had much to do with the population politics that framed the election long before any ballots were cast and any victory speeches were delivered. This political and cultural work made it possible to imagine the outcome of a single election as on a demographic trajectory.[1]

National Latino civil rights leaders and organizations contributed to this imaginary trajectory, as we saw in the previous chapter. Mobilizing voters and statistics, they specifically foreshadowed a political future without sleeping giants. With only growth on the horizon, the Latino vote was—it was claimed—fated to determine elections to come. But this was no idle futurology. The future was summoned, as is often the case, to affect the present.

Advocates had no shortage of needs and wants. Three months before the election, NHLA and its member organizations published their *2012 National Hispanic Leadership Agenda*. The report contained policy prescriptions on a range of issues, including economic security and empowerment, education, immigration, government accountability, civil rights, and health. Of these, immigration weighed arguably the heaviest, not least because it had been used to motivate Latino voters.

These political actors immediately set out to capitalize on the post-election consensus, proclaiming 2013 the year of immigration reform. As one told congressional leaders, "No more excuses, no delaying tactics, no partisan semantics that have held us back for decades. The time to act is now!" However, translating their foreshadowed future into a legislative victory was far from straightforward. No matter how compelling or seemingly unavoidable, such futures are not the future as such; they are, by definition, glimpses of it. This means that there is some time between the present and said future. As such, the foreshadowed future may be ignored, delayed, and forgotten as much as anything else. Confronted with this reality, advocates, I contend, made a determined effort to remind congressional leaders of the election and the consequences of forgetting the future. I call these efforts *forewarning.*

Forewarning is analytically distinct from the temporal tactics I have discussed thus far. To forewarn is not simply to encourage people to envision the future in a particular way, as forecasting aims to do. Nor is it meant to signal the presence of the future, as foreshadowing intends. Whereas those tactics respectively address the content and closeness of the future, forewarning deals with the consequences of the future. To be certain, there is some overlap among these, and I believe that without having engaged in forecasting and foreshadowing, Latino advocates would not have been able to forewarn.

I employ this concept in ways that are both resonant with and different from a growing body of scholarship on "anticipatory action."[2] Focused on the politics of anticipation, researchers have explored responses to future threat (e.g., economic crisis, environmental disasters, terrorism). In many of these studies, the future of interest is uncertain yet probable, a condition that invites practices and discourses of "preparedness."[3] In this case, Latino advocates considered the future certain. But, as they would argue, the political ramifications of Latino population growth and demographic change, more generally, were not set in stone. As a consequence, officials had some "volition" to shape the implications of the future.[4] Forewarning was thus not about preparing for an uncertain but probable future but responding to an *inevitable but malleable* one. In this way, advocates departed from the entrenched idea that ethnoracial demographic change necessarily favored the Democratic Party. Republican officials, at this point the primary obstacles to reform, were told that, if they so desired, they could reinvigorate their party by throwing their support behind comprehensive immigration reform. But, conversely, they were warned that resisting reform would—by consequence of the demographic imperative—seal the political fate of the GOP.

Demographic Imperative

Advocates didn't wait long after the election to forewarn officials on Capitol Hill. On December 12, 2012, they gathered for a press conference at the headquarters of the National Council of La Raza, located blocks from the White House. *New York Times* journalist Julia Preston would later write, "Latino Groups Warn Congress to Fix Immigration, or Else."

Standing shoulder to shoulder—as if embodying unity—the leaders addressed the press. NCLR's Janet Murguía began by noting that, with her colleagues, she had entered the past election season with "one common goal": ensuring that "Latino voters were well represented." And delivered they did: "A record number of Hispanic voters turned out in this election. The Hispanic voter made a considerable difference in this year's election, especially in many of the key swing states." Murguía was not simply reiterating a now-acknowledged fact but pointing to what had *moved* Latino voters—what had awakened a giant. "Latino voters," she stated, "went to the polls with the economy on their minds, but with immigration reform in their hearts." Their collective action made a strong "political case" for a "bipartisan solution" to immigration. The language reminded me of the conversation I had months earlier, where Eliseo Medina spoke about no longer needing to rest their arguments for reform on moral appeals. Murguía then added, "Given the demographics, it is clearly in the best interests of both parties to do so as well."

Murguía's statement was direct enough for all listening, but her colleagues became increasingly assertive. With the next midterm election in mind, Medina, the second to speak, declared: "Our voices will become stronger and louder, now, in 2014, and well into the future." Voto Latino's president Maria Teresa Kumar added: "We have time on our side, we have numbers on our side, we have allies on our side, and we have individuals that are standing before you that work very hard day and night to make sure that we're representing our community wisely, but more importantly that we're here in front of them to organize." And then, reaching a crescendo, Max Sevillia, from the Mexican American Legal Defense and Educational Fund, avowed: "Latino voter engagement will continue to grow in the coming years, ensuring that the candidates who ignore the voting block will do so at their own peril."

The Republican Party, the leaders warned, was facing an extinction-level event, which could be averted should they undertake a shift on immigration policy. Anita Estes, a Puerto Rican activist and member of the Labor Council for Latin American Advancement in Florida, for example, described the

FIGURE 5.1. "Demographic Meteor Hits GOP" cartoon, 2013. Used by permission of Lalo Alcaraz.

GOP to me in an interview as "dinosaurs." Sipping coffee, she elaborated, "They have to bring themselves to reality to compete because if not, they are going to cease to exist because the old people are going to pass away and *lo que se van a quedar son los jovenes*" (what will be left are the youth). Her distinction between "old people" and "jovenes" was not simply generational but implicitly raced. Old and white were synonymous, as were young folks and Latinos. Anita's desire to see Republican leaders respond to the demographic imperative was deeply personal. Her husband had been deported to Mexico, and she had seen firsthand the labyrinth of immigration law. For this reason, she hoped Republican officials would embrace immigration reform over political extinction. Their demise, Anita believed, was not destiny, as one cartoon from the syndicated Chicano cartoonist Lalo Alcaraz expressed metaphorically in 2013 (fig. 5.1). Rather, she maintained it was a matter of choice, in other words, a self-fulfilling prophecy.

Postelection diagnoses in the mainstream press seemed to agree with the peril facing Republicans unwilling to embrace the Latino future of the country. In the *New York Times*, journalists Jeff Zeleny and Jim Rutenberg wrote, "The Republican Party seemed destined for a new round of self-reflection over how it approaches Hispanics going forward, a fast-growing portion of the voting population that senior party strategists had sought to woo before a strain of intense activism against illegal immigration took hold within the Republican grass roots."[5] In *Foreign Affairs*, Ray Suarez argued that Latinos were transforming the electoral map, making it all but "impossible for Republicans to win enough Electoral College votes to put a candidate in the White House."[6] And *Washington Post* editorial board member Jonathan Capehart, picking up on the fifty-thousand-new-Latino-voters-per-month statistic explored in chapter 4, titled his postelection commentary, "50,000 Shades of Dismay for the GOP."[7] To survive the demographic imperative, the Republican Party would have to change.

Republican Makeover

In the immediate postelection period, the foreshadowed future was on the mind's of many Republican leaders and operatives. The conservative polling group Resurgent Republic called 2012 the year that "changing demographics caught up with Republicans." Alongside a series of election turnout graphs, it claimed that while Mitt Romney "did a superb job of winning the support of white voters," this "was not enough to win a presidential election in the America of 2012."[8] A leaked Republican memo included the phrase "demographic change is real" and noted that in Florida alone, more than 200,000 more Latinos went to the polls than in 2008—and the majority endorsed Obama.[9] Drawing on the words of former Secretary of State Condoleezza Rice, the memo concluded that the Republican Party was going to have to create "an even bigger tent" to survive.[10]

These anxieties became the basis of the Republican National Committee's (RNC) so-called autopsy report, published in March 2013. Formally titled *The Growth and Opportunity Project*, the report claimed to offer an "honest review of the 2012 election cycle." Based on its analysis, it concluded that "unless changes are made" the GOP would be unable to win the presidency in the "near future." The major source of its "precarious" prospects was population change. "America is changing demographically, and unless Republicans are able to grow our appeal the way GOP governors have done, the changes tilt the playing field even more in the Democratic direction."[11] This exercise in population politics tellingly described the Latino population as "imperative" to engage. Indeed, this was the first "demographic partner" it discussed. For all its prognostication of decline and defeat, the report did not propose any radical change. Most recommendations boiled down to tone and messaging. One exception was immigration. Noting that the RNC was "not a policy committee," it nonetheless urged, "We must embrace and champion comprehensive immigration reform."[12] Without that, there was little hope in increasing "Hispanic" support for the Republican Party.

Advocates were pleased to hear such proclamations from Republican leaders—it was evidence that their election gambit had paid off. The parties were taking notice of the electoral power of the Latino electorate, and that meant immigration reform was now on the national agenda in a new way. In early 2013 Eliseo Medina was elated. At his office in the national headquarters of SEIU near DuPont Circle in Washington, DC, he likened the election to a boxing match. Surrounded by labor posters and Cesar Chávez quotes, he remarked, "They say the biggest punch is the one you don't see. That's the one that knocks you out." I wasn't surprised by the analogy of a fight but by the idea that no one had seen Latinos' "punch" coming. If anything, Medina and his colleagues had worked hard to telegraph what pundits later viewed as the knockout blow. In any case, he was convinced Republicans had gotten some sense knocked into them. He recalled his first meeting with Arizona senator John McCain, around 2007. McCain shared with him a newspaper article about border crossings and told him it was a tragedy that people were dying in the desert. Not long after, the two participated in a Florida rally in support of a new bill for comprehensive immigration reform, the Secure Borders, Economic Opportunity and Immigration Reform Act of 2007.[13] However, a challenge from a Tea Party–endorsed candidate three years later led this one-time ally to fall in line with the GOP's increasingly more anti-immigrant stance.[14] That changed after the 2012 election, which Medina believed returned McCain to "where his heart was originally."

The apparent Republican makeover was a frequent talking point at Latino advocacy and immigrant rights events in Washington. In February 2013 LULAC hosted a panel explicitly on immigration reform. Medina's colleague Josh Bernstein, director of SEIU's immigration advocacy, claimed that the election—and most notably the participation of Latino and Asian voters—had placed immigration reform in "a totally new, different situation." Bernstein insisted that it was no time to let up on the pressure and simply relish the moment. Angela Kelly of the Center for American Progress painted the transformation even more starkly: "The terms of the debate changed literally overnight. There is no policy issue that I can think of that from the day before the election to the day after the election flipped like a light switch. You have seen the very stampede of Republicans and conservatives running to this issue." Kelly implored the audience to embrace the shift rather than penalize representatives for their past positions. No matter what metaphor was employed, advocates expressed their conviction that the election had altered the legislative landscape. For Latino civil rights groups in particular, it was time to seize this legislative opening.

Writing in *Huffington Post*, NHLA chair Héctor Sánchez Barba enjoined reelected President Obama to "quickly take advantage of the momentum now that Republicans seem to understand the basic lesson that extremism has no future."[15] When I spoke to Sánchez Barba in 2013, he reiterated that anti-immigrant rhetoric was no longer an electorally viable strategy. Republicans might win some conservative districts with that rhetoric but now understood there was "no possibility" to win another presidential election without the Latino vote. It had become too big to anger or alienate.

Advocates welcomed Republican policy change but were under no illusions. Sitting outside a café on a warm spring day, Gilberto Ocampo, a consultant who worked closely with national Latino organizations, expressed his amazement with the sudden "love fest" on Capitol Hill for Latinos. Every time he bumped into his Republican colleagues, they would express profuse embarrassment. While Ocampo wondered whether the new tone was purely cosmetic, he was not at all worried. As one leader expressed in an interview:

> Some of these anti-immigrant politicians didn't all of a sudden wake up with love in their hearts for Latinos. What changed their minds is the politics. They saw we were not defenseless. Latinos were not defenseless. They probably still harbor the same opinions about us. But they know that their *political survival* now depends on having a different relationship with our community and they're desperately trying to figure out how to do that.

For this veteran advocate, "sometimes it's better to be feared than loved." That the GOP's shift was a "political calculation" wasn't really a concern so long as it greased the legislative wheels for immigration reform. At that moment, it seemed that this was, in fact, the case. How could the future—so definitively foreshadowed through the election—be forgotten?

Reform on the Horizon

Republican pronouncements and confidence in their newfound position fueled advocates' belief that immigration reform was on the near horizon. Speaking to Spanish-language journalists, a leader announced, *"Nosotros estamos absolutamente convencidos de que va ver reforma migratoria. El fracaso no es una opción para nosotros"* (We are absolutely convinced that there will be immigration reform. Failure is not an option for us). Then, in English, he added, "[Republicans] will come to vote for immigration reform. They can come out on their own will because it's the right thing to do or they can come kicking and screaming, but they will come. I guarantee you that." To be sure, such statements were performative, in that they sought to create an outcome professed as certain. But I believe it also expressed a real conviction.

While not readily apparent to me at the time, this conviction was on display at a LULAC staff meeting in May 2013. The meeting was focused on preparations for the organization's summer convention. Twenty staffers, along with Brent Wilkes, the national executive director, sat around a long conference table. At one point in the meeting Wilkes, who had been toggling between typing on a small laptop and making occasional eye contact with his team, interjected that an online company had expressed interest in helping undocumented immigrants fill out their residency paperwork. The comment sparked a conversation about what would happen *after* immigration reform. One staff member, a woman in her twenties, proposed that LULAC continue to host town halls, which at the time were a key part of the national strategy to build support for immigration reform. After legislation passed, the town halls could be repurposed to educate immigrants on the new mechanics of applying for residency and perhaps even citizenship. Another longtime staffer mentioned that a group of lawyers had volunteered to offer legal clinics after the legislation became law. This discussion was not merely about being prepared for the possibility of reform and what that would demand of the organization. It also revealed strong confidence that reform would happen in that year's legislative cycle. In a sense, the real question for advocates was not *when* immigration reform would happen but *what kind* of reform it would be.

Advocates knew to expect intense struggles and negotiations over the substance of any proposed legislation. They immediately made the content of their vision for reform known. By and large, their vision centered on what is known as "comprehensive immigration reform" (CIR) and the chief demand for a "path" to citizenship.

Since the mid-2000s, national Latino civil rights groups have—almost universally—supported comprehensive reform. Generally, CIR bills contain four elements: (1) border security and enforcement directives, (2) employer sanctions, (3) guest worker provisions, and (4) legalization measures. These components more or less reflect the distinct, and sometimes crisscrossing, demands of different constituencies and interest groups.[16] Business leaders, for example, have long demanded access to cheap immigrant labor and thus have opposed efforts to restrict immigration outright. Labor unions, meanwhile, have historically resisted the importation of immigrant labor and have favored sanctions on employers that hire undocumented workers. Immigration restrictionists have pushed for punitive and exclusionary measures. Finally, some groups have advocated increasing access to legal immigration and providing status regularization, if not legalization, for the undocumented. Immigrant rights groups, including Latino civil rights advocacy groups, are among the most visible entities holding this position.

Attempts to bridge these competing, often antagonistic positions, have generated massive and unwieldy pieces of legislation. This has required the formation of what political scientist Daniel Tichenor has described as "strange bedfellows."[17] The process is especially fraught as major constituencies have not been equally influential. For instance, restrictionists have more powerfully dictated the terms of debate and the content of legislation than those favoring legalization.[18] One of the most visible signs of this asymmetry is the embrace of the concept of "earned citizenship." As legal scholar Muneer Ahmad notes, "amnesty" has not always been politically radioactive in U.S. immigration policy. Since the 9/11 attacks especially, mainstream immigrant and civil rights groups have entirely abandoned the language of amnesty. Instead, they have embraced the language of "earned citizenship" or a "path to citizenship," which Ahmad correctly demonstrates "implicitly subscribes to the core claim of restrictionists, namely, that undocumented immigrants have committed moral transgressions that require some form of moral recompense."[19] This is one of the concessions made to secure bipartisan support for immigration reform.

With reform seemingly on the horizon, Latino advocacy groups expressed once again their commitment to CIR and tactical opposition to "piecemeal" approaches, which focus on a single issue or a subset of immigration-related issues rather than on immigration as a whole. This position—shared by the major labor unions and immigrant rights advocacy organizations—has been a source of tension with some sectors of the Dreamer movement, who have grown understandably disillusioned with comprehensive bills after several repeat failures.[20]

This time around advocates began the push for CIR with a more forceful critique against the prioritization of border security over other aspects of reform. At the December 2012 press conference discussed earlier, Hispanic Federation's Chris Espinosa called out the imbalance: "We have secured our borders. It is time to get to the other elements of comprehensive immigration reform, which should include a path to citizenship." Early into the new year, with the foreshadowed future still fresh in the memory of congressional leaders, advocates professed that the time for "enforcement-only" policies was over.

Bipartisan Openings

Less than a month into 2013, two bipartisan immigration reform proposals were unveiled: the first from a group of senators and the second from the Obama administration, fresh off its second inauguration ceremony. Along with others in the broader immigrant rights movement, Latino civil rights advocates followed the news closely. They knew the players and understood the major fissures and factions. But most important for them, the proposals confirmed their legislative optimism.

On January 28, eight senators—four Democrats and four Republicans—made public a bipartisan framework for immigration reform. After nearly two months of internal negotiations, Senators Chuck Schumer (D-NY), John McCain (R-AZ), Lindsey Graham (R-SC), Bob Menendez (D-NJ), Michael Bennet (D-CO), Dick Durbin (D-IL), Marco Rubio (R-FL), and Jeff Flake (R-AZ) came to a provisional agreement on four "basic legislative pillars" to fix the country's "broken" immigration system. These pillars were the foundation of what became the Border Security, Economic Opportunity, and Immigration Modernization Act (S. 744), introduced the following month. Dubbed the "Gang of Eight," the senators outlined the pillars in a brief document and a news conference: establishing "a tough but fair path to citizenship" for undocumented immigrants, reforming the "legal immigration system" in ways that would "help build the American economy and strengthen American families," creating an "effective employment verification system," and building an "improved process for admitting future workers to serve our nation's workforce needs, while simultaneously protecting all workers." The path to citizenship, they noted, was "contingent upon securing our borders and tracking whether legal immigrants have left the country when required." All in all, the pillars were largely reboots from earlier bills, although more skewed toward "merit" rather than family-based immigration.

Before a congested room of journalists and long-lens cameras, the senators framed reform as "difficult, but achievable." Although Senator Schumer described the working group and its framework as a "major breakthrough," he cautioned that seizing the "window of opportunity" would require a willingness to "meet in the middle." In that spirit, the senators claimed the proposal was genuinely bipartisan, in line with the country's "legacy as a nation of laws and a nation of immigrants." Still more, it had the support of a "majority of the American public," as determined through recent polls. When a journalist asked what would make this iteration of reform successful where others had failed, Senator McCain, the once presidential candidate and Vietnam War veteran, took the question. Echoing the RNC "autopsy" report, he responded: "The Republican Party is losing the support of our Hispanic citizens" for whom immigration reform was the "preeminent issue." Among this sector of the U.S. population, support for legalization and citizenship was high. But the senators were clear that a path to citizenship provision was still the "most controversial" aspect of reform. Evidencing the influence of the anti-immigration lobby, they stressed that the proverbial "path" would be contingent on border security, which as a consequence would receive an infusion of resources, personnel, and technology. On cue, the gang insisted—explicitly and obliquely—that their proposal would avoid the purported weaknesses of the Immigration Reform and Control Act (IRCA), signed by President Ronald Reagan in 1986. Restrictionists have long derided IRCA as an "amnesty" bill that encouraged rather than resolved the problem of undocumented immigration. With ramped up enforcement and a more modernized and streamlined immigration system that could help attract the "best and brightest" immigrants from around the world, the senators asserted their framework would bring an end to the problem of "illegal immigration" and ensure, in the words of Senator Rubio, "that we are never here again."[21]

The day after the Gang of Eight unveiled their framework, President Obama presented his vision for immigration reform at a Las Vegas high school. "I'm here today because the time has come for common-sense, comprehensive immigration reform. The time is now. Now is the time. Now is the time. Now is the time." The mostly Latino audience responded with fervent applause and chants of "¡Sí se puede!" Very much in step with the rhetoric of mainstream immigrant rights advocates, Obama declared the United States a "country of immigrants" with an "out-of-date and badly broken" immigration system, which he argued was neither economically nor ethically sound. His administration, he boasted, had already taken steps: it had strengthened the border, putting "more boots on the ground on the southern border than at any time in our history"; it had "focused enforcement on criminals who are here illegally"; and it had taken up "the cause of the Dreamers" (he did not, however, point out that Dreamer activism, rather than the president's generosity, had led to the Deferred Action for Childhood Arrivals program, or DACA). Obama then laid out three "straightforward" principles, which he saw as "very much in line" with the tenets of the senators.

The first principle was continued enforcement and stronger sanctions for employers that hired undocumented immigrants. The second principle dealt with the undocumented people already in the country. Couching this in the language of fairness, Obama endorsed a path that allowed undocumented immigrants to "earn" their citizenship. As in the Senate framework, this benignly described path would demand that undocumented immigrants submit biometrics, pass national security and criminal background checks, pay back taxes and a penalty, learn English, abstain from public welfare benefits, and finally go to "the back of the line."[22] The final principle called for the complete overhaul of the "legal" immigration system, from family unity and reunification policies to processes to attract and retain immigrants who were high-skilled professionals. As the president admitted, there were many similarities between his administration's proposals and those of the senators.[23] Listening to these proposals, it wasn't evident that the election and what it foreshadowed had done more than place immigration reform back on the national legislative agenda. Indeed, neither plan broke with the prevailing security consensus that has defined the past two decades of immigration policy.[24] For the more radical and militant sectors of the immigrant rights movement, the proposals were a nonstarter. But for national Latino advocates, as well as the broader Alliance for Citizenship coalition they were part of, the proposals were starting points for negotiation.[25]

Although the terrain seemed not to have shifted as much as one might have expected given postelection discourse, Latino advocates remained "energized and optimistic."[26] The proposals were welcomed but imperfect. They questioned the arduous and lengthy path to citizenship, and the decision to make legalization dependent on ramped-up, further militarized border security. In their view, the border was already secure and enforcement well-funded. A LULAC press release said this much: "There is sufficient data to indicate that border states are already safe—in fact the safest in the country—and misspending billions on apprehension and enforcement is nothing but an expensive attempt to win over immigration opponents."[27] Many felt that citizenship was again taking the "back seat," as one of LULAC's former presidents had once remarked.[28] Still, they knew that a plan without border security and enforcement was dead on arrival for Republicans.[29]

Leaders voiced other concerns. The proposed shift from family to "merit" visas, which would eliminate the family reunification policy for sponsoring siblings and children over age thirty, as well as for LGBT partners, was rather troubling. They were also disappointed that the proposed Senate legislation was stacked against low-income immigrants, who were unlikely to be the "high-skilled professionals" of "merit" admissions and for whom the requirements of the path to citizenship could be prohibitively expensive.[30]

Yet, notwithstanding such reservations, these political actors expressed a willingness to work with Republican and Democratic legislators to pass comprehensive immigration reform. An NHLA press release stated: "After years of hard work and patience by the Latino community, our role in the 2012 election, Monday's unveiling of a bipartisan framework for immigration reform by the Senate, and yesterday's speech by President Obama, the momentum is clearly in our favor."[31]

Latinos for Immigration Reform

In March 2013 NHLA launched "Latinos for Immigration Reform." By this point, several of its coalition members, such as NCLR and LULAC, had already developed their own campaigns, which would be more or less folded into the broader NHLA campaign. NHLA touted its campaign as "the largest Latino grass roots mobilization in our nation's history to pass fair and just immigration reform."[32] It involved several elements: local and Capitol Hill congressional visits, online and phone advocacy, town halls across the country, and testimony at legislative hearings.

Through this well-worn repertoire, advocates made a broad case for comprehensive immigration reform. This case rested on three distinct appeals or arguments that local and national immigrant rights activists have made, in one form or another, for decades: moral, economic, and political. As already seen, the political appeal was inseparable from the demographic imperative. After a brief description of each, I will narrate how these appeals were voiced in legislative advocacy following the futurized 2012 election.

Moral arguments appealed to the conscience of legislators and to the "American public." Reform, advocates claimed, was a way to "bringing people out of the shadows" and unify families. Such arguments were especially prone to engage in what political scientist Amalia Pallares called "tangling." In her study of the mobilization of the concept of "family" to resist deportation, Pallares found that activists emphasized "the role played by the undocumented in the lives and caretaking of residents and citizens, and the ways in which deporting the undocumented leads to dramatic decline in the affective, economic, and social conditions of the documented."[33] Tangling, typically expressed through emotionally powerful stories, tends to pivot toward valorized depictions of undocumented immigrants. The first generation of the Dreamer movement was a case in point: it focused on exceptional youth, such as valedictorians and members of the military, as the face of the movement. Sociologists Walter Nicholls and Justus Uitermark have observed that scaling up immigrant activism from local struggles to the national stage in this way motivated mainstream advocacy groups to adopt a nationalist "master frame" that could "resonate with a broad, mainstream, and thoroughly American audience."[34] Thus the moral arguments for immigration reform have often hinged on crafting a portrait of the "deserving" immigrant.[35] These immigrants were framed as hardworking, innocent (in the case of immigrant children) and, in essence, "Americans in waiting."[36]

The economic argument framed immigrants, Latino immigrants in particular, as hardworking contributors to the U.S. economy. Meant to debunk and push back on old and persistent claims that undocumented immigration was an economic drain that lowered wages for "native" workers, this longstanding rhetoric gained greater traction after the release of the Congressional Budget Office's economic assessment of S. 744.[37] The CBO's report was presented as evidence that the bill would generate "significant economic benefits."[38] As stated by LULAC president Margaret Moran, the CBO concluded that it would "decrease the budget deficit by 197 billion dollars within the first ten years after becoming a law, and by an additional 700 billion dollars over the next decade." Moran added, "Immigration reform would repair this country's recovering economy." Not surprisingly, the CBO report also provided fuel for opponents of the bill. It projected that reform would reduce deficits but also "slightly raise unemployment through 2020" and decrease wages through 2025. As with demographic statistics, economic numbers and analyses can also be selectively and strategically used by political projects to shape public perception.[39]

The *political* case for immigration reform was inseparable from the demographic imperative. It was here that *forewarning* came into the picture. The moral and economic points were espoused by other, non-Latino immigration groups, but this part of the argument was seen as uniquely theirs. Although woven together, for the first half of 2013, the political argument anchored Latino advocates' case for comprehensive immigration reform. This was evident in their events and legislative meetings.

In early March NCLR held its annual "advocacy days." More than two hundred affiliates from around the country descended on Washington, DC.

The first of two days of events took place at Gallaudet University, located in the Trinidad neighborhood. Participants, ranging from seasoned community leaders to novice activists, listened to speeches and presentations from the firebrand representative Luis Gutiérrez (D-IL) and NCLR staff, and took part in workshops designed to prepare affiliates for the following day's congressional visits. Most of the activities were held in a large hall filled with circular tables reserved for specific states. Fresh from my time in Orlando, I asked the handful of participants from Florida if I could sit with them. A group of mostly middle-aged women from throughout the state welcomed me to their table, intrigued, so it seemed, about my research during the election.

The election and Latino demographics were major themes throughout the day. This began with Janet Murguía's short yet impassioned opening remarks. Waxing triumphant about the decisiveness of the Latino vote earned her enthusiastic applause from our table and throughout room. She promised more was on the horizon:

> *We've only just begun.* A lot of you in this room represent the fact that for the *next twenty years*, every year, 900,000 Hispanic Americans will turn eighteen and will be eligible to vote. We're going to make an impact into the future because of our demographic power. But we also know that those numbers are just statistics if we don't bring them to life. And part of what you're doing here today, part of what we did in November, is to [make] those statistics that people read in the census . . . come alive.

Murguía summoned a variant of the fifty-thousand figure popularized during the election to forecast two decades into the future. The force behind this project was, as always, demography, what she labeled "demographic power." As I listened to her, I was most struck by the claim that the election brought census data to life. I couldn't have thought of a more evocative way to describe the practice of foreshadowing discussed in the previous chapter. As rousing as Murguía's words were, affiliates would be without her during their meetings on Capitol Hill. Fortunately, NCLR staff organized a workshop on how to have an effective congressional visit. The workshop sought to teach us how to bring those numbers, once more, to life.

The facilitators were direct and clear. We were asked to tap into the "power of numbers." Personal stories were useful but they had their limits. They were useful for making moral arguments; numbers, for political arguments. The lead facilitator wanted us to see the cold calculus of representative democracy: "I think it would be nice to think that members of Congress are always just focused on the truth and doing the right thing, but the reality is that they are responsible to the constituencies that help elect them, the folks who help fund their campaign, and the folks who vote for them." He added, "If we really want to be heard, we have to be able to reference our power in numbers during these meetings." Accordingly, we were instructed to not represent ourselves as individuals but to emphasize we were part of an "institution" and state how many people that institution served. One example given: "I'm from the Latino health clinic, we serve ten thousand people in your district." It is "really important to reference those numbers." But even more powerful, "If you have Latino vote figures from the district or even from the state, or figures of the Latino population in the district or the state, make sure to bring those in as well." If we were not yet convinced, the facilitator declared, "It is really, ultimately, about numbers in many ways. You want to base and project that power in numbers during the meeting." And base and project those numbers we did.

In congressional meetings, electoral and demographic figures were routinely and ritualistically cited (fig. 5.2). This happened whether or not participants had been explicitly instructed to invoke them, as they had at NCLR's workshop. I found no difference regardless of what organization's offices I visited. Statistical rhetoric was woven in and out of conversations with officials and their staff. Take, for instance, a series of visits I observed and participated in with members of LULAC. On this particular occasion, I was part of a small group led by Sindy Benavides, who at the time was the organization's civic engagement director. Benavides crossed the U.S.-Mexico border with her mother as a young child, after a long journey from Honduras. Following a stint working at the Democratic National Committee and then for Virginia governor Tim Kaine, she began doing nonpartisan civic engagement work, first with Voto Latino and then with LULAC (where, by now, she had long been a council member). Persistently upbeat and principled, this proud Virginian led us through the austere halls of the Longworth Building on Capitol Hill. Before every meeting, she would huddle us up and share what kind of reception we could expect to receive.

On our first visit that day, she prepared us: we were not meeting a sympathetic legislator. This Republican member of Congress from the South was staunchly opposed to immigration reform. We arrived on time but were made to wait about fifteen minutes before a staffer led us into a small conference room. The staffer, a white woman in her twenties, greeted us warmly and apologized for the delay. She informed us that the senior staffer with

FIGURE 5.2. LULAC Leadership on Capitol Hill, circa 2015. Used by permission of the League of United Latin American Citizens.

whom we had been scheduled to speak had been reassigned. Worse still, she admitted to having little knowledge about immigration. Given the strong opinions of the congressman, I wasn't sold. Sindy began the conversation. LULAC, she told the staffer, was the "oldest Latino civil rights group in the country," a familiar refrain among "LULACers," as they sometimes refer to each other. Hoping to make a connection, she stated that the organization had its "roots in the South" (indeed, it was founded and has remained strongest in Texas). The staffer nodded and smiled, if stiffly. Combining moral and political claims, Sindy expressed that, while LULAC works on a lot of issues, immigration was "critical for many families" and, she added, for the country's "fifty-three million" Latinos.

Demographic claims were not only directed at Republican officials. Later that afternoon we arrived at the office of a newly elected Democratic congressman from Texas. Sitting on brand-new leather chairs in a mostly undecorated office, we met with a legislative aide. Efrain de Leon, a LULAC staff member from the West Coast, asked me, as the resident researcher, to comment briefly on the "Latino vote," its impact, and the importance of immigration reform. I obliged, sticking close to the talking points we had received in the training sessions. When I finished, Carlos Herrera, a longtime LULAC council member and leader from Texas, jumped in and stated that the bill needed to "move away from punitive" measures. Another member called on the congressman to go as "far to the left as possible." The rationale: "so that we can meet somewhere in the middle." Endorsing her colleague's point, another member reiterated the organization's opposition to more "criminalization." Carmen Vega, a New York member, stressed that LULAC did not want a path to citizenship that "doesn't become a reality." Dramatizing the long waits proposed by the Gang of Eight, she worried that many *abuelas* (grandmothers) would die without ever becoming U.S. citizens. Shifting from a moral to a political register, Carmen invoked a familiar figure: "It's a numbers game . . . fifty thousand Latinos turn eighteen every month! We'll continue playing numbers and get the vote." Despite this point, Efrain de Leon felt compelled to underscore after this visit that we could not forget to "remind them of our vote . . . the power of our demographics."

As members and affiliates communicated Latino "demographic power" in legislative visits, so did the leaders and spokespersons. In February 2013 Janet Murguía testified before the U.S. Senate Judiciary Committee. Her prepared remarks touched on all of the major immigration policy positions of Latino advocacy groups. She challenged the need for additional enforcement, described the situation on the border as "already intolerable," and spoke about the contributions already being made by immigrants, including undocumented immigrants, to the country. "Their lives are inextricably linked with ours," she reiterated. Murguía characterized a path to citizenship as "the single most essential element of immigration," urging the path be made "clear," "achievable," and "direct"—all descriptors at odds with the punitive language coming out of the Senate and White House. Anything less, she warned, would not be "legitimate" to the Latino community.

All these points about the content of the proposed legislation came after Murguía had articulated the demographic stakes:

> As the recent election clearly demonstrated, the issue of immigration is a galvanizing one for the nation's Hispanic community. There is a precious opportunity to address it humanely and responsibly. The toxicity in this debate has affected us deeply, regardless of immigration status, and we see getting this debate on the right course as a matter of fundamental respect for the presence and role of Latinos in the U.S. Latino voters generated the game-changing moment for immigration last November,

creating an opening to finally achieve the solution our country longs for. And our role is *growing*. An average of 878,000 Latino citizens will turn eighteen each year between 2011 and 2028. Our community is engaged and watching this debate closely.

Noticeably, Murguía only implied the impact of Latino demographics and voter growth. She did not marshal the phrase "demographic power" or explicitly forewarn the senators in the room. The consequences of ignoring the Latino electorate were not precisely described. Certainly, it was easy enough to read between the lines. Such subtlety was not unusual, even when these actors seemed to have the upper hand. Most of the time demographic forewarnings were dispensed cautiously and subtly, as Latino advocates did not want to appear menacing. As with how they forecast the future, forewarning was constrained by persistent concerns over inflaming white backlash and demographobia. All this, however, was at odds with the belief that demographics were tied to political recognition and the edict to enunciate the power of numbers. Although I never observed someone sanctioned for how they invoked the demographic imperative, such subtlety and carefulness was not confined to leaders. This was illustrated in a humorous exchange between a LULAC mother and daughter. Upon learning that our next visit would be to the office of Senator Jeff Flake (R-AZ), a member of the Gang of Eight, the mother called us into a huddle and proposed that the first thing we should tell the senator was that Latinos were growing by fifty thousand a month. Her daughter agreed, jokingly adding that we had better mention that "with a smile."

Challenge or Compromise

In congressional visits and public events, advocates told a story, however circumspect at times, about the demographic-political consequences of inaction. While confident that immigration reform was close, they nonetheless had to navigate a politically polarized legislative process. This involved confronting different expectations and recommendations about how they should pursue and promote reform (and their priorities). As the following vignettes illustrate, their bipartisan interlocutors on the Hill and advocates themselves were not of one mind.

On one occasion with LULAC, we visited the office of a representative who personally knew one of the members of the group. The vibe was relaxed, unlike the unspoken tension and awkwardness of some meetings with Republican staffers. As we found seats around a conference table, the staffer inquired about our visits. She was particularly interested to hear our reactions to the meeting with one of the Democrats on the Gang of Eight. Leaning into the table, the advocate familiar with the staffer responded that our group was "very satisfied" with the conversation. Before she could elaborate, the staffer interrupted: "Never be satisfied until you actually see the language." The bill was not yet public. "Keep the pressure on." Thrusting her hands into the air, as if dumbfounded, she shared her experience with a group from another Latino advocacy organization. She said those visitors caved in on their demands before negotiations even started. "Who *does* that?" she asked with a mix of puzzlement and exasperation.

Hearing this, the LULAC members shared the organization's positions on immigration reform, which we had received in a handout at the beginning of the day. The staffer was delighted to hear that LULAC considered a path to citizenship "nonnegotiable" and that it supported AgJobs, a piece of legislation that would legalize the status of immigrant agricultural workers. Her boss, she said, wanted to ensure that "workers are protected," even though she knew that "owners don't want citizenship . . . they want temporary workers." Our group was advised to concentrate on the senators "crafting the bill," especially the Republican members. Without stating it outright, the staffer alluded to tensions among the Gang of Eight. Peeved to learn that Senator Rubio's DC office did not accept LULAC's request to meet, she suggested we contact his local office to complain about the refusal.

In response to a question about how to build congressional support, the staffer recommended the organization create a "buzz" that would capture the "national spotlight." She gave the example of the Dreamers, who were increasingly adopting confrontational and newsworthy actions: staging civil disobedience, hunger strikes, and publicly shouting down politicians, including President Obama. The staffer hastened to suggest less confrontational methods—maybe holding public briefings on the Hill and working with celebrities. A member interpreted the advice as a call to be "more provocative and sexy." Perhaps town hall meetings and legislative visits were not enough to move the needle.

Internally, some advocates had serious concerns about their own tactics. While assuredly not all of the same mind, they were cautious to express to me any disunity within the leadership ranks. Moments of candor were rare but more common during impromptu conversations than in formal interviews. One such moment took place during NALEO's annual conference, held June 2013 in my hometown of Chicago. During a luncheon attended by several hundred elected officials from around the country, I had the fortune to be seated next to a longtime advocate and NHLA member. To my surprise, he recognized me, and we struck up a conversation about his thoughts on prospects for immigration reform, considering that the Senate had passed S. 744 the day before. He did not answer immediately. His long pause made me think he was uninterested in the question or perhaps was queuing up a stock reply. Neither was the case. He looked at me, lowered his head, and grumbled that something would pass in the House of Representatives. However, he was afraid that whatever made it out of that gauntlet would not be what they wanted. Sooner or later Latinos would be "thrown under the bus." President Obama, he complained, had done this, by his estimation, at least five times. But neither Obama nor congressional representatives were the main source of his frustration or the target of his ire. He was most angry with and disappointed in his colleagues. Summoning the old trope of the politically "passive" Latino, he described his colleagues as too submissive, too humble, and too willing to accept disregard from people in power.[40] He claimed that this was an engrained disposition, rooted in "Hispanic culture." Before I could ask what he meant, he looked around the room, raised his voice, and stated that political change demanded more aggressiveness. Leaders had to be willing to "pinch the nose and kick the ass." He lamented, in a macho midwestern manner, they "don't have the balls." Latino civil rights advocates, he believed, were incapable of making Democrats bow to them the way the Tea Party had done to Republicans. As half-eaten salad plates were being removed from our table, he thundered that Latinos needed to act more like the Jewish and LGBT communities, populations with fewer "votes" but apparently more influential and combative political tactics.

Where some, including advocates themselves, desired more forceful actions, Republican officials mostly advised trusting the process. Antagonism would be counterproductive, especially in the House. Compromise and flexibility were described as essential political values—values that could be found inward. A particularly poignant example came in the fall of 2013, as LULAC members visited the office of an influential Republican senator from one of the Rocky Mountain states. As always, Sindy Benavides had informed our group that the senator supported a path to citizenship and DREAM Act but was also a strong proponent of the controversial E-Verify program.[41] The senator was widely credited with helping corral enough Republican support in the Senate to pass S. 744 earlier that year, and his chief of staff—with whom we would be speaking—had been closely involved in drafting the bill.

The chief of staff, a balding white man in his early forties, brought us into a large but dim meeting room with ceiling-high wooden bookshelves. Seated at the head of the table, he set off on a monologue before we could make a single point. Monopolizing the time, he spoke about his confusion about his own party's opposition to immigration reform. He named a few economic and moral reasons for reform, none unfamiliar to the advocates and activists in his presence. Tellingly, he made no mention of any political reasons. Almost rhetorically, he asked what made some of his colleagues so "nervous." Though hardly "Christ-like," his colleagues were, he hoped, "better than that." He volunteered that his personal reason for supporting immigration reform was that "Hispanics" were "so warm, kind, and loving." As he told it, he gained this essentialist insight on a "mission trip" to Chicago where a group of Mexican grandmothers introduced him to corn tortillas, which had since become a staple of his diet.

A pause invited an interjection. A LULAC member raised that families were being torn apart. "When did our country become *that*?" he asked. The chief of staff nodded sympathetically and, it seemed, in all seriousness proposed that LULAC host a cultural night at a Latin American embassy. I suppose he misunderstood what "Latin American citizen" meant in LULAC's name. "They haven't experienced your culture, your food and dress." Such an experience would somehow teach them that Latinos were a "God-fearing people." So astonished by the essentialism and paternalism, I almost failed to glance at the reactions of the council members. Judging by facial expressions and body language, the reactions were varied. A few nodded their heads in what seemed like approval, while others glanced, confusedly, from person to person. Others were clearly uneasy. Gloria Busto, an ever-busy Mexican American from Virginia, was one of them. Almost jumping out of her chair, she shouted out a single word: "Racism!" Silence overtook the room. Racism, not a lack of intercultural exchange, she argued, was the reason this staffer's colleagues opposed immigration reform. Even if the word made some "uncomfortable," you had to call it like it is, Gloria said. Later she told me that her husband didn't understand the hesitation of advocates to call out racism.

The chief of staff did not engage the point, so Sindy, seeking to salvage the strange meeting, asked a direct question: "How can comprehensive immigration reform be messaged to conservatives?" Given growing Republican opposition to the reform in the House, this was a sensible question, but she didn't receive a sensible response. "Focus on the heart. All too often we talk past one another. Love. Focus on that," the chief of staff advised.

For "you"—Hispanics—he said, it is "easy to love." Americans love, but it doesn't come as easy, not like Hispanics, who "exude" love. Thick with condescension, he advised the group not to go "tit-for-tat" with their opponents. Let them yell and be angry. Stooping to that level "takes away from you . . . the goodness of your culture." Love, he told us, was our "secret weapon."

Still Sleeping?

As these groups carried out their postelection advocacy, the political consensus about the Latino vote in the 2012 election was coming under scrutiny. The most severe challenge came with the release of voter data from the Census Bureau in May 2013, during the thick of debates and negotiations over S. 744.[42] Widely considered the most accurate source on election turnout, the data revealed that the Latino vote neither met the projection of 12.2 million nor accounted for 10 percent of the vote—statistics that had been mobilized extensively before and after the election. Days after the release, the Pew Hispanic Center revised the conclusions it had previously drawn from exit poll data. While maintaining that the Latino vote was impactful, Pew analysts acknowledged the impact was smaller than once thought.[43] In raw numbers, the Latino electorate had grown, but this was mainly due to a demographic rather than a political increase.

The news media immediately made the election data a story. In contrast with the postelection coverage's emphasis on the Latino vote, media accounts after the census data came out focused largely on the African American vote, which was found to have surpassed white voter turnout rates for the first time. Coverage that did address the Latino vote was mostly unflattering. *Fox News* carried the headline "'Record' Hispanic Voter Turnout in 2012 a Misnomer, Census Numbers Show." The headline of journalist Chris Cillizza's article in the *Washington Post* was even more pointed: "The Hispanic Vote Is a Sleeping Political Giant. It Might Never Wake Up."[44] Cillizza wrote: "While the rapid growth of the Hispanic community is, without question, the demographic story of the last 10 years and the next 10 years, it's less clear that Latinos are showing any signs of realizing the political influence that goes along with that population increase. Need one stat to prove that point? Hispanics comprised 17.2 percent of the nation's population but were just 8.4 percent of all voters in 2012."

Critiques also came from some quarters of Latino research and advocacy. In a memo, Antonio González, president of the William C. Velásquez

Institute, the research wing of the Southwest Voter Registration Education Project, openly criticized the "awakened" narrative promulgated by national Latino organizations: "Contrary to the claims of hyper mobilized Latino participation in the Nov. 2012 elections the data show Latino voter participation while continuing to grow apace consistent with historic patterns didn't come close to post-election pronouncements." González framed his memo as an attempt to "separate fact from fiction."[45]

This new data forced national Latino groups to recalibrate how they spoke about the turnout and impact of the Latino vote. For the most part, they ceased using the 10 percent figure and the claim—once a projection—that 12.2 million Latino voters took part in the 2012 election. On occasion, however, these figures would resurface, as in a widely circulated 2014 *Huffington Post* op-ed from NCLR's then–deputy director of civic engagement that used both figures to claim, "The 2012 elections were a powerful demonstration of the growing electoral influence of Latinos."[46] Advocates, recognizing the adjusted numbers, nonetheless maintained that the size of the turnout had been the largest to date. NALEO-EF, the organization that had produced the 12.2 million voter projection, claimed in a press release that the Census Bureau's data confirmed "record Latino vote in Election 2012." The size of the electorate had grown by 15 percent, and the Latino vote had been "particularly decisive" in the battlegrounds of Colorado, Florida, and Nevada, it went on. Still, the press release conceded, more work was needed "before the nation's second largest population group reaches its full political potential."[47] Yet despite these modifications, the census data revived stubborn ideas about the "sleeping giant" and provided defensible reasons to forget the demographic future, at least in the short term.

Forgetting the Future

Even before the census report, debate was bubbling in the Republican Party about the 2012 election and consensus about the demographic ascendancy of the Democratic Party. These debates did not just coincide with negotiations over immigration reform; they provided space for dissent from the party line put forth by the RNC. The foreshadowed future, for dissenters, seemed less certain and thus easier to forget.

The dominant takeaway from the 2012 election was initially that the GOP had alienated or ignored too many constituencies. Its stances had moved too far to the right to offset demographic decline among whites. Not all conservatives were convinced. Slowly at first, dissenters began to gain steam for an alternative explanation, one not entirely at odds with voter data from the Census Bureau: Mitt Romney lost because of a decrease in the white vote, not an increase in the Latino vote, among other constituencies. In the conservative-leaning *RealClearPolitics*, analyst Sean Trende argued in an essay published immediately after the election that appeasing Latinos and other "minority" voters (i.e., passing comprehensive immigration reform) was a fool's mission for the GOP. Its efforts would be better spent seeking out "missing" white voters. "As it stands, the bigger puzzle for figuring out the path of American politics is who these non-voters are, why they stayed home, and whether they might be reactivated in 2016 (by either party)."[48] Rich Lowry, editor of the conservative stalwart the *National Review*, called Trende's analysis a "must-read," adding that seven million fewer whites voted in 2012 than in 2008. "This isn't readily explainable by demographic shifts either; although whites are declining as a share of the voting-age population, their raw numbers are not." In June 2013, after new census data was released, Trende published a four-part series on the election that further argued that, besides softening its tone, the Republican Party would not benefit from political concessions to the Democrats. Instead, it should focus on the apparently natural base of the GOP (i.e., whites).[49] For those outside of the Republican-conservative bubble, the 2012 primaries and Romney's campaign—with its talk of "self-deportation" and dog-whistle rhetoric about government freeloaders—that recommendation seemed already in practice.

The new narrative, while comforting to some, was viewed by other Republican strategists and leaders as wrongheaded. Seeking to stop the bleeding, Karl Rove penned a *Wall Street Journal* op-ed, "More White Votes Alone Won't Save the GOP." Senior Republican South Carolina senator Lindsey Graham warned about a "demographic death spiral."[50] Graham told reporters, "The only way we can get back in good graces with the Hispanic community, in my view, is pass comprehensive immigration reform. If you don't do that, it really doesn't matter who we run in my view." But the positions of Rove and Graham were becoming increasingly minoritarian. The future was not necessarily the one that had been foreshadowed. There was, by extension, no demographic imperative to bend to. This was the message that Michael Barone, a senior political analyst for the conservative newspaper *Washington Examiner* expressed on a panel on the "future of the Republican Party" in August 2013, as signs became evident that the Republican-controlled House of Representatives was not prepared to advance comprehensive immigration reform. Challenging the demography-is-destiny thesis that underlay the 2012 election postmortem, Barone asserted:

> So nobody's going to own the future. Conservatives would like to rent some more of it than they have right now, and I think the prospects for that are fairly good. I mean, we've been told constantly since the 2012 election that the demographic trends mean that the Democrats inevitably are going to become the natural majority party in the country. We also heard after the 2004 election that demographic trends meant that the Republicans were going to become the natural majority party in the country and that didn't turn out to be true in 2006 and 2008. And it did not turn out to be true for the Democrats in 2010.

Barone continued: "Whites have been told for quite a while now hey, you're going to be a minority in America today. Well, they're starting to vote like a minority. They voted 59/39 percent for Mitt Romney, Republicans carried the House popular vote 60/37 in 2010, so I don't think that there's anything inevitable about the so-called nonwhites and young [people] taking over the electorate and making Republican victories impossible."

Just months after the RNC report, key sectors of the party increasingly questioned the demographic death spiral thesis. Operatives set their sights on reenergizing white voters and, where possible, adding support among other ethnoracial populations. In this new calculus, immigration reform was not necessary. Along with doubts about the impact of the Latino vote, this dissent made it easier to forget the future foreshadowed in the election.

Death by Deferral

Advocates celebrated the news that S. 744 passed the Senate by a vote of sixty-eight to thirty-two. The process took almost half a year, from the time the Gang of Eight announced its proposal in January 2013 to the vote at the end of June. Excitement was tempered, however, by the recognition that the political climate was decidedly harsher in the House, where the bill would have to pass, then go through reconciliation, before it would even arrive at the president's desk. There remained cautious hope, but the 2012 election was far in the rearview, already forgotten by increasingly vocal Republicans and conservatives.

Immediately after the 2012 election, as in the Senate, a group of representatives in the House, including Luis Gutiérrez (D-IL) had begun bipartisan discussions and negotiations. Speaker John Boehner (R-OH) publicly attested to his newfound support for comprehensive immigration reform. "I'm confident that the president, myself, others, can find the common ground to take care of this issue once and for all."[51] Yet less than a year later House Republicans refused to conference with the Senate and opted instead to craft their own immigration reform legislation. They chose to pursue a piecemeal rather than comprehensive approach. Boehner initially expressed willingness to bring up individual bills on border security, the Dreamers, and agricultural workers, in that order. But GOP leaders in the House eventually decided, in line with the security consensus, to pursue only border enforcement and a guest-worker program with no path to legalization. House Republicans refused to support the DREAM Act and instead attacked President Obama's popular DACA program, which had been passed in 2012. Boehner even refused to allow a vote on an immigration reform bill introduced by House Democrats.

The Republican retreat enraged national Latino leaders. Janet Murguía said Republicans were "playing a game, a political game, and intentionally delaying immigration reform." At an event held in the stunning lobby of the AFL-CIO's headquarters in Washington, DC, MALDEF's president and general counsel Thomas Saenz railed against the hypocrisy of the Republican Party. Representatives who "built their careers around the notion of color blindness" seemingly had no problem supporting "through their inaction an immigration system that discriminates against immigrants primarily from Mexico and Latin America." He asked, "Can you imagine leaders accepting that in another context? Can you imagine House leaders accepting in any university, public or private, anywhere across this country, saying to applicants, 'We've already admitted enough of people from your background so you will wait twenty years to be admitted to this university.' It would not last one minute." Saenz questioned how the same leaders had "built their political careers around a bedrock devotion to family values" but were "nowhere to be seen as family upon family is devastated and torn apart daily by our broken immigration system." He concluded his remarks by returning to the words of Martin Luther King, Jr., on the white liberal politics of delay and gradualism:[52]

> Nearly fifty-one years ago Martin Luther King, Jr., gave a speech in the March on Washington. We often focus on certain statements from that speech, but I want to focus on one not often referenced. Dr. King, who at the time was facing those who would argue for a slower, more deliberate

approach to solving the defining issue of civil rights for African Americans. And he warned us fifty-one years ago to reject what he called the tranquilizing drug of gradualism. That's where we are today. The urgency is now. We need bold leadership. We need aggressive action to ensure that our principles as a nation are vindicated through recognizing the need to address the injustice that daily occurs from our immigration system.

With the doors of the House closing and media outlets proclaiming the death of immigration reform, national Latino leaders turned their attention to the president. They called on Obama to take "big and bold" steps to provide executive relief in lieu of legislative reform. Maria Teresa Kumar of Voto Latino wrote in an op-ed: "Our message to the president is to be brave. Go big. Act fast."[53] Time was of the essence. In an exchange with Murguía, Representative Gutiérrez claimed, "We lose eleven hundred people every day waiting for Republicans." Advocates began to demand that the president exercise what they argued was part of his authority—a position vehemently opposed by Republican leaders—and they began calling him out for overseeing mass deportations. Up until this moment, these groups had remained focused on securing a broad legislative fix rather than on stopping deportations, which was the focus of grassroots campaigns, such as the #not1more campaign, led by the National Day Laborer Organizing Network (NDLON).

But things began to change. The most evocative signal came during Janet Murguía's speech at NCLR's Capital Awards Gala in 2014. With attendees dressed in their finest, Murguía called President Obama the "deporter-in-chief." While she also admonished House Republicans for delaying and then pulling the plug on reform, she made clear that the president must agree to "stop unnecessary deportations." She continued, "Any day now, this administration will reach the two million mark for deportations. It is a staggering number that far outstrips any of his predecessors and leaves behind it a wake of devastation for families across America." The directness of Murguía's critique was unexpected. She and NCLR did not originate the label. Progressive and radical activist groups had already derided Obama as the "deporter-in-chief." But this appropriation marked the first time a leader of a mainstream national organization had used it.[54] The comment generated a wave of media coverage.[55] It set up what scholars have described as a "seismic shift" among national organizations.[56] Suddenly, steadfast proponents of comprehensive immigration reform, such as the Center for Community Change, the AFL-CIO, and America's Voice, began to critique the administration's atrocious record on deportation. Frank Sherry, the executive director of America's Voice, asserted that deportations were placing "Obama's legacy's on the line." "Does he really want to go down as the 'deporter-in-chief,' and the only thing that happened during his second term was beefed-up enforcement and deportations? He's the president. He's got to take action."

On the ropes, President Obama retorted that he was, in fact, "the champion-in-chief." He claimed that Republicans had killed immigration reform and that he was legally "constrained in what I am able to do."[57] For a time at least, the once-close relationship between the NCLR and the administration had chilled.

Two months after Murguía's controversial speech, in May 2014, MAL-DEF, NDLON, and NHLA released a joint report, *Detention, Deportation, and Devastation: The Disproportionate Effect of Deportations on the Latino Community*.[58] Its most cited finding was that almost 97 percent of deportees in 2013 were of Latin American descent. As national Latino groups tried to pressure Obama from within, the most militant sectors of the Dreamers movement and other sectors in the wider immigrant rights movement pressured from outside. They worked independently for the most part, but together they communicated that *immediate* executive action was necessary. Obama eventually set a date to issue an expansion of DACA, only to later delay it until after the 2014 midterm elections. Along with the Republican deferral on immigration reform, Obama's delay on executive relief struck advocates hard. Relief came months later, after the election, in the form of the Deferred Action for Parents of Americans and Lawful Permanent Residents (DAPA), a short-lived program meant to protect parents with citizen or legal resident children from deportation. It was considered a major victory by immigrant rights groups, but everyone understood that immigration would require legislative reform and, by the end of 2014, openings for reform had disappeared. With attention turning to the next presidential election, comprehensive immigration reform was proclaimed all but "dead."[59]

———

Within a span of two years, national Latino advocates went from being on the verge of their greatest legislative victory to having suffered a stinging defeat. Their sense of progress and acceleration toward political relevance and influence gave way to frustration and stagnation. At least temporarily, moderate Republican officials were done worrying over demographic peril like that forewarned by Latino advocates; they had to face the more imme-diate problem of electoral challenges from Tea Party candidates. In short order, Latino leaders went from the "future is now" and the "time for reform is now" to the "time is running out."

And yet, by the start of 2015, as Washington began to pivot to the next presidential election, they regrouped. Once again, advocates argued that the road to 1600 Pennsylvania Avenue ran through the Latino community. Latino empowerment had been delayed, but time and demography were on the side of the nation's ever-expanding Latino population. Advocates grew confident that inaction on immigration reform, the callousness against unac-companied minors, and anti-Latino rhetoric would have, as Maria Teresa Kumar prophesied, "a huge impact on political elections for years to come."[60] As the 2016 election came into sight, they believed it was time, again, to focus on the future.

Present

6

Reaction and Reversal

Another election night. We have entered the final stretch. Everyone has their ears pressed to cellphones and eyes fixed on their computers. We are in Washington, DC, the national office of LULAC, to be exact, but calls to NALEO-EF's hotline are coming in from all across the country. For basic questions, such as helping someone find their polling station, the voter application on our assigned computers is usually sufficient. It is far less so for more difficult calls, such as when a frightened voter reported to me earlier in the day that they were threatened with deportation if they didn't vote for Donald Trump. In between calls, I watch two volunteers reach for their *ayuda* signs. One thrusts her hand and sign straight up, the other moves them from side to side. Two styles, same purpose. They have a challenging call and hope to catch the eyes of senior staff, who have noticed more calls about voter intimidation compared to past elections.[1]

Our phone lines have now begun to calm. We can all catch a breath. I doubt this is the case farther west, where polls are still open. Most working at this temporary call center are what pollsters and pundits call "Latino millennials," but some of us, myself included, are older. Answering the phones are LULAC staff and council members from DC and Virginia, a small but rambunctious group from LCLAA, a few staff from NALEO-EF, and some from the American Federation of Teachers. Over the past two days, somewhere around thirty individuals have volunteered to staff the phones here.

Computers and voter hotline materials are no longer on the conference table. They have been replaced with plates overflowing with food. The room's transformation is incomplete; its walls are still papered with helpful Spanish translations of voter terminology and state-specific information. State returns are coming in. A handwritten tally is being kept on the door. Although Hillary Clinton has won fewer states than Donald Trump, she is leading in Electoral College votes. The front half of the room excitedly watches the returns and the back half bursts with loud conversations and laughter. Voto Latino's Maria Teresa Kumar appears on MSNBC, where she frequently comments on political issues, to speak about the turnout in Florida. As in 2012, most of the major Latino civil rights groups invested heavily in civic engagement there. I can't help but reminisce about election night four years ago with Mi Familia Vota in Orlando. Tonight is different. Besides this segment on MSNBC, we haven't heard much talk about the Latino vote.

The mood shifts. Trump has picked up some more states, some big upsets. Concern is growing. The tally doesn't seem to have been updated in a while. I can feel the disbelief in the room and in myself. Glazed looks, teary eyes, and dropped jaws are all around me. A fifty-something volunteer near me murmurs, "I'm gonna have a heart attack." The conference room begins to empty. Can it be that a candidate who called Mexican immigrants "rapists," "murderers," and "bad hombres" is on the verge of winning the presidency? What happened to the road to the White House going through Latino communities?

———

November 8, 2016, ushered in an utterly unanticipated, perhaps unimaginable, reality for many. This includes advocates in national Latino civil rights organizations. Barely a year earlier, one leader had pronounced: "Let me be clear, we know Donald Trump will never be president." Two months before the election, another had told his colleagues with comparable certitude that Republicans would, "one way or another," learn to treat Latinos and immigrants better, or be "locked out of the White House for forty to fifty years." Their confidence was rooted in demography, in the belief that an emergent electoral-demographic firewall made a president like Trump—who replaced the dog whistle with the bullhorn—a political impossibility. Demography, so it seemed, had not yet become destiny. Was this a bump in the trajectory, or a U-turn? Said differently, had the future been forestalled or foreclosed?

For a political project that has for so long tried to "turn the clock forward," these questions were no doubt considered, but more pressing was how to make sense of this seemingly impossible "present." How should they respond? What could they hope to accomplish? How could they reassert and reestablish their path of political acceleration? This final chapter explores the answers that national Latino civil rights groups have given to these questions.

This unsettled and unsettling time resurfaced internal tensions and external critiques.[2] Within the first two years of the Trump administration, the focus of my analysis in this chapter, we find both continuity and change in Latino advocacy. Of most direct concern for me are the temporal orientations—implicit but occasionally explicit—in responses to the Trumpian challenge. Some have insisted on the need to stay the course, to redouble the use of well-worn tactics, such as civic engagement and insider politics. Others have turned to the past for lessons and inspiration, a notable departure for a political project so focused on the future. The future—the demographic future in particular—has not entirely fallen out of favor, but it has been recalibrated in several ways. These responses cannot be understood apart from what the French historian François Hartog has called "presentism."[3] Faced with an all-consuming barrage of attacks and challenges, advocates struggled to advance their agenda of political acceleration. Against this ensnarement of the present, some initiatives have sought to project new paths forward to realize "Latino power."

Clash of the Polls

Before advocates could respond to Trump, they first had to respond to the election and how it was interpreted by the news media and the pundit class. As in 2012, the leadership of the National Latino Civic Engagement Table held a press conference to offer their perspective on the election. Most of the same leaders and organizations were involved, too, but their edge was gone. The apparent shock, I am sure, had not settled in. Four years ago they had provocatively forewarned that political "peril" would befall any elected official and party that opposed or obstructed comprehensive immigration reform. Yet the prospects of reform came and went, and peril never arrived.

Advocates came to the press conference with a direct message. Although the presidential outcome was "unexpected," Latino voters turned out in "record numbers," a phrase repeated several times. They exceeded NALEO-EF's projection of thirteen million. The "surge" in Latino voters once more revealed "a powerful constituency." Latino and Latina candidates won races all over the country, from the Senate on down. Anti-Latino officials like Sheriff Joe Arpaio of Maricopa County, Arizona, were denied reelection. There was news to celebrate, in other words. But that wasn't the news the media was reporting. Instead, the postelection coverage about the Latino vote was eclipsed by national exit polls.

The National Election Poll (NEP), sponsored by major media outlets, found that Trump received nearly 30 percent of the Latino vote. Based on that figure, he garnered more Latino support than Republican presidential candidate Mitt Romney had in 2012. This news upended months of discourse about the politically energizing effects of Trump's inflammatory rhetoric against Mexican and Latin American immigrants. From naturalization rates to surveys of voter enthusiasm, the prediction had been, as one headline put it, "Trump Awakens a Sleeping Giant."[4] Over and over, pundits and advocates alike warned that Trump and the Republican Party were playing with demographic fire. Indeed, days before the election the conservative standard-bearer, the *National Review*, agonized on its cover, "Demographic changes are threatening to turn traditional red states blue. How do Republicans survive?" This question overlaid a drawing of a tsunami-like blue wave about to crash into a small wooden boat with one frightened passenger—the GOP elephant. According to the NEP poll, however, that Latino-propelled wave never materialized.[5]

An explosion of press coverage and political commentary followed the NEP polling data.[6] Syndicated columnist Ruben Navarrette wrote that he woke up with "huevos rancheros" on his face the day after the election. Well aware that Latino voters were not a monolith, he was nonetheless puzzled that "so many Latinos ended up voting for their tormentor."[7] Rejecting its own pre-election prognostication, the *National Review*'s editor-at-large John O'Sullivan clutched the poll to criticize what he called the "Latino-surge theory," which his magazine, as noted earlier, had endorsed. The Democratic wave, he and others posited, not only had failed to occur, it might never actually come to pass.[8]

At their press conference, Latino advocates disputed the NEP data and the media's embrace of it as an uncontested fact. They put forth data from Latino Decisions, which was described as the "gold-standard firm for polling our community."[9] Latino Decisions is a polling agency founded by the well-respected Latino political scientists Gary Segura and Matt Barreto. Advocacy organizations regularly contract the agency to conduct polls, and it is common to see its principals present at their events.[10] In fact, Barreto conveyed to me that their earlier polling work for these organizations laid the foundation for the establishment of Latino Decisions. In the words of one leader at the press conference, it was an "insult as Latinos to keep hearing the media ignoring empirical data that was presented by Latino

Decisions and presenting an alternative number that we do not accept and we reject."[11] Their frustration was not just about the NEP poll but with a longer history of mainstream polls that had failed to accurately and adequately poll Latinos. Common limitations of these polls are that they tend not to reach enough Spanish speakers, not sample enough precincts with a high Latino population density, and also tend to oversample Latinos with a higher socioeconomic status than the population as a whole.[12] When asked at the news conference about future elections, an advocate shot back, first get "this election right." The advocate recalled the controversy about the exit polls in 2004 that fueled discourse about the rise of Hispanic conservatism.[13]

For advocates, the Latino Decisions Election Eve Poll painted a more accurate picture of Latino voters.[14] In contrast to the NEP poll, Latino Decisions found that "79% supported Clinton, while only 18% voted for Trump." That number—less than a fifth of Latino votes going for Trump—was the lowest share for a Republican presidential candidate in decades, including Romney. Based on that figure, they argued that Latino voters "overwhelmingly" rejected Trump's bigotry and supported "American values of tolerance and inclusiveness."[15]

Internally, the post-election narrative was a major source of frustration. I observed this at NHLA's board meeting in December 2016, the first after the election. Similar to the press conference, the discussion began positively as members congratulated one another on their civic engagement efforts and pointed to electoral victories at the federal, state, and local levels. The election of Nevada's Catherine Cortez Masto, who would become the first Latina to serve in the U.S. Senate, received the most vigorous applause. Members spoke about a "historic" turnout and "surge" of Latino voters. "The main line is: we delivered," said one firmly. He lamented, however, the "manipulation of numbers" and how "polls can mislead national conversations." At no point were specific polls mentioned, but the discrepancy among them was raised. There were other laments. Many in the meeting felt that Latino and Black voters were being unfairly blamed for Trump's victory, and too few people were talking about the lack of voter outreach funding for these very communities.

The media and pundit embrace of the NEP poll robbed advocates of some of the rhetorical force of their arguments about the Latino vote. Try as they might, advocates complained, they couldn't seem to get anyone to focus on the fact that, even if the NEP poll was right, 70 percent of Latino voters voted *against* Trump. Yet much of the national discourse proceeded as if the opposite were true. Trump himself has since boasted on numerous occasions about his deep support among "the Hispanics." Years after, advocates tell me they are "still dealing with that 30 percent."

Demographic Rewind

In their press conferences, op-eds, and other public forums, advocates not only put forth their own account of Latino voters, they also advanced their own ideas about the rise and machinations of Trump. Although rarely stated explicitly, their account challenged the "economic" argument for Trump's victory.[16] For them, Trump support was fueled by fears about ethnoracial demographic change, and specifically Latino advance. As discussed earlier, these political actors have spent years promoting demo-utopian narratives that characterize Latino population growth as a "boon" for the country. But this narrative has not—as of yet—prevailed over the demodystopias that white supremacists have long communicated. Many Trump supporters, they claimed, had been won over by the campaign's explicit and implicit signals about the future of the country.

Now in power, Trump, they argued, represented not merely a demographic backlash but a concerted effort to turn the nation backward. In an op-ed, Jessica González-Rojas of the National Latina Institute for Reproductive Health, wrote: "The Trump administration sees the country's changing demographics—the rising number of nonwhite and foreign-born people—as the chief internal threat." As one leader publicly stated, "They see the future, and they're trying to hold it back." Janet Murguía told NCLR affiliates, for example, "Change threatens the status quo." She added, "We are challenged by voices who, because of fear, lack of understanding or even hate, would turn *back the clock* to a less tolerant time when the color of one's skin, their accent or the sound of their surname defined their place in history." Exercising what sociologist Crystal Fleming has theorized as "racial temporality," Murguía marked a radical disjuncture between the past and the future that Trump presumably interrupted. Somewhere between a euphemistically described "less tolerant time" and a post-racial utopia in which skin color, accent, and surname no longer determine one's "place in history," the country got Trump. Speaking at an NHLA event in 2017, MALDEF's Thomas Saenz similarly expressed:

> This is an attempt to take the progress in integrating the Latino community, the immigrant community, into the fabric of the United States and reverse it. In other words, *going backwards with respect to the progress that*

the Latino community has made. With white nationalists well represented in the White House and in leadership positions in the Department of Justice, it's perhaps not surprising that [the] goal about disintegrating the Latino community, the largest minority community for more than a decade, the fast growing Latino community viewed by white nationalists then as the greatest threat to their goals, would come to the forefront in this administration.

Ever creative with his turns of phrase, Saenz played with the meanings of dis-integration. Was Trump seeking to exclude Latinos and make them feel as if they do not belong, or, more sinisterly, was he seeking to disintegrate them, as in rid the country of their existence? This leader saw this disintegration project as centered but not exclusively focused on the "Latino community." The Trumpian project, he and his colleagues insisted, did not merely seek to slow down or stall change; it sought to *reverse* it. What else could Trump be calling for when he exhorted his base to "Make America Great *Again*"?

As a fomenter of demographobia, Trump was thus an unexpected but familiar foe. In much of their public discourse, advocates have thus resisted framing Trump as an aberration. Instead, they have relied on "historical analogies" to characterize him as simply the latest incarnation of a seemingly vanquished past.[17] Even before Trump's election, Murguía described him as a "new face of an old threat." On another occasion she declared, "Donald Trump is Joe McCarthy, George Wallace, and Pete Wilson all rolled into one." Trump was therefore not unique. Of all the figures to which he analo-gized, the most frequent has been former Republican California governor Pete Wilson. In his 1994 reelection campaign, Wilson rallied against Mexican and Central American immigration and campaigned on Proposition 187, a highly controversial state bill that sought to prohibit undocumented immi-grants from accessing public services, such as emergency care and schools.

The Trump-as-Pete-Wilson analogy served a couple of purposes. First, it served as a threat to the Republican Party. As Thomas Saenz warned in a 2016 op-ed, "The Latino vote, much of which might have been up for grabs previously, became a solid anti-Republican vote, as Pete Wilson became an all-purpose bogeyman and party symbol for Latinos, to the great and endur-ing detriment of the Republican Party in California."[18] Second, it provided a sense of optimism. On numerous occasions, Maria Teresa Kumar, like her colleagues, has spoken about the present as the national "Pete Wilson moment." As Latinos in California brought down Wilson, so could Latinos bring down Trump. At an NHLA meeting, Kumar forcefully stated: "I'm from California and I lived through the Pete Wilson experience where he came squarely after the Latino community. We got to work. Latinos became citizens, Latinos registered to vote, and there's no question that you can't do anything in California now without Latino participation." Like Wilson, Trump could be defeated with the vote. Already, these advocates were eyeing the 2018 midterms and the 2020 presidential election. In these articulations, the past, rather than the future, was serving as means to threaten and mobilize.[19] The imagined past, I will discuss shortly, had still other uses.

Even as Trump was situated in a longer history or trajectory of white supremacist population politics, he was also depicted as a violator of the country's long-standing values. On an NHLA teleconference that took place on the eve of Trump's inauguration, several participants expressed that Trump betrayed American values. José Calderon of the Hispanic Federation expressed confidence that "people of conscience" would declare "this is not the America that we grew up in. These are not the values that we hold dear. We're going to do everything within our power to fulfill the promise of America and what we expect America to be." To give one more example of many, a UnidosUS/NCLR blog post after Trump's first State of the Union speech read, "Tomorrow we return to the regularly scheduled programming of bigotry, divisiveness and denigration of American values that has been the hallmark of the Trump administration thus far."[20]

From these statements, Trump was not a blast from a shameful American past. Rather, he was "un-American." Such claims were not so much historical as they were mythic. They express what scholars have called "creedal nationalism," a variety of nationalism that is associated with color-blind liberal principles of democracy, universalism, and civil rights.[21] Debra Thompson writes, "The 'creedal story,' so deeply embedded in the American democratic ethos, is premised on the idea that America is defined by equality of opportunity and a long-standing commitment to the principle that 'all men are created equal.'"[22] As the historical analogies recognized, Trump's rhetoric and policies were far from un-American. No doubt aspirational, their articulation contested the meaning of "Americanness." Framing Trump as such positioned Latinos—who are often viewed as perpetually foreign—as, on the contrary, custodians of American values. In this matter, advocates called on creedal nationalism to challenge the White House's white nationalist claim on "America." This rhetorical move has its costs. It sustains a nonetheless racialized myth that minimizes and omits the colonial violence and racial capitalism on which "America" was built and lives.

Although contradictory, these characterizations have been applied to other "un-American" figures in the past. But while they have contended with nativists and white supremacists of various stripes, Trump was different. He was not a fringe actor, a conservative commentator, or even a state official. He was the president, one that had deliberately surrounded himself with acolytes and architects of white demographobia. For these advocates, how to characterize him proved simpler than how to confront him.

Staying the Course

In the midst of an intense discussion after the election, an NHLA member commented, in exasperation, "We are playing [the game of] Life, but someone shredded the instruction manual. . . . We are playing the same game [with] new rules." Her words, offered at a board meeting, gave the room a pause. She creatively captured what for many advocates was a major conundrum. Should NHLA and its constituent entities continue to make the same political moves or tactics even though the rules had apparently changed? Or should they change how they move, or refuse to play the game altogether? These were far from abstract or rhetorical questions. Faced with a seemingly nonstop onslaught of rhetoric and policy, advocates had to make decisions about how to best respond to the Trump administration. As one might expect from a coalition composed of a range of political entities, there were different, sometimes competing, ideas about how to proceed.

The dominant response to the Trumpian challenge has been to *stay the course*. From this perspective, the coalition and its member organizations needed to press forward. There was no need to forfeit or throw out their game plan. NHLA had an agenda and a method to stop the madness. It was a position not without contention.

At the December 2016 board meeting previously discussed, Héctor Sánchez Barba framed the meeting as a time to reflect on "next steps." Born in the Mexican state of Guanajuato—a state that he boasted had a rich and radical political history—to middle-class parents who owned a drugstore, he became chair of the coalition in 2012, a year after becoming the executive director of LCLAA at the age of thirty-five. As he tells it, this political science major and instructor found his calling during a short visit to Washington, DC. At the meeting, Sánchez Barba exclaimed to his colleagues, "Our priorities don't change." The election of Trump, he insisted, should not alter their advocacy agenda. He was referring explicitly to the coalition's 2016 public policy report. At over eighty-three glossy pages, the document

FIGURE 6.1. NHLA 2016 Policy Agenda Press Conference, 2016.
Photo by author.

was the largest and most extensive the coalition had ever produced. It was
unveiled at a well-attended press conference on Capitol Hill prior to the
2016 Democratic and Republican conventions in 2016 (fig. 6.1). During the
announcement and in the document, demographics were invoked to give
weight to the policy prescriptions.[23] The agenda was touted as the group's
most gender- and LGBTQ-inclusive and thematically expansive one to date.
It was also the first NHLA policy agenda that included a section on the envi-
ronment and addressed the issue of mass incarceration.[24]

The election of Trump did not entirely unsettle consensus around its
policy agenda. However, some tactical questions arose. One particular issue
that sparked debate at the December meeting was whether to push for
Latino representation in the Trump cabinet. At any other time, this would
not have even been a question. During Obama's second term, for example,
NHLA sent the White House a list of nineteen potential candidates for con-
sideration along with a letter.[25] It later successfully blitzed the Obama White
House, demanding that Tom Perez be nominated as secretary of labor. Four

years later the coalition was on the verge of becoming, as one member put it, "the only major population without a cabinet position."[26] Opinions varied about how to respond.

One leader called the developing Trump cabinet a "clown car" and expressed relief that there were "no Latinos" involved. The addition of a Latino cabinet member, some worried, would give the administration "cover" to say it "care[d] about diversity." Contrasting what political theorists distinguish as "descriptive" versus "substantive" representation, one leader loudly exclaimed, "[It is] not about having a Latino! It is about having a Latino reflective of our priorities."[27] Among those who argued for representation, one member reminded the group of its commitment to increase Latina representation. Another argued that if the group was "serious about representation," it had to advocate for inclusion. Eventually a compromise was proposed. Rather than entirely abandon the appointment campaign it had been working toward for years, NHLA would adopt a less "publicly aggressive" and "scaled-back" campaign. As far as I can tell, the coalition adopted this position. On numerous occasions, NHLA and its member organizations openly criticized Trump for failing to include Latinos in the cabinet, but without the fervor of 2012.[28]

Staying the course was not confined to policy demands. It also included tactical commitment to civic engagement. This conviction was on full display during a two-part public event that NHLA organized to discuss the new administration as it approached its 100th day. In the first session, leaders gave legislative updates on immigration, gender equity, the economy, and the environment. The second session—the session on "action"—centered entirely on civic engagement and the vote. One speaker discussed NHLA's initiative to increase the number of Latinas in public office. She claimed that the significance of "Latinas Represent"—a campaign the coalition launched in 2014—was not limited to the immediate present but to the future, given that one in three women in the country would be Latina by 2060. Another leader spoke about the need to grow the Latino electorate "in order to build political power." Another still, stressed the importance of maintaining contact with officials in between elections. Overall, at this event and others, advocates claimed civic engagement as the vehicle to bring an end to Trump.

Although there was strong consensus to stay the course, some felt that the coalition needed to do more, to be more assertive. At a September 2017 board meeting, a senior member voiced his frustration at the news that the coalition's executive council had postponed a scheduled act of civil disobedience. The leader took the decision as an indication of NHLA's failure to respond appropriately to the Trumpian challenge. Capturing the attention of everyone in the room, the leader belted, "This is a defining moment for NHLA! This is where we show what we're made of!" All over the country, he said, people were asking him, "What is our national leadership doing?" He continued:

> That's a question that I get most often, because they don't see us doing something that they can relate to, something that really resonates. I can say, "press conference." They say, "*ya basta con los* press conferences!" You just say things at the press conference. You announce things at press conferences, but you don't *do* anything at press conferences. Our community is looking for something that shows that our collective leadership is standing up for them. . . . We need to do something that shows our community that we are willing stand up for them.

This leader was not concerned with press coverage or how the administration responded. He wanted to demonstrate to the Latino population "*quienes somos* and that we are standing up for our community at whatever the cost may be." After he finished, he was reassured that the reason for the postponement was not a lack of member support. It was the need for more preparation. Indeed, nearly half of its members had signed on to the act.

Although a misunderstanding triggered the leader's remarks, the frustration it conveyed was shared by several others within NHLA and in its periphery. For example, Mark Magaña believed that advocates in the past had a "positive effect" doing "traditional Beltway advocacy." He didn't think that was still the case anymore. Magaña was the founder-president and CEO of GreenLatinos, an environmental coalition. Making an impact now required more nonviolent direct action. He worried that national Latino advocacy wasn't well-suited for the challenge. "I like to say we've become indoor cats, play the inside game, we lost our claws, we've gotten fed, we're fat and happy, but now it's like the whole system's changed and we got to get our claws back. . . . It's not genteel anymore. Genteel gets you nothing." The circumstances called for a change of tactics.

Similarly, a former staff member of one of the major Latino civil rights groups expressed aggravation with what she perceived as a politics as usual attitude among the organizations. As we spoke in a Washington, DC, coffee shop, she described her frustration through a scene in the popular HBO show *Game of Thrones*. In the scene, the character Sam pleaded with a council of wise men known as "maesters" to leverage their authority and issue an alarm to confront the rapidly approaching army of White Walkers.

Paraphrasing Sam's exhortation, she said, "People listen to you, and if you say this is [a crisis]. . . . If you were to put all the resources the maesters have, this could be a turning point. You have the ability to save humanity." The maesters, whom she likened to the civil rights leaders, have the power to declare and respond to the crisis, but they won't. They would rather take their time and study it. "I've been Sam, in meetings where I'm like, 'Are you serious?' It's like no matter how much you say," it doesn't make a difference.

These critiques were not so much about what civil rights groups were doing as much as about what they were not. The entire project wasn't called into question. What was being questioned, however, was whether the tactics the groups had relied on until then were enough to meet the challenge of the present. Those who raised these critiques believed that these leaders and organizations needed to more directly confront the Trumpian project. At the same time, however, there were some who saw compromise with it as a potentially more productive tactic.

Insider Politics

One of the features of staying the course was what political scientist Ken Kollman once described as "old-fashioned inside lobbying."[29] Advocates have long engaged in insider politics, which rests on relationships and negotiations with elected officials. In the first two years of the Trump administration, NHLA members continued to communicate and meet with congressional leaders. They recognized, however, that the context was different. When I spoke to NALEO-EF policy analyst, Ashley Genoa, she remarked having the "same" relationships with Republican congressional offices but that the "environment in which they operate" had changed. This affected what officials and aides were "willing and able to do, what we get back from them." With regard to the White House, there was great ambivalence about what could be gained. Access to the White House was virtually nonexistent under Trump, who refused every invitation to meet with the NHLA since he announced his candidacy. This was fundamentally different from the Obama White House, with which they had lines of communication and occasional invitations to participate in events or confer with the president. Absent all this, most leaders saw little to no promise in dealings with the Trump administration. But the stance was not universal.

In January 2018, when Trump outlined his proposal for immigration reform during his State of the Union address, NHLA immediately denounced it. Trump proposed a path to citizenship for only Dreamers, enhanced and expanded border security, a "merit"-based system to replace the diversity visa lottery, and restricted family-based immigration. Immigrant rights advocates, including NHLA leaders, saw the play: trade protections for the Dreamers—whom Trump himself endangered through his termination of DACA—for other measures long sought by immigration restrictionists. NHLA issued a press statement that charged Trump of holding the "DREAMers hostage to push forward a xenophobic, racist agenda." Leaders were unequivocal in their public repudiation. The statement quoted Brent Wilkes of LULAC: "President Trump's immigration framework is an unacceptable wish list of far right anti-immigrant policies that will impose draconian measures on hardworking immigrants, separate families, slash legal immigration and build an offensive US tax-payer funded wall on our border with Mexico." The quote was later used in an NHLA graphic shared on social media. Jessica González-Rojas of NLIRJ further expressed: "Dreamers are not bargaining chips. They deserve more than a White House that continues holding their health and safety hostage in an attempt to advance its white supremacist agenda. We urge Congress to prioritize passing a clean Dream Act without compromising the future or safety of our communities."[30] To invoke the "game" metaphor once more, NHLA, as a coalition, was not willing to play with Trump. But one leader was. It resulted in a major debacle for one of NHLA's anchoring organizations.

Days after the State of the Union, then-president of LULAC Roger Rocha sent a letter congratulating the president for "setting out a reasonable framework on immigration reform and border security." Describing Trump's framework as a "compromise," this leader from Laredo, Texas, pledged that his organization would do "our part in making your vision a reality." News of the letter came to light when the Senate majority leader, Mitch McConnell (R-KY), told the press:

> The endorsement of LULAC—not just of the President's DACA proposal, but the whole—is enormously significant. . . . Honestly I've always thought LULAC was sort of a subsidiary of the Democratic Party. Apparently I was wrong about that, but I hope they do listen to the leaders of LULAC, who said here in effect that what the President is offering is a reasonable proposal. That ought to break the ice. That ought [to] give us chance to get an outcome.[31]

McConnell's comment set off a Twitter storm. Many expressed dismay, while others thought the letter was unsurprising—only the latest example of the organization's failings and disconnect with the community and social movements. One tweet read: "LULAC never ever disappoints with their haste in falling in line. Trump called our people RAPISTS and called countries, including El Salvador, Shitholes. He continuously feeds Brown people to his rabid supporters and you THANK him? *Que vergüenza*." The radical grassroots Latinx organization Mijente issued a petition demanding that "LULAC stop aligning with white supremacy, attempting to speak for our people, and keep their respectability-vendido-outdated selves out of issues and those of the people they have never represented."[32] More sympathetically, commenters wondered what was happening inside LULAC. Frank Sharry of America's Voice, a liberal immigration group, tweeted: "Hispanic organization president supports WH proposal that cuts legal immigration of Hispanics by 58%. Yikes. More likely to hurt the organization than boot the WH proposal. Sending love to LULAC staff, who are so much better than this."

LULAC's membership and leadership—including its executive director Brent Wilkes—were caught completely off guard. Rocha had never consulted the board. Brent Wilkes, LULAC's longtime executive director, made his own public statement: "As for Mr. Rocha's statement that 'We at LULAC will continue to do our part in making your vision a reality,' I want to be very clear: the 'we' that Mr. Rocha referred to does not include me personally, nor in my role as CEO of LULAC."[33] A LULAC member created a meme in which the entire board (listed in the left-hand column of the letter) was blacked out and Rocha's name was circled in red, next to the words, "One Person Only." Responding to a tweet stating that LULAC had shifted from Democratic to Republican, a young leader in the organization wrote: "Correction: One man—Roger Rocha @NatlPresLULAC—supports this. He acted on his own, and his support for the Trump proposal does not represent the position of the general membership of LULAC. The NON-PARTISAN civil rights org supports the Dreamers." LULAC Young Adults and Collegiate LULAC issued their own condemnation: "As is the consensus among the overwhelming number of immigrant activists, we would not bargain a pathway to citizenship if it meant increased terror in immigrant communities and the dismantling of the immigration system, as the White House proposal intends and which you endorsed unilaterally."[34] These younger leaders went further, calling for Rocha's "immediate resignation."

Rocha refused to resign but issued an apology to the organization and the broader immigrant rights movement. He claimed no "malicious intent" only an "eleventh hour" attempt to protect the Dreamers from the administration's deadline to end DACA protections, set to expire in March of that year.[35] Rocha's refusal to resign triggered others to resign instead. A tearful Wilkes was out, as was Abigail Zapote, the head of LULAC Young Adults, who was still pained over her decision a year later.[36] When I spoke to her then she shared, "It felt awful. It felt like I was letting all of the young leaders that I mentored, I felt like I was letting them all down. I felt like I was letting down the entire commission of trying to pass the DREAM Act. I felt just completely . . . I don't know, I also felt just like tearing myself away from that title that I had earned." Those who remained similarly voiced how the ordeal had affected them and damaged their organization's reputation. Determined, those that remained began to pick up the pieces and chart a new course for the organization, which included selecting Sindy Benavides, the organization's director of civic engagement, as its new CEO. She was, it was often noted, the first woman to assume that position of leadership, and a Honduran American woman to boot.

Advocates did not abandon insider politics entirely, but there was awareness of its limitations and pitfalls in Trumpian times. Most believed that the times called for them to continue to publicly denounce the administration and invest in civic engagement, seen as the solution. But some, as we saw in the critiques discussed earlier, called for tactical escalation. These calls often looked not to the future but to the past for inspiration.

Escalations

The past has many uses.[37] As already noted, historical analogies were used to position Trump as a familiar foe and one who could be defeated, just as Pete Wilson was, through the ballot box. But the past was also mined as a source of tactical inspiration and innovation. At the NHLA board meeting in September 2017 several calls for escalation were made.

In an ornate room studded with stained glass, far from the border and the frontlines of mobilizations against white nationalism, Héctor Sánchez Barba opened the meeting with a question—not at all rhetorical—about how NHLA should confront the extremism and attacks on Latinos and the immigrant community. What was the "best way" to take their response to the "next level"? The mere fact that these questions were raised indicates there was support for doing more than staying the course. Perhaps anticipating some discomfort, he assured his colleagues that the strength of the coalition was its "unity" and "transparency." Although members were free to respond, float ideas, and discuss, he pressed the group to become more tactically aggressive: "They are not afraid of us." There seemed to be no disagreement in the room. He added that "all tactics should be welcomed," with the caveat that there be coordination between those in the "streets" and those in the "halls."

Sánchez Barba's opening provocation was followed, by design, with an extended discussion on civic engagement. The topic provided a space to reassert both tactical consensus and the primacy of voter registration and mobilization. This was, more or less, stable terrain. But when the meeting's agenda arrived at the subject of economic boycotts and civil disobedience, it was less so. As noted earlier, at least one member was outwardly frustrated with the postponement of civil disobedience. But what concerns me here is not critique but how the past was invoked to think about and pressure for escalation.

The tactic of boycotts was broached first. In support of the idea, one leader remarked, money, rather than politics, was the way to hurt Trump. Others recommended a broader target—why not boycott all companies that worked with him and his band of white supremacists? As the conversation unfolded, the issue of whom to target became secondary to the more basic questions of whether and when to boycott. Some questions were raised about the capacity of the coalition to effectively carry out such an action. Was the group well enough prepared? Would it be more successful to collaborate with other organizations and communities? Both support and reservations about the boycott were heightened because NHLA was scheduled to rally in front of the White House the following day. Those in support saw the rally as the perfect opportunity to announce the boycott. For those still unsure, announcing a poorly planned and unsuccessful boycott could do more harm than good. At this moment, there seemed to be more support for the *idea* than the *act* of a boycott. Capturing some of the spoken and unspoken hesitation in the room, a member ventured that a boycott would be difficult to carry out and could provoke "strong opposition." At this, a colleague interrupted, incensed, "I am f-ing tired of hearing that things are difficult! Good things, tough things, successful things, and big history-making things are difficult, and they take sacrifice."

NHLA, he continued, was out of step with the Latino community: "We're nowhere near where the community is. They want to do the difficult shit because they're in it; their daily lives are difficult. So if we're not ready to step in it. We're not ready to sacrifice a little bit of ourselves, give up something, give up something financial, something, time wise. Then we're not at the point where we think we're at." With palpable frustration, he continued:

"This is personal and I'm sorry, but I don't want to hear that's *difficult*. Yes. Take all the great people in history who did progressive, difficult things. Everyone said there's no way they can do that. Gandhi, Martin Luther King, Cesar Chávez." Sitting at the edge of his seat, this leader urged his colleagues to respond forcefully to Trump and his agenda: "Let's do the difficult stuff. Let's not do the easy stuff and this is difficult, but let's think big about it . . . let's do it with the entire progressive community and let's hurt him economically, let's humiliate him. Let's also humiliate his friends and associates. No one should be willing to touch this guy. [He] should be toxic." More preparation was fine with this member, but it shouldn't be raised to prevent more assertive actions. "If we can't stick our neck out *now*, then when can we?" No one responded directly. Instead, the conversation remained centered on the need for greater preparation and brainstorming alternative advocacy action items to announce. Soon after, the conversation shifted to other agenda items. This frustrated member associated transformative "big" and "difficult" change with the movements of the past. He used major historical figures as "models for" rather than merely "models of" action.[38] Gandhi, Martin Luther King, Jr., and Cesar Chávez should be emulated, not simply remembered.

The past was also invoked during the conversation about civil disobedience. One leader with extensive experience as a participant and legal advisor to civil disobedience was asked to provide context for the tactic. This educational session was targeted specifically at those members, perhaps the majority, without activist backgrounds. The leader's baritone voice carried the weight of the topic. Civil disobedience, he stated, was a "tradition that goes as far back as we can remember." In the United States, though, it could be traced to "the amazing lessons that we have learned as a community from the African American community." Here it wasn't individuals but a community that offered models for action. With this legacy in mind, the advocate characterized the act as one that "forces us to interrupt the common, normal course of business or government. It is meant to interrupt." He designated civil disobedience a necessary escalation to confront "an element of this country that is fighting its last gasp about white supremacy. There's a section of this country that still believes that white people are racially superior to all of us, and we have a president, in my opinion, who believes that wholeheartedly." In times of uncertainty and backlash, this leader drew inspiration from the Black Civil Rights movement. He was not alone. In fall 2019 LULAC drew on the memory of the Freedom Riders for a women-led civic engagement campaign. Sindy Benavides expressed, alongside former Freedom Riders, "LULAC kicks off the Freedom Walks for Justice to both pay homage to the Freedom Riders of the Civil Rights Movement and to mobilize diverse communities across the country facing the same acute threat: hate and injustice." This case shows that the past, and the history of the Black freedom struggle in particular, inspired not only tactical escalation but more conventional tactics of the coalition as well.

For national Latino civil rights groups, the future has long been the dominant temporal register. Confronted with a figure and political project understood to be bent on reversing civil rights gains and animated by demographic fears, some actors turned to the past. But what about the future, and specifically the demographic future? And, more generally, what role did population politics play in Trumpian times?

Population Politics Recalibrated

The day after the September 2017 board meeting, NHLA members and their staff marched from AFL-CIO's headquarters to Lafayette Park in front of the White House. Although without civil disobedience, the march and rally evidenced a willingness to do more than hold press conferences. It also manifested the coalition's stated desire to deepen its relationship and collaborations with other movements and populations. At the event, NHLA was joined by representatives from the AFL-CIO, Women's Law Center, Navajo Nation, Asian Pacific American Labor Alliance, National Center for Transgender Equality, Climate Action Network, Human Rights Campaign, and Lambda Legal. When it was Maria Teresa Kumar's turn to speak, the Voto Latino executive director scanned the diverse crowd and shouted into the bullhorn, "*This* is what America looks like!" (fig. 6.2).

Speeches delivered at the rally consistently emphasized civic engagement. If past discourse was any guide, one would have expected advocates to also make strong statements about the demographic power of the Latino vote. But with one exception—that "one in six Americans are Latino"—and a couple of other allusions, the content of the speeches was bereft of population politics.

Recall that, after the 2012 election, Latino advocates were quick to threaten Republican officials with the "demographic imperative." But thus far into the Trump presidency, these claims were noticeably infrequent. And when articulated, they tended to be less strident. Take, for instance, LULAC's Roger Rocha's remarks at the postelection press conference (well before he thought it wise to endorse the administration's stance on immigration): "The Latino community's voting strength will only continue to grow in the coming

FIGURE 6.2. NHLA White House Rally, September 17. Used by permission of the National Hispanic Leadership Agenda.

years, and as such, politicians would be wise to begin addressing issues which are important to the Latino community."[39] It is difficult not to conclude that this shift or tactical recalibration was, at least in part, a consequence of the heightened visibility and reach of white supremacist population politics. Yet although advocates have not entirely given up on forewarning, they have employed it much less than one might have expected to challenge Trump.

In Trumpian times, leaders and organizations recalibrated their population politics. I do not know whether this was a conscious shift; when asked, leaders seemed not to have noticed. There are several features of this recalibration. The first, as noted earlier, was a limited use of forewarning. This temporal tactic, as we saw in the previous chapter, was confined to electoral and legislative matters, in which democratic participation rather than raw demographics was emphasized. To be sure, these warnings rested on population trends, but they were legitimated in relation to representative democracy: If you don't "represent" our interests, we will vote you out of office.

This fact makes all the more noteworthy the general absence of forewarning in their response to Trump.

Second, advocates at times mobilized demographic figures without explicit mention of the future. This connects with a longstanding use of population data to highlight disparities and inequalities. To illustrate this use, I turn to an NHLA-supported boycott of Paramount Pictures. In 2018, NHLA issued a letter to Paramount criticizing the movie company for its refusal to work with the NHLA member organizations, the National Hispanic Media Coalition and the National Latino Media Council. The former released a report that found that Paramount had the "worst studio record in hiring Latinos in front [of] and behind camera."[40] Its letter expressed:

> As you know, Latinos represent over 18 percent of the United States population, and Latinos have been the largest racial/ethnic minority group in the country for more than a decade. In addition, Latinos comprise over one quarter of all public school students from kindergarten through 12th grade nationwide. Not surprisingly then, surveys indicate that Latinos represent nearly a quarter of all moviegoers in the United States. These statistics render all the more shocking—and insulting to all Latinos—Paramount's abysmal representation of Latinos both in front of and behind the camera in your movies.[41]

The action, and the considerable press it garnered, inveighed against the lack of Latino inclusion not in the name of abstract justice but in terms of demography.[42] Even though the future was sometimes alluded to, this use of demographics concerned more the present state of representation (or lack thereof).

Third, advocates have, in some cases, expanded their demographic scope. As in the NHLA rally, this shift followed desires to grow collaboration with other targeted groups. The most explicit example of this recalibration is NCLR's name change. In the summer of 2017, as the organization held its annual conference in Phoenix, Arizona, NCLR unexpectedly announced that its new name would be UnidosUS. The organization's leaders claimed the name change was not taken lightly; it was informed by a desire to remain "relevant." Demographic changes within the Latino population, Janet Murguía stated, the label "raza" rendered a "barrier" to their mission. Latino millennials and non–Mexican Americans were said not to vibe with the Chicano-era term. On numerous occasions UnidosUS leaders pushed back against the idea that the change capitulated to right-wing attacks.

But just as the name UnidosUS was framed as more inclusive for Latinos—a term that at the same time was undergoing modification by the gender nonbinary Latinx—it also aspired to gain a broader constituency. In a speech, Murguía claimed that the new name not only reinforced "Latinos' role as a unifying force and voice, it also signaled a message for others to join us and come together united in the best interests of our country and all Americans." The organization continues to circulate figures about Latino population growth and still understands itself as a "Latino" civil rights organization, but one that extends beyond the panethnic to a wider multicultural horizon and future.

The name change provoked a range of opinions. Some have endorsed it, considering it a "smart, inclusive move."[43] Others accused the organization of "kissing up to corporate America." Still others saw the decision as disavowing its history and roots in the Chicano movement. *Washington Post* writer Bianca Betancourt wondered if rebranding alone would help the organization attract millennials, one of the populations said to have motivated the change. "It will take more than a new name to mobilize the community to fight for its interests. Younger Latinos already have been gradually distancing themselves from legacy activist groups in favor of digital organizing and more inclusive leadership."[44] Similarly, one advocate based in Washington, DC, told me, "I don't mind the name change, but what bothers me is that it doesn't seem to be in conjunction with any kind of real strategy for change." The change also received attention from conservative and right-wing authors and news media. Writing in the *National Review*, Victor Davis Hanson, the author of *Mexifornia*, long a staple in nativist diets, described the organization's former name as "racialist" and interpreted UnidoUS as an attempt to "convey an inclusive message exactly the opposite from the inferences of its prior tribalist nomenclature."[45]

Still, in other ways, the population politics of national Latino groups have not changed in content, only in emphasis. These actors continue to project a discourse of demographic optimism. Take, for example, Maria Teresa Kumar's opening remarks at a plenary panel during the UnidosUS conference in 2018. The panel, titled "Unidos We Stand: Fighting Back with Courage," featured prominent leaders from other civil rights and policy organizations. These included Neera Tanden of the Center for American Progress, Chad Griffin of Human Rights Campaign, Sherrilyn Ifill of the NAACP Legal Defense and Educational Fund, and Vanita Gupta of the Leadership Conference on Civil and Human Rights. The discussion was moderated by UnidosUS president Janet Murguía. Each presenter spoke on an assigned a discussion theme. Kumar delivered her theme, "progress," in the style of a TED Talk. She claimed that Latinos were under attack because of the progress they had made. Looking ahead, she said:

We are built for this moment. We are strong. Because progress is recognizing our potential at the voting booth. Eighty percent of Latinos who register vote. The mean age of the white American voter is fifty-four. The mean age of the Latino voter is eighteen years old. That is progress. Because when we come together as a community, when we're running young candidates, when we're setting ourselves high into the office of the president, when we are making sure that we are executives and mobilizing each other, uplifting each other like we did in Tornillo, we're unstoppable.

Kumar's remarks built on long-standing tropes of Latino youthfulness and its growing electoral capacity, explicitly contrasted to a graying white electorate. She further linked this demographic horizon to familiar indices of progress among national Latino advocacy organizations: more and more Latinos were running for office, occupying prominent political positions, and becoming corporate executives. Her mention of Tornillo was telling: one of the major immigrant detention camps, it had been the target of Latino advocates' and allies' protests against youth detention and family separation just weeks prior to the conference. Her inspirational words were meant to communicate that progress remained within grasp, if for no other reason than continuing demographic trends.

But expressions of demographic optimism have also been subjected to critique. These critiques, it is important to note, tend to come from individuals and movements outside of Latino civil rights advocacy. On the same UnidosUS panel as Kumar, Sherrilyn Ifill, president and director-counsel of the NAACP Legal Defense and Educational Fund, scrutinized demographic optimism. Responding to a question from Murguía about what to do "differently, or in a new way" to carve a "path forward for all of us," Ifill identified two issues. The first directly responded to Kumar's speech:

I think that notwithstanding our very optimistic picture of what will happen in this country demographically, and Maria Teresa was referring to some of that in terms of the median age of the Latino voter, and we talk about the browning of America, and we talk about being a majority minority country and so forth, and I think we have to rely less on the idea that demography is destiny, because it is not. There is such a thing as minority rule. It's very ugly. Many of us know it from South Africa. It's brutal. We shouldn't assume that just because there are numbers that there's power. If you want power, you have to decide that you're going to exercise power.

Ifill questioned the conflation with demography with power. Using the historical case of South Africa's apartheid regime, she suggested an alternative future, one of white "minority" rule. Others have also critiqued the "demography as destiny" thesis. Outside the advocacy network, some progressive groups have pushed back against the demographic story of Latino progress. The group Mijente, for example, stated in its principles that "transformative change requires more from us, not just more of us."[46] Population change, in other words, was not enough alone to change political conditions. Most national Latino advocates would agree with this point but their rhetoric, however, has often painted—and deliberately so—bright futures framed in largely demographic terms.

Overall, population politics remained part of their arsenal. But as seen earlier, they have recalibrated, in subtle and explicit ways, how Latino demographics were invoked. In the first two years of the Trump administration, Latino advocates largely chose not to forewarn Trump and his Republican colleagues. This hesitation, I argue, stemmed from long-standing worries about triggering white backlash. Even so, demographic rhetoric continues to be seen as rhetorically useful, particularly to highlight disparities and to instill optimism in unsettled times.

The Latino Power Project

The Trumpian challenge has elicited numerous responses from NHLA and its member organizations. There have been, as discussed earlier, strong commitments to maintain its legislative agenda and tactical repertoire, most significantly civic engagement. But it has also received critiques demanding more direct confrontation that have often drawn inspiration on the past, specifically the Black civil rights tradition. Advocates have also recalibrated their population politics and how they mobilize demographic futures. Although distinct, these different threads share the same context of "presentism." François Hartog describes presentism as "the sense that only the present exists, a present characterized at once by the tyranny of the instant and by the treadmill of an unending now."[47] Hartog's concern was with the current stage of modernity and its erasure of the future. Though his societal or even global scale is broader than what I have in mind, the concept, I believe, is fruitful for reflecting on moments of crisis. In situations that demand all-consuming attention, it is difficult, perhaps even imprudent, to think long-term.

Some leaders, however, such as Héctor Sánchez Barba, have been preoccupied with the absence of a long-term strategy for Latino empowerment. This concern predates Donald Trump but has only been intensified since his election. Collaborating with the influential Washington-based consultant and strategist Robert Raben of the Raben Group, Sánchez Barba sought and secured the NHLA board's approval to develop what was initially called the Latino Power Project 2050. I observed and participated in its earliest phases. The 2050 in the name was a reference not only to the century's midpoint but also to the popularized demographic chronology that placed the country as becoming "majority-minority" in 2050. By that point the Latino population is projected to make up between 25 and 30 percent of the total U.S. population. The Latino Power Project aimed to ensure that, by that year, Latino representation corresponds to Latino demographics. As one Raben Group visualization expressed, in 2060 the Latino population should be 30 percent, and consequently so should the U.S. Senate (fig. 6.3).

Sánchez Barba announced the initiative in a *Huffington Post* op-ed in 2015:

> In order to advance the Latino agenda in the long-term, we will create a plan that analyzes the existing Latino paths to power, defines what Latino power looks like going forward and develops a framework to increase Latino influence. NHLA will spearhead a Latino Power Project that will be guided by Latino leaders, visionaries and professionals around our great country. Together we will take stock of where Latinos stand today on our nation's "power meter." We will identify the structural and systemic changes that are required to allow us to reach our full potential. Finally, we will create an advocacy plan that guarantees the fair representation of Latinos at the most important tables and in the spaces where major decisions are made.[48]

The problem with "short-termism," as Hartog phrases it, was further elaborated in a page-long concept statement on the Power Project:

> Given the demands of the millions we represent, as Hispanic leaders we find far too much of our daily time and resources spent on the effort of meeting yesterday's and today's needs, fighting crucial, but too frequently remedial, battles—fair housing, inadequate education, restrictions on voting, anti-immigrant measures, employment, and more. Ameliorating these past problems, and their current effects, is essential. But it is only a start. It does not address the needs of the future, and the core question of our place in America's pluralistic democracy: what our power is and how we will exercise it.

Latino advocates, the statement noted, had too long focused on amelioration, an essential concept but lacking action. Struggles for housing and education and defense against anti-immigrant measures were understood

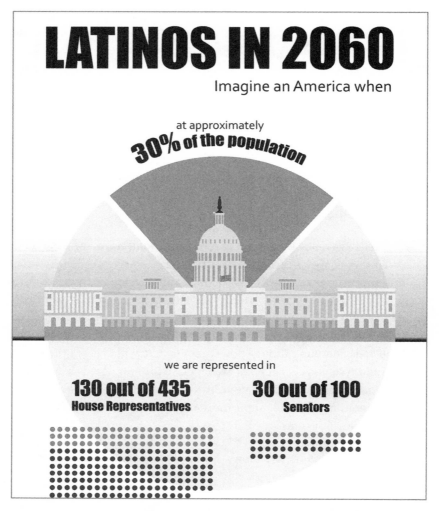

LATINOS IN 2060

Imagine an America when

at approximately
30% of the population

we are represented in

130 out of 435
House Representatives

30 out of 100
Senators

FIGURE 6.3. "Latinos in 2060" infographic. Latino Power Project, circa 2016. Used by permission of the Raben Group.

as crucial but were unlikely to grow the "power" of the Latino population and its ability to exercise that power.

The organizers of the Latino Power Project have struggled to "socialize" many of its participants to think beyond the immediate and to place strategy over tactics. Moreover, they have worried that the *timing* of the project might be seen as a direct response to Trump. At several daylong discussions with Latino leaders around the country, advocates have reiterated that the Power Project transcended the current administration, no matter how hard it was to endure its daily demands, attacks, and challenges.

Part of the project's long-term orientation is rooted in its emphasis on the longue durée of Latino marginality. Sánchez Barba grounded the project in a longitudinal assessment of Latino representation over time. To this end, he requested I collect data on the number of Latinos in what he called "spaces of power," influential political, economic, and intellectual sites. The data we collected revealed that the rate of progress had been negligible across many, if not all, focal spaces. Raw numbers had increased marginally (e.g., there are more Latinos on Fortune 500 boards today than in the past), but Sánchez Barba insisted that the real test was whether the gap between population size and representation had increased or decreased over time.

The exercise, I would later learn, was meant to raise a critique and stimulate introspection among Latino advocates and their peers in other fields. The data were used to question the narrative of progress. It was not simply that progress had been slow—no one would debate that point—but that things *had gotten worse*. Sánchez Barba mobilized "proof" of a persistent and growing gap in Latino representation to argue for a new, longer-term strategy of Latino empowerment. Although never explicitly stated, the data was meant to affirm that demography was not destiny.

The Latino Power Project has set out to develop a long-term strategy for "Latino" empowerment. Among other items, it has explored the formation of an "accountability" or "watchdog" organization, similar in some ways to the Anti-Defamation League, which was founded to combat anti-Semitism. The entity would be charged with monitoring and responding to cases of anti-Latino discourse and practice. Although this initiative and the project as a whole remains under development, it has pushed advocates and colleagues in other fields to think beyond the immediate—an especially difficult proposition during the Trump administration. Part of the rhetorical argument behind its call for longer-term planning was its challenge to demographic optimism. The growth of the Latino population was not framed as the basis and engine for "Latino power." Demography did not guarantee proportional representation, and the power that would presumably afford. Achieving representation, its organizers passionately argued, demanded a new strategic vision untethered from the constraints of the present.

———

The Trump administration severely tested national Latino advocacy. The exhausting array of attacks on Latinos and immigrants unearthed and heightened both internal tensions and external critiques in advocacy organizations. Time and temporality were central to these tensions and critiques.

These ranged from questions about tactics to questions of strategy, as well as issues of rhetoric. Different interpretations about the present inspired different conclusions about the best ways to react and respond to the bewildering, unfocused onslaught of the administration. Even the shared belief that Trump's project has, at least for the time being, stalled, if not reversed, some of the political gains Latinos have made (or believed they were about to make) was unable to assuage these differences.

Nonetheless, the organizational and ideological inertia of NHLA and its leading organizations kept the coalition unified and from changing dramatically during the Trump's presidency. To be sure, voices for a more activist approach to politics have become louder. But the emphasis on civic engagement and insider activity remained the chief tactic of the coalition, and national Latino advocacy, writ large. Where we have seen change is in the rhetoric of advocacy, particularly abstaining from invoking demographic futures to threaten political opponents. Instead, Latino demographics were used to both convey optimism and, in one case, unsettle narratives of progress.

Conclusion

On the morning of August 3, 2019, Patrick Crusius, a twenty-one-year-old white man, arrived in El Paso, Texas. He had driven over ten hours from his home in an affluent suburb of Dallas. Armed with a "civilian" cousin of the AK-47 assault rifle, Crusius opened fire in a popular shopping mall miles from the U.S.-Mexico border and detention centers housing hundreds of unaccompanied minors. His killing spree left twenty-two dead, another twenty-two injured, and a community in trauma.

The first wave of media coverage characterized the massacre as the latest in the country's ever-growing list of mass shootings. Yet it was soon after discovered that, shortly before the act, Crusius had reportedly uploaded a manifesto of sorts on 8chan, an internet haven for white supremacists and others on the extreme right. Titled "The Inconvenient Truth," the document was short but muddled. As one journalist put it, it contained a "jumble of positions and ideologies," on topics ranging from automation to environmental degradation to interracial relationships, among other things.[1] The document, however, was clear as to the primary motive behind the massacre: "This attack is a response to the Hispanic invasion of Texas. They are the instigators, not me. I am simply defending my country from cultural and ethnic replacement brought on by an invasion." The hollow-point bullets Crusius indiscriminately and discriminately unleashed, he reasoned, were an act of white demographic self-defense.

———

Crusius's tract contained many of the major tropes and themes that have anchored white supremacist population politics for decades, if not longer. These included and exceeded the elements of what Leo Chavez has theorized as the "Latino Threat Narrative." There was the language of invasion, and the specific characterization of immigrants—and "Hispanic" immigrants in particular—as an invading force.[2] Like the Christchurch mosque massacre in New Zealand, which had taken place months earlier, and the alt-right protest at Charlottesville, Virginia, two years prior, the document invoked the "great replacement," a conspiracy theory that claims whites are being replaced by nonwhites, Muslims, and a Jewish cabal.[3] And last, there was the call for the creation of a white ethnostate free of the threat of race mixture.[4] The racist demodystopia it cobbled together contrasts sharply with the imagined demographic future that has been the subject of this book.

National Latino advocacy organizations have constructed and communicated a decidedly utopian forecast. In their scenario, the Latino population does not pose a threat to the white population or to the country as a whole. Even in its most combative formulation, it depicts only *partisan* loss for those who ignore or attack this projected population-on-the-rise. Yet while otherwise diametrically opposed, these manifestations of population politics share some similarities. Both employ numbers and narratives to give credence and potency to their respective images of the future. Both center on the same population, which is characterized as either threatening or rejuvenating on the basis of its size and projected growth. These parallels, I stress, do not diminish the chief difference between them, a difference that, as El Paso teaches, is a matter of life and death. Only one scenario is deliberately articulated to instill fear and trigger violence.

Latino civil rights advocates have long contended with white supremacist projects. As in past responses to its violence, they immediately condemned the El Paso massacre and the ideologies that fuel such atrocities. NHLA's public statement included messages from over half of the coalition's forty-five organizations.[5] On the whole, the statement placed blame for the attack on the White House, and to a lesser extent the Republican Party, for its silent complicity. Since the Trump campaign, Latino advocates have warned about increased anti-Latino aggression and the likelihood of such an event. In the statement, the newly elected LULAC president Domingo García expressed, "The blood that was spilled through this deadly attack lies in the hands of President Trump and the Administration." Gabriela Lemus, then Mi Familia Vota's board president and former NHLA chair, stated, "Responsibility for the current violence like that which happened in El Paso—led by an individual espousing a white nationalist agenda—starts at the top."[6] Similarly, Janet Murguía of UnidosUS, writing in the *New York Times*, argued that Trump's rhetoric and disdain for the Latino population—evidenced by his treatment of Central American immigrants border and Puerto Ricans after Hurricane Maria—provided fodder for anti-Latino violence and sentiment.[7]

In person and through public channels, NHLA leaders also sent messages of support to the victims and the broader "Latino community." Several were among some two hundred prominent signatories of an open letter penned by actors and filmmakers America Ferrera, Eva Longoria, Diane Guerrero, Alex Martinez Kondracke, and Olga Segura, as well as immigrant rights activist Mónica Ramírez, who has ties to NHLA. Addressed to "Querida Familia Latina," the letter validated feelings of fear and hurt caused not only by the massacre but also by ICE raids, family separation, children in cages, and hate speech: "Though real pain and fear are sweeping through our communities, we remain powerful."[8] The letter and advocates more generally stressed that the El Paso massacre was not a singular event that could be separated from the larger political climate and the workings of an administration willing to inflict violence on unwanted populations.

Their responses to white supremacist agendas and actions were not limited to reactive condemnations of violence and expressions of solidarity. Historically, advocates have tried to defuse white anxiety over demographic change and thus dampen its galvanizing capacity. As discussed in chapter 3, narratives about the national benefits of Latino population growth and pronouncements of its fidelity and cultural commensurability have served as a defensive tactic against enunciations of Latino threat. As further evidence that imagined demographic futures are always relational, it is impossible to understand the population politics of national Latino civil rights groups apart from the ever-present concern with white reaction and the mainstreaming of overtly anti-Latino discourses and white demodystopias more generally.

Mitigating white demographobia, however, is only part of what has motivated their investment in population politics. Arguably, the major motivation stems from an old conviction that population growth is and should be a means to political empowerment. It is this conviction that I will turn to next. Ultimately, the message I want to impart is the need to denaturalize how we—academics and nonacademics—talk and think about demography. I believe more attention needs to be given to the historically sedimented and contemporaneously inflected struggles through which our knowledge of, perceptions about, and reactions to purported population change are being publicly cultivated and contested.

Latino Futures

Population politics are an integral part of national Latino civil rights advocacy. As I have argued, the reliance on demographic knowledge and the emphasis on the future began during the establishment of this political network between the late 1960s and early 1980s. What commenced as civil rights demands for statistical proof of inequality expanded to making claims provisioned with demographic projections. Talk about the future elevated the status of and interest in the newly constituted "Hispanic" population and its emergent spokespersons. Media coverage increased. Political elites and corporations grew more attentive. Even as this development coincided with a rise in stigmatizing representations about Mexican and Latin American immigrants, particularly undocumented laborers, the first generation of Latino civil rights advocates increasing spoke about population growth as a catalyst for political and social advancement.

The uptake of this progressively taken-for-granted sentiment can be seen in the statements and publications of advocacy organizations at the time. One poignant example can be found in the January/February 1980 issue of the National Council of La Raza magazine, *Agenda*. Dedicated to the topic of Latino political power and progress, it was published on the eve of the first census to ask a question about "Spanish/Hispanic origin or descent."[9] On its third page, a short section titled "Looking Ahead" was encased in a graphical rendering of the sun. Its first paragraph read: "A new decade is beginning, one which has been called 'The Hispanic Decade' or 'Our Decade in the Sun.' Predictions of rapid increases in numbers and in the power that accompanies numerical strength have given reason for optimism and expectation among Hispanics. Will the optimism be warranted? Will the expectations be fulfilled? Will numbers, after all, make such a difference?"

These weighty questions were not posed rhetorically. The editorial statement quickly resolved any uncertainty about the relationship between demography and progress, instructing readers that the remainder of the issue would explore "some of the ways that Hispanic numbers can make a difference: in unity, in politics, and in hemispheric relations." Forty years later, advocates remain largely convinced that numbers can and will make a positive difference.

Latino population growth grounds this largely hopeful view about the future of the "Latino community." As it continues to numerically grow and geographically expand, it will play an increasingly significant role in U.S. social and political life. This claim has not only been used to mobilize support and draw public attention. Most of the advocates I spoke with also expressed a strong personal belief that demographic trends represent a trajectory of progress. To be sure, they have been plenty frustrated at the rate of improvement and empowerment, and certainly troubled by the post-Obama politics of white resentment. Although tested, confidence remains that a bright future is on the horizon. Far from unique, this presumption of linear progress has long dominated intellectual and political discourses of race and racism in the United States.[10] From this conception of social change, the question becomes its speed—whether progress comes slow or fast.

Indeed, advocates are not content with waiting for this demographically secure future to arrive. They believe and publicly insist, as previous chapters have shown, that its arrival can be politically accelerated. Above all, increased participation in censuses and elections is considered the preeminent means of acceleration. In other words, political engagement determines the speed of progress laid by demographic growth. Through concerted, collective action, advocates argue, this population can determine the *when* of Latino political power and influence. An awakened giant, as opposed to a sleeping one, can determine whether this is achieved soon or in "two or three generations," as Janet Murguía claimed in the 2011 speech quoted at the opening of this book.

All these claims and convictions are proof of population politics. Demographic trends are not objective conduits for political progress, just as they are not objective harbingers of disaster. That these interpretations, among a host of others, are favored or rejected at any given moment and by any given social grouping is, to a great extent, the result of practical and political attempts to make sense of population dynamics, which themselves are outcomes of particular ways of organizing and imagining social relations.[11] In the case of these civil rights advocates, I argue that population politics—a term they do not use—represent one of the means by which they have tried to accelerate the perceived promise of demography. Translating growth into influence and recognition requires, in part, managing how the "Latino" population and the future are understood and felt.

During the period I conducted fieldwork, advocacy organizations used three temporal tactics of population politics. The first, *forecasting*, supplied an answer to the question: What is to come? A bright future. As noted earlier, this forecast was meant to both reassure non-Latinos—especially whites— and convey the future strength of the Latino population. The second tactic, *foreshadowing*, answered a different question: How close is the future? On the near horizon. Less concerned with how the future is envisioned than with how it is enacted, foreshadowing aimed to transform present events into signs of a soon-to-arrive future. The third tactic, *forewarning*, harnessed the preceding two tactics to answer another question: what will happen if we do not heed the future? Political fates will be decided. This tactic sought to compel political opponents to respond favorably to their demands in light of projected futures. These tactics communicated not one imagined Latino future but several, mobilized together to accelerate the political power that demography, it is believed, will afford this population in the decades to come.

Temporal Tensions

Acceleration has been a fraught and frustrated project. The preceding chapters have described numerous challenges and obstacles. White demographobia, as we have seen, has remained an ever-present problem. This has encouraged expressions of *demographic respectability*: that is, the representation of the Latino population in white-appeasing and marketable ways. Voter suppression laws and exclusion from major funding streams for civic engagement have also hindered their ambitions, replenishing tired ideas about the "sleeping" Latino vote. In addition, advocates have struggled to navigate the straits of partisan polarization, in which one party takes them for granted and the other ignores and attacks them. There is little evidence that this condition will subside in the near future.

Along with such challenges, several temporal tensions mar and mark their efforts. Latino forecasts presume that there will be a self-recognizing and identifying Latino population in the future. Will this category have continued salience and resonance? Will the descendants of those who today identify or are classified as such carry this category?[12] These questions, I should add, are not unique to the category "Latino." While it is impossible to answer such questions definitively, what we know is that currently there is serious political contention over this category and whether one can speak legitimately and comprehensively about a "Latino community" or "Latino population." These debates have raised important issues about historical exclusions and the hegemony of particular and often narrow ways of being, looking, and sounding "Latino." Although still meaningful, at least nominally for millions, some have called for the label's outright cancellation or its profound re-envisioning. Read through current debates, a "Latino" future seems less inevitable and more fragile than the projections of advocacy groups. Whether this category survives and in what, if any, form remains an open question. So is how the population politics of Latino advocacy organizations will or will not change in response to these challenges to the meaning and utility of the category on which their futures have been built. Signs suggest they are listening. Already it is increasingly common to see the appearance of terms like Latinx and Afro-Latino in their public-facing materials.[13] Time will tell what these categorical embraces will mean for their programs and projections, and whether they will satify longstanding critiques.

The final tension to note pertains to the ways in which the Latino population has been tensed as a population of the future. In public discourse, it is routine to hear questions such as the following: What impact will this population have on the U.S. economy in the future? How will it remake party politics? How will it transform ideas about race? What role will it have in the coming labor force? The emphasis on futurity helps to explain the perpetual discovery and newness of this population. It also fuels the population's ongoing depiction as soon to arrive or to come of age. As political theorist Cristina Beltrán has noted, this population has been depicted as ever on "on the cusp of political power and influence." Latino civil rights groups regularly voice similar points. Thus, even as they have attempted to accelerate their political power, they have inadvertently contributed to the idea that the Latino population matters *most* to the future. This temporal register renders Latino presents as always lacking in relation to the future. Moreover, it traps its avowed impact, significance, and influence in the future, which as Jonathan Rosa has written, "positions the Latino population in relation to a distinctive social tense of always not yet, or perhaps, never quite yet."[14]

These and other tensions will play out in a context determined not by these political actors but by others. And this context will include the 2020 census, which has turned into an important beachhead in the struggle to secure white minority rule in the face of ethnoracial demographic change.

The Siege of Census 2020

Much of this book took place in the shadow of the 2010 census. The demographic knowledge it produced, such as the figure of 50.5 million "Hispanics," was charged and communicated throughout the decade by diverse agents. By the time that data became public in 2011, the laborious infrastructural work for the next census was already underway. Census making, as we have seen, is an act and a site of population politics. Negotiations and struggles over categories and other aspects of the process of enumeration can profoundly color the kinds of demographic futures that can be subsequently imagined and made intelligible. Advocates are veterans of these struggles, having worked for decades to ensure the production of statistical knowledge about the Latino population. Yet they did not expect to have to confront a racially interventionist administration seeking to control the future through the 2020 census.

In January 2018 the Census Bureau announced that its proposed changes to how race and ethnicity were counted would not appear in the upcoming census. The decision dismissed almost a decade of research, negotiation, and preparation that would have combined the "Hispanic-origin" and "race" questions and introduced a new and long sought category for Middle Eastern and North African identifying individuals, known as MENA.[15] For some time, census officials have sought to reduce the number of individuals that select "Some other race" in the census, the overwhelming majority of whom identify as Hispanic-origin.[16] National Latino advocacy groups historically opposed the combination of these questions, citing decreases to the overall numbers for the Latino population. Unlike past tests of combined formats, however, the 2010 Census Race and Hispanic Origin Alternative Questionnaire Experiment (AQE) and 2015 National Content Test revealed no numerical loss and dramatically lowered the size of the hard-to-interpret "Some other race" response. The results of these tests, combined with extensive internal discussion and meetings with census officials, led most national Latino civil advocates to support the combined question.[17] NALEO-EF, for instance, characterized the combined question as the "best option for improving data on Latinos."[18] The changes received support from the broader advocacy and academic community, as evidenced by the endorsement of the Census Bureau's National Advisory Committee and the Leadership Conference on Civil and Human Rights, a coalition of the country's major civil rights organizations.

Although it was the Census Bureau that notified the public that the 2020 census would follow, with only slight modification, the format of the previous census, the decision was made elsewhere.[19] Any proposed changes to federal standards on race and ethnic classification require approval from the Office of Management and Budget. In advance, OMB was provided with analyses from the Census Bureau and proposals from an OMB-convened Interagency Working Group charged with studying the topic. Its officials stated that OMB would come to a decision on the combined question by the middle of 2017—in time to meet the deadline for inclusion in the Census Bureau's final test before the decennial census. No decision came before the deadline, however, a fact that effectively blocked the proposed changes.

Despite numerous requests from journalists and advocates, OMB never gave an explanation for the delayed response.[20] Moreover, the White House never took a public position on the proposed changes, which had been initiated during the Obama presidency.[21] Even so, the episode heightened concerns about the role of the administration in the process.[22] It was well-known and widely cited that the Census Bureau's tests of the MENA category and the combined question had witnessed significantly lower rates of white identification among Latino- and MENA-identifying individuals. Advocates criticized the reversal, but another administration intervention arose to command their attention.[23]

On the heels of news about race and ethnic questions, Commerce Secretary Wilbur Ross—serving, in effect, as the head of the Census Bureau since it was without a director—declared in March 2017 that the census would ask a question on citizenship. The last time such a question appeared on the full census was in 1950.[24] The order was notable for several reasons. As sociologist Cristina Mora writes, the Census Bureau did not request the question, and its census advisory committees were not consulted. In addition, the question was not only inserted late in the planning process but also without any prior testing—something at odds with the Census Bureau's own practice. As some Arab American advocates were quick to point out, the Census Bureau claimed that the MENA category needed more testing before it could be included in the census but were willing to add a completely untested question. The question also contradicted the position of recent Census Bureau directors.[25] Indeed, six former directors sent a collective letter to Secretary Ross expressing their belief that "adding a citizenship question to the 2020 census will considerably increase the risks to the 2020 enumeration."[26] While the decision departed from conventional practice and wisdom, Republican officials and anti-immigrant groups have sought a citizenship question for decades.[27] It also appears to have been an early desire of the Trump administration. A leaked White House memo, dated three days after Trump's inauguration, stated that "the U.S. Census Bureau shall include questions to determine U.S. citizenship and immigration status" on the census.[28]

Latino advocates immediately and vehemently objected to the citizenship question. They argued that it was a blatant and politically motivated attempt to instill fear and depress Latino participation in the census. Far from being an isolated act, advocates saw the question as another example of the administration's anti-Latino and anti-immigrant agenda. Maria Teresa Kumar, for example, characterized the question as a ploy to "hijack the integrity of the census in pursuit of its perverse nativist, ideological agenda hoping to bully the second largest group of Americans from accurate representation." When I spoke to Thomas Saenz, MALDEF's president and general counsel, he likened the Trump administration's efforts to an attempt at "statistical genocide." He figured that some would take the phrase as a gross overstatement but believed it captured what was involved and at stake. "Again, I use it advisedly, I say statistical genocide, not real genocide, but I do add there are real-world consequences that threaten livelihoods and lives from statistical genocide. . . . It is a statistical genocide, or an attempt at it, because it was targeting a particular group, and seeking to eliminate them, a significant proportion of them, from the demographic statistics of the country." Saenz expressed a key point about population politics—they can be as much about creating populations as erasing them.

Advocates pushed back against the citizenship question in numerous ways. They held press conferences, wrote opinion pieces, and conducted research to document the negative impact the question would have on Latino participation rates. Although their primary target was Secretary Ross and the Trump administration, they also confronted census officials. For instance, during his response to a Census Bureau presentation during a summer 2018 meeting, NALEO-EF's Arturo Vargas voiced that the 2020 census was no longer the one that they and their collaborators had been planning for the past decade. Owing to the decisions of the administration, census officials were, in essence, "building a plane in flight." While he repeatedly acknowledged the work of the census and vowed to support it, he pleaded with the officials in the room not to forsake their "scientific integrity and mission." They had a responsibility, Vargas added, to "stand up and indicate when its mission is being undermined for purposes other than the collection of accurate data." He warned, "History is watching." The late Angelo Falcón of NiLP floated the idea of "Latino Statistical Disobedience," in case the citizenship question went forward. The act called for not boycotting the census outright but rather "massively lying" on the citizenship question. "If enough people do this, it would render the question unusable by the Trump Administration without affecting the overall count."[29] The need for such a response never came to pass, but had it been implemented, it would have been a historic departure for these civil rights groups.

Most consequential, advocates and their colleagues in other civil rights organizations turned to the courts. They filed numerous amicus briefs for a wave of lawsuits that were filed around the country, the first of which was by New York State.[30] In its amicus brief for the New York lawsuit, the civil rights litigation group and NHLA member LatinoJustice outlined how the question would harm the Latino community. The brief argued that the question would likely reduce participation in the census, lead to a loss of federal funding and commercial investment in Latino communities, and dilute its political power. In May 2018 MALDEF filed a lawsuit in conjunction with Asian Americans Advancing Justice (AAJC), a leading Asian American civil rights group. Representing over two dozen organizations and individuals, civil rights litigators argued that "the inclusion of a citizenship question in the decennial Census violates the equal protection guarantee of the Fifth Amendment because it is motivated by racial animus towards Latinos, Asian Americans, and animus towards non-U.S. citizens and foreign-born persons." As evidence, they used public statements made by Trump and other government officials. Upon the discovery of new evidence, the lawsuit was subsequently amended to state that the original impulse to add the citizenship question did not come at the request of the Department of Justice for purposes of enforcing the Voting Rights Act, as government officials had testified. Rather, the amendment claimed, it was part of a conspiracy to "deprive minorities of their constitutional rights to equal representation and fair allocation of federal funds."[31] It further named Trump and other high-level government officials, including former White House advisor Steve Bannon, then attorney general Jeff Sessions, and then Kansas secretary of state Kris Kobach, as coconspirators.

The MALDEF and AAJC suit was later consolidated into another suit filed in Maryland. The trial judge for that case ruled that the Trump administration violated the enumeration clause in the U.S. Constitution and the Administrative Procedure Act but dismissed the charge of intentional racial discrimination. However, in June 2019 the Supreme Court, in a 5-4 ruling on the New York State lawsuit against the Commerce Department, blocked the citizenship question on the basis of the administration's "contrived" rationale. Advocates breathed a momentary sigh of relief, but this was short lived as the administration continued to pursue citizenship data and curtail the duration of enumeration.[32] In addition, Trump officials sought to exclude noncitizens from congressional apportionment.[33] The move went against historical precedent and constitutional mandate. It was inspired by the Republican Party's "Michelangelo of gerrymandering," Thomas B. Hofeller, who, it was discovered, had written that redistricting Texas districts with citizen-only population statistics "would be advantageous to Republicans and non-Hispanic whites."[34] At each juncture, the civil rights community aggressively opposed this siege of the census. Although not always victorious, their efforts slowed and sometimes halted implementation of the administration's plans.

FIGURE 7.1. "Stand up for our community!" poster. ¡HAGASE CONTAR!, circa 2019. Used by permission of the National Association for Latino Elected and Appointed Officials Educational Fund.

Along with contributing to these legal and political challenges to the administration, Latino advocates worked—as they have for decades—to encourage mass participation in the census. With fewer resources available from the Census Bureau, they tried to address intensified fears about the census triggered by the citizenship question debacle and logistical challenges posed by the coronavirus. Reviving tactics used to promote the 2010 census, advocacy groups once again launched national and local campaigns and collaborated with Spanish-language media to educate the public on the value and safety of the census. Similar to past censuses, promotions emphasized themes of community empowerment, hopeful futures, and resources for social welfare (fig. 7.1). Against great odds, advocates worked toward achieving a complete count of the Latino population.

At the time of writing, it is unknown what impact the Trump administration's schemes had on the 2020 census. Yet eventually, the Census Bureau will produce and release a cascade of statistics. If the past is any indication, its new figures will help reanimate public debate about the meaning of ethnoracial demographic change and its seemingly inevitable transformation of the country.

It's Population Politics!

This book has peered into the population politics of national Latino civil rights organizations. This network, I hope to have illustrated, does not exist in a silo. It is part of, and shaped by, a broader political field and history. With this account, I sought to not only foreground population politics, to focus attention on the wielding of figures of the future. It was also to provide an alternative to naturalistic treatments of demographic change, which often conceive populations and their trends as a wholly unmediated causal force. Commonplace phrases and slogans such as "demography is destiny" or "it's demography, stupid!" express this questionable sentiment.[35]

These phrases need not be present to naturalize populations and demography. There are many examples to draw from; a few should suffice. In 2019 journalist Yoni Appelbaum published the essay "How America Ends." It was the first article to appear in the issue's lead section, titled "On the Forces That Pull Us Apart."[36] In his pensive essay, Appelbaum reflects on the apparent divisiveness and incivility of current U.S. politics. Behind this "rancor" are several culprits—globalization, economic inequality, the "hyperbolizing force of social media," "geographic sorting," and the "demagogic provocations" of Trump. All have played a part, but none represents the "biggest driver." That dubious honor belongs to ethnoracial demographic change. With spirited American exceptionalism, Appelbaum writes, "The United States is undergoing a transition perhaps no rich and stable democracy has ever experienced: its historically dominant group is on its way to becoming a political minority—and its minority groups are asserting their co-equal rights and interests." The country's survival, so Appelbaum believes, hangs in the balance as it confronts a "tectonic demographic shift."[37] The implication is that demographic changes, among but not limited to ethnoracial population changes, are responsible for present and portended political instability.

The attribution of power to demographics is not just a symptom of popular demography. It is very much part of many discussions of academic writings on the subject. This is especially the case in work on white anxieties and fears about the growth of nonwhite populations. For example, in their recent book *National Populism*, European political scientists Roger Eatwell and Matthew Goodwin argue that populist "revolts," such as the election of Trump and Brexit in the United Kingdom, are responses to four "deep-rooted" societal changes. One of these changes is demographic. They argue that what they call "hyper-ethnic change" is "unsettling traditional norms, values, and ways of life and is stoking a backlash from citizens who see it as a demographic and cultural risk."[38] Writing about major upsurges in nativist movements, historical demographer Brian Gratton argues that these surges are "first and foremost products of two necessary and near sufficient demographic forces: very high volume of arrivals and sharp changes in immigrant origins."[39] A similar argument is made by Eric Kaufmann, who concludes that "in most times and places, ethno-demographic change breeds an anti-immigration response among the majority."[40] The point I am making is not that these arguments are entirely unreasonable or empirically unsupported. Rather, it is to highlight how they attribute causal power to demographic trends to spark feelings of anxiety or fear. These responses, along with the political alignments they are often linked to, are framed as seemingly automatic and unmediated outcomes.[41] Lost or downplayed in these analyses are the historical sediments and contemporary sources of population politics, which actively recruit individuals and groups to view trends as transformative, inevitable, and driven by different and often "inferior" or "menacing" populations. Moreover, these conclusions often rest on unstated assumptions about the nature of "racial difference."[42] As sociologist and legal scholar Osagie Obasogie writes, dominant conceptions presume that race is *visually* obvious. Take, for example, the following assertion: "many whites and minorities experience an everyday visual diversity on the street or in public places that is likely to affect their perception."[43] Against this view, Obasogie argues that the capacity to "see" race is socially, politically, and institutionally enabled.[44]

In contrast to the "it's demography, stupid" position, this book has built on and extended work on the cultural and temporal politics of demography. Its point of departure has been that many of the powers ascribed to raw demographics cannot be explained or well understood without first accounting for population politics, past and present. Whether demographic futures inspire hope and fear depends on the discursive and structural waters in which we—you and I—swim. It is population politics that furnish what categories and populations are in play and how these are understood. I have focused on deliberate efforts to enroll peoples and publics to envision and experience U.S. population change in politically specific ways. As the case of national Latino civil rights groups illustrates, demographic interpellations are not always successful. For sociologically discernable reasons, individuals may consider some characterizations and visions more compelling, more resonant than others. Population politics may also generate unexpected identifications and reactions. Nonetheless, it is these messages and materials out of which demographic imaginaries are fashioned, transformed, and pursued.

This approach, I believe, has important implications for how we relate to the issue of demographic change. It implies that there is no neutral position from which to announce or project futures. It applies not only to political movements but also to academics, even those not formally or expressly affiliated with movements. While scholars generally find it easy to point out the interested and situational nature of political ideologies, we generally find it more difficult to admit that academic knowledge and we ourselves are politically implicated as well. The serious social scientist may balk at the demodystopias of political leaders or the sometimes stylized and simplified stories offered by journalists, all the while believing that we can talk about demographics more objectively and more accurately. Perhaps. But while there is meaningful space between willful manipulation and good-faith efforts to understand demographic realities, no account can promise objective, unobstructed truth on the matter. If this point is embraced, the question is not simply better data. While important and useful, such knowledge cannot alone answer how we should think about and relate to purported trends. Good data may offer a sound foundation on which to consider competing forecasts, but again this cannot resolve the normative issues that inescapably exceed numerical representations. As historian Mary Poovey once wrote,

"Statistics *produces* excess in two senses. First, as the 'raw material' for other 'sciences,' statistics enables others to generate theories and legislation that are figured nowhere in the numbers themselves. Secondly, as a discourse that *claims* a transparent relation to the objects it represents, statistical representation masks the meanings it does produce at the same time that it puts these meanings into play."[45] In other words, a retreat to methods will not succeed. The more complicated challenge is to evaluate the political utility and ethical consequences of different conceptions of the demographic future.

Recent calls to move away from "majority-minority" prognostication, such as the important work of Richard Alba and others, exhibit an awareness of the normative conundrums that confront all demographic representations. At stake, Alba contends, is not only better ways to count existing populations but also better narratives. In *The Great Demographic Illusion*, he proposes his own: rather than become a minority, whites may come to form a new majority along with those of "mixed minority-white backgrounds."[46] This narrative is meant, in part, to minimize white anxiousness, to reassure them of the future. Although Eric Kaufmann's book *Whiteshift* comes to somewhat different conclusions, a similar impulse drives it to offer a vision of the future in which whites will remain the symbolic custodians of Western nations among "mixed-race majorities."[47] Each author marshals extensive empirical data, but their arguments transcend them. This is unavoidable. Scholarly analyses cannot adjudicate what are eminently political questions about how we relate to one another, how social and political life should be arranged, and what we envision for the time ahead. As such, these and other accounts need to be judged not only on their empirical foundations and theoretical breadth but also on their normative implications. By the latter criteria, I hold reservations about white appeasement narratives. Such narratives run the risk of legitimating sentiments of white loss and victimhood and reinscribing the sense of entitlement to dictate the terms of the future.

More generally, demographic narratives—whether assurances of little change or declarations of revolution—often encourage a sense of inevitability. Is this, itself, inevitable? Can we relate to the demographic, and therefore to the democratic, otherwise? Can we envision demography without guarantees?[48] In this spirit, this book does not tell what the future holds. Its author does not have the powers of Tiresias.[49] I am only confident that the shape of what is to come will bear, in some way, the signature of the racialized population politics being carried out today in its name.

ACKNOWLEDGMENTS

I dedicate this book to my late mother, Nellie B. Muñiz. My mother was a proud, brilliant Puerto Rican woman. Equally dangerous with a *chancleta* and a red pen, she taught me how to read and write. For her, words were only worth their weight in conviction. Half-hearted writing was not writing at all. I try to live by her many lessons and can only wonder what she would have thought about this book and the questions it takes up and leaves unanswered. All I know is that without her love and insistence, neither I nor it would exist.

———

I have spent the better part of the past decade thinking and researching about the future, how it is envisioned and struggled over. This book is, in some sense, the culmination of that effort. Of course, nothing in these pages was birthed in isolation. It is, very much like the future, a product of a thicket of social relationships. In the span of a few pages, it is impossible to acknowledge every person who has helped me—in large and small ways—along the way. I hope that you can accept this partial accounting here.

The type of research on which this book rests lives or dies on the generosity of what were, at least initially, strangers. Fortunately, many of those I met and sought to speak with were generous to engage with me, to share their thoughts and feelings, and to put me in touch with their colleagues and initiatives. In Rhode Island, where the ideas for this research began, I am especially appreciative of Anna Cano-Morales, Marta Martínez, Pablo Rodríguez, and Doris de Los Santos. Within the Washington, DC, scene, I want to acknowledge Francela Chinchilla, Patricia Foxen, Leni González, Gabriela Lemus, Clarissa Martínez, Eliseo Medina, Ben Monterroso, Tom Saenz, Héctor Sánchez Barba, Arturo Vargas, and Brent Wilkes. In particular, I am grateful to Sindy Benavides for her support and friendship. In Florida, I thank, among others, Yulissa Arce, Doña Fela, Soraya Marquez, the late Rico Piccard, Ben Pusey, Zoraida Rios-Andino, Yanidsi Vélez, and

Marcos Vilar. Without all these and other individuals, I would have had nothing to write about. My hope is that they will find some value in my conclusions and find that I approached their perspectives and efforts with the seriousness and rigor that they demand.

I have been blessed with many intellectual mentors. Four individuals, in particular, encouraged and sharpened my ideas as a Brown University PhD student. From the first day we met, José Itzigsohn has been an unwavering source of support and a model of integrity. Gianpaolo Baiocchi reassured me that I belonged and had something to say, ever encouraging me to take on big questions. With every comment and inquiry, Michael Kennedy pushed me in new and ethically dense directions. Ann Morning's signature is found throughout this book, and I am grateful for her investment in it. Along with other academic mentors who have supported my work and career, I also thank Arlene Dávila, Amanda Lewis, Tyrone Forman, and Amalia Pallares. A special debt of gratitude is owed to Nilda Flores-González. It is because of her foresight and support that I am today a sociologist and professor. Equal parts mentor and friend, Victoria-María MacDonald opened her home to me while I conducted research in Washington, DC, and has read just about everything I've written.

Various intellectual communities have contributed to this work. At Brown, I thank Sinem Adar, Nitsan Chorev, David Ciplet, Ricarda Hammer, Weeam Hammoudeh, Patrick Heller, Paget Henry, Yara Jarallah, Peter Klein, Johnnie Lotesta, Josh Pacewicz, Andrew Schrank, Bhrigupati Singh, Gayatri Singh, and Mark Suchman. After completing my PhD degree, I became a Provost Postdoctoral Fellow at the University of Chicago. The experience was enriching, in no small part thanks to, among others, Kimberly Hoang, Andreas Glaeser, Karin Knorr-Cetina, Xi Song, Robert Vargas, and the terrific undergraduate students of SOC 20246 and 20266.

My colleagues at Northwestern have extended themselves, offered sage advice about life in the academy, and supported my intellectual and pedagogical pursuits. Among the sociological community, I want to acknowledge Claudio Benzecry, Pablo Boczkowski, Larissa Buchholz, Chas Camic, Héctor Carrillo, Tony Chen, Steve Epstein, Wendy Espeland, Gary Alan Fine, Wendy Griswold, Brayden King, Aldon Morris, Ann Orloff, Andy Papachristos, Mary Pattillo, Christine Percheski, Monica Prasad, Quincy Stewart, and all the graduate students I have had the honor to work with for their intellectual generosity and much needed messages of encouragement. The assistance I have received from departmental staff, in particular Murielle Harris and Ryan Sawicki, has saved me time and headaches on numerous occasions. The Latina/o Studies Program has been a second home, where I have counted on the comradeship and mentorship of Frances Aparicio, Carlos Ballinas, Gerry Cadava, Alejandro Carrion, John Cutler Alba, and Myrna Garcia, among others.

Over the years, I have benefited from countless conversations with and comments from colleagues and friends: Gabriel Abend, Abigail Andrews, Mabel Berezin, Yarimar Bonilla, Héctor Cordero-Guzmán, Bruce Curtis, Eileen Díaz-McConnell, Julie Dowling, Kim Ebert, Marion Fourcade, Deborah Gould, Dan Hirschman, Tony Jack, Celia Lacayo, Marisol LéBron, Anat E. Leibler, Mara Loveman, Ann Mische, Cristina Mora, Dina Okamoto, Tianna Paschel, Jan-Hendrik Passoth, Isaac Reed, Nicholas Rowland, Atef Said, Patricia Silver, Ariana Valle, Sylvia Zamora, and Nick Vargas, among others. From the time I began graduate school to the final days of writing this book, Jonathan Rosa has pushed my thinking with his incisive insights and provocations.

Beginning with my time at Brown and Rhode Island, I have drawn inspiration and strength from a group of scholars who have become family. Among these are Tatiana Andia, Marcelo Bohrt, Aisalkyn Botoeva, Karida Brown, Orly Clerge, Brian Conor, Cedric de Leon, Diana Graizbord, Tina Park, Elena Shih, Oscar Sosa, and Trina Vithayathil. Pages could be written about how each of them has sustained me through this wild journey. Writing with Aisalkyn, Cedric, Diana, and Trina has made all the difference at key moments. In Chicago, I've leaned on some good friends in this academic hustle. They've helped keep me sane and smart: Claudio Benzecry, Andy Clarno, Claire Decoteau, Kimberly Hoang, Jennifer Jones, Julie Lee Merseth, Juan Martinez, Robert Vargas, and Angel Vélez.

The book you hold is very much marked by the feedback I received—most fortunately—at three separate manuscript workshops. The first took place relatively early in the book-writing process, and it revived my enthusiasm for the project. It was a huge honor to have Latinx scholars of the caliber of Frances Aparicio, Cristina Beltrán, Gerry Cadava, Leo Chávez, and Amalia Pallares read my work and share their brilliant and generative thoughts with me. The second workshop was no less an honor. I shared my manuscript with students in my fall 2019 undergraduate course on the politics of racial knowledge. Their sophisticated and earnest engagement with my work brought me to tears. I hope they see that I tried to heed their advice and assert my voice. The final workshop, organized by José Itzigsohn and prabhdeep singh kehal, returned me to Brown, where I received the exact feedback I needed to complete the manuscript. Many thanks to José and prab and the graduate students and faculty who participated in the workshop: Amanda Ball, Katie Duarte, Laura Garbes, Elena Shih, Nabila Islam, Subadevan, Nicole González-Van Cleve, and Clare Wan.

Several individuals provided invaluable research assistance at various stages of the project. I want to recognize the fine work of Melia Agudelo, Juliana Cardona, Dori-Taylor Carter, Melissa Cintrón, Sarah Fernández, and Elizabeth Guthrie. Jason Kruse at the Northwestern Library was an invaluable resource.

The content of the book also benefited from audiences at the American Bar Foundation, Brown University, Indiana University-Bloomington, Miami University, New York University, Northwestern University, Notre Dame University, University of California, Berkeley, University of Chicago, University of Connecticut, University of Georgia, University of Illinois-Chicago, University of Oregon, University of San Diego, Worcester State University, and Yale University (Program in the History of Science and Medicine), as well as at conferences of the American Sociological Association, Latinx Studies, Latin American Studies Association, the Social Science and History Association, and the Society for Social Studies of Science. Many thanks to Leslie R. Hinkson and the rest of the 2016 ASA Dissertation Award committee and Leisy Abrego and the rest of the award committee for the 2014 Cristina Maria Riegos Graduate Student Paper of ASA Section on the Sociology of Latinas/os.

Of course, this book would not be in your hands without the talented folks at Princeton University Press. I want to express my sincerest appreciation to my editor Meagan Levinson, Jackie Delaney, Brigitte Pelner, and all those who saw the book to publication. A special thanks to Anita O'Brien for her careful copyediting.

I have to also acknowledge Letta Page for improving the prose and helping me better see what I had been trying (and hoping) to say all along.

This research was made possible with generous funding and support from the Beatrice and Joseph Feinberg Memorial Fund, Ford Foundation, National Science Foundation, and University of Chicago Provost's Career Enhancement Postdoctoral Fellowship.

To conclude, I return to my foundations: my community and my family. I want to thank all the mentors and comrades in the Humboldt Park/Paseo Boricua community and at the Puerto Rican Cultural Center. To José López, thank you for the ever critical questions about the academy and your example of struggle. To Alejandro Molina, your mentorship has been indispensable, and hopefully worth your effort. To Margaret Power and Laura Ruth

Johnson, thank you for the lessons of solidarity and scholarship you have given me. Steve Whitman, you are severely missed. I look forward to working with you all to build the Puerto Rican Chicago Archive.

I am also indebted to friends who have been steadfast in their support and understanding of my long absences: Melissa Cintrón, Matthew and Judy Rodríguez-Díaz, Daryl Stewart, and Ricky Venegas.

And finally, I want to recognize my wonderful family. Those who know me well know that I come from a small and tight-knit family. To my sisters Yvette and Cindy, my tio Tony and tio Albert and adopted uncle Ricardo, my brothers-in-law Pablo and Jeff, and my niece and nephew Mia and Alex, I am grateful for a lifetime of love and laughter.

And to my partner Diana Castillo, thank you for your infinite patience and love. I wouldn't have managed to finish this book without you.

NOTES

Introduction

1. I employ the notion of *ethnoracial* throughout. While "race" and "ethnicity" are often treated as obviously and ontologically distinct, they are historically and conceptually entangled. Indeed, "racial" taxonomies were colonially fashioned through not only through bodily markers but also putative ethnic criteria, such as language and custom. See Barnor Hesse, "Racialized Modernity." For formulations and applications of the notion, see David Theo Goldberg, *Racist Culture*; Linda Alcoff-Martin, *Visible Identities*; and Nilda Flores-González, *Citizens but Not Americans*.

2. Aquatic or hydraulic metaphors have long colored how ethnoracial demographic trends are imagined. These metaphors, have naturalized racialized conceptions of certain populations as threatening and dangerous. Here, I use such metaphors to describe population discourse, not populations themselves. See Eileen Díaz McConnell, "Numbers, Narratives, and Nation"; Otto Santa Ana, *Brown Tide Rising*; Roger Daniels, "Two Cheers for Immigration," 7.

3. Jonathan Vespa, David M. Armstrong, and Lauren Medina, *Demographic Turning Points for the United States*, 6.

4. Sabrina Tavernise, "Why the Announcement of a Looming White Minority Makes Demographers Nervous."

5. It is analytically possible to distinguish those entities that deliberately seek to influence public demographic imaginaries to achieve particular political ends from those that influence without an explicit strategic motivation. Whether this distinction holds in practice or what entities can be placed on either side is an empirical—and not always straightforward—question.

6. See Leo R. Chavez, *Covering Immigration*; Santa Ana, *Brown Tide Rising*; Díaz McConnell, "Numbers, Narratives, and Nation."

7. Josh Sanburn, "U.S. Steps Closer to a Future Where Minorities Are the Majority"; Sabrina Tavernise, "Fewer Births than Deaths among Whites in Majority of U.S. States"; Rafael Bernal, "Hispanic Population Reaches New High of Nearly 60 Million."

8. For example, in 2017, the *New York Times* data blog Upshot featured a "census time machine" in the form of a choropleth map that showed "which counties today resemble what America will look like in decades ahead, and which ones most resemble the nation's ethnic composition as it once was." Niraj Chokshi and Quoctrung Bui, "A Census Time Machine." *TIME* magazine's Time Lab featured a similar story but with an interactive map to illustrate whether a given state was demographically in the "past or future." Unlike the *New York Times*, which claimed Las Vegas, it claimed that current Texas demographics were most indicative of the future. *TIME*, "Find Out If Your State Is America's Past or Future."

9. Sociologists of the media understand "newsworthiness" as constructed rather than inherent to events and issues. Among others, see David L. Altheide, *Creating Fear*.

10. Philip Bump, "Rep. Steve King Warns That 'Our Civilization' Can't Be Restored with 'Somebody Else's Babies.'" King's tweet, in support of a far-right candidate for prime minister

of the Netherlands, is one of many anti-immigrant and racist remarks he has made. To the joy of many civil rights advocates, King failed to win the primary for his 2020 reelection bid.

11. Pierre Bourdieu, *On the State*, 3.

12. The attitude of demographic naturalism is closely enveloped in attitudes of statistical realism. See Alain Desrosières, "How Real Are Statistics?"

13. Bruce Curtis, *The Politics of Population*, 24. See also Bruce Curtis, "The Politics of Demography."

14. Curtis, *The Politics of Population*, 28. Moreover, the academic field of demography has always been concerned with policy and politics. Dennis Hodgson, "Demography as Social Science and Policy Science."

15. William Alonso and Paul Starr, eds., *The Politics of Numbers*, 3.

16. Ann Morning, *The Nature of Race*, 10.

17. Morning has found that the social constructionism has been far less influential than typically assumed. The rise of genomic conceptions of race over the past two decades has raised concerns about the future of racial essentialism.

18. Étienne Balibar, "Is There a Neo-Racism?"

19. Susanne Schultz, "Demographic Futurity," 648.

20. Barnor Hesse, "Counter-Racial Reformation Theory," viii.

21. Barnor Hesse, "Racialized Modernity."

22. Patrick Wolfe, *Traces of History*, 18. See also Dorothy Roberts, *The Fatal Invention*.

23. David Theo Goldberg, *Racist Culture*, 149.

24. Alaka M. Basu, "Demography for the Public." On "garbled demography," see Michael S. Teitelbaum, "The Media Marketplace for Garbled Demography."

25. As anthropologist and demographer Philip Kreager has written about the production of population statistics, "We should not underestimate the feat of imagination this entailed: first, to imagine society as consisting of an idealized and discrete physical substrate of events; second, to create a formal mathematics of this imagined substrate; third, to present the products of these abstract considerations not only as pertaining to real world events, but as a deeper reality in some way capturing the inherent structure and nature of events; and, finally, to introduce these constructs into society in a way that ordinary people—bureaucrats, physicians, householders, grandmothers—would use them to identify themselves and everyday features of their lives." Kreager, "Objectifying Demographic Identities," 38–39.

26. For a broader review of the scholarship on politics and demography, see Michael Rodríguez-Muñiz, "Towards a Political Sociology of Demography."

27. Myron Weiner, "Political Demography," 597.

28. On political demography, see Michael S. Teitelbaum, "Political Demography"; Myron Weiner and Michael S. Teitelbaum, *Political Demography, Demographic Engineering*; Jack A. Goldstone, Eric P. Kaufmann, Monica Duffy Toft, *Political Demography*.

29. On the concept of demographic engineering, see Weiner and Teitelbaum, *Political Demography, Demographic Engineering*; and Paul Morland, *Demographic Engineering*.

30. On innumeracy, see Daniel Herda, "How Many Immigrants?" Richard and R. Alba, Rubén. G. Rumbaut, and Karen. Marotz, "A Distorted Nation." On perceptions of demographic change, see, for example, Maureen A. Craig and Jennifer A. Richeson, "Information about the US Racial Demographic Shift Triggers Concerns about Anti-White Discrimination"; Craig and Richeson, "Hispanic Population Growth Engenders Conservative Shift"; Maria Abascal, "Us and Them"; and H. Robert Outten et al., "Majority Group Members' Negative Reactions to Future Demographic Shifts."

31. See, among others, Joshua Cole, *The Power of Larger Numbers*; Libby Schweber, *Disciplining Statistics*; Susan Greenhalgh, "The Social Construction of Population Statistics"; Emily Klancher Merchant, "A Digital History of Anglophone Demography and Global Population

Control"; Emily A. Marshall, "Population Projections and Demographic Knowledge in France and Great Britain." This scholarship has been closely linked, and overlaps to some extent, with work on the historical emergence of statistics. See Alain Desrosières, *The Politics of Large Numbers*; Mary Poovey, *A History of the Modern Fact*; Ian Hacking, *Taming Chance*; Theodore M. Porter, *The Rise of Statistical Thinking*; Stephen M. Stigler, *The History of Statistics*. For an excellent account of the linkage between statistical techniques and eugenics, see Tukufu Zuberi, *Thicker than Blood*.

32. Paul Starr, "Social Categories and Claims in the Liberal State."

33. Paul Schor, *Counting Americans*; Trina Vithayathil, "Counting Caste"; Patrick Simon, "The Choice of Ignorance."

34. Milica Zarkovic Bookman describes three ways that political actors have tried to shape population counts: decrease through partitioning into subpopulations, increase through aggregation, or erase altogether through refusals to count certain categories or peoples. Bookman, *The Demographic Struggle for Power*.

35. Richard Alba, *The Great Demographic Illusion*. See also Mark Ellis, "What Future for Whites?"; Dowell Myers and Levy Morris, "Racial Population Projections and Reactions."

36. Even so, old decisions can at times be called into question. The shift across Latin America from putatively "color-blind" to "race-conscious" census making provides one example. See Tianna Paschel, *Becoming Black Political Subjects*; Mara Loveman, *National Colors*; and Edward Telles, "Multiple Measures of Ethnoracial Classification in Latin America."

37. Pierre Bourdieu, *Outline of a Theory of Practice*, 79.

38. Anat Leibler, "Disciplining Ethnicity"; Loveman, *National Colors*; Jacob Davey and Julia Ebner, "The Great Replacement."

39. See Susanne Schultz, "Demographic Futurity"; Schultz, "Reproducing the Nation."

40. In *The Textures of Time*, Michael G. Flaherty defines "timework" as "interpersonal and interpersonal effort directed toward provoking or preventing various temporal experiences. The concept implicates the agentic micromanagement of one's own involvement with self and situation" (11). Actors and organizations can also engage in timework to provoke and prevent certain temporal experiences. To distinguish between self- and other-directed timework, particularly those conducted by political projects, I define the latter as temporal tactics.

41. Auyero, *Patients of the State*.

42. Elizabeth Cohen, *The Political Value of Time*.

43. By "racial time," Michael Hanchard means "the inequalities of temporality that result from power relations between racially dominant and subordinate groups. Unequal relationships between dominant and subordinate groups produce unequal temporal access to institutions, goods, services, resources, power, and knowledge, which members of both groups recognize." Hanchard, "Afro-Modernity," 253. See also Charles Mills, "White Time"; Debra Thompson, "Critical Race Temporality"; P. J. Brendese, "Black Noise in White Time."

44. Rahsaan Mahadeo, "Why Is the Time Always Right for White and Wrong for Us?"

45. E. P. Thompson, "Time, Work-Discipline, and Industrial Capitalism."

46. Crystal Marie Fleming, *Resurrecting Slavery*.

47. Debra Thompson includes continuity and disjuncture as two dimensions of her "temporal racial schematics." Thompson, "Critical Race Temporality." For a fascinating account of elite-driven claims to racialized temporal rupture, see Maximilian Viatori, "Rift, Rupture and the Temporal Politics of Race in Ecuador."

48. On the notion of "invented traditions," Eric Hobsbawm, "Introduction." On nationalism and material culture, see, for example, Peggy Levitt, *Artifacts and Allegiances*; Geneviève Zubrzycki, *National Matters*; Nuala Johnson, "Cast in Stone"; Fiona Rose-Greenland, "The Parthenon Marbles as Icons of Nationalism." Statues and other material representations of the nation can also become objects of dispute. Geneviève Zubrzycki, *Beheading the Saint*.

49. This problem is not unique to sociology. As Arjun Appadurai writes, anthropology "remains preoccupied with the logic of reproduction, the force of custom, the dynamics of memory, the persistence of habitus, the glacial movement of the everyday, and the cunning of tradition in the social life of even the most modern movements and communities." Appadurai, *The Future as a Cultural Fact*, 285. As in sociology, this has begun to change. For a recent exegesis, see Rebecca Bryant and Daniel M. Knight, *The Anthropology of the Future*.

50. See, among other works, Barbara Adam and Chris Groves, *Future Matters*; Ann Mische, "Projects and Possibilities"; Gary Alan Fine, *Authors of the Storm*; Iddo Tavory and Nina Eliasoph, "Coordinating Futures"; David Gibson, *Talk at the Brink*; Jens Beckert, *Imagined Futures*; Javier Auyero and Débora Swistun, "Tiresias in Flammable Town"; John Hall, "Social Futures of Global Climate Change"; Johnnie Lotesta, "The Myth of the Business Friendly Economy"; Grégoire Mallard and Andrew Lakoff, "How Claims to Know the Future Are Used." For an account of the earlier "futurist" sociology, see Barbara Adam, "Wendell Bell and the Sociology of the Future."

51. See, for example, Nik Brown and Mike Michael, "A Sociology of Expectations"; Mads Borup, Nik Brown, Kornelia Konrad, and Harro Van Lette, "The Sociology of Expectations in Science and Technology"; Vincanne Adams, Michelle Murphy, Adele E. Clarke, "Anticipation"; Carla Alvial-Palavicino, "The Future as Practice"; Nicholas J. Rowland and Mathew J. Spaniol, "The Future Multiple"; Kaethe Selkirk, Cynthia Selin, and Ulrike Felt, "A Festival of Futures."

52. Mische's dimensions of projectivity are *reach* ("extension into short, medium, long term"); *breadth* ("range of possible alternatives considered"); *clarity* ("degree of elaboration and detail"); *contingency* ("pre-fixed vs. flexible, uncertain, dependent futures"); *expandability* ("expanding vs. contracting futures"); *volition* ("relations of motion, influence and control"); *sociality* ("consideration of future actors, relations and interactions"); *connectivity* ("imagined logic of temporal connection"); and *genre* ("recognizable narrative conventions or dramatic templates"). Ann Mische, "Measuring Futures in Action."

53. Mike Michael, "Futures of the Present."

54. Demographic projections are often taken as predictions rather than forecasts. Nathan Keyfitz, "The Social and Political Context of Population Forecasting."

55. Desrosières, "How Real Are Statistics?"

56. For a starting point into this now vast scholarship, see Theodore M. Porter, *Trust in Numbers*; Ian Hacking, *Taming Chance*; Mary Poovey, *A History of the Modern Fact*; Sarah E. Igo, *Averaged American*; Patricia Cline Cohen, *A Calculating People*.

57. While worthwhile, books such as Joel Best's *Damned Lies and Statistics* have their limits. They can, inadvertently or not, encourage people to reify statistics rather than confront the more politically and ethically complicated reality that all numbers are, to some extent, "cooked." Accordingly, the power of numbers cannot be reduced to their apparent "truth." Even numbers that are deemed valid can produce a wide range of intended and unintended consequences. For this reason, some scholars have called for greater attention to the utility of numbers rather than simply their accuracy. Crystal Biruk, *Cooked Data*; Curtis, *The Politics of Population*.

58. In sociology, the "sociology of quantification" is a relatively recent development. As Wendy Espeland and Mitchell Stevens write, "Quantification is a constitutive feature of modern science and social organization, yet sociologists have generally been reluctant to investigate it as a sociological phenomenon in its own right." Espeland and Stevens, "The Sociology of Quantification, 402." For recent reviews, see Elizabeth Popp Berman and Daniel Hirschman, "A Sociology of Quantification"; Andrea Mennicken and Wendy Nelson Espeland, "What's New with Numbers?"; Rainer Díaz-Bone and Emmanuel Didier, "Introduction."

59. Curtis, "The Politics of Demography."

60. Michel Foucault, *Security, Territory, Population*, 109. As Bruce Curtis shows, Foucault naturalized "populations," considering it something that statistical methods discovered rather than constructed. See Curtis, "Foucault on Governmentality and Population."

61. James C. Scott, *Seeing Like a State.*

62. Debra Thompson, *The Schematic State.* There is growing interest in statistics as a tool of critique and emergent forms of what has been called "statactivism." See Alain Desrosières, "Statistics and Social Critique"; Isabelle Bruno, Emmanuel Didier, and Tommaso Vitale, "Statactivism."

63. Ian Hacking, *Taming Chance,* 3.

64. Sarah E. Igo, *Averaged American.*

65. See, for examples, David Theo Goldberg, *Racial Subjects*; Jacqueline Urla, "Cultural Politics in an Age of Statistics"; David I. Kertzer and Dominique Arel, "Censuses, Identity Formation, and the Struggle for Political Power"; Arjun Appadurai, "Number in the Colonial Imagination"; Tom Waidzunas, "Young, Gay, and Suicidal"; Geoffrey C. Bowker and Susan Leigh Star, *Sorting Things Out.*

66. Nikolas Rose, "Governing by Numbers"; David Scott, *Refashioning Futures*; Julia Paley, "Making Democracy Count."

67. See Wendy Espeland and Vincent Jung, "Ethical Dimensions."

68. Martin de Santos, "Fact-Totems and the Statistical Imagination."

69. Daniel Hirschman, "Stylized Facts in the Social Sciences."

70. Over the past decade, social scientists and political theorists have turned to the term "affect" to capture the nonlinguistic and noncognitive dimensions of human social existence. See William Connolly, *A World of Becoming*; Deborah B. Gould, *Moving Politics*; Brian Massumi, *Parables for the Virtual.* Similar to many scholarly concepts, "affect" has been defined in numerous ways and should not be confused with Affect Control Theory. While most recent works distinguish affect from emotions, I treat them here as closely related.

71. On the emotive and affective properties of numbers, see Kathleen Woodward, *Statistical Panic*; Wendy Nelson Espeland and Michael Sauder, *Engines of Anxiety*; Sung-Joon Park, "Nobody Is Going to Die."

72. Michal Kravel-Tovi, "Accounting of the Soul," 713.

73. James M. Jasper, "Emotions and Social Movements."

74. Gould, *Moving Politics.*

75. Arjun Appadurai, *The Future as Cultural Fact.*

76. Sara Ahmed, "Affective Economies," 119.

77. In his recent work, cultural critic Jeff Chang credited the term to Stanford anthropologist H. Samy Alim, who defined demographobia as "the irrational fear of changing demographics," Chang, *Who We Be.* But, to my knowledge, it appears that the origins of the term lie outside of the United States. The term seems to have been first used by the former Israeli diplomat Yoram Ettinger as the title of a 2006 commentary. In the commentary, Ettinger argued against Israeli territorial concessions to Palestinians, charging that these decisions are rooted in a "demographic fatalism" he contends is unsupported by population trends. Ettinger, "The Case Against Demographobia." From a critical perspective, scholar Shourideh C. Molavi has described the centrality of racialized demographobia to the Israeli state: "In addition to control over the land, demographic control is also a cornerstone to the Zionist project. The Zionist settler-colonial paradigm dictates that the 'right' people—namely Jews—must settle the land and that this population must constitute a majority of the total population of the state to maintain its Jewish character. A recurring concern for Israeli national security officials, and a stimulant of periodic geographic and topographic changes to the state, demographobia, or the pathological fear of and concern around non-Jewish (i.e. Palestinian-Arab) births, has shaped Israel's public debate." Molavi, *Stateless Citizenship,* 138–39.

78. Hiro Saito, "Reiterated Commemoration," 373.

79. Eduardo Bonilla-Silva, "Feeling Race."

80. John David Skrentny, *The Minority Rights Revolution.* An exception is the League of United Latin American Citizens (LULAC), founded in 1929. Jack L. Walker, *Mobilizing Interest Groups in America.*

81. NHLA was formed out of the union of the National Hispanic Leadership Conference and the National Hispanic Agenda. Rodolfo O. de la Garza and Louis DeSipio, "Latinos and the 1992 Election," 38.

82. Several of these organizations have both 501c3 and 501c4 status, which allows for some partisan work. For example, Voto Latino, which was originally a 501c3 organization, recently became a 501c4 group. It subsequently created the Voto Latino Foundation as its 501c3 component. My focus in this book is on their nonpartisan work.

83. John McCarthy and Mayer Zald, "The Trend of Social Movements in America," 20.

84. There has been some debate about whether such organizations should be considered social movements. Kenneth T. Andrews and Bob Edwards argue for a synthetic approach that sees interest groups, social movements, and nonprofit organizations as sharing "a core focus on the pursuit of a collective good framed in the public interest." Andrews and Edwards, "Advocacy Organizations in the U.S. Political Process," 485.

85. Among this network of organizations, UnidosUS/NCLR's budget of $36 million dwarfs the others. The next largest is NALEO-EF, with over $12 million, and the rest are under $5 million. All figures as of 2016.

86. LULAC has hundreds of semiautonomous councils around the country. Members elect its national board and president at its annual convention. All these positions are volunteer. This board empowers a national office led by a paid CEO. I focus on the national office and its leadership. On debates about membership versus nonmembership organizations, see Edward T. Walker, John D. McCarthy, and Baumgartner, "Replacing Members with Managers?"

87. Francis, "The Price of Civil Rights." In the 1960s and 1970s the major concern was the pacifying influence of philanthropy, particularly the Ford Foundation, which funded the founding of what became the National Council of La Raza and the Mexican American Legal Defense and Educational Fund. See Benjamin Marquez, "Mexican-American Political Organizations and Philanthropy"; Benjamin Marquez, "Trial by Fire"; and Victoria-María MacDonald and Benjamin Polk Hoffman, "Compromising La Causa?" Today, the major concern is the influence of corporate donors.

88. See, for example, Craig Allan Kaplowitz, *LULAC, Mexican Americans, and National Policy*; Benjamin Marquez, *LULAC*; G. Cristina Mora, *Making Hispanics*.

89. See also Samantha L. Perez and Joshua Murray, "Latino Faces, Corporate Ties."

90. In this sense, advocacy organizations can be conceptualized as "boundary organizations." Thomas Medvetz, "Murky Power."

91. Chavez, *Latino Threat Narrative*; and Dávila, *Latino Spin*.

92. One underpinning liberal assumption is that representation should rest on numercial majorities. As David Scott theorized in the context of colonial Sri Lanka, numbers came to be seen as rational and modern, embued with the capacity to manage "primordial" ethnic strife through an "abstract egalitarian ratio." However, such numbers normalized the very idea of "majorities" and "minorities," and the accompanying sense that demography should structure democratic governance. This, in turn, intensifed ethnopolitical tensions. David Scott, *Refashioning Futures*.

93. It is an emotionally challenging enterprise, which at times requires, as Erving Goffman famously remarked, a willingness "to be a horse's ass." Goffman, "On Fieldwork." The "costs" of ethnographic research are not, as Kimberly K. Hoang argues in *Dealing in Desire*, equally distributed. As challenging as I found fieldwork, I no doubt benefited from the fact that I am a light-skinned Puerto Rican, cis-male researcher, at the time from an Ivy League institution.

94. Although sociology and anthropology have a long tradition of ethnographies of political life, interest in "political ethnographies" has grown over the past two decades. For useful introductions in sociology, see Javier Auyero, "Introductory Note to Politics under the Microscope"; Gianpaolo Baiocchi and Brian Connor, "The Ethnos in the Polis." Claudio Benzecry and Gianpaolo

Baiocchi argue that self-designated political ethnograpies rarely discuss what is political in political ethnography. Lacking reflexivity, researchers impose their conception of what is and is not political on the social world being studied. They propose a "lowest common denominator definition" that involves "following actors and taking their activities and understandings seriously" and remaining, at least initially, agnostic "about what might be the privileged social location of political activity." Claudio Benzecry and Gianpaolo Baiocchi, "What Is Political about Political Ethnography?"

95. The word "peopled" is an allusion to Gary Alan Fine, "Towards a Peopled Ethnography." Fine advances a conception of ethnography that is theoretically ambitious and focused on the interactions of small groups of people. As evidenced in his own work, nonhuman objects can mediate interactions and meaning making. See, for example, Gary Alan Fine, *Players and Pawns*. Science studies, and in particular Actor-Network Theory, has been a major influence on the recent "material turn" in ethnographic research; see Terence E. McDonnell, *Best Laid Plans*; Antina Von Schnitzler, *Democracy's Infrastructure*; Diana Graizbord, Michael Rodríguez-Muñiz, and Gianpaolo Baiocchi, "Expert for a Day"; Alex V. Barnard, "Making the City 'Second Nature'"; Wendy Griswold, Gemma Mangione, and Terence E. McDonnell, "Objects, Words, and Bodies in Space."

96. I say uneven because I assumed authorial power to represent both. On "landscapes of meaning," see Isaac Ariail Reed, *Interpretation and Social Knowledge*.

97. As Claudio Benzecry writes, "We don't record the totality of social life in a particular place. We organize a reality that is multiform, complex and contradictory, according to (and as such limited by) the questions we want to answer. It is this limitation—the fact that we are limited by theory, language and selfhood—that actually allows us to produce this kind of knowledge." Benzecry, "What Did We Say They've Said?," 31.

98. On Puerto Rican and Latinx Orlando, see Patricia Silver, *Sunbelt Diaspora*; Simone Delerme, *Latino Orlando*; Ariana J. Valle, "Race and the Empire-State"; Jorge Duany, "The Orlando Ricans."

99. As Michael Whyte writes, returns to the "field" to update information are "not a simple linear process: more stories, more events, more money, and greater insight. It is more than continually capturing the latest installment in an ongoing story. By returning again and again, we are not simply being brought up to date. We participate in a temporal process that is also transformative: we are ourselves updated. The two processes are linked. By returning again and again, we learn more—and we become capable of understanding more." Whyte, "Episodic Fieldwork, Updating, and Sociability," 120.

100. Robert K. Merton and Patricia L. Kendall, "The Focused Interview."

101. Cristina Beltrán, *The Trouble with Unity*.

Chapter 1. Demographic Futures Past

1. Reinhart Koselleck, *Futures Past*.

2. Reinhart Koselleck, *Sediments of Time*, 3. Analytically, Koselleck distinguished between three layers. The first was the singularity of events. The second was structures of repetition. He maintained that singular moments, or events, could transform landscapes, but these rested on repetition—itself a source not only of stability but of change. Some layers of historical experience, he added, can outlive individual lifespans and generational cohorts. Such layers, the third in his framework, were metahistorical.

3. Stefan-Ludwig Hoffman and Sean Franzel, "Introduction: Translating Koselleck," in *Sediments of Time*, xiv. Translators Franzel and Hoffman chose "sediments" to capture the German word *zeitschichten*. "It is in good part to access this process of accretion (and erosion) over time that we have chosen to translate *Zeitschichten* as 'sediments' of time rather than the more geologically precise 'strata.'"

4. Natalia Molina, *How Race is Made in America*.

5. David Scott, *Conscripts of Modernity*, 4. Problem-space is a conceptual device, a way of thinking about the intellectual and political parameters and possibilities available within a given historical context. As anthropologist Scott writes, the concept refers to "the ensemble of questions and answers around which a horizon of identifiable stakes (conceptual as well as ideological-political stakes) hangs." The specific questions raised and answers given, in the course of any political struggle, are neither infinite nor free-floating. Rather, problem-spaces are historically and situationally circumscribed, loosely tethered to material, institutional, and practical exigencies. These pressures are not, however, wholly determinative. Some latitude to challenge and critique always exists.

6. Andreu Domingo, "Demodystopias." Domingo, a demographer, discusses demodystopias as a "literary subgenre" that emerged in the first half of the twentieth century. I am using the term more broadly as any discourses that cast demographic trends as threatening and negative.

7. Dennis Hodgson, "Benjamin Franklin on Population," 639.

8. Matthew Connelly, *Fatal Misconception*, 6.

9. Erika Lee, *America for Americans*, 18, 34. It is a historical irony, and perhaps cautionary tale for Franklin's ideological descendants today, that his anti-German diatribes, which fueled German political opposition, led to the demise of Franklin's electoral career.

10. Peggy Pascoe, *What Comes Naturally*.

11. Rickie Solinger, "Bleeding across Time," 64; see also Pascoe, *What Comes Naturally*; and David A. Hollinger, "Amalgamation and Hypodescent."

12. See Melissa Nobles, *Shades of Citizenship*; Paul Shor, *Counting Americans*. Antimiscegenation laws were also passed to prohibit marriage between whites and nonwhites. On prohibition against Asian-white marriages, see Deenesh Sohoni, "Unsuitable Suitors."

13. George Fredrickson, *The Black Image in the White Mind*, 5.

14. Cedric de Leon, "Why 1861?"

15. J. Mills Thornton, *Politics and Power in a Slave Society*, 206.

16. George Fredrickson, *The Black Image in the White Mind*, 244, 254.

17. Sang Hea Kil, "Fearing Yellow, Imagining White," 672.

18. Although commonly known as the Chinese Exclusion Act, the 1882 act only restricted Chinese immigration. It was the subsequent 1888 act that instituted exclusion. Beth Lew-Williams, *The Chinese Must Go*. See also Erika Lee, *At America's Gates*.

19. Lew-Williams, *The Chinese Must Go*, 9.

20. Mark Ellis, "What Future for Whites?," 218.

21. Connelly, *Fatal Misconception*, 44.

22. Nell Irvin Painter contends that the idea of a single "white race" would be consolidated in the U.S. public imagination after the First World War. Painter, *The History of White People*.

23. Madison Grant, *The Passing of the Great Race*.

24. Jean-Guy Prévost and Jean-Pierre Beaud, *Statistics, Public Debate and the State, 1800–1945*.

25. Mae M. Ngai, *Impossible Subjects*.

26. Lothrop Stoddard, *The Rising Tide of Color against White World-Supremacy*, 5.

27. Ian Frazier, "When W.E.B. Du Bois Made a Laughingstock of a White Supremacist."

28. For a distillation of Du Bois as a theorist of racialized modernity, see José Itzigsohn and Karida L. Brown, *The Sociology of W.E.B. Du Bois*.

29. Koselleck, *Sediments of Time*.

30. Edmund Ramsden, "Social Demography and Eugenics in the Interwar United States."

31. Carole R. McCann, *Figuring the Population Bomb*; Connelly, *Fatal Misconception*; Emily Klancher Merchant, "A Digital History of Anglophone Demography."

32. Solinger, "Bleeding across Time," 70.

33. Solinger, "Bleeding across Time," 76.

34. The speech was drafted by Daniel Patrick Moynihan, Nixon's urban affairs advisor and the author of the controversial report *The Negro Family: The Case for National Action*. Derek S. Hoff, "Kick That Population Commission in the Ass."

35. Hoff, "Kick That Population Commission in the Ass," 30.

36. Charles Westoff, "The Commission on Population Growth and the American Future," 494.

37. Commission on Population Growth and the American Future, *Population and the American Future*, 1.

38. Connelly, *Fatal Misconception*, 251. For an excellent discussion of public and scientific discourse about "ghetto containment," see Solinger, "Bleeding across Time," 70–75.

39. Commission on Population Growth and the American Future, *Population and the American Future*, 108, 113.

40. Ozzie Edwards, "The Commission's Recommendations from the Standpoint of Minorities," 466.

41. Commission on Population Growth and the American Future, *Population and the American Future*, 293–94. Olivárez, a figure about whom little has been written, anchored her pointed criticism on the facts of U.S. history: "Many of us have experienced the sting of being 'unwanted' by certain segments of our society. Blacks were 'wanted' when they could be kept in slavery. When that ceased, blacks became 'unwanted'—in white suburbia, in white schools, in employment. Mexican-American (Chicano) farm laborers were 'wanted' when they could be exploited by agri-business. Chicanos who fight for their constitutional rights are 'unwanted' people. One usually wants objects and if they turn out to be unsatisfactory, they are returnable. How often have ethnic minorities heard the statement: 'If you don't like it here, why don't you go back to where you came from'? Human beings are not returnable items. Every individual has his/her rights, not the least of which is the right to life, whether born or unborn."

42. Charles Westoff, "The Commission on Growth and the American Future," 494.

43. Westoff, "The Commission on Growth and the American Future."

44. In a 1970 letter to the president of the Sierra Club, Phillip Berry, Patrick Moynihan expressed: "In the United States the distribution of the population is at least as important as its absolute size. We are one of the least densely populated countries in the world and will likely remain so, with one of the slowest rates of growth. Yet we are highly concentrated, with a large majority of our people living on a small fraction of our land." Hoff, "Kick That Population Commission in the Ass," 33.

45. See Hoff, "Kick That Population Commission in the Ass," 22.

46. Commission on Population Growth and the American Future, *Population and the American Future*, 199.

47. Commission on Population Growth and the American Future, *Population and the American Future*, 200, 203.

48. Elena R. Gutiérrez, *Fertile Matters*.

49. On the popularization of the notion "illegal," see Edwin Ackerman, "What Part of Illegal Don't You Understand?"

50. Paul R. Ehrlich, Loy Bilderback, and Ann H. Ehrlich, *The Golden Door*, xiii.

51. Ehrlich, Bilderback, and Ehrlich, *The Golden Door*, 236; Chavez, *The Latino Threat*, 85.

52. The connection between eugenics and conservation has a long history, including figures like Madison Grant. See Jade S. Sasser, *On Infertile Ground*, 55.

53. Gutiérrez, *Fertile Matters*, 83.

54. Tanton tried numerous times to convince the conservationist Sierra Club to adopt an immigration control policy, most recently in the early 2000s. Gutiérrez, *Fertile Matters*, 93.

55. The book seems to have helped spark Tanton's concern with the environmental impacts of immigration. *The Camp of the Saints* witnessed a revival on the extreme right and was endorsed by former Trump aide Steve Bannon. For an insightful cultural sociological analysis of the novel and Bannon's anti-enlightenment thought, see Jeffrey C. Alexander, "Raging against the Enlightenment."

56. John Tanton, "WITAN Memo III."

57. Alfonso Gonzales, *Reform without Justice*, 28.

58. Gutiérrez, *Fertile Matters*, 93.

59. Adam Goodman, *The Deportation Machine*, 111.

60. The characterization of Mexican immigration as an "invasion" is old. As noted earlier, the Chinese had been described as an "unarmed invasion." In the 1920s Samuel J. Holmes, a University of California zoologist, applied this trope to the fertility of Mexican immigrants. At the time, news outlets like the *New York Times* prognosticated that since Mexicans were "largely Indian in blood," their immigration could lead "to a new 'race' problem." Arguments like these, growing in popularity alongside concerns with labor competition, led census officials to statistically segregate Mexicans from whites in the 1930 census and motivated the newly formed Immigration and Naturalization Services (INS) to ramp up deportations in the decades that followed.

61. Leo R. Chavez, *Covering Immigration*. Chavez offers the most in-depth cultural analysis of media discourse on immigration in the post-1965 period. He found an increasingly alarmist depiction in text and images beginning in the late 1970s. For a quantitative account that confirms this finding, see Douglas S. Massey and Karen A. Pren, "Unintended Consequences of US Immigration Policy."

62. G. Cristina Mora, *Making Hispanics*.

63. Leo Grebler, Joan W. Moore, and Ralph Guzmán, *The Mexican-American People*.

64. Mora, *Making Hispanics*, 23.

65. The promised "White House Conference on Mexican Americans" never took place. Instead, an event was held in El Paso, more pomp than substance, doing little to convince leaders that the administration took this population and its needs seriously. Indicative of the state of panethnic solidarity in 1966, the White House's push to have the event include Puerto Ricans was rebuffed by Mexican American leaders. See Benjamin Francis-Fallon, *The Rise of the Latino Vote*, 127–30.

66. John Skrentny, *The Minority Rights Revolution*, 123.

67. National Education Association, *The Invisible Minority . . . Pero No Vencibles*.

68. Helen Rowan, *The Mexican American*, 4, 5.

69. Julian Samora, "Conclusion," in *La Raza*, 206.

70. *National Journal*, "The Growing Hispanic Population," 549.

71. Khalil Gibran Muhammad, *The Condemnation of Blackness*; Debra Thompson, *The Schematic State*; David Theo Goldberg, "Taking Stock."

72. Hugh Davis Graham, *The Civil Rights Era*, 199.

73. Thompson, *The Schematic State*, 103.

74. NCLR, *Impact of Limited Federal Statistical Data/Information on Hispanic Americans*, 2, 3.

75. On the concept of "legibility" and modern statecraft, see James C. Scott, *Seeing Like a State*. With regard to the census and ethnoracial legibility, see Thompson, *The Schematic State*; and Michael Rodríguez-Muñiz, "Cultivating Consent."

76. President Johnson established the U.S. Interagency Committee on Mexican-American Affairs (ICMAA) in 1967. He appointed Vicente Ximenes, a Texas-born Mexican American with ties to LULAC, as chair of the committee. The announcement came on the same day that Johnson also appointed Ximenes to the Equal Employment Opportunity Commission. Two years later the ICMAA was renamed the Cabinet Committee on Opportunities for Spanish Speaking People and given a more explicitly panethnic mandate. For a historical account of the formation and work

of the ICMAA and CCOSSP, see Benjamin Francis-Fallon, *The Rise of the Latino Vote*, and Mora, *Making Hispanics*.

77. Nixon's intervention was no doubt part of a concerted effort to court Mexican voters. For a detailed history of the role of party politics in creating the "Latino vote," see Francis-Fallon, *The Rise of the Latino Vote*.

78. On Mexicans and Mexican Americans, among others, see Cybelle Fox and Thomas A. Guglielmo, "Defining America's Racial Boundaries"; Natalia Molina, "Medicalizing the Mexican"; Laura E. Gómez, *Manifest Destinies*. On Puerto Ricans, among others, see Laura Briggs, *Reproducing Empire*; Hilda Lloréns, *Imagine the Great Puerto Rican Family*; Julian Go, *American Empire and the Politics of Meaning*; Mara Loveman, "The U.S. Census and the Contested Rules of Racial Classification."

79. Brian Gratton and Emily Klancher Merchant, "La Raza."

80. Julie Dowling, *Mexican Americans and the Question of Race*.

81. Jennifer Leeman, "Racializing Language."

82. For instance, in the 1960 census only in New York City did the Census Bureau include a "redundant nativity question that distinguished 'U.S., Puerto Rico, Elsewhere' as places of birth, and asked whether those born 'Elsewhere' were U.S. citizens." Ira S. Lowry, *The Science and Politics of Ethnic Enumeration*.

83. H. M. Choldin, "Statistics and Politics."

84. Leeman, "Racializing Language." Leeman interprets the reliance of linguistic markers in the face of linguistic variation as evidence of the close linkage between race and language historically upheld by census administrators. By the turn of the twentieth century the Census Bureau had already begun to treat "mother tongue as a hereditary characteristic passed from one generation to the next, *regardless of actual language use*" (519, emphasis in original). This essentialist, hereditary, binding of language to group would attach most firmly to Mexicans and other Latinos, serving as a primordial rationale for panethnic categorization. The existing historical record does not tell us if leaders shared or disagreed with essentialist readings of "Latino" origins. We only know that they felt that many members of their communities could not be adequately counted through "Spanish language" measures.

85. Mora, *Making Hispanics*.

86. Mora, *Making Hispanics*, 89.

87. U.S. Commission on Civil Rights, *Counting the Forgotten*, iii.

88. Frank Del Olmo, "Spanish-Origin Census Figures Revised by U.S." In the article, Mario Obledo, then director of MALDEF and a member of the Mexican-American Population Commission of California, was quoted as saying, "I'm glad the Census Bureau took us seriously and that our efforts have been vindicated."

89. Nobles, *Shades of Citizenship*, 79.

90. Federal Interagency Committee on Education, *Report of the Ad Hoc Committee on Racial and Ethnic Definitions*, 13, 12.

91. Francis-Fallon, *The Rise of the Latino Vote*; Mora, *Making Hispanics*.

92. Even the choice of "Hispanic" was much more complex and contested than admitted in the report. Some members of the FICE ad-hoc committee preferred Latino and Hispano. One member later recalled, "There was never any consensus in that group to the very end. . . . We came up with an agreement, but . . . there were some bad feelings. I know two people who didn't speak for up to a year after it was over." Victoria Hattam, *In The Shadow of Race*, 117–18.

93. Mora, *Making Hispanics*, 100–101.

94. Rubén Rumbaut, "Making a People," 21.

95. Mora, *Making Hispanics*.

96. NCLR, *Impact of Limited Federal Statistical Data/Information on Hispanic Americans*, 11.

97. Carlos Conde, ed., *The Spanish Speaking People of the United States*, 9.

98. Francis-Fallon, *The Rise of the Latino Vote*.

99. Mora and Okamoto argue that *Agenda* and other pan-Latino publications were comparatively less critical of the U.S. state and less concerned with international relations compared to pan-Asian magazines of the same period. These differences are grounded in different structural conditions and the political fields in which these projects developed and navigated. See Cristina Mora and Dina Okamoto, "Postcolonialism, Racial Political Fields, and Panethnicity."

100. Guadalupe Saavedra, "On Powerlessness."

101. Reynaldo F. Macías, "U.S. Hispanics in 2000 A.D.—Projecting the Number," 16.

102. There is some debate about whether Yzaguirre pioneered the expression. *Los Angeles Times* columnist and editor Frank Del Olmo attributed it to Maria Elena Torano, a Cuban American official in the Carter administration: "We haven't had the Vernon Jordans and the Jesse Jacksons. We haven't had the civil-rights battles. But we are being sensitized. The blacks had the decade of the '60s; women had the '70s. The '80s will be the decade for Hispanics." Frank Del Olmo, "Latino 'Decade' Moves into '90s"; *U.S. News & World Report*, "Hispanics Push for Bigger Role in Washington."

103. Raúl Yzaguirre, "The Decade for Hispanics," 2.

104. Conde, *The Spanish Speaking People of the United States*, 1.

105. Joel Kotkin, "Lack of Clout."

106. Raul Yzaguirre, "Letter to the Editor." Referring to demographic projections about the future size of the Black and Latino populations, respectively, Yzaguirre commented: "We've been powerless because the media have never picked up on it. Somehow it has never been a sexy issue. So, for the first time, it looks like we're going to be the nation's largest minority, and we're finally beginning to make some kind of impact."

107. Robert García, "Hispanics: Diversity and Unity."

108. Frank Del Olmo, "City, County to be One-Fourth Latin by 1980, Study Predicts."

109. Robert Lindsey, "Hispanics Lead U.S. Minorities in Growth Rate."

110. Reid Miles, *Hispanic Americans Soon*.

111. George Russell, "It's Your Turn in the Sun," 48.

112. Russell, "It's Your Turn in the Sun," 48.

113. Russell, "It's Your Turn in the Sun," 50.

114. Chavez, *The Latino Threat*.

115. Russell, "It's Your Turn in the Sun," 58.

116. Samuel Huntington, "Hispanic Challenge," 30.

117. Matthew Connelly, "To Inherit the Earth," 318.

118. Koselleck, *Futures Past*.

Chapter 2. Strength in Numbers

1. Claims about representation cannot be separated from the fact that this political project exists within a liberal democratic system indentured to the numerically based "majoritarian principle." As the anthropologist David Scott writes, "In the late modern political world we inhabit it appears self-evident to us that rule ought to be in the hands of the largest number, that is, of the majority. There is a relationship between abstract number and political representation that we take for granted as defining the field of possible argument about justice, and there is a calculus of probabilities that we can invoke to supply—and ground—the rationality that connects the distribution of number and political outcomes." Scott, *Refashioning Futures*, 162.

2. Rodríguez-Muñiz, "Cultivating Consent."

3. Eric Newburger, *2010 Census Integrated Communications Program*, 6.

4. NiLP was originally known as the Institute for Puerto Rican Policy, an important center for policy analysis and research in New York founded in 1982.

5. In the late 1970s, race and ethnicity advisory committees were established by the Census Bureau to diffuse political controversy over undercounts and to change public opinion about the census in minoritized communities. Sociologist Harvey Choldin writes, census officials believed that "if these minority leaders could be persuaded that the census was valuable and trustworthy, perhaps they could influence their groups to cooperate." See Harvey Choldin, *Looking for the Last Percent*. In 2012 REAC was reconstituted as the National Advisory Committee on Racial, Ethnic, and Other Populations.

6. U.S. Census Bureau, "Census Information Centers." Established in 1990, this little-known Census Bureau initiative was developed to share data and provide technical assistance to under-served populations. In a 2010 assessment of the program, Falcón notes that "people of color are projected to become a majority of the US population in the not too distant future," and access to "timely and useful data and tools for analysis increases in urgency if they are to have a greater voice in public policy discussions." Angelo Falcón, *Data Dissemination to Communities of Color*.

7. In 2009 testimony before the U.S. House of Representatives Oversight and Government Reform Committee, Subcommittee on Information Policy, Census, and National Archives, Vargas stated that only 6 percent of the Census Bureau staff identifies as Latino, rendering it the "most under-represented segment of the Bureau's permanent workforce."

8. NALEO-EF, "NALEO Educational Fund Urges Swift Confirmation of Dr. Robert Groves."

9. Vargas's point is strongly supported by empirical scholarship on the subject. See, for example, Michael Hajime Miyawaki, "Part-Latinos and Racial Reporting in the Census"; Steven Hitlin, J. Scott Brown, and Glen H. Elder, Jr., "Measuring Latinos"; and Clara E. Rodríguez, Michael H. Miyawaki, and Grigoris Argeros, "Latino Racial Reporting in the US."

10. Tim Padgett, "Still Black or White." While Voto Latino softly encouraged Latinos to self-identify racially as "some other race," most national Latino advocacy did not promote identification with particular categories. Other organizations, such as the Afro-Latin@ Forum, a coalition of intellectuals and community activists primarily based in New York City, produced bilingual public service announcements encouraging Latinos and Latinas of African descent to identify as "Latino" and "Black" on the census. Concerns with ethnic and racial classification were not limited to Latinos. The Arab Complete Count Committee in Orange County, California, garnered national media coverage with its slogan "Check it right; you ain't white!" John Blake, "Arab- and Persian-American Campaign."

11. NALEO-EF, "NALEO Educational Fund Urges Swift Confirmation of Dr. Robert Groves."

12. Harvey Choldin, "Statistics and Politics."

13. Historically, fear of the state has motivated evasion of or resistance to censuses. See Patrick Carroll, *Science, Culture, and Modern State Formation*; Scott, *Seeing Like a State*; Curtis, *The Politics of Population*; and Mara Loveman, "The Modern State and the Primitive Accumulation of Symbolic Power." Although census promoters, including Latino advocates, stress the legal protections of census participation, there are several examples of direct or indirect collaboration and communication between the Census Bureau and intelligence agencies. Recent scholarship paints a more complicated picture of the census, revealing, for instance, moments of interagency collaboration, such as the case of World War II Japanese internment and more recent post-9/11 surveillance of Muslim and Arab Americans. See William Seltzer and Margo Anderson, "The Dark Side of Numbers"; Margo Anderson, *The American Census*, 194; Samia El-Badry and David A. Swanson, "Providing Census Tabulations to Government Security Agencies in the United States."

14. ICE was the successor to the Immigration and Naturalization Service (INS).

15. Underwritten by conservative anti-immigration groups, such as FAIR, state-level anti-immigrant ordinances and bills increased dramatically in the mid-2000s. The defeat of the punitive "Sensenbrenner Bill" and the political mobilization it triggered across the country contributed to the shift from federal to state policy among restrictionists. See Pratheepan Gulasekaram and S. Karthick Ramakrishnan, *The New Immigration Federalism*; Alfonso Gonzales, *Reform without Justice*.

16. One of S.B. 1070's most controversial provisions required local and state police to act as immigration authorities when "reasonable suspicion exists that the person is an alien and is unlawfully present." Although in 2012 the U.S. Supreme Court ruled in *Arizona v. United States* (11-182) that certain aspects of the bill were unconstitutional, the "show me your papers" provision, as it was termed by civil rights advocates concerned with racial profiling, was spared. Among national and local Latino advocates, S.B. 1070 exemplified a pervasive anti-immigrant and anti-Latino sentiment in U.S. society. For more on S.B. 1070 and its effects, see Rogelio Sáenz, Cecilia Menjívar, and San Juanita Edilia Garcia, "Arizona's SB 1070"; Cassaundra Rodriguez, "Fueling White Injury Ideology."

17. U.S. Census Bureau, "Census Bureau Announces Award of 2010 Census Communications Contract."

18. U.S. Census Bureau, *2010 Census Integrated Communications Campaign Plan*, 34.

19. The eight "Diverse America" clusters were (1) All Around Average I (homeowner skewed), (2) All Around Average II (renter skewed), (3) Economically Disadvantaged I (homeowner skewed), (4) Economically Disadvantaged II (renter skewed), (5) Ethnic Enclave I (homeowner skewed), (6) Ethnic Enclave II (renter skewed), (7) Single Unattached Mobiles, and (8) Advantaged Homeowners. Clusters 3 and 7 were considered hard to count relative to the others and thus deserving of more attention.

20. U.S. Census Bureau, *2010 Census Integrated Communications Campaign Plan*, 10.

21. Jonathan Rosa, *Looking like a Language, Sounding like a Race*, 7. See also Jonathan Rosa and Nelson Flores, "Unsettling Race and Language."

22. Michael Rodríguez-Muñiz, "Cultivating Consent."

23. Pierre Bourdieu, "Rethinking the State," 4.

24. For a detailed account of the campaign's formation, see David R. Ayón, "Mobilizing Latino Immigrant Integration."

25. Miriam Jordan, "Groups Seek Better Count of Hispanics."

26. Núria Net, "Make Your Pledge."

27. U.S. Census Bureau, "Complete Count Committee Guide," 8.

28. Ross Novie, *Voto Latino Presents*.

29. Christina Bellantoni, "Republican Senators Vitter, Bennett Attempt to Force Census to Ask Immigration Status"; NALEO-EF, "NALEO Condemns Vitter-Bennett Amendment."

30. Latino advocates were not alone in their opposition to the amendment. See the *New York Times* editorial "How to Waste Money and Ruin the Census."

31. LULAC, "Victory in the Senate with the Halt of the Vitter Amendment."

32. Adelle M. Banks, "Hispanic Groups Divided over 2010 Census."

33. Esteban Israel, "Fearful, Angry Latinos Might Shun Census."

34. ¡HAGASE CONTAR!, *Census 2010*.

35. NALEO-EF, "Largest Hispanic Evangelical Networks in the Nation Support an Accurate Count of the Latino Community in the 2010 Census."

36. Julia Preston, "Latino Leaders Use Churches in Census Bid."

37. Frank James, "Census Poster Tie-in to Jesus, Mary and Joseph Inflame Some"; Haya El Nasser, "Group's Census Promo Called 'Blasphemous.'"

38. Eric Young, "Faith Groups Mobilized to Raise Census Awareness with Jesus Story."

Chapter 3. A New American Reality

1. Reflecting on the position of the African American people in the United States, W.E.B. Du Bois famously wrote, "One ever feels his two-ness,—an American, a Negro; two souls, two thoughts, two unreconciled strivings; two warring ideals in one dark body, whose dogged strength alone keeps it from being torn asunder." W.E.B. Du Bois, *The Souls of Black Folk*.

2. In her 2006 autobiography, Salinas described demographic and linguistic change as the most monumental development she has witnessed as a journalist. "The uncontainable growth of the Latin population would change the face and, yes, also the North American accent" (my translation). Maria Elena Salinas and Liz Balmaseda, *Yo Soy la Hija de Mi Padre (I Am My Father's Daughter)*.

3. Others also drew ethnic meaning from the video. A Puerto Rican voter registration coordinator in Florida told me that when she first saw it, she cried: "It's really empowering. It's about damn time that we get recognized as these types of people, the in-betweeners, and we should be proud of that. I mean, I'm proud of it now. I wasn't before because I just always thought I had to be so Puerto Rican or I had to be so American."

4. Guy García, "Are Hispanics the New American Reality?"

5. Fred Polak, *The Image of the Future*.

6. Eviatar Zerubavel, "Lumping and Splitting."

7. Qualification has some resonance with notions like "qualculation." Michel Callon and John Law, "On Qualculation, Agency, and Otherness."

8. This is not to suggest that numbers simply await narration; in particular contexts, numbers can also "elicit new narratives, new stories about what they mean, how they unfold, and if they are fair or unfair, or who made them." Wendy Espeland, "Narrating Numbers," 56.

9. Mikhail M. Bakhtin, *The Dialogic Imagination*, 250.

10. Although Bakhtin explored chronotopes in literature, social scientists, led by linguistic anthropologists, have demonstrated the broader utility of the concept for understanding social narratives. See, for example, Ilkka Tuomi, "Chronotopes of Foresight"; Jonathan Rosa, "Racializing Language, Regimenting Latinas/os"; Ryan Blanton, "Chronotopic Landscapes of Environmental Racism"; Jan Blommaert, "Chronotopes, Scales, and Complexity in the Study of Language in Society."

11. Nicholas Jones is currently the director and senior advisor of race and ethnic research and outreach in the Census Bureau's Population Division.

12. These standards are inscribed in Directive 15, which was originally adopted in 1977 and last revised in 1997. For historical background, see Victoria Hattam, "Ethnicity & the Boundaries of Race"; Ann Morning and Daniel Sabbagh, "From Sword to Plowshare"; Mora, *Making Hispanics*.

13. Paul Starr, "Social Categories and Claims in the Liberal State." Starr argues that official categories—those generated or sanctioned by governmental agencies—are distinct in several ways from everyday and scientific categories.

14. Mora, *Making Hispanics*.

15. At a minimum, the Census Bureau provides the materials with which social actors and organizations assemble and articulate images of the future. At a maximum, it is, instead, an active contender in these struggles over how the country's demographic future should be perceived, felt, and acted on. Historically, as political scientist Melissa Nobles has shown, census officials have oscillated between these positions. Melissa Nobles, *Shades of Citizenship*.

16. Dan Keating and Carol Morello, "Census Offers New Proof That Hispanic, Asian Growth Skyrocketed"; Susan Saulny, "Census Data Presents Rise in Multiracial Population of Youths"; Wendell Marsh, "U.S. Hispanic Population Tops 50 million."

17. Keating and Morello, "Census Offers New Proof."

18. Ronald Brownstein, "America's New Electorate."

19. Associated Press, "Census: Hispanics Now Comprise 1 in 6 Americans."

20. Michael Martinez and David Ariosto, "Hispanic Population Exceeds 50 Million."

21. Similar to other media representations of Latino demographic growth, the title used Spanish ("los") to communicate that population change would have linguistic consequences. It also homogenized the Latino population as a Spanish-speaking population.

22. On Black and Latino juxtaposition after 2000, see Ilia Rodríguez, "Telling Stories of Latino Population Growth in the United States." Although Latinos are supposedly of any race and had identified racially as both White and Black, these categories were treated as mutually exclusive. Far more than in 2010, this practice has increasingly been challenged, most notably by the rise in Afro-Latinx identification and political organizing.

23. Danielle Kurtzleben, "7 Ways the U.S. Population Is Changing."

24. Conor Dougherty, "Population Leaves Heartland Behind."

25. U.S. Census Bureau, "Most Children Younger than Age 1 Are Minorities."

26. My discussion focuses on a few "ideal types." I understand these valences as relational and operating on a continuum.

27. Patrick J. Buchanan, *Suicide of a Superpower*, 132, 166.

28. Ann Coulter, *¡Adios, America!*, 28.

29. Kathleen Woodward, *Statistical Panic*.

30. Vanessa Cárdenas, Julie Ajinkya, and Daniella Gibbs, *Progress 2050*, 6, 12.

31. William H. Frey, *Diversity Explosion*, ix, x, 245.

32. Some GOP forecasters hold out hope for the possibility of moving some populations to the right, thereby replenishing the conservative base.

33. Alain Desrosières, "How Real Are Statistics?"

34. In 2013 Latino advocates, led by NALEO's Education Fund, raised awareness about the undercount of Latino youth.

35. U.S. Census Bureau, "Most Children Younger than Age 1 Are Minorities." News of the Census Bureau's claim that nonwhite births in 2011 exceeded those of whites generated a wave of U.S. and international media coverage. Here is a sampling: Carol Morello and Ted Mellnik, "Census: Minority Babies Are Now Majority in United States"; Conor Dougherty and Miriam Jordan, "Minority Births Are New Majority"; Tavernise, "Whites Account for Under Half of Births in U.S."; Dennis Cauchon and Paul Overberg, "Census Data Shows Minorities Now a Majority of U.S. Births"; *BBC News*, "Non-Hispanic US White Births Now the Minority in US."

36. NALEO-EF, "Nevada Latino Population Skyrockets"; "New Jersey Owes Population Growth to Latino Community"; "Latinos Fuel Illinois Population Growth"; "North Carolina Latino Population Swells"; and "Latinos Key to Texas Population Growth."

37. NALEO-EF, "Latinos Play Major Role in Nation's Growth."

38. De Santos, "Fact-Totems and the Statistical Imagination."

39. This claim to largeness contrasts with the "fear of small numbers" that generates anxiety among American Jewish leaders. Michal Kravel-Tovi, "Accounting of the Soul."

40. Arturo Vargas, "This Is the New Face of America."

41. As scholars have shown, aesthetic aspects of statistical presentation are nearly as important as their informational dimensions. Edward R. Tufte, *The Visual Display of Quantitative Information*.

42. Wendy Nelson Espeland and Mitchell L. Stevens, "A Sociology of Quantification."

43. Espeland, "Reverse Engineering and Emotional Attachments," 298.

44. Although analytically distinct, curatorial choices, such as the decision to present data on the "Latino" population, can also work to *qualify* data.

45. Sharon R. Ennis, M. Rios-Vargas, and Nora G. Albert, "The Hispanic Population: 2010."

46. The 2016 version of this fact sheet does include subgroup information. It is one of a handful of exceptions to the singular emphasis on panethnicity. This is likely due to the fact sheet's continued use of the same format.

47. Janet Murguía, "Hispanic Values Are American Values."

48. Mora, *Making Hispanics*.

49. Vargas, "This Is the New Face of America."

50. Héctor E. Sánchez, Andrea L. Delgado, and Rosa G. Saavedra, *Latino Workers in the United States*, 8.

51. Patricia Foxen and Sara Benitez, *The 2010 Census*.

52. Mara Loveman, *National Colors*, 180.

53. NCLR, *Using NCLR's Latino Kids Data Explorer*, 2.

54. Wendy Espeland and Michael Sauder, *Engines of Anxiety*, 37.

55. Vargas, "This Is the New Face of America."

56. Patricia Foxen, Sara Benitez, and Clarissa Martinez de Castro, "Nationwide Growth in the Latino Population," 1.

57. Foxen, Benitez, and Martinez de Castro, "Nationwide Growth in the Latino Population," 4.

58. Foxen, Benitez, and Martinez de Castro, "Nationwide Growth in the Latino Population," 4.

59. Arlene Dávila, *The Latino Spin*, 4.

60. Michael C. Dawson, *Behind the Mule*.

61. Jennifer A. Jones, *The Browning of the New South*.

62. Henry Cisneros, "Latinos and the Law of Large Numbers."

63. Erasmo Nieves-Martinez, *Encouraging Science Education and Careers among Latinos*.

64. During the speech, audience members challenged Obama's refusal to issue an executive order ceasing deportation. Playing with the Cesar Chávez quote, which the 2008 Obama campaign appropriated, the crowd began to repeatedly chant "Yes you can!" Obama responded, "Believe me—believe me, the idea of doing things on my own is very tempting. I promise you. Not just on immigration reform. But that's not how—that's not how our system works." Despite that, on two occasions, political pressure moved Obama to undertake executive action on immigration: his executive order, Deferred Action for Childhood Arrivals (DACA), was issued in summer 2012 and expanded in November 2014. After this speech, Obama never returned to speak at NCLR (Vice President Joe Biden, Attorney General Eric Holder, and Michelle Obama have spoken in his stead).

65. Henry Cisneros, *Latinos and the Nation's Future*, 6.

66. Ernest Gurulé, "Latinos 50 Million Strong."

67. For Mikhail Bakhtin, the chronotope of crisis was the "most fundamental instance" of the broader chronotope of threshold. Bakhtin, *The Dialogic Imagination*, 248.

68. Michael Omi and Howard Winant, *Racial Formation in the United States*.

69. Dávila, *The Latino Spin*.

70. Ruben Navarrete, "Don't Be Afraid of America's Changing Demographics."

71. Murguía, "Hispanic Values Are American Values."

Chapter 4. Awakening a Giant

1. Jonathan Rosa writes, the video "delivers an emphatic message about the importance of the Latina/o vote while also speaking to disparate audiences whose perspectives are understood to be fundamentally distinct from one another." Jonathan Rosa, "Racializing Language, Regimenting Latinas/os," 116.

2. English translation: "I don't understand why we don't vote as though we were the majority. / Our people represent 12% of the army. / We are 50 million and growing. But we only vote at 7%?"

3. David Stark and Verena Paravel, "PowerPoint in Public."

4. Science and technology studies scholars have noted that demonstrations have a future-oriented character. See Noortje Marres, *Material Participation*. In a related vein, Andrew Barry

has highlighted that the suffix "demo," among various connotations, also "implies provisionality." As in a music demo, a demonstration is "a display of the possibility of a real object, rather than its actualization." Andrew Barry, "Demonstrations"

5. Ann Mische, "Measuring Futures in Action," 438.

6. Proactive mobilization includes both electoral and nonelectoral political participation. Ricardo Ramírez, *Mobilizing Opportunities*, 8.

7. Lisa Garcia-Bedolla and Melissa R. Michaelson, *Mobilizing Inclusion*.

8. Hector Becerra, "Latino Vote Not Set in Stone for Obama."

9. Field observations conducted in Florida prior to the 2012 election revealed that get-out-the-vote coordinators and canvassers were extremely vigilant against partisanship. During door-to-door visits, in fact, canvassers adamantly refused to give endorsements, even when repeatedly asked by potential voters. While it is possible that canvassers were performing nonpartisanship in my presence, I have no reason to believe this was the case.

10. Daniel Kreiss, *Prototype Politics*; Kreiss, *Taking Our Country Back*.

11. Julián Castro is the former mayor of San Antonio and former U.S. secretary of housing and urban development, and Joaquín Castro is a Texas congressman. The Castros emerged in this period as a Democratic counterpoint to Republican Latino and Latina figureheads, such as Florida senator Marco Rubio and former New Mexico governor Susana Martinez.

12. NALEO is, to be sure, not unique in this regard. Voto Latino has hosted several "Power Summits" in recent years, and the respective annual meetings of NCLR and LULAC routinely feature sessions on Latino political empowerment, which, explicitly or implicitly, take as their point of departure the vexing question of demographics-to-power translation.

13. As noted in chapter 1, the existence of and interest in statistics about the Latino electorate is historical development, aided by the institutionalization and popularization of the panethnic category "Hispanic/Latino" and the formation of a knowledge production industry focused on "Latinos" and their economic and electoral preferences. In the political field, Latino-targeted polling has grown exponentially since the 2004 presidential election—the election that controversially found Latinos moving closer to Ronald Reagan's famous assertion that "Hispanics are Republican. They just don't know it yet." For a discussion of the debate about Latino support for George W. Bush in the 2004, see Arlene Dávila, *The Latino Spin*. For a longer history of the role of partisan politics in constituting the idea of a "Latino Vote", see Francis-Fallon, *The Rise of the Latino Vote*.

14. Gustavo Valdes, "Latino Officials See Big Hispanic Vote in 2012."

15. Bruno Latour, *Science in Action*.

16. *TIME*, "Yo Decido: Why Latinos Will Pick The Next President." The cover sparked considerable controversy, not only in claiming a specific group as the election's deciding factor but also because of its inclusion of a non-Latino among the twenty faces that adorn the cover. Dylan Stableford, "Time Magazine Apologizes for Putting Non-Latino on 'Yo Decido' Cover."

17. Richard Stengel, "America's New Decisionmakers."

18. Hector Becerra, "Obama Says Latinos Could Be 'Big Reason' He Wins Second Term."

19. Cristina Beltrán, *The Trouble with Unity*, 4.

20. Janell Ross, "Latino Voters 2012."

21. Sara Benitez, "Latino Children Will Add Nearly 15.8 Million Potential Voters to the Electorate."

22. There are ideological and structural reasons for their commitment to this vision. "Confronted by an interest-group paradigm that rewards national over regional interests and cohesive voting blocs that can be quickly mobilized around a recognizable set of issues, Latino elites have found it useful to present themselves as a politically cohesive national minority group equivalent to African Americans." Beltrán, *The Trouble with Unity*, 101.

23. Paul Taylor et al., *When Labels Don't Fit*.

24. See Michael Jones-Correa and David L. Leal. "Becoming 'Hispanic'"; José Itzigsohn, *Encountering American Faultlines*.

25. The Pew report, and specifically its findings about racial identity, was widely discussed in relation to the murder of Trayvon Martin. Martin's killer, George Zimmerman, was born to Euro-American and Peruvian parents. See Michael Martin, "In Trayvon Martin Case, Who's Considered White?"; Jorge Ramos Avalos, "The Nameless Many"; Ilan Stavans, "George Zimmerman, Hispanics, and the Messy Nature of American Identity."

26. Paloma Esquivel, "Latino or Hispanic?"

27. Jorge Ramos Avalos, "The Nameless Many."

28. Beltrán, *The Trouble with Unity*, 106. The Pew report was also critiqued in the press. The popular online media outlet *Latino Rebels*, for example, responded: "Because the type of information Pew spewed out (yes, we have always wanted to use the verb 'spewed' next to 'Pew') did very little to what the BIG GOAL is now for the 50 million: true unity and true political power. (If indeed those are the goals that US Latinos/Hispanics truly want, which we think they do.)" *Latino Rebels*, "The Problem with Pew Polls about Being Latino."

29. Eileen Diaz McConnell and Edward A. Delgado-Romero, "Latino Panethnicity."

30. Beltrán, *The Trouble with Unity*, 127.

31. Janet Murguía, "Diverse Identities but Much Common Ground."

32. Beltrán, *The Trouble with Unity*, 127.

33. Donna St. George and Brady Dennis, "Growing Share of Hispanic Voters Helped Push Obama to Victory"; Elise Foley, "Latino Voters in Election 2012 Help Sweep Obama to Reelection"; Elizabeth Llorente, "Election 2012"; Cindy Y. Rodriguez, "Latino Vote Key to Obama's Re-election."

34. Jeff Zeleny and Jim Rutenberg, "Divided U.S. Gives Obama More Time."

35. *La Opinión*, "El Voto Latino Pesó."

36. Elizabeth Llorente, "Obama Victory Proof That the Sleeping Latino Giant Is Wide Awake."

37. Paul Taylor et al., "An Awakened Giant."

38. *Fox News*, "Latinos Highlight America's Changing Face"; Nancy Benac and Connie Cass, "Face of US Changing."

39. Josh Levs, "The New America."

40. Roberto Suro, "The Power of the Latino Vote."

41. Rodriguez, "Latino Vote Key to Obama's Re-election."

42. Julia Preston and Fernanda Santos, "A Record Latino Turnout, Solidly Backing Obama."

43. Preston and Santos, "A Record Latino Turnout, Solidly Backing Obama."

44. Janet Murguía, "The Latino Vote."

45. Arturo Vargas, "Election 2012 and the Future of Latino Politics."

Chapter 5. Dreams Deferred

1. Social actors can envision short-term futures or "place themselves within larger time frames." Population politics, I argue, can enable the formation of demographic trajectories, which can connect the present to a faraway future. Iddo Tavory and Nina Eliasoph, "Coordinating Futures," 913.

2. Ben Anderson, "Preemption, Precaution, Preparedness."

3. Vincanne Adams, Michelle Murphy, and Adele E. Clarke, "Anticipation"; Andrew Lakoff, "Preparing for the Next Emergency."

4. Mische, "Measuring Futures in Action."

5. Jeff Zeleny and Jim Rutenberg, "Divided U.S. Gives Obama More Time."

6. Ray Suarez, "Hispanics and National Politics."

7. The title of the article played on the widely popular E. L. James romance trilogy, *50 Shades of Grey*.

8. Whit Ayres, Jon McHenry, and Luke Frans, *2012*.

9. Benjy Sarlin, "RNC Memo Cites Demographics, Bush, Sandy in Romney Loss."

10. Kevin Cirilli, "Condi: GOP Sent 'Mixed Messages.'"

11. The report is referring here to the 2011 election of two Latino Republican state governors, Brian Sandoval (Nevada) and Susana Martinez (New Mexico).

12. Republican National Committee, *The Growth and Opportunity Project*, 4, 7, 8.

13. S. 1348 was a failed bipartisan bill, led by McCain and Democrat Ted Kennedy.

14. Medina also commented on McCain's shift to the right on immigration in a 2010 op-ed. See Eliseo Medina, "Immigration Policy a GOP Weak Spot."

15. Héctor Sánchez, "Latinos Delivered, Now It is Your Turn Mr. President."

16. Daniel J. Tichenor, *Dividing Lines*.

17. Tichenor, *Dividing Lines*.

18. As political scientist Alfonso Gonzales has written, an "anti-immigrant bloc" composed of think tanks, intellectuals, pundits, and state officials has made concerns with security and border control hegemonic. He argues that immigration reformers, including national Latino advocacy groups, are "structurally locked into a game of perpetual compromise" that demands they "accept and lobby for state practices and policy proposals that include militarization of the U.S.-Mexico border and interior enforcement as a 'fair compromise' for immigration reform." Gonzales, *Reform without Justice*.

19. Muneer I. Ahmad, "Beyond Earned Citizenship," 259.

20. On the Dreamer movement, see Walter J. Nicholls, *The DREAMers*. For a sociological account of the formation of the contemporary immigrant rights movement, see Walter J. Nicholls, *The Immigrant Rights Movement*.

21. Their document used the phrase "unauthorized immigrants," but most of the senators used "illegal immigrants" throughout the press conference.

22. Elizabeth F. Cohen, "Out of Line." Cohen finds that the line-standing frame, which predominates in debate about undocumented legalization, began to proliferate no earlier than 2005. This framing, she writes, "encourages some people to think of affirmative action or immigration amnesties as unfair because they mistakenly regard those programs as violating line-standing and 'firstness' principles" (11).

23. One key difference: the administration's principles did not stipulate that certain security metrics had to be met before the path to citizenship would begin.

24. Gonzales, *Reform without Justice*.

25. The Alliance for Citizenship was the successor to Reform Immigration for America, a coalition developed after the successive failures to pass comprehensive immigration reform in 2006 and 2007. Led by Washington, DC-based organizations like the Center for Community Change and the National Council of La Raza and funded by major liberal foundations such as the Ford Foundation and Open Society, these coalitions nationalized the immigrant rights movement in support for CIR. For an account of this process and its political consequences, see Nicholls, *The Immigrant Rights Movement*.

26. NHLA, "NHLA Statement on Bipartisan Senate Immigration Reform Plan."

27. LULAC, "Latino Groups Issue House of Representatives 'Incomplete' Grade."

28. LULAC, "LULAC Decries Obama's Militarization of the US Border with Mexico."

29. NHLA, "NHLA Launches Latinos United for Immigration Reform Campaign."

30. LULAC, "LULAC Applauds Gang of Eight's Consensus."

31. NHLA, "NHLA Statement on President Obama's Immigration Proposal."

32. NHLA, "NHLA Launches Latinos United for Immigration Reform Campaign."

33. Amalia Pallares, *Family Activism*, 17.

34. Walter J. Nicholls and Justus Uitermark, "A Virtuous Nation and Its Deserving Immigrants."

35. For recent research on the politics and consequences of "deservingness" frames, see Sébastien Chauvin and Blanca Garcés-Mascareñas, "Becoming Less Illegal"; Caitlin Patler and Roberto G. Gonzales, "Framing Citizenship"; Abigail L. Andrews, "Moralizing Regulation"; Pallares, *Family Activism*; and Grace Yukich, "Constructing the Model Immigrant."

36. Hiroshi Motomura, *Americans in Waiting*.

37. Benjamin Page and Felix Reichling, *The Economic Impact of S. 744*.

38. LULAC, "Senate Passes Historic Bipartisan Immigration Reform; LULAC Urges House to Do the Same."

39. Tom K. Wong, *The Politics of Immigration*, 30–31. Some recent scholarship has found that economic arguments, however, may not be as potent as often believed. See, for example, Irene Bloemraad, Fabiana Silva, and Kim Voss, "Rights, Economics, or Family?"

40. This idea of passivity fuels the notion of the sleeping giant. See Beltrán, *The Trouble with Unity*.

41. E-Verify is a federal program designed to ascertain whether a prospective or existing employee is legally eligible to work in the United States. While the program is mandated for federal agencies and employers receiving funds from the federal government, states have shown considerable variation in uptake, as some require all employers to participate in the program and others chose to abstain from it.

42. Thom File, *The Diversifying Electorate*.

43. Mark Hugo López and Ana González-Barrera, *Inside the 2012 Latino Electorate*.

44. Bryan Llenas, "'Record' Hispanic Voter Turnout in 2012 a Misnomer"; Chris Cillizza, "The Hispanic Vote Is a Sleeping Political Giant."

45. Antonio González, "Why the Latino Vote Underperformed in 2012."

46. Loren McArthur, "The Latino Vote Can Make a Difference in the 2014 Elections."

47. NALEO-EF, "New Census Analysis Confirms Record Latino Vote."

48. Sean Trende, "The Case of the Missing White Voters."

49. Sean Trende, "The Case of the Missing White Voters, Revisited."

50. Cheryl K. Chumley, "Sen. Lindsey Graham." Graham's choice phrasing perhaps originated in an *Economist* editorial, "Death Spiral."

51. Jennifer Steinhauser, "Speaker 'Confident' of Deal."

52. Martin Luther King, Jr., *Why We Can't Wait*.

53. Maria Teresa Kumar, "Mr. President, Sign Immigration Executive Action."

54. Walter J. Nicholls, Justus Uitermark, and Sander van Haperen note that the phrase first appeared in 2011 but received little fanfare. Two years later, in May 2013, Dreamers used it in a banner drop in a Chicago rally, after which it began to gain currency. Nicholls, Uitermark, and van Haperen, "The Networked Grassroots," 15. Exactly a month before Murguía's speech, in February 2014, Joanne Lin, a legislative counsel with the American Civil Liberties Union, published a commentary in the *Huffington Post* titled "Deporter-in-Chief."

55. Among many, see Reid J. Epstein, "NCLR Head"; Donna Cassata, "Head of NCLR Calls Obama the 'Deporter in Chief'; Latino Rebels, "Immigration Activists Applaud NCLR Leader's 'Deporter-in-Chief' Obama Comments"; Justin Sink, "Obama Rebukes Deportation Criticism"; Michael Shear and Julia Preston, "Deportation Policy Shift Is Signaled by Obama."

56. Nicholls, Uitermark, and van Haperen. "The Networked Grassroots," 16.

57. David Nakamura, "Obama: 'I'm the Champion-in-Chief' on Immigration Reform."

58. José Magaña-Salgado, *Detention, Deportation, and Devastation*.

59. Shannon O'Neil, "Immigration Reform Is Dead"; David Nakamura and Ed O'Keefe, "Immigration Reform Effectively Dead"; Burgess Everett and Seung Min Kim, "Immigration Reform Looks Dead."

60. LULAC, "Latino Groups Issue House of Representatives 'Incomplete' Grade."

Chapter 6. Reaction and Reversal

1. A later NALEO-EF analysis found that 8 percent of eleven thousand unique calls were "flagged as potential violations of the law or a breach of sound and fair election administration." NALEO-EF, "New Report Outlines Problems Experienced by Latino Voters."

2. On "unsettled times," see Ann Swidler, "Culture in Action."

3. François Hartog, *Regimes of Historicity*, xv.

4. Kenneth R. Timmerman, "Trump Awakens the Sleeping Giant of America."

5. The lead article framed "Hispanic" voters as the "major driver" of ethnoracial and electoral diversification. Tim Albert, "Can the GOP Overcome Demographic Change in Red States?"

6. Alan Gomez, "Another Election Surprise"; John Paul Brammer, "'The Latino Vote' Didn't Overwhelm Trump"; Harry Enten, "Trump Probably Did Better with Latino Voters than Romney Did"; Roberto Suro, "Here's What Happened with the Latino Vote"; Laura Meckler and Aaron Zitner, "Donald Trump's Win Bucks Warnings from GOP"; Asma Khalid, "Latinos Will Never Vote for a Republican, and Other Myths."

7. Ruben Navarrette, Jr., "The Latino Vote Didn't Save America." Before the election, Navarrette notes, he had likened "Latinos for Trump" to "Chickens for Colonel Sanders." Having expected that Latino voters would help "save the republic from Donald Trump," he worried they would now be in need of saving.

8. John O'Sullivan, "The Latino Voting Surge That Never Happened."

9. Janet Murguía, "Your Voice Is More Important Now than Ever Before."

10. National Latino organizations have contracted Latino Decisions to poll identified Latinos on voter habits, political attitudes, perspectives on the economy, among other topics.

11. Sarah Wheaton and Steven Shepard, "Latino Groups Argue Exit Polls Were Too Generous to Trump."

12. Matt A. Barreto, Tyler Reny, and Bryan Wilcox-Archuleta, "Survey Methodology and the Latina/o Vote."

13. After the 2004 presidential election there was prolonged contention over how many Latino voters had supported George W. Bush and whether the Latino vote was shifting toward the Republican Party. See Dávila, *The Latino Spin*.

14. In op-eds and blog posts, Latino Decisions principals also critiqued the NEP, reiterating critiques they have previously made about how mainstream agencies poll Latinos. See Latino Decisions, "Lies, Damn Lies, and Exit Polls." See also Gabriel Sánchez and Matt A. Barreto, "In Record Numbers, Latinos Voted Overwhelmingly Against Trump." This elicited methodological challenges and claims that Latino Decisions' work for the Clinton campaign made them less objective.

15. National Latino Civic Engagement Table, "National Latino Civic Engagement Table Reacts to 2016 Election."

16. This idea, popular in academic and political circles, was connected to the discovery of the "white working class." The emphasis on this sector failed to recognize or willfully ignored the fact that it was middle-class whites who delivered the White House to Trump. For an excellent critique of the "economic" argument, see Gurminder K. Bhambra, "Brexit, Trump, and 'Methodological Whiteness.'"

17. Grégoire Mallard, "From Europe's Past to the Middle East's Future," distinguished between "historical" and "forward" analogies, the difference being that in the former similitude has been observed and in the latter it is assumed or anticipated. Or, in the language of Koselleck, the forward analogy belongs to the horizon of expectation and the historical one to the space of experience.

18. Thomas A. Saenz, "Rust Belt to Brown Belt."

19. The historical analogies that advocates used contrast with some articulations of anti-immigrant and white supremacist discourse, which have often employed "forward analogies" about demographic catastrophes to build support. Among the right, California has long been

employed to forewarn about ethnoracial demographic change. See, for example, Victor Davis Hanson, *Mexifornia*.

20. UnidosUS, "Trump's Plea for Unity in State of the Union Rings Hollow."

21. Bart Bonikowskia and Paul DiMaggio, "Varieties of American Popular Nationalism."

22. Debra Thompson, "An Exoneration of Black Rage," 467.

23. NHLA, *Hispanic Public Policy Agenda*, 5. For example, the "Message from the Chair" stated: "More than 58 million Latinos reside in and make meaningful contributions to the nation every single day. In the last ten years, Latinos represented more than half of total U.S. population growth. This significant demographic change signals a shift in community attitudes, political representation, and electoral power. Indeed, the Census estimates that by 2050 Latinos will comprise nearly one third of the entire nation's population."

24. Each theme was subdivided into subthemes. For example, the theme of civil rights included sections on voting rights, the census, criminal justice, and mass incarceration, among others. For each theme and subtheme, a narrative of the problem or challenges was provided, along with recommendations endorsed by the entire coalition.

25. NHLA, "Letter to President Barack Obama." NHLA was concerned that the cabinet would be left without any Latino representation after the departures of Secretary of Labor Hilda Solis and Interior Secretary Ken Salazar.

26. To respect the privacy of participants, I will not directly attribute any statements to particular individuals from my observations of NHLA board meetings.

27. See Cristina Beltrán, "Racial Presence versus Racial Justice."

28. Thomas A. Saenz, "Trump Brown-Out."

29. Ken Kollman, *Outside Lobbying*, 3.

30. NHLA, "Latino Leaders Condemn White House's Proposed Immigration Framework."

31. Alice O'llstein, "Latino Org in Chaos after Its Prez Goes Rogue."

32. *Latino Rebels,* "LULAC President's Letter to Trump."

33. National Institute of Latino Policy, "LULAC Responds to Rocha Letter."

34. *Latino Rebels*, "Despite Trump Letter Being Retracted."

35. Julio Ricardo Varela, "LULAC President Says He Won't Resign."

36. Suzanne Gamboa, "LULAC President Refuses to Resign Despite Outcry from Members."

37. Jacquelyn Dowd Hall, "The Long Civil Rights Movement and the Political Use of the Past."

38. Clifford Geertz, *Interpretation of Cultures*, 125.

39. National Latino Civic Engagement Table, "National Latino Civic Engagement Table Reacts to 2016 Election."

40. Jonathan Handel, "Latinx Groups Picket Paramount Pictures."

41. Beltrán, "Racial Presence Versus Racial Justice."

42. Ross A. Lincoln, "Latino Group NHLA Joins Call for Greater Diversity"; Handel, "Latinx Groups Picket Paramount Pictures."

43. Martín Quezada and Daniel Ortega, "La Raza or UnidosUS."

44. Bianca Betancourt, "La Raza Couldn't Rally Young Activists."

45. Victor Davis Hanson, "Never What?"; Alex Clark, "La Raza Rebrands as 'UnidosUS.'"

46. Mijente, "Principles of Unity."

47. Hartog, *Regimes of Historicity*, xv.

48. Héctor E. Sánchez Barba, "NHLA'S Latino Leaders Chart Bold Strategy."

Conclusion

1. Yasmeen Abutaleb, "What's Inside the Hate-Filled Manifesto."

2. See chapter 1.

3. The "great replacement" was coined by the French author Renaud Camus but has a long history. For scholarly accounts of this notion and its political effects, see Jacob Davey and Julie Ebner, "The Great Replacement"; Andreu Domingo, "From Replacement Migrations to the 'Great Replacement'"; Leo Chavez, "Fear of White Replacement." For a broader history of contemporary white nationalist violence and militant groups, see Kathleen Belew, *Bring the War Home*.

4. On white ethnostates, see Alexandra Minna Stern, *Proud Boys and the White Ethnostate*.

5. Exhibiting the coalition's ideological diversity, the messages spanned milquetoast "condolences and solidarity" from its more conservative members to emphatic denouncements of "white male supremacy" from its most progressive members. NHLA, "Latino Leaders Mourn the Deaths."

6. NHLA, "Latino Leaders Mourn the Deaths."

7. Janet Murguía, "The El Paso Shooting Is the Violence Latinos Have Been Dreading."

8. Julio Ricardo Varela, "More than 200 Entertainers, Activists and Leaders Sign Letter."

9. The predecessor to this question appeared in the 1970 census but only in the long form, which was sent to just a sample of households. The question asked: "Is this person's origin or descent" and offered the following response choices: "Mexican," "Puerto Rican," "Cuban," "Central or South American," "Other Spanish," and "No, none of these." See chapter 1 for further discussion.

10. Louise Seamster and Victor Ray, "Against Teleology in the Study of Race."

11. Curtis, *The Politics of Population*.

12. Although Alba does not offer firm forecasts, his work points to the prospect that the children of a substantial portion of those currently officially classified as Latino will be, as the result of Latino/white intermarriage, so deeply integrated in non-Hispanic white spaces and networks that they may not identify or live in meaningful ways as Latinos. Alba, *The Great Demographic Illusion*. Research on identity preferences among "half-Latinos" and Latino and non-Latino white intermarriage suggests alternative trajectories. See, for example, Michael Hajime Miyawaki, "Part-Latinos and Racial Reporting in the Census," and Jessica M. Vasquez, "The Whitening Hypothesis Challenged."

13. For example, the most recent NHLA policy agenda, released in fall 2020, opened with a statement on "Inclusivity and the Terms Hispanic and Latino/a/x." Expressing a desire for inclusion and diversity, it stated, "When terms such as 'Latino,' 'Hispanic,' 'Latino/a,' or 'Latinx' are used throughout the public policy agenda, we intend them to represent all persons of Latino/a/@/e/x or Hispanic heritage, and those who identify as Hispanic or Latino/a/@/e/x, while also acknowledging the shortcomings of these terms." NHLA, *2020–2024 Hispanic Public Policy Agenda*.

14. Rosa, *Looking Like a Language, Sounding Like a Race*, 15.

15. Arab and Middle Eastern American advocacy groups argue that the classification of the Middle Eastern and North Africa population as white has led to severe undercounting and underrepresentation. Among those that support the MENA category, there is ongoing debate about whether it should be defined as an ethnic or a racial category. See Erik Love, *Islamophobia and Racism in America*; Randa Kayyali, "US Census Classifications and Arab Americans." On the complexities of Middle Eastern American racial identity formation, see Neda Maghbouleh, "From White to What?"; Amina Zarrugh, "Racialized Political Shock."

16. See Hitlin, Brown, and Elder, "Measuring Latinos"; and Rodríguez, Miyawaki, and Argeros, "Latino Racial Reporting in the US."

17. Support for the combined question is not universal. Some Latino advocates and academics have raised concerns about the question, both because the AQE test revealed some loss of subgroup information (e.g., Puerto Rican, Ecuadorian) and potential loss of data on socioeconomic differences among variously racialized Latinos. See Nancy López, "Killing Two Birds with One Stone?"; Edward Telles, "Latinos, Race, and the U.S. Census."

18. NALEO-EF, "Census Bureau Proposed Combined Race and Ethnicity Question Offers Best Option for Improving Data on Latinos." While supportive, the organization claimed there were several "outstanding concerns" about the proposed changes. These include "the manner in which the Bureau presents and tabulates the data derived from the combined question; the comparability of these data to historical data derived from the two separate questions approach; and the fact that the combined question still includes a 'some other race, ethnicity, or origin' category, which raised continuing issues with regard to the comparability of Census data and the OMB race and ethnicity standards."

19. Modifications that were included, and have been long sought by civil rights groups, were the ability to identify as more than one Hispanic-origin group and the removal of "negro" from the Black/African American category.

20. Hansi Lo Wang, "2020 Census to Keep Racial, Ethnic Categories"; Paul Overberg, "Census Change to Race, Ethnicity Questions."

21. The OMB-convened Interagency Working Group charged with exploring the possible changes never issued a final report and seems to have been terminated without notice. NALEO-EF, "The Hispanic Origin and Race Questions in the Census 2020."

22. Already civil rights advocates writ large were concerned with the Trump administration's role in the census, including its political appointees, its long delay on appointing a census director, and the fiscal constraints it placed on the bureau and its decennial enumeration.

23. The issue has not been forgotten. For example, in January 2020, two months before census enumeration began, Arturo Vargas addressed the House Committee on Oversight and Reform. In his testimony, he called for a congressional investigation of OMB's Office of Information and Regulatory Affairs, which had, in his words, left the Census Bureau's proposal "gathering dust."

24. Beginning in 1960, the Census Bureau developed a long and short census questionnaire. The long form was sent to a sample of the overall population, whereas the short form was used to enumerate the whole population. A citizenship question appeared only in the long form between 1970 and 2000. The Census Bureau terminated the long form after the 2000 census and began to use the American Community Survey (ACS) as its replacement. ACS is sent to a sample of the country several times between censuses and has included a citizenship question.

25. Cristina Mora, "Latinx and the US Census."

26. Sam Adler-Bell, "The Supreme Court Will Decide if Census Citizenship Question Is Legal."

27. For example, as discussed in chapter 2, Republican senators David Vitter and Robert Bennett submitted an amendment to a Census Bureau appropriations bill that would have required the inclusion of a citizenship question in the 2010 census. On prior attempts and legal decisions, see also Mora, "Latinx and the US Census." In 2018 Stephen A. Camarota of the anti-immigration Center for Immigration Studies testified in support of the citizenship question at the House Judiciary Committee Subcommittee on the Constitution and Civil Justice.

28. The memo was among several that outlined the administration's desire to revoke the DACA program and to limit immigration from Muslim-dominant countries. Hansi Lo Wang, "How the 2020 Census Citizenship Question Ended Up in Court."

29. Angelo Falcón, "Prepare (Just in Case) for a Mass Act of Latino Statistical Disobedience."

30. Hansi Lo Wang, "More than 2 Dozen States, Cities Sue."

31. MALDEF, "Lawsuit on 2020 Census Citizenship Question Updated."

32. On October 13, 2020, the Supreme Court overturned rulings that blocked the administration's plan to end the census enumeration ahead of schedule. Hansi Lo Wang, "How Trump Officials Cut the 2020 Census Short" and "Supreme Court Permits Trump Administration to End Census."

33. Adam Liptak, "Supreme Court Speeds Case on Excluding Undocumented Immigrants."

34. Michael Wines, "Deceased G.O.P. Strategist's Hard Drives Reveal New Details."

35. The saying "it's demography stupid" modifies James Carville's famous line, "The economy, stupid," which he drilled into presidential candidate Bill Clinton in 1992. To my knowledge, the first known usage of this phrase was a *Jerusalem Post* interview in 2004 with the controversial Israeli geographer Arnon Soffer. Soffer gained notoriety for writing about Palestinians as a "demographic threat" to the state of Israel. Ruthie Blum, "It's the Demography, Stupid." It then appeared as the headline of an inflammatory *Wall Street Journal* commentary by the conservative Canadian author Mark Steyn in 2006, who likened Middle Eastern and Muslim immigration to Europe to a "neutron bomb": "The grand buildings will still be standing, but the people who built them will be gone. We are living through a remarkable period: the self-extinction of the races who, for good or ill, shaped the modern world." Use of the phrase has spread beyond racist doomsday narratives to partisan politics, such as the reelection of Barack Obama in 2012. Demography, most specifically changes to the country's ethnoracial voter composition, were cited as the chief explanatory factor for this outcome. See, for example, Bill Vandenberg, "It's the Demography, Stupid"; Joseph Yackley, "A Republican Post-Mortem"; and Annabel Crabb, "It's the Demography, Stupid."

36. The cover of the issue featured a dripping, paint-drenched red-and-blue handprint above the text, "How to Stop a Civil War."

37. Yoni Appelbaum, "How America Ends."

38. Roger Eatwell and Matthew Goodwin, *National Populism*, 133.

39. Brian Gratton, "Demography and Immigration Restriction in American History," 159.

40. Eric Kaufmann, "It's the Demography, Stupid," 275.

41. Along this vein, there is in the social sciences a long tradition of scholarship on group threat that sees "minority" population size and growth as predictive of dominant group sentiments of threat. See Hubert M. Blalock, *Toward a Theory of Minority-Group Relations*; Fosset and Kiecolt, "The Relative Size of Minority Populations and White Racial Attitudes"; Lincoln Quillian, "Prejudice as a Response to Perceived Group Threat." While many of these works claim Herbert Blumer's "sense of group position" theory as a chief inspiration, as Lawrence Bobo writes, they have "mistakenly reduce[d] the theory to a purely structural-level claim of objective threat." Herbert Blumer, "Race Prejudice as a Sense of Group Position"; Lawrence Bobo, "Prejudice as Group Position," 450.

42. It is noteworthy that some of the scholars are suspicious or openly dismissive of critical race theory.

43. Alba, *The Great Demographic Illusion*, 49. Eric Kaufmann, who is more explicit about his conception, affirms the ocular basis of race. With some caveats, he writes, "broadly speaking, there is cross-cultural consensus around colour and I don't believe this can be deconstructed. Is the same true for our established racial groups? Broadly speaking, I think so." Kaufmann, *Whiteshift*, 26.

44. Obasogie, *Blinded By Sight*. See also Jonathan Rosa and Vanessa Díaz, "Raciontologies."

45. Mary Poovey, "Figures of Arithmetic, Figures of Speech," 275. Emphasis in original.

46. Alba, *The Great Demographic Illusion*.

47. Kaufmann, *Whiteshift*.

48. Far afield from Stuart Hall's concerns, I am drawing inspiration from his incisive essay, "The Problem of Ideology."

49. In Greek mythology, the gods blinded Tiresias for seeing Athena naked but gave him the "gift of seercraft." Ironically, he could see into the future but not see in the present. See Alfred Schütz, "Tiresias, or Our Knowledge of Future Events."

REFERENCES

Abascal, Maria. "Us and Them: Black-White Relations in the Wake of Hispanic Population Growth." *American Sociological Review* 80, no. 4 (2015): 789–813.

Abutaleb, Yasmeen. "What's Inside the Hate-Filled Manifesto Linked to the Alleged El Paso Shooter." *Washington Post*, August 4, 2019.

Ackerman, Edwin. "'What Part of Illegal Don't You Understand?': Bureaucracy and Civil Society in the Shaping of Illegality." *Ethnic and Racial Studies* 37, no. 2 (2014): 181–203.

Adam, Barbara, and Chris Groves. *Future Matters: Action, Knowledge, Ethics.* Leiden: Brill, 2007.

Adam, Barbara. "Wendell Bell and the Sociology of the Future: Challenges Past, Present and Future." *Futures* 43, no. 6 (2011): 590–95.

Adams, Vincanne, Michelle Murphy, and Adele E. Clarke. "Anticipation: Technoscience, Life, Affect, Temporality." *Subjectivity* 28 (2009): 246–65.

Adler-Bell, Sam. "The Supreme Court Will Decide If Census Citizenship Question Is Legal. Democrats Should Also Work to Block It." *Intercept*, February 15, 2019. https://theintercept.com /2019/02/15/2020-census-citizenship-question/.

Ahmad, Muneer I. "Beyond Earned Citizenship." *Harvard Civil Rights-Civil Liberties Law Review* 52 (2017): 257.

Ahmed, Sara. "Affective Economies." *Social Text* 79, vol. 2, no. 22 (2004): 117–39.

Alba, Richard. *The Great Demographic Illusion: Majority, Minority, and the Expanding American Mainstream.* Princeton, NJ: Princeton University Press, 2020.

———. "The Likely Persistence of a White Majority." *American Prospect* 27, no. 1 (2016): 67–71.

Alba, Richard, Brenden Beck, and Duygu Basaran Sahin. "The U.S. Mainstream Expands—Again." *Journal of Ethnic and Migration Studies* 44, no. 1 (2018): 99–117.

Alba, R., R. G. Rumbaut, and K. Marotz. "A Distorted Nation: Perceptions of Racial/Ethnic Group Sizes and Attitudes toward Immigrants and Other Minorities." *Social Forces* 84, no. 2 (2005): 901–19.

Alberta, Tim. "Can the GOP Overcome Demographic Change in Red States?" *National Review*, October 31, 2016. https://www.nationalreview.com/2016/10/voter-demographics-diversifying -republicans-falling-behind/.

Alcaraz, Lalo. *Fuertes with the 2010 Census.* Los Angeles: MALDEF, 2010.

Alcoff Martín, Linda. *Visible Identities: Race, Gender, and the Self.* New York: Oxford University Press, 2006.

Alexander, Jeffrey C. "Raging against the Enlightenment: The Ideology of Steven Bannon." In *Politics of Meaning/Meaning of Politics*, edited by Jason L. Mast and Jeffrey C. Alexander, 137–48. New York: Palgrave Macmillan, 2019.

Alonso, William, and Paul Starr. "Introduction." In *The Politics of Numbers*, edited by William Alonso and Paul Starr, 1–6. New York: Russell Sage Foundation, 1987.

Altheide, David L. *Creating Fear: News and the Construction of Crisis.* Piscataway, NJ: Transaction, 2002.

Alvial-Palavicino, Carla. "The Future as Practice. A Framework to Understand Anticipation in Science and Technology." *TECNOSCIENZA: Italian Journal of Science & Technology Studies* 6, no. 2 (2016): 135–72.

Anderson, Ben. "Preemption, Precaution, Preparedness: Anticipatory Action and Future Geographies." *Progress in Human Geography* 34, no. 6 (2010): 777–98.

Anderson, Margo J. *The American Census: A Social History.* New Haven, CT: Yale University Press, 1988.

Andrews, Abigail L. "Moralizing Regulation: The Implications of Policing 'Good' versus 'Bad' Immigrants." *Ethnic and Racial Studies* 41, no. 14 (2018): 2485–2503.

Andrews, Kenneth T., and Bob Edwards. "Advocacy Organizations in the US Political Process." *Annual Review of Sociology* 30 (2004): 479–506.

Appadurai, Arjun. *The Future as Cultural Fact: Essays on the Global Condition.* London: Verso, 2013.

———. "Number in the Colonial Imagination." In *Orientalism and the Postcolonial Predicament: Perspectives on South Asia*, edited by Carol A. Breckenridge and Peter van der Veer, 314–39. Philadelphia: University of Pennsylvania Press, 1993.

Appelbaum, Yoni. "How America Ends." *Atlantic*, November 12, 2019. https://www.theatlantic.com/magazine/archive/2019/12/how-america-ends/600757/.

Auyero, Javier. *Patients of the State: The Politics of Waiting in Argentina.* Durham, NC: Duke University Press, 2012.

Auyero, Javier, and Débora Swistun. "Tiresias in Flammable Shantytown: Toward a Tempography of Domination." *Sociological Forum* 24, no. 1 (2009): 1–21.

Ayón, David R. "Mobilizing Latino Immigrant Integration: From IRCA to the Ya Es Hora Citizenship Campaign, 1987–2007." *Research Paper Series on Latino Immigrant Civic and Political Participation*, no. 1 (2009): 1–23.

Ayres, Whit, Jon McHenry, and Luke Frans. "2012: The Year Changing Demographics Caught Up with Republicans." *Resurgent Republic*, January 10, 2012.

Bakhtin, Mikhail Mikhailovich. *The Dialogic Imagination: Four Essays.* Austin: University of Texas Press, 1981.

Balibar, Étienne. "Is There a Neo-Racism?" In *Race, Nation, Class: Ambiguous Identities*, edited by Étienne Balibar and Immanuel Wallerstein, 17–28. London: Verson, 1991.

Banks, Adelle M. "Hispanic Groups Divided over 2010 Census." *Christianity Today*, April 30, 2009. https://www.christianitytoday.com/ct/2009/aprilweb-only/117-42.0.html

Barnard, Alex V. "Making the City 'Second Nature': Freegan 'Dumpster Divers' and the Materiality of Morality." *American Journal of Sociology* 121, no. 4 (2016): 1017–50.

Barreto, Matt A., and Gary M. Segura. *Latino America: How America's Most Dynamic Population Is Poised to Transform the Politics of the Nation.* New York: PublicAffairs, 2014.

Barreto, Matt A., Tyler Reny, and Bryan Wilcox-Archuleta. "Survey Methodology and the Latina/o Vote: Why a Bilingual, Bicultural, Latino-centered Approach Matters." *Aztlan: A Journal of Chicano Studies* 42, no. 2 (2017): 211–27.

Barry, Andrew. "Demonstrations: Sites and Sights of Direct Action." *Economy and Society* 28, no. 1 (1999): 75–84.

Basu, Alaka M. "Demography for the Public: Literary Representations of Population Research and Policy." *Development and Change* 45, no. 5 (2014): 813–37.

BBC News. "Non-Hispanic U.S. White Births Now the Minority in U.S.," May 17, 2012. https://www.bbc.com/news/world-us-canada-18100457.

Becerra, Hector. "Latino Vote Not Set in Stone for Obama." *Los Angeles Times*, September 4, 2012. https://www.latimes.com/politics/la-xpm-2012-sep-04-la-pn-latino-vote-romney-obama-20120904-story.html.

———. "Obama Says Latinos Could Be 'Big Reason' He Wins Second Term." *Los Angeles Times*, October 26, 2012. https://www.latimes.com/politics/la-xpm-2012-oct-26-la-pn-obama-latinos-second-term-20121024-story.html.

Beckert, Jens. *Imagined Futures: Fictional Expectations and Capitalist Dynamics.* Cambridge, MA: Harvard University Press, 2016.

Belew, Kathleen. *Bring the War Home: The White Power Movement and Paramilitary America.* Cambridge, MA: Harvard University Press, 2019.

Bellantoni, Christina. "Republican Senators Vitter, Bennett Attempt to Force Census to Ask Immigration Status." *TPM*, October 8, 2009. https://talkingpointsmemo.com/dc/republican-senators-vitter-bennett-attempt-to-force-census-to-ask-immigration-status.

Beltrán, Cristina. "Racial Presence versus Racial Justice: The Affective Power of an Aesthetic Condition." *Du Bois Review* 11, no. 1 (2014): 137–58.

———. *The Trouble with Unity: Latino Politics and the Creation of Identity.* Oxford: Oxford University Press, 2010.

Benac, Nancy, and Connie Cass. "Face of U.S. Is Changing; Elections to Look Different." *San Diego Union-Tribune*, November 12, 2012. https://www.sandiegouniontribune.com/sdut-face-of-us-changing-elections-to-look-different-2012nov12-story.html.

Benitez, Sara. *Latino Children Will Add Nearly 15.8 Million Potential Voters to the Electorate.* Washington, DC: National Council of La Raza, 2012.

Benzecry, Claudio E. "What Did We Say They've Said? Four Encounters between Theory, Method and the Production of Data." *Ethnography* 18, no. 1 (2017): 24–34.

Benzecry, Claudio E., and Gianpaolo Baiocchi. "What Is Political about Political Ethnography? On the Context of Discovery and the Normalization of an Emergent Subfield." *Theory and Society* 46, no. 3 (2017): 229–47.

Berman, Elizabeth Popp, and Daniel Hirschman. "The Sociology of Quantification: Where Are We Now?" *Contemporary Sociology* 47, no. 3 (2018): 257–66.

Bernal, Rafael. "Hispanic Population Reaches New High of Nearly 60 Million." *The Hill*, July 9, 2019. https://thehill.com/latino/452223-hispanic-population-reaches-new-high-of-nearly-60-million.

Best, Joel. *Damned Lies and Statistics: Untangling Numbers from the Media, Politicians, and Activists.* Berkeley: University of California Press, 2001.

Betancourt, Bianca. "La Raza Couldn't Rally Young Activists. It Will Take More than a Name Change to Fix That." *Washington Post*, August 3, 2017. https://www.washingtonpost.com/news/post-nation/wp/2017/08/03/to-rally-younger-latino-activists-unidosus-needs-to-do-more-than-change-its-name/.

Bhambra, Gurminder K. "Brexit, Trump, and 'Methodological Whiteness': On the Misrecognition of Race and Class." *British Journal of Sociology* 68, no. S1 (2017): S214–32.

Biruk, Crystal. *Cooking Data: Culture and Politics in an African Research World.* Durham, NC: Duke University Press, 2018.

Blake, John. "Arab- and Persian-American Campaign: 'Check It Right' on the Census." CNN, April 1, 2010. https://www.cnn.com/2010/US/04/01/census.check.it.right.campaign/index.html.

Blalock, Hubert M. *Toward a Theory of Minority-Group Relations.* New York: Wiley, 1967.

Blanton, Ryan. "Chronotopic Landscapes of Environmental Racism." *Journal of Linguistic Anthropology* 21, no. Supl (2011): 76–93.

Bloemraad, Irene, Fabiana Silva, and Kim Voss. "Rights, Economics, or Family? Frame Resonance, Political Ideology, and the Immigrant Rights Movement." *Social Forces* 94, no. 4 (2016): 1647–74.

Blommaert, Jan. "Chronotopes, Scales, and Complexity in the Study of Language in Society." *Annual Review of Anthropology* 44, no. 1 (2015): 105–16.

Blum, Ruthie. "It's the Demography, Stupid: An Interview with Geographer/Demographer Arnon Soffer." *Jerusalem Post*, May 20, 2004.

Blumer, Herbert. "Race Prejudice as a Sense of Group Position." *Pacific Sociological Review* 1, no. 1 (1958): 3–7.

Bobo, Lawrence D. "Prejudice as Group Position: Microfoundations of a Sociological Approach to Racism and Race Relations." *Journal of Social Issues* 55, no. 3 (1999): 445–72.

———. "Somewhere between Jim Crow & Post-Racialism: Reflections on the Racial Divide in America Today." *Daedalus* 140, no. 2 (2011): 11–36.

Bonikowski, Bart, and Paul DiMaggio. "Varieties of American Popular Nationalism." *American Sociological Review* 81, no. 5 (2016): 949–80.

Bonilla-Silva, Eduardo. "Feeling Race: Theorizing the Racial Economy of Emotions." *American Sociological Review* 84, no. 1 (2019): 1–25.

Bookman, Milica Zarkovic. *The Demographic Struggle for Power: The Political Economy of Demographic Engineering in the Modern World.* London: Frank Cass, 1997.

Borup, Mads, Nik Brown, Kornelia Konrad, and Harro Van Lente. "The Sociology of Expectations in Science and Technology." *Technology Analysis and Strategic Management* 18, no. 3–4 (2006): 285–98.

Bourdieu, Pierre. *On the State: Lectures at the Collège De France, 1989–1992.* Cambridge, MA: Polity Press, 2015.

———. *Outline of a Theory of Practice.* New York: Cambridge University Press, 1977.

———. "Rethinking the State: Genesis and Structure of the Bureaucratic Field." *Sociological Theory* 12, no. 1 (1994): 1–18.

———. "The Social Space and the Genesis of Groups." *Theory and Society* 14, no. 6 (1985): 723–44.

Bowker, Geoffrey C., and Susan Leigh Star. *Sorting Things Out: Classification and Its Consequences.* Cambridge, MA: Massachusetts Institute of Technology Press, 1999.

Brammer, John Paul. "'The Latino Vote' Didn't Overwhelm Trump, Because We're Not All the Same." *Guardian*, November 9, 2016. https://www.theguardian.com/commentisfree/2016 /nov/09/the-latino-vote-didnt-overwhelm-trump-because-were-not-all-the-same.

Brendese, P. J. "Black Noise in White Time: Segregated Temporality and Mass Incarceration." In *Radical Future Pasts: Untimely Political Theory*, edited by Romand Coles, Mark Reinhardt, and George Shulman, 112–45. Lexington: University of Kentucky Press, 2014.

Briggs, Laura. *Reproducing Empire: Race, Sex, Science, and U.S. Imperialism in Puerto Rico.* Berkeley: University of California Press, 2002.

Brown, Nik, and Mike Michael. "A Sociology of Expectations: Retrospecting Prospects and Prospecting Retrospects." *Technology Analysis and Strategic Management* 15, no. 1 (2003): 3–18.

Brownstein, Ronald. "America's New Electorate." *Atlantic*, April 1, 2011. https://www.theatlantic .com/politics/archive/2011/04/americas-new-electorate/73317/.

Buchanan, Patrick J. *Suicide of a Superpower: Will America Survive to 2025?* New York: Macmillan, 2011.

Bump, Philip. "Rep. Steve King Warns That 'Our Civilization' Can't Be Restored with 'Somebody Else's Babies.'" *Washington Post*, March 12, 2017.

Bruno, Isabelle, Emmanuel Didier, and Tommaso Vitale. "Statactivism: Forms of Action between Disclosure and Affirmation." *PArtecipazione e COnflitto* 7, no. 2 (2014): 198–220.

Callon, Michel. "Some Elements of a Sociology of Translation: Domestication of the Scallops and the Fisherman of St. Brieuc Bay." *Sociological Review* 32 (1984): 196–223.

Callon, Michel, and John Law. "On Qualculation, Agency, and Otherness." *Environment and Planning D: Society and Space* 23, no. 5 (2005): 717–33.

Capehart, Jonathan. "50,000 Shades of Dismay for the GOP." *Washington Post*, November 19, 2012. https://www.washingtonpost.com/blogs/post-partisan/post/50000-shades-of-dismay-for -the-gop/2012/11/19/9a5826ba-3270-11e2-bb9b-288a310849ee_blog.html.

Cárdenas, Vanessa, Julie Ajinkya, and Daniella Gibbs Léger. *Progress 2050: New Ideas for a Diverse America*. Washington, DC: Center for American Progress, 2011.

Carroll, Patrick. *Science, Culture, and Modern State Formation*. Berkeley: University of California Press, 2006.

Cassata, Donna. "Head of Latino Group Calls Obama 'Deporter in Chief,' Criticizes GOP Inaction on Immigration." *Huffington Post*, March 4, 2014. https://www.huffingtonpost.ca/2014/03/04 /head-of-latino-group-call_n_4899656.html.

Cauchon, Dennis, and Paul Overberg. "Census Data Shows Minorities Now a Majority of U.S. Births." *USA Today*, May 17, 2012. https://usatoday30.usatoday.com/news/nation/story/2012 -05-17/minority-births-census/55029100/1.

CBS News. "Census: Hispanics Now Comprise 1 in 6 Americans," March 24, 2011. https://www .cbsnews.com/news/census-hispanics-now-comprise-1-in-6-americans/.

Chang, Jeff. *Who We Be: The Colorization of America*. New York: St. Martin's Press, 2014.

Chauvin, Sébastien, and Blanca Garcés-Mascareñas. "Becoming Less Illegal: Deservingness Frames and Undocumented Migrant Incorporation." *Sociology Compass* 8, no. 4 (2014): 422–32.

Chavez, Leo R. *Covering Immigration: Popular Images and the Politics of the Nation*. Berkeley: University of California Press, 2001.

———. "Fear of White Replacement: Latina Fertility, White Demographic Decline, and Immigration Reform." In *A Field Guide to White Supremacy*, edited by Ramon Gutiérrez and Kathleen Belew. Berkeley: University of California Press, forthcoming.

———. *The Latino Threat: Constructing Immigrants, Citizens, and the Nation*. Stanford, CA: Stanford University Press, 2008.

Choldin, Harvey M. *Looking for the Last Percent: The Controversy over Census Undercounts*. New Brunswick, NJ: Rutgers University Press, 1994.

———. "Statistics and Politics: The 'Hispanic Issue' in the 1980 Census." *Demography* 23, no. 3 (1986): 403–18.

Chokshi, Niraj, and Quoctrung Bui. "A Census Time Machine: Sioux Falls Is the Past, Staten Island the Present, Las Vegas the Future." *New York Times*, June 22, 2017. https://www.nytimes.com /interactive/2017/06/22/upshot/Census-Time-Machine-Demographics-in-America.html.

Chumley, Cheryl K. "Sen. Lindsey Graham: GOP Facing 'Demographic Death Spiral.'" *Washington Times*, June 17, 2013. https://www.washingtontimes.com/news/2013/jun/17/sen-lindsey -graham-gop-facing-demographic-death-sp/.

Cillizza, Chris. "The Hispanic Vote Is a Sleeping Political Giant. It Might Never Wake Up." *Washington Post*, June 4, 2013. https://www.washingtonpost.com/news/the-fix/wp/2013/06/04 /the-hispanic-vote-is-a-sleeping-political-giant-it-might-never-wake-up/.

Cirilli, Kevin. "Condi: GOP Sent 'Mixed Messages.'" *Politico*, November 9, 2012. https://www .politico.com/story/2012/11/condi-gop-sent-mixed-messages-083627.

Cisneros, Henry. "Latinos and the Law of Large Numbers." *Al Día News*, April 8, 2009. https:// aldianews.com/articles/opinion/latinos-and-law-large-numbers/6055.

———, ed. *Latinos and the Nation's Future*. Houston: Arte Publico Press, 2009.

Clark, Alex. "La Raza Rebrands as 'Unidos US.'" *Breitbart*, July 10, 2017. https://www.breitbart .com/politics/2017/07/10/la-raza-rebrands-unidosus/.

Cohen, Elizabeth F. "Out of Line: Populist Rhetoric, Immigration, and the Line-Standing Frame." Paper presented at Immigration and Populism Conference, Stanford University, June 8, 2018.

———. *The Political Value of Time: Citizenship, Duration, and Democratic Justice*. Cambridge: Cambridge University Press, 2018.

Cole, Joshua. *The Power of Large Numbers: Population, Politics, and Gender in Nineteenth-Century France*. Ithaca, NY: Cornell University Press, 2000.

Commission on Population Growth and the American Future. *Population and the American Future: The Report of the Commission on Population Growth and the American Future.* New York: New American Library, 1972.

Conde, Carlos, ed. *The Spanish Speaking People of the United States: A New Era.* Washington, DC: Cabinet Committee on Opportunities for Spanish Speaking People, 1970.

Connelly, Matthew. *Fatal Misconception: The Struggle to Control World Population.* Cambridge, MA: Harvard University Press, 2010.

———. "To Inherit the Earth: Imagining World Population, from the Yellow Peril to the Population Bomb." *Journal of Global History* 1 (2006): 299–319.

Connolly, William E. *A World of Becoming.* Durham, NC: Duke University Press, 2011.

Coulter, Ann. *¡Adios, America!: The Left's Plan to Turn Our Country into a Third World Hellhole.* Washington, DC: Regnery, 2015.

Crabb, Annabel. "It's the Demography, Stupid." *ABC News*, November 7, 2012. https://mobile .abc.net.au/news/2012-11-08/crabb-us-election/4360796.

Craig, Maureen A., and Jennifer A. Richeson. "Hispanic Population Growth Engenders Conservative Shift among Non-Hispanic Racial Minorities." *Social Psychological and Personality Science* 9, no. 4 (2018): 383–92.

———. "Information about the US Racial Demographic Shift Triggers Concerns about Anti-White Discrimination among the Prospective White 'Minority.'" *PLoS ONE* 12, no. 9 (2017): 1–20.

Crampton, Jeremy W. "Rethinking Maps and Identity: Choropleths, Clines, and Biopolitics." In *Rethinking Maps: New Frontiers in Cartographic Theory*, edited by Martin Dodge, Rob Kitchin, and Chris Perkins, 26–49. New York: Routledge, 2009.

Curtis, Bruce. "Foucault on Governmentality and Population: The Impossible Discovery." *Canadian Journal of Sociology* 27, no. 4 (2002): 505–33.

———. "The Politics of Demography." In *Complexities of Contextual Political Analysis*, edited by Robert E. Goodin and Charles Tilly, 1066–90. Oxford: Oxford University Press, 2006.

———. *The Politics of Population: State Formation, Statistics and the Census of Canada, 1840–1975.* Toronto: University of Toronto Press, 2001.

Daniels, Roger. "Two Cheers for Immigration." In *Debating American Immigration, 1882–Present*, edited by Roger Daniels and Otis L. Graham, 5–69. Lanham, MD: Rowman & Littlefield, 2001.

Davey, Jacob, and Julia Ebner. "'The Great Replacement': The Violent Consequences of Mainstreamed Extremism." *Institute for Strategic Dialogue* 7 (2019). https://www.isdglobal.org /wp-content/uploads/2019/07/The-Great-Replacement-The-Violent-Consequences-of -Mainstreamed-Extremism-by-ISD.pdf.

Dávila, Arlene. *The Latino Spin: Public Image and the Whitewashing of Race.* New York: New York University Press, 2008.

———. *Latinos Inc.: The Marketing and Making of a People.* Berkeley: University of California Press, 2001.

Dawson, Michael C. *Behind the Mule: Race and Class in African-American Politics.* Princeton, NJ: Princeton University Press, 1994.

de la Garza, Rodolfo O., and Louis DeSipio. "Latinos and the 1992 Elections: A National Perspective." In *Ethnic Ironies: Latino Politics in the 1992 Elections*, edited by Rodolfo O. de la Garza and Louis DeSipio, 3–50. Boulder, CO: Westview Press, 1996.

De Man, Hendrik. *The Psychology of Socialism.* London: Allen & Unwin, 1928.

de Leon, Cedric. "Why 1861?: Racial Capitalism and the Timing of the U.S. Civil War." Colloquium Talk, Northwestern University, September 2019.

de Santos, Martin. "Fact-Totems and the Statistical Imagination: The Public Life of a Statistic in Argentina 2001." *Sociological Theory* 27, no. 4 (December 2009): 466–89.

Del Olmo, Frank. "City, County to Be One-Fourth Latin by 1980, Study Predicts." *Los Angeles Times*, June 22, 1973.

———. "Latino 'Decade' Moves into '90s." *Los Angeles Times*, December 14, 1989. https://www.latimes.com/archives/la-xpm-1989-12-14-ti-1-story.html.

———. "Spanish-Origin Census Figures Revised by U.S.: 1.5 Million Added to 1970 Count of Latin Americans." *Los Angeles Times*, January 15, 1974.

Delerme, Simone. *Latino Orlando: Suburban Transformation and Racial Conflict.* Gainesville: University Press of Florida, 2020.

Desrosières, Alain. "How Real Are Statistics? Four Possible Attitudes." *Social Research* 68, no. 2 (2001): 339–55.

———. *The Politics of Large Numbers: A History of Statistical Reasoning.* Cambridge, MA: Harvard University Press, 1998.

———. "Statistics and Social Critique." *PArtecipazione e COnflitto* 7, no. 2 (2014): 348–59.

Diaz-Bone, Rainer, and Emmanuel Didier. "Introduction: The Sociology of Quantification-Perspectives on an Emerging Field in the Social Sciences." *Historical Social Research/Historische Sozialforschung* 41, no. 2 (2016): 7–26.

Domingo, Andreu. "'Demodystopias': Prospects of Demographic Hell." *Population and Development Review* 34, no. 4 (2008): 725–45.

———. "From Replacement Migrations to the 'Great Replacement': Demographic Reproduction and National Populism in Europe." *Advances in Social Sciences Research Journal* 7, no. 6 (2020): 671–85.

Dougherty, Conor. "Population Leaves Heartland Behind." *Wall Street Journal*, April 11, 2011. https://www.wsj.com/articles/SB10001424052748704843404576251150723518240.

Dougherty, Conor, and Miriam Jordan. "Minority Births Are New Majority." *Wall Street Journal*, May 17, 2012. https://www.wsj.com/articles/SB100014240527023038796045774083630033351818.

Dowling, Julie A. *Mexican Americans and the Question of Race.* Austin: University of Texas Press, 2014.

Duany, Jorge. "The Orlando Ricans: Overlapping Identity Discourses among Middle-Class Puerto Rican Immigrants." *Centro Journal* 22, no. 1 (2010): 85–115.

Du Bois, W.E.B. *The Souls of Black Folk.* New York: Penguin, 2018 [1903].

Eatwell, Roger, and Matthew Goodwin. *National Populism: The Revolt against Liberal Democracy.* London: Penguin Books, 2018.

Economist. "Death Spiral," May 19, 2009. https://www.economist.com/democracy-in-america/2009/05/19/death-spiral.

Edwards, Ozzie. "The Commission's Recommendations from the Standpoint of Minorities." *Social Science Quarterly* 53, no. 3 (1972): 465–69.

Ehrlich, Paul R., and Loy Bilderback. *The Golden Door: International Migration, Mexico, and the United States*, edited by Anne H. Ehrlich. New York: Ballantine Books, 1979.

El-Badry, Samia, and David A. Swanson. "Providing Census Tabulations to Government Security Agencies in the United States: The Case of Arab Americans." *Government Information Quarterly* 24, no. 4 (2007): 470–87.

El Nasser, Haya. "Group's Census Promo Called 'Blasphemous.'" *USA Today*, December 14, 2009. https://usatoday30.usatoday.com/news/nation/census/2009-12-14-xmas_N.htm.

Ellis, Mark. "What Future for Whites? Population Projections and Racialised Imaginaries in the US." *International Journal of Population Geography* 7, no. 3 (June 2001): 213–29.

Enchautegui, María E. "Legalization Programs and the Integration of Unauthorized Immigrants: A Comparison of S. 744 and IRCA." *Journal on Migration and Human Security* 2, no. 1 (March 2014): 1–13.

Ennis, Sharon R., Merarys. Rios-Vargas, and Nora G. Albert. "The Hispanic Population: 2010." *Census Briefs*, U.S. Census Bureau, May 2011.

Enten, Harry, "Trump Probably Did Better with Latino Voters than Romney Did." *FiveThirtyEight*, November 18, 2016. https://fivethirtyeight.com/features/trump-probably-did-better-with-latino-voters-than-romney-did/.

Epstein, Reid J. "NCLR Head: Obama 'Deporter-in-Chief.'" *Politico*, March 4, 2014. https://www.politico.com/story/2014/03/national-council-of-la-raza-janet-murguia-barack-obama-deporter-in-chief-immigration-104217.

Espeland, Wendy. "Narrating Numbers." In *The World of Indicators: The Making of Governmental Knowledge through Quantification*, edited by Richard Rottenburg, Sally E. Merry, Sung-Joon Park, and Johanna Mugler, 56–75. Cambridge: Cambridge University Press, 2015.

———. "Reverse Engineering and Emotional Attachments as Mechanisms Mediating the Effects of Quantification." *Historical Social Research / Historische Sozialforschung* 41, no. 2 (2016): 280–304.

Espeland, Wendy Nelson, and Michael Sauder. *Engines of Anxiety: Academic Rankings, Reputation, and Accountability*. New York: Russell Sage Foundation, 2016.

Espeland, Wendy Nelson, and Mitchell L. Stevens. "A Sociology of Quantification." *European Journal of Sociology* 49, no. 3 (2008): 401–36.

Esqueivel, Paloma. "Latino or Hispanic? For Many Americans, Neither Feels Quite Right." *Los Angeles Times*, April 5, 2012. https://www.latimes.com/local/la-xpm-2012-apr-05-la-me-latino-hispanic-20120405-story.html.

Ettinger, Yoram. "The Case against Demographobia." *Ettinger Report*, June 19, 2006. http://theettingerreport.com/the-case-against-demographobia/.

Everett, Burgess, and Seung Min Kim. "Immigration Reform Looks Dead." *Politico*, March 9, 2015. https://www.politico.com/story/2015/03/immigration-reform-congress-115880.

Falcón, Angelo. *Data Dissemination to Communities of Color: The Role of the Census Information Centers*. New York: National Institute for Latino Policy, 2010.

———. "Prepare (Just in Case) for a Mass Act of Latino Statistical Disobedience for an Accurate 2020 Census!" *NiLP Report on Latino Politics and Policy*, April 8, 2018. https://myemail.constantcontact.com/NiLP-Commentary--Census-2020-May-Need-an-Act-of-Latino-Statistical-Disobedience.html.

Federal Interagency Committee on Education. *Report of the Ad Hoc Committee on Racial and Ethnic Definitions*. Washington, DC: U.S. Department of Health, Education, and Welfare, 1975.

File, Thom. *The Diversifying Electorate—Voting Rates by Race and Hispanic Origin in 2012 (and Other Recent Elections)*. Washington, DC: U.S. Census Bureau, 2013.

Fine, Gary Alan. *Authors of the Storm: Meteorologists and the Culture of Prediction*. Chicago: University of Chicago Press, 2009.

———. *Players and Pawns: How Chess Builds Community and Culture*. Chicago: University of Chicago Press, 2015.

———. "Towards a Peopled Ethnography: Developing Theory from Group Life." *Ethnography* 4, no. 1 (2003): 41–60.

Flaherty, Michael G. *The Textures of Time: Agency and Temporal Experience*. Philadelphia: Temple University Press, 2011.

Fleming, Crystal Marie. *Resurrecting Slavery: Racial Legacies and White Supremacy in France*. Philadelphia: Temple University Press, 2017.

Flores, Juan. *From Bomba to Hip-Hop: Puerto Rican Culture and Latino Identity*. New York: Columbia University Press, 2000.

Flores-González, Nilda. *Citizens but Not Americans: Race and Belonging among Latino Millennials*. New York: NYU Press, 2017.

Fogel, Aaron. "The Prose of Populations and the Magic of Demography." *Western Humanities Review* 47, no. 4 (1993): 312–37.

Foley, Elise. "Latino Voters in Election 2012 Help Sweep Obama to Reelection." *Huffington Post*, November 7, 2012. https://www.huffpost.com/entry/latino-voters-election-2012_n_2085922.

Fossett, Mark A., and K. Jill Kiecolt. "The Relative Size of Minority Populations and White Racial Attitudes." *Social Science Quarterly* 70, no. 4 (1989): 820–20.

Foucault, Michel. *Security, Territory, Population: Lectures at the College De France 1977–1978.* New York: Picador, 2007.

Fox, Cybelle, and Thomas A. Guglielmo. "Defining America's Racial Boundaries: Blacks, Mexicans, and European Immigrants, 1890–1945." *American Journal of Sociology* 118, no. 2 (2012): 327–79.

Fox News. "Latinos Highlight America's Changing Face," November 10, 2012.

Foxen, Patricia. *Using NCLR's Latino Kids Data Explorer to Teach Demographic and Social Change.* Washington, DC: National Council of La Raza, 2013.

Foxen, Patricia, and Sara Benitez. *The 2010 Census: Let's Put Those Numbers to Use.* Powerpoint presentation. Washington, DC: National Council of La Raza, 2011.

Foxen, Patricia, Sara Benitez, and Clarissa Martinez de Castro. *Nationwide Growth in the Latino Population Is a Boon for the Country.* Washington, DC: National Council of La Raza, 2011.

Franklin, Benjamin. "Observations Concerning the Increase of Mankind, Peopling of Countries, Etc." *Perspectives in Biology and Medicine* 13, no. 4 (1970 [1751]): 469–75.

Francis, Megan Ming. "The Price of Civil Rights: Black Lives, White Funding, and Movement Capture." *Law & Society Review* 53, no. 1 (2019): 275–309.

Francis-Fallon, Benjamin. *The Rise of the Latino Vote: A History.* Cambridge, MA: Harvard University Press, 2019.

Frazier, Ian. "When W.E.B. Du Bois Made a Laughingstock of a White Supremacist." *New Yorker*, August 19, 2019. https://www.newyorker.com/magazine/2019/08/26/when-w-e-b-du-bois-made-a-laughingstock-of-a-white-supremacist.

Frey, William H. *Diversity Explosion: How New Racial Demographics Are Remaking America.* Rev. 2d ed. Washington, DC: Brookings Institution Press, 2018.

Gabriel, Trip. "Before Trump, Steve King Set the Agenda for the Wall and Anti-Immigrant Politics." *New York Times*, January 10, 2019. https://www.nytimes.com/2019/01/10/us/politics/steve-king-trump-immigration-wall.html.

Gamboa, Suzanne. "LULAC President Refuses to Resign Despite Outcry from Members." *NBC News*, February 16, 2018. https://www.nbcnews.com/news/latino/lulac-president-refuses-resign-despite-outcry-members-n848641.

García, Guy. "Are Hispanics the New American Reality? Claro Que Si! But Will They Get Their Own Museum? Quien Sabe." *Huffington Post*, May 20, 2011. https://www.huffpost.com/entry/national-american-latino-museum_b_864657.

García, Robert. "Hispanics: Diversity and Unity." *Washington Post*, August 24, 1983. https://www.washingtonpost.com/archive/politics/1983/08/24/hispanics-diversity-and-unity/fb6d3eb9-4e82-4739-8023-ccf714f250c9/.

Garcia-Bedolla, Lisa, and Melissa R. Michaelson. *Mobilizing Inclusion: Transforming the Electorate through Get-Out-the-Vote Campaigns.* New Haven, CT: Yale University Press, 2012.

Geertz, Clifford. *The Intepretation of Cultures.* New York: Basic Books, 1973.

Gibson, David R. *Talk at the Brink: Deliberation and Decision during the Cuban Missile Crisis.* Princeton, NJ: Princeton University Press, 2012.

Go, Julian. *American Empire and the Politics of Meaning: Elite Political Cultures in the Philippines and Puerto Rico during U.S. Colonialism.* Durham, NC: Duke University Press, 2008.

Goffman, Erving. "On Fieldwork." *Journal of Contemporary Ethnography* 18 (1989): 123–32.

Goldberg, David Theo. *Racial Subjects: Writing on Race in America.* New York: Routledge, 1997.

———. *Racist Culture: Philosophy and the Politics of Meaning*. Malden, MA: Blackwell, 1993.

Goldstone, Jack A., Eric P. Kaufmann, and Monica Duffy Toft. *Political Demography: How Population Changes Are Reshaping International Security and National Politics*. Oxford: Oxford University Press, 2012.

Gomez, Alan. "Another Election Surprise: Many Hispanics Backed Trump." *USA Today*, November 9, 2016. https://www.usatoday.com/story/news/politics/elections/2016/2016/11/09/hispanic-vote-election-2016-donald-trump-hillary-clinton/93540772/.

Gómez, Laura E. *Manifest Destinies: The Making of the Mexican American Race*. 2d ed. New York: NYU Press, 2018.

Gonzales, Alfonso. *Reform without Justice: Latino Migrant Politics and the Homeland Security State*. Oxford: Oxford University Press, 2014.

González, Antonio. "Why the Latino Vote Underperformed in 2012, a Critical Analysis (Part 1)." News release, William C. Velásques Institute, May 22, 2013.

Goodman, Adam. *The Deportation Machine: America's Long History of Expelling Immigrants*. Princeton, NJ: Princeton University Press, 2020.

Gould, Deborah B. *Moving Politics: Emotion and Act Up's Fight against AIDS*. Chicago: University of Chicago Press, 2009.

Graham, Hugh Davis. *The Civil Rights Era: Origins and Development of National Policy, 1960–1972*. New York: Oxford University Press, 1990.

Graizbord, Diana, Michael Rodríguez-Muñiz, and Gianpaolo Baiocchi. "Expert for a Day: Theory and the Tailored Craft of Ethnography." *Ethnography* 18, no. 3 (2017): 322–44.

Grant, Madison. *The Passing of the Great Race: Or, the Racial Basis of European History*. New York: Scribner, 1916.

Gratton, Brian, and Emily Klancher Merchant. "La Raza: Mexicans in the United States Census." *Journal of Policy History* 28, no. 4 (2016): 537–66.

Grebler, Leo, Joan W. Moore, and Ralph Guzmán. *The Mexican-American People: The Nation's Second Largest Minority*. New York: Free Press, 1970.

Greenhalgh, Susan. "The Social Construction of Population Science: An Intellectual, Institutional, and Political History of Twentieth-Century Demography." *Comparative Studies in Society and History* 38, no. 1 (1996): 26–66.

Gulasekaram, Pratheepan, and S. Karthick Ramakrishnan. *The New Immigration Federalism*. Cambridge: Cambridge University Press, 2015.

Gurulé, Ernest. "Latinos 50 Million Strong." *La Voz*, January 5, 2011.

Gutiérrez, Elena R. *Fertile Matters: The Politics of Mexican-Origin Women's Reproduction*. Austin: University of Texas Press, 2008.

Hacking, Ian. *Taming Chance*. Cambridge: Cambridge University Press, 1990.

¡Hagase Contar! *Census 2010: Talking Points—General Awareness*. Los Angeles: Ya es hora, 2009.

Hall, Jacquelyn D. "The Long Civil Rights Movement and the Political Use of the Past." *Journal of American History* 91, no. 4 (2005): 1233–63.

Hall, John R. "Social Futures of Global Climate Change: A Structural Phenomenology." *American Journal of Cultural Sociology* 4, no. 1 (2016): 1–45.

Hall, Stuart. "The Problem of Ideology-Marxism without Guarantees." *Journal of Communication Inquiry* 10, no. 2 (1986): 28–44.

Hanchard, Michael. "Afro-Modernity: Temporality, Politics, and the African Diaspora." *Public Culture* 11, no. 1 (1999): 245–68.

Handel, Jonathan. "Latinx Groups Picket Paramount Pictures for Second Time in Two Months." *Hollywood Reporter*, October 17, 2018. https://www.hollywoodreporter.com/news/nhmc-nhla-picket-paramount-pictures-second-time-two-months-1153274.

Hanson, Victor Davis. *Mexifornia: A State of Becoming*. New York: Encounter Books, 2007.

———. "Never What?" *National Review*, March 12, 2019.

Hartog, François. *Regimes of Historicity: Presentism and Experiences of Time*. New York: Columbia University Press, 2015.

Hattam, Victoria. "Ethnicity & the Boundaries of Race: Rereading Directive 15." *Dædalus* 134, no. 1 (2005): 61–69.

———. *In the Shadow of Race: Jews, Latinos, and Immigrant Politics in the United States*. Chicago: University of Chicago Press, 2007.

Herda, Daniel. "How Many Immigrants? Foreign-Born Population Innumeracy in Europe." *Public Opinion Quarterly* 74, no. 4 (2010): 674–95.

Hesse, Barnor. "Counter-Racial Formation Theory." In *Conceptual Aphasia in Black: Displacing Racial Formation*, edited by P. Khalil Saucier and Tyron P. Woods, vii–xi. Lanham, MD: Lexington Books, 2016.

———. "Racialized Modernity: An Analytics of White Mythologies." *Ethnic and Racial Studies* 30, no. 4 (2007): 643–63.

Hillygus, D. Sunshine, Norman H. Nie, Kenneth Prewitt, and Heili Pals. *The Hard Count: The Political and Social Challenges of Census Mobilization*. New York: Russell Sage Foundation, 2006.

Hirschman, Daniel. "Stylized Facts in the Social Sciences." *Sociological Science* 3 (2016): 604–26.

Hitlin, Steven, J. Scott Brown, and Glen H. Elder, Jr. "Measuring Latinos: Racial vs. Ethnic Classification and Self-Understandings." *Social Forces* 86, no. 2 (2007): 587–611.

Hobsbawm, Eric. "Introduction: Inventing Traditions." In *The Invention of Tradition*, edited by Eric Hobsbawm and Terence Ranger, 1–14. Cambridge: Cambridge University Press, 1992.

Hodgson, Dennis. "Benjamin Franklin on Population: From Policy to Theory." *Population and Development Review* 17, no. 4 (1991): 639–61.

———. "Demography as Social Science and Policy Science." *Population and Development Review* 9, no. 1 (1983): 1–34.

Hoff, Derek S. "'Kick That Population Commission in the Ass': The Nixon Administration, the Commission on Population Growth and the American Future, and the Defusing of the Population Bomb." *Journal of Policy History* 22, no. 1 (January 2010): 23–63.

Hoffmann, Stefan-Ludwig, and Sean Franzel. "Introduction: Translating Koselleck." In *Sediments of Time: On Possible Histories*, iv–xxxi. Stanford, CA: Stanford University Press, 2018.

Hollinger, David A. "Amalgamation and Hypodescent: The Question of Ethnoracial Mixture in the History of the United States." *American Historical Review* 108, no. 5 (December 2003): 1363–90.

Huntington, Samuel P. "Hispanic Challenge." *Foreign Policy*, October 28, 2009, 30–45. https:// foreignpolicy.com/2009/10/28/the-hispanic-challenge/.

Igo, Sarah E. *The Averaged American: Surveys, Citizens, and the Making of a Mass Public*. Cambridge, MA: Harvard University Press, 2007.

Israel, Esteban. "Fearful, Angry Latinos Might Shun Census." *Reuters*, March 31, 2010. https://www .reuters.com/article/us-usa-latinos/fearful-angry-latinos-might-shun-census-idUSTRE62 U4RY20100331.

Itzigsohn, José, and Karida L. Brown. *The Sociology of WEB Du Bois: Racialized Modernity and the Global Color Line*. New York: NYU Press, 2020.

James, Frank. "Census Poster Tie-in to Jesus, Mary and Joseph Inflames Some." NPR, December 2009. https://www.npr.org/sections/thetwo-way/2009/12/census_poster_tiein_to_jesus _m.html.

Jasper, James M. "Emotions and Social Movements: Twenty Years of Theory and Research." *Annual Review of Sociology* 37 (2011): 285–303.

Johnson, Nuala. "Cast in Stone: Monuments, Geography, and Nationalism." *Environment and Planning D: Society and Space* 13, no. 1 (1995): 51–65.

Jones, Jennifer A. *The Browning of the New South*. Chicago: University of Chicago Press, 2019.

Jordan, Miriam. "Groups Seek Better Count of Hispanics." *Wall Street Journal*, 2009. https://www.wsj.com/articles/SB125435725382154619.

Judis, John B., and Ruy Teixeira. *The Emerging Democratic Majority*. New York: Scribner, 2002.

Kaplowitz, Craig Allan. *LULAC, Mexican Americans, and National Policy*. Austin: Texas A&M University Press, 2005.

Kaufmann, Eric P. "'It's the Demography, Stupid': Ethnic Change and Opposition to Immigration." *Political Quarterly* 85, no. 3 (2014): 267–76.

———. *Whiteshift: Populism, Immigration and the Future of White Majorities*. New York: Abrams Press, 2018.

Kayyali, Randa. "US Census Classifications and Arab Americans: Contestations and Definitions of Identity Markers." *Journal of Ethnic and Migration Studies* 39, no. 8 (2013): 1299–1318.

Keating, Dan, and Carol Morello. "Census Offers New Proof That Hispanic, Asian Growth Sky-rocketed in the Past Decade." *Washington Post*, March 24, 2011. https://www.washingtonpost.com/local/new-census-portrait-hispanics-and-asians-skyrocketed-over-past-decade/2011/03/23/ABpKDQOB_story.html.

Kertzer, David I., and Dominique Arel. "Censuses, Identity Formation, and the Struggle for Political Power." In *Census and Identity: The Politics of Race, Ethnicity, and Language in National Censuses*, edited by David I. Kertzer and Dominique Arel, 1–42. Cambridge: Cambridge University Press, 2001.

Keyfitz, Nathan. "The Social and Political Context of Population Forecasting." In *The Politics of Numbers*, edited by William Alonso and Paul Starr, 235–58. New York: Russell Sage Foundation, 1987.

Khalid, Asma. "Latinos Will Never Vote for a Republican, and Other Myths about Hispanics from 2016." NPR, December 22, 2016. https://www.npr.org/2016/12/22/506347254/latinos-will-never-vote-for-a-republican-and-other-myths-about-hispanics-from-20.

Kil, Sang Hea. "Fearing Yellow, Imagining White: Media Analysis of the Chinese Exclusion Act of 1882." *Social Identities* 18, no. 6 (2012): 663–77.

King, Jr., Martin Luther. *Why We Can't Wait*. London: Penguin Books, 2000.

Kollman, Ken. *Outside Lobbying: Public Opinion and Interest Group Strategies*. Princeton, NJ: Princeton University Press, 1998.

Koselleck, Reinhart. *Futures Past: On the Semantics of Historical Time*. Translated by Keith Tribe. New York: Columbia University Press, 1979.

———. *Sediments of Time: On Possible Histories*. Edited by Sean Franzel and Stefan-Ludwig Hoffmann. Stanford, CA: Stanford University Press, 2018.

Kotkin, Joel. "Lack of Clout: Leaders Blame Reluctance to Use Electoral Process." *Washington Post*, March 29, 1978.

Kravel-Tovi, Michal. "Accounting of the Soul: Enumeration, Affect, and Soul Searching among American Jewry." *American Anthropologist* 120, no. 4 (2018): 711–24.

Kreager, Philip. "Objectifying Demographic Identities." In *Categories and Contexts: Anthropological and Historical Studies in Critical Demography*, edited by Simon Szreter, Hania Sholkamy, and A. Dharmalingam, 33–56. Oxford: Oxford University Press, 2004.

Kreiss, Daniel. *Prototype Politics: Technology-Intensive Campaigning and the Data of Democracy*. New York: Oxford University Press, 2016.

———. *Taking Our Country Back: The Crafting of Networked Politics from Howard Dean to Barack Obama*. New York: Oxford, 2012.

Kumar, Maria Teresa. "Mr. President, Sign Immigration Executive Action." MSNBC, November 13, 2014. http://www.msnbc.com/msnbc/obama-sign-immigration-executive-action.

Kurtzleben, Danielle. "7 Ways the U.S. Population Is Changing." *US News*, May 13, 2011. https://www.usnews.com/news/slideshows/7-ways-the-us-population-is-changing.

La Opinión. "El Voto Latino Pesó," November 7, 2012. https://laopinion.com/2012/11/07/el-voto -latino-peso-2/.

Lakoff, Andrew. "Preparing for the Next Emergency." *Public Culture* 19, no. 2 (2007): 247–71.

Latino Decisions. "Lies, Damn Lies, and Exit Polls," November 10, 2016. https://latinodecisions. com/blog/lies-damn-lies-and-exit-polls/

Latino Rebels. "Despite Trump Letter Being Retracted, LULAC Young Adults and Collegiate Groups Call for Rocha's Resignation," February 1, 2018. https://www.latinorebels.com/2018 /02/01/despite-trump-letter-being-retracted-lulac-young-adults-and-collegiate-groups-call -for-rochas-resignation/.

———. "Immigration Activists Applaud NCLR Leader's 'Deporter-in-Chief' Obama Comments," March 4, 2014. https://www.latinorebels.com/2014/03/04/immigration-activists-applaud -nclr-leaders-deporter-in-chief-obama-comments/.

———. "LULAC President's Letter to Trump Says His Organization Agrees with White House Immigration Framework," January 31, 2018. https://www.latinorebels.com/2018/01/31/lulac -presidents-letter-to-trump-says-his-organization-agrees-with-white-house-immigration -framework/.

———. "The Problem with Pew Polls about Being Latino (or Hispanic) in America: Too Many Labels," April 6, 2012.

Latour, Bruno. *Science in Action.* Cambridge, MA: Harvard University Press, 1987.

Laurent, Brice. "Technologies of Democracy: Experiments and Demonstrations." *Science and Engineering Ethics* 17, no. 4 (2011): 646–66.

League of United Latin American Citizens (LULAC). "Latino Groups Issue House of Representatives 'Incomplete' Grade on Immigration and a Pledge Card for Action." News release, December 10, 2013.

———. "LULAC Applauds Gang of Eight's Consensus Leading to Swift Immigration Reform." News release, May 22, 2013.

———. "LULAC Decries Obama's Militarization of the US Border with Mexico." News release, May 26, 2010.

———. "LULAC Responds to Rocha Letter." News release, February 1, 2018.

———. "Senate Passes Historic Bipartisan Immigration Reform; LULAC Urges House to Do the Same." News release, June 27, 2013.

———. "Victory in the Senate with the Halt of the Vitter Amendment." News release, November 5, 2009.

Lee, Erika. *At America's Gates: Chinese Immigration during the Exclusion era, 1882–1943.* Chapel Hill: University of North Carolina Press, 2003.

———. *America for Americans: A History of Xenophobia in the United States.* New York: Basic Books, 2019.

Lee, Jennifer, and Frank D. Bean. *The Diversity Paradox: Immigration and the Color Line in Twenty-First Century America.* New York: Russell Sage Foundation, 2010.

Leeman, Jennifer. "Racializing Language: A History of Linguistic Ideologies in the US Census." *Journal of Language and Politics* 3, no. 3 (2004): 507–34.

Levitt, Peggy. *Artifacts and Allegiances: How Museums Put the Nation and the World on Display.* Berkeley: University of California Press, 2015.

Levs, Josh. "The New America: What the Election Teaches Us about Ourselves." CNN, November 9, 2012. https://www.cnn.com/2012/11/09/politics/election-new-america/index .html.

Lew-Williams, Beth. *The Chinese Must Go: Violence, Exclusion, and the Making of the Alien in America.* Cambridge, MA: Harvard University Press, 2018.

Lin, Joanne. "Deporter-in-Chief." *Huffington Post*, February 5, 2014. https://www.huffpost.com/entry/deporter-in-chief_b_4733456.

Lincoln, Ross A. "Latino Group NHLA Joins Call for Greater Diversity at Paramount." *Wrap*, October 16, 2018. https://www.thewrap.com/latino-group-nhla-joins-call-for-greater-diversity-at-paramount/.

Lindsey, Robert. "Hispanics Lead U.S. Minorities in Growth Rate." *New York Times*, February 18, 1979. https://www.nytimes.com/1979/02/18/archives/hispanics-lead-us-minorities-in-growth-rate-hispanic-minority.html.

Liptak, Adam. "Supreme Court Speeds Case on Excluding Undocumented Immigrants in Redistricting." *New York Times*, October 14, 2020. https://www.nytimes.com/2020/09/30/us/supreme-court-census-undocumented.html.

Llenas, Bryan. "'Record' Hispanic Voter Turnout in 2012 a Misnomer, Census Numbers Show." *Fox News*, May 9, 2013. https://www.foxnews.com/politics/record-hispanic-voter-turnout-in-2012-a-misnomer-census-numbers-show.

Lloréns, Hilda. *Imaging the Great Puerto Rican Family: Framing Nation, Race, and Gender during the American Century*. Lanham, MD: Lexington Books, 2014.

Llorente, Elizabeth. "Election 2012: Obama Wins Re-Election, Clinches Latino Vote." *Fox News*, November 6, 2012. https://www.foxnews.com/politics/election-2012-obama-wins-re-election-clinches-latino-vote.

———. "Obama Victory Proof That the Sleeping Latino Giant Is Wide Awake." *Fox News*, November 8, 2012. https://www.foxnews.com/politics/obama-victory-proof-that-the-sleeping-latino-giant-is-wide-awake.

"Looking Ahead." *Agenda: A Journal of Hispanic Issues* 10, no. 1 (January/February 1980).

López, Mark Hugo, and Ana González-Barrera. *Inside the 2012 Latino Electorate*. Washington, DC: Pew Hispanic Center, 2013.

López, Nancy. "Killing Two Birds with One Stone? Why We Need Two Separate Questions on Race and Ethnicity in the 2020 Census and Beyond." *Latino Studies* 11, no. 3 (2013): 428–38.

Lotesta, Johnnie. "The Myth of the Business Friendly Economy: Making Neoliberal Reforms in the Worst State for Business." *American Journal of Cultural Sociology* 7, no. 2 (2019): 214–45.

Love, Erik. *Islamophobia and Racism in America*. New York: NYU Press, 2017.

Loveman, Mara. "The Modern State and the Primitive Accumulation of Symbolic Power." *American Journal of Sociology* 110, no. 6 (2005): 1651–83.

———. *National Colors: Racial Classification and the State in Latin America*. Oxford: Oxford University Press, 2014.

———. "The U.S. Census and the Contested Rules of Racial Classification in Early Twentieth-Century Puerto Rico." *Caribbean Studies* 35, no. 2 (2007): 79–114.

Lowry, Ira S. *The Science and Politics of Ethnic Enumeration*. Santa Monica, CA: Rand Corporation, 1980.

Lujan, Carol Chiago. "American Indians and Alaska Natives Count: The US Census Bureau's Efforts to Enumerate the Native Population." *American Indian Quarterly* 38, no. 3 (2014): 319–41.

Macdonald, Victoria-María, and Benjamin Polk Hoffman. "'Compromising La Causa?': The Ford Foundation and Chicano Intellectual Nationalism in the Creation of Chicano History, 1963–1977." *History of Education Quarterly* 52, no. 2 (2012): 251–81.

Macías, Reynaldo F. "U.S. Hispanics in 2000 A.D.—Projecting the Number." *Agenda: A Journal of Hispanic Issues* 7, no. 3 (May/June 1977): 16–19.

Magaña-Salgado, José. *Detention, Deportation, and Devastation: The Disproportionate Effect of Deportations on the Latino Community*. Mexican American Legal Defense and Educational Fund, National Day Laborer Organizing Network, and National Hispanic Leadership Agenda, 2014.

Maghbouleh, Neda. "From White to What? MENA and Iranian American Non-White Reflected Race." *Ethnic and Racial Studies* 43, no. 4 (2020): 613–31.

Mahadeo, Rahsaan. "Why Is the Time Always Right for White and Wrong for Us? How Racialized Youth Make Sense of Whiteness and Temporal Inequality." *Sociology of Race and Ethnicity* 5, no. 2 (2019): 186–99.

Mallard, Grégoire. "From Europe's Past to the Middle East's Future: The Constitutive Purpose of Forward Analogies in International Security." *American Journal of Cultural Sociology* 6 (October 2018): 532–62.

Mallard, Grégoire, and Andrew Lakoff. "How Claims to Know the Future Are Used to Understand the Present: Techniques of Prospection in the Field of National Security." In *Social Knowledge in the Making*, edited by Charles Camic, Neil Gross, and Michèle Lamont, 339–77. Chicago: University of Chicago Press, 2011.

Marshall, Emily A. "Population Projections and Demographic Knowledge in France and Great Britain in the Postwar Period." *Population and Development Review* 41, no. 2 (2015): 271–300.

Marquez, Benjamin. *LULAC: The Evolution of a Mexican American Political Organization*. Austin: University of Texas Press, 1993.

———. "Mexican-American Political Organizations and Philanthropy: Bankrolling a Social Movement." *Social Service Review* 77, no. 3 (2003): 329–46.

———. "Trial by Fire: The Ford Foundation and MALDEF in the 1960s." *Politics, Groups, and Identities* 8, no. 4 (2020): 661–76.

Marres, Noortje. *Material Participation: Technology, the Environment, and Everyday Publics*. New York: Palgrave Macmillan, 2012.

Masi de Casanova, Erynn. "Spanish Language and Latino Ethnicity in Children's Television Programs." *Latino Studies* 5 (2007): 455–77.

Massumi, Brian. *Parables for the Virtual: Movement, Affect, Sensation*. Durham, NC: Duke University Press, 2002.

Marsh, Wendell. "U.S. Hispanic Population Tops 50 Million." *Reuters*, March 24, 2011. https://www.reuters.com/article/us-census-hispanics/u-s-hispanic-population-tops-50-million-idUSTRE72N5OC20110324.

Martinez, Michael, and David Ariosto. "Hispanic Population Exceeds 50 Million, Firmly Nation's No. 2 Group." CNN, March 24, 2011. http://www.cnn.com/2011/US/03/24/census.hispanics/index.html.

Massey, Douglas S., and Karen A. Pren. "Unintended Consequences of US Immigration Policy: Explaining the Post-1965 Surge from Latin America." *Population and Development Review* 38, no. 1 (March 2012): 1–29.

McArthur, Loren. "The Latino Vote Can Make a Difference in the 2014 Elections." *Huffington Post*, January 23, 2014. https://www.huffpost.com/entry/the-latino-vote-can-make-_b_4654424.

McCann, Carole R. *Figuring the Population Bomb: Gender and Demography in the Mid-Twentieth Century*. Seattle: University of Washington Press, 2016.

McCarthy, John D. and Mayer N. Zald. *The Trend of Social Movements in America: Professionalization and Resource Mobilization*. Morristown, NJ: General Learning Press, 1977.

McConnell, Eileen Díaz. "Numbers, Narratives, and Nation: Mainstream News Coverage of U.S. Latino Population Growth, 1990–2010." *Sociology of Race and Ethnicity* 5, no. 4 (2018): 500–517.

———. "An 'Incredible Number of Latinos and Asians': Media Representations of Racial and Ethnic Population Change in Atlanta, Georgia." *Latino Studies* 9, no. 2–3 (2011): 177–97.

McConnell, Eileen Díaz, and Edward A. Delgado-Romero. "Latino Panethnicity: Reality or Methodological Construction?" *Sociological Focus* 37, no. 4 (2004): 297–312.

McDonnell, Terence E. *Best Laid Plans: Cultural Entropy and the Unraveling of Aids Media Campaigns*. Chicago: University of Chicago Press, 2016.

Meckler, Laura, and Aaron Zitner. "Donald Trump's Win Bucks Warnings from GOP, Democrats to Improve Hispanic Outreach." *Wall Street Journal*, November 18, 2016. https://www.wsj.com/articles/trumps-win-calls-warnings-over-hispanic-voter-disconnect-into-question-1479414368.

Medina, Eliseo. "Immigration Policy a GOP Weak Spot." *Politico*, April 21, 2010. https://www.politico.com/story/2010/04/immigration-policy-a-gop-weak-spot-036096.

Medvetz, Thomas. "Murky Power: 'Think Tanks' as Boundary Organizations." *Research in the Sociology of Organizations* 34 (2012): 113–33.

Mennicken, Andrea, and Wendy Nelson Espeland. "What's New with Numbers? Sociological Approaches to the Study of Quantification." *Annual Review of Sociology* 45 (2019): 223–45.

Merchant, Emily Klancher. "A Digital History of Anglophone Demography and Global Population Control, 1915–1984." *Population and Development Review* 43, no. 1 (2017): 83–117.

Merton, Robert K., and Patricia L. Kendall. "The Focused Interview." *American Journal of Sociology* 51, no. 6 (1946): 541–57.

Mexican American Legal Defense and Educational Fund (MALDEF). "Lawsuit on 2020 Census Citizenship Question Updated to Include Native American Groups and Charge Government Conspiracy." News release, July 9, 2018. https://www.maldef.org/2018/07/lawsuit-on-2020-census-citizenship-question-updated-to-include-native-american-groups-and-charge-government-conspiracy/.

Mijente. "Principles of Unity," June 30, 2018. https://mijente.net/2018/06/mijente-principles/

Miles, Reid. "Hispanic Americans Soon: The Biggest Minority." *TIME*, October 16, 1978.

Mills, Charles W. "White Time: The Chronic Injustice of Ideal Theory." *Du Bois Review* 11, no. 1 (2014): 27–42.

Minta, Michael D. "Diversity and Minority Interest Group Advocacy in Congress." *Political Research Quarterly* 73, no. 1 (2020): 208–20.

Mische, Ann. "Measuring Futures in Action: Projective Grammars in the Rio+20 Debates." *Theory and Society* 43, no. 3 (2014): 437–64.

———. "Projects and Possibilities: Researching Futures." *Sociological Forum* 24, no. 3 (2009): 694–704.

Miyawaki, Michael Hajime. "Part-Latinos and Racial Reporting in the Census: An Issue of Question Format?" *Sociology of Race and Ethnicity* 2, no. 3 (2016): 289–306.

Molavi, Shourideh C. *Stateless Citizenship: The Palestinan-Arab Citizens of Israel*. Boston: Brill, 2013.

Molina, Natalia. *How Race Is Made in America: Immigration, Citizenship and the Historical Power of Racial Scripts*. Berkeley: University of California Press, 2014.

———. "Medicalizing the Mexican: Immigration, Race, and Disability in the Early-Twentieth-Century United States." *Radical History Review* 2006, no. 94 (2006): 22–37.

Mora, G. Cristina. "Cross-Field Effects and Ethnic Classification: The Institutionalization of Hispanic Panethnicity, 1965 to 1990." *American Sociological Review* 79, no. 2 (2014): 183–210.

———. "Latinx and the US Census." *Oxford Research Encyclopedia of American History* (forthcoming).

———. *Making Hispanics: How Activists, Bureaucrats, and Media Constructed a New American*. Chicago: University of Chicago Press, 2014.

Mora, G. Cristina, and Dina G. Okamoto. "Postcolonialism, Racial Political Fields, and Panethnicity: A Comparison of Early 'Asian American' and 'Hispanic' Movements." Sociology of Race and Ethnicity 6, no. 4 (2020): 450–67.

Mora, G. Cristina, and Michael Rodríguez-Muñiz. "Latinos, Race, and the American Future: A Response to Richard Alba's 'The Likely Persistence of a White Majority.'" *New Labor Forum* 20, no. 2 (2017): 40–46.

Morales, Ed. *Latinx: The New Force in American Politics and Culture*. London: Verso, 2019.

Morello, Carol, and Ted Mellnik. "Census: Minority Babies Are Now Majority in United States." *Washington Post*, May 17, 2012. https://www.washingtonpost.com/local/census-minority-babies-are-now-majority-in-united-states/2012/05/16/gIQA1WY8UU_story.html.

Morello, Carol and Ed O'Keefe. "Hispanic Leaders Disagree over Christmas-themed Census Poster." *Washington Post*, December 16, 2009. https://www.washingtonpost.com/wp-dyn/content/article/2009/12/15/AR2009121502928.html

Morning, Ann. *The Nature of Race: How Scientists Think and Teach about Human Difference*. Berkeley: University of California Press, 2011.

Morning, Ann, and Daniel Sabbagh. "From Sword to Plowshare: Using Race for Discrimination and Antidiscrimination in the United States." *International Social Science Journal* 57, no. 183 (2005): 57–73.

Motomura, Hiroshi. *Americans in Waiting: The Lost Story of Immigration and Citizenship in the United States*. New York: Oxford University Press, 2006.

Muhammad, Khalil Gibran. *The Condemnation of Blackness*. Cambridge, MA: Harvard University Press, 2010.

Murguía, Janet. "Diverse Identities but Much Common Ground." Pew Hispanic Research Center, 2012. http://www.pewhispanic.org/2012/05/31/janet-murguia-diverse-identities-but-much-common-ground/.

———. "The El Paso Shooting Is the Violence Latinos Have Been Dreading." *New York Times*, August 6, 2019. https://www.nytimes.com/2019/08/06/opinion/el-paso-shooting-latino.html.

———."Hispanic Values Are American Values." *Wall Street Journal*, April 22, 2011. https://www.wsj.com/articles/SB10001424052748703916004576270451847726580.

———. "The Latino Vote: 'The New Normal.'" *Huffington Post*, November 16, 2012. https://www.huffpost.com/entry/the-latino-vote-the-new-n_b_2145251.

———. "Your Voice Is More Important Now than Ever Before." UnidosUS, November 10, 2016.

Myers, Dowell, and Morris Levy. "Racial Population Projections and Reactions to Alternative News Accounts of Growing Diversity." *Annals of the American Academy of Political and Social Science* 677, no. 1 (2018): 215–28.

NAACP Legal Defense and Educational Fund. *Count on Change! Why You Should Participate in the 2010 Census*. New York: NAACP, 2010.

Nakamura, David. "Obama: 'I'm the Champion-in-Chief' on Immigration Reform." *Washington Post*, March 6, 2014. https://www.washingtonpost.com/news/post-politics/wp/2014/03/06/obama-im-the-champion-in-chief-on-immigration-reform/.

Nakamura, David, and Ed O'Keefe. "Immigration Reform Effectively Dead until after Obama Leaves Office, Both Sides Say." *Washington Post*, June 26, 2014. https://www.washingtonpost.com/politics/immigration-reform-deal-now-unlikely-until-after-obama-leaves-office-both-sides-say/2014/06/26/945d1210-fc96-11e3-b1f4-8e77c632c07b_story.html.

National Association of Latino Elected and Appointed Officials Educational Fund (NALEO-EF). "Census Bureau Proposed Combined Race and Ethnicity Question Offers Best Option for Improving Data on Latinos." News Release, June 12, 2017.

———. *Hispanic Origin and Race Questions in Census 2020*. 2019. https://hagasecontar.org/wp-content/uploads/2019/12/The-Hispanic-Origin-and-Race-Questions-in-Census-2020-Final.pdf.

———. "Largest Hispanic Evangelical Networks in the Nation Support an Accurate Count of the Latino Community in the 2010 Census." News release, December 15, 2009.

———. "Latinos Fuel Illinois Population Growth." News release, February 16, 2011.

———. "Latinos Key to Texas Population Growth." News release, February 18, 2011.

———. "Latinos Play Major Role in Nation's Growth." News release, March 25, 2011.

———. "NALEO Condemns Vitter-Bennett Amendment as Effort to Suppress Latino Census Count." News release, October 16, 2009.

———. "NALEO Educational Fund Urges Swift Confirmation of Dr. Robert Groves as Director of U.S. Census Bureau." News release, May 19, 2009.

———. "Nevada Latino Population Skyrockets." News release, February 25, 2011.

———. "New Census Analysis Confirms Record Latino Vote in Election 2012." News release, May 8, 2013.

———. "New Jersey Owes Population Growth to Latino Community." News release, February 4, 2011.

———. "New Report Outlines Problems Experienced by Latino Voters in Election 2016." News release, November 21, 2016.

———. "North Carolina Latino Population Swells." News release, March 3, 2011.

National Council of La Raza (NCLR). *Impact of Limited Federal Statistical Data/Information on Hispanic Americans*. Washington, DC: National Council of La Raza, June 1974.

———. *Using NCLR's Latino Kids Data Explorer to Teach Demographic and Social Change*. Washington, DC: National Council of La Raza, 2013.

National Education Association. *The Invisible Minority . . . Pero No Vencibles: Report of the Nea-Tucson Survey on the Teaching of Spanish to the Spanish-Speaking*. Washington, DC: National Education Association, 1966.

National Hispanic Leadership Agenda (NHLA). "Latino Leaders Condemn White House's Proposed Immigration Framework." News release, January 29, 2018.

———. "Latino Leaders Mourn the Deaths in El Paso and Dayton, Demand Unequivocal Opposition to Hate-Filled Rhetoric and Dehumanizing Policies." News release, August 6, 2019.

———. "Letter to President Barack Obama." News release, January 16, 2013.

———. "NHLA Launches Latinos United for Immigration Reform Campaign and Plans for Unprecedented Mobilization of the Latino Community." News release, March 27, 2013.

———. "NHLA Statement on Bipartisan Senate Immigration Reform Plan." News release, January 28, 2013.

———. "NHLA Statement on President Obama's Immigration Proposal." News release, January 30, 2013.

———. *2012 Hispanic Public Policy Agenda*. Washington, DC: National Hispanic Leadership Agenda 2012.

———. *2016 Hispanic Public Policy Agenda*. Washington, DC: National Hispanic Leadership Agenda, 2016.

———. *2020–2024 Hispanic Public Policy Agenda*. Washington, DC: National Hispanic Leadership Agenda, 2020.

National Journal. "The Growing Hispanic Population," April 7, 1979.

National Latino Civic Engagement Table. "National Latino Civic Engagement Table Reacts to 2016 Election and the Latino Vote." News release, November 10, 2016.

Navarrette, Ruben. "Don't Be Afraid of America's Changing Demographics." CNN, August 18, 2014. http://www.cnn.com/2014/08/18/opinion/navarrette-majority-minority-students -public-schools/index.html.

———. "Why The Latino Vote Didn't Save America." *Daily Beast*, November 6, 2016. https://www .thedailybeast.com/why-the-latino-vote-didnt-save-america.

Net, Núria. "Make Your Pledge: Census 2010." *Remezcla*, February 4, 2010. https://remezcla.com /culture/voto-latino-census-2010/.

New York Times. "How to Waste Money and Ruin the Census," editorial, October 19, 2009. https:// www.nytimes.com/2009/10/20/opinion/20tue1.html.

Newburger, Eric. *2010 Census Integrated Communications Program 2010 Census Website Assessment Report*. Washington, DC: U.S. Department of Commerce, 2012.

Ngai, Mae M. *Impossible Subjects: Illegal Aliens and the Making of Modern America.* Princeton, NJ: Princeton University Press, 2004.

Nicholls, Walter J. *The Dreamers: How the Undocumented Youth Movement Transformed the Immigrant Rights Debate.* Stanford, CA: Stanford University Press, 2013.

———. *The Immigrant Rights Movement: The Battle over National Citizenship.* Stanford, CA: Stanford University Press, 2019.

Nicholls, Walter J., and Justus Uitermark. "A Virtuous Nation and Its Deserving Immigrants: How the Immigrant Rights Movement Embraced Nationalism." *Social Movement Studies* (October 2019): 1–18.

Nicholls, Walter J., Justus Uitermark, and Sander van Haperen. "The Networked Grassroots: How Radicals Outflanked Reformists in the United States' Immigrant Rights Movement." *Journal of Ethnic and Migration Studies* 42, no. 6 (May 2016): 1036–54.

Nieves-Martinez, Erasmo. *Encouraging Science Education and Careers among Latinos.* Washington, DC: Congressional Hispanic Caucus Institute, 2011.

Nobles, Melissa. *Shades of Citizenship: Race and the Census in Modern Politics.* Stanford, CA: Stanford University Press, 2000.

Novie, Ross. *Voto Latino Presents: Be Counted Census PSA.* Voto Latino, March 14, 2010.

Obasogie, Osagie K. *Blinded by Sight: Seeing Race through the Eyes of the Blind.* Stanford: Stanford, CA: Stanford University Press, 2014.

O'Brien, Eileen. *The Racial Middle: Latinos and Asian Americans Living Beyond the Racial Divide.* New York: NYU Press, 2008.

Ollstein, Alice. "Latino Org in Chaos after Its Prez Goes Rogue, Endorses Trump Immigration Plan." *TPM*, January 30, 2018. https://talkingpointsmemo.com/dc/latino-org-in-chaos-after -its-prez-goes-rogue-endorses-trump-immigration-plan.

Omi, Michael, and Howard Winant. *Racial Formation in the United States: From the 1960s to the 1990s.* 2nd ed. New York: Routledge, 1994.

O'Neil, Shannon. "Immigration Reform Is Dead, Precisely When We Need It Most." *Foreign Policy*, June 13, 2014. https://foreignpolicy.com/2014/06/13/immigration-reform-is-dead-precisely -when-we-need-it-most/.

The Onion. "Hispanics Expected to Become Majority of U.S. Population by Middle of Father-in-Law's Rant," August 7, 2014. http://www.theonion.com/articles/hispanics-expected-to -become-majority-of-us-popula,36633/.

O'Sullivan, John. "The Latino Voting Surge That Never Happened." *National Review*, November 22, 2016. https://www.nationalreview.com/2016/11/hispanic-turnout-disappoints -democrats-undermines-permanent-majority-theory/.

Outten, H. Robert, Timothy Lee, Rui Costa-Lopes, Michael T. Schmitt, and Jorge Vala. "Majority Group Members' Negative Reactions to Future Demographic Shifts Depend on the Perceived Legitimacy of Their Status: Findings from the United States and Portugal." *Frontiers in Psychology* 9, no. FEB (2018): 1–12.

Overberg, Paul. "Census Change to Race, Ethnicity Questions Shelved by Trump Administration Delay." *Wall Street Journal*, January 30, 2018. https://www.wsj.com/articles/census-change -to-race-ethnicity-questions-shelved-by-trump-administration-delay-1517262931.

Padgett, Tim. "Still Black or White: Why the Census Misreads Hispanics." *TIME*, March 29, 2010. http://content.time.com/time/nation/article/0,8599,1975883,00.html.

Page, Benjamin, and Felix Reichling. *The Economic Impact of S. 744, the Border Security, Economic Opportunity, and Immigration Modernization Act.* Washington, DC: Congressional Budget Office, June 2013.

Painter, Nell Irvin. *The History of White People.* New York: Norton, 2010.

Paley, Julia. "Making Democracy Count: Opinion Polls and Market Surveys in the Chilean Political." *Cultural Anthropology* 16, no. 2 (2001): 135–64.

Pallares, Amalia. *Family Activism: Immigrant Struggles and the Politics of Noncitizenship.* New Brunswick, NJ: Rutgers University Press, 2014.

Pallares, Amalia, and Nilda Flores-González, eds. *¡Marcha!: Latino Chicago and the Immigrant Rights Movement.* Urbana: University of Illinois Press, 2010.

Park, Sun-Joon. "'Nobody Is Going to Die': An Ethnography of Hope, Indicators and Improvisations in HIV Treatment Programmes in Uganda." In *The World of Indicators: The Making of Governmental Knowledge through Quantification,* edited by Richard Rottenburg, Sally E. Merry, Sung-Joon Park, and Johanna Mugler, 188–219. Cambridge: Cambridge University Press, 2015.

Paschel, Tianna S. *Becoming Black Political Subjects: Movements and Ethno-Racial Rights in Colombia and Brazil.* Princeton, NJ: Princeton University Press, 2016.

Pascoe, Peggy. *What Comes Naturally: Miscegenation Law and the Making of Race in America.* New York: Oxford University Press, 2009.

Patler, Caitlin, and Roberto G. Gonzales. "Framing Citizenship: Media Coverage of Anti-Deportation Cases Led by Undocumented Immigrant Youth Organisations." *Journal of Ethnic and Migration Studies* 41, no. 9 (2015): 1453–74.

Perez, Samantha L., and Joshua Murray. "Latino Faces, Corporate Ties: Latino Advocacy Organizations and Their Board Membership." *Sociological Forum* 31, no. 1 (2015): 117–37.

Phillips, Steve. *Brown Is the New White: How the Demographic Revolution Has Created a New American Majority.* New York: New Press, 2016.

Polak, Fred. *The Image of the Future.* Translated by Elise Boulding. Amsterdam: Elsevier, 1973.

Poovey, Mary. "Figures of Arithmetic, Figures of Speech: The Discourse of Statistics in the 1830s." *Critical Inquiry* 19, no. 2 (1993): 256–76.

———. *A History of the Modern Fact: Problems of Knowledge in the Sciences of Wealth and Society.* Chicago: University of Chicago Press, 1998.

Porter, Theodore M. *The Rise of Statistical Thinking: 1820–1900.* Princeton, NJ: Princeton University Press, 1986.

Preston, Julia. "Latino Groups Warn Congress to Fix Immigration, or Else." *New York Times,* December 13, 2012. https://thecaucus.blogs.nytimes.com/2012/12/12/latino-groups-warn-congress-to-fix-immigration-or-else/.

———. "Latino Leaders Use Churches in Census Bid." *New York Times,* December 22, 2009. https://www.nytimes.com/2009/12/23/us/23latino.html.

Preston, Julia, and Fernanda Santos. "A Record Latino Turnout, Solidly Backing Obama." *New York Times,* November 8, 2012. https://www.nytimes.com/2012/11/08/us/politics/with-record-turnout-latinos-solidly-back-obama-and-wield-influence.html.

Prévost, Jean-Guy, and Jean-Pierre Beaud. *Statistics, Public Debate and the State, 1800–1945: A Social, Political and Intellectual History of Numbers.* New York: Routledge, 2015.

Prewitt, Kenneth. "Race in the 2000 Census: A Turning Point." In *The New Race Question: How the Census Counts Multiracial Individuals,* edited by Joel Perlmann and Mary C. Waters, 354–62. New York: Russell Sage Foundation, 2002.

———. *What Is Your Race? The Census and Our Flawed Efforts to Classify Americans.* Princeton, NJ: Princeton University Press, 2013.

Quezada, Martin, and Daniel Ortega. "La Raza or UnidosUS: What's in a Name?" *AZ Central,* July 14, 2017. https://www.azcentral.com/story/opinion/op-ed/2017/07/14/la-raza-unidosus-whats-name/469079001/.

Quillian, Lincoln. "Prejudice as a Response to Perceived Group Threat: Population Composition and Anti-Immigrant and Racial Prejudice in Europe." *American Sociological Review* 60, no. 4 (1995): 586–611.

Quisumbing King, Katrina. "Recentering U.S. Empire: A Structural Perspective on the Color Line." *Sociology of Race and Ethnicity* 5, no. 1 (January 2019): 11–25.

Ramírez, Ricardo. *Mobilizing Opportunities: The Evolving Latino Electorate and the Future of American Politics.* Charlottesville: University of Virginia Press, 2013.

Ramirez, Ricardo, and Olga Medina. *Catalysts and Barriers to Attaining Citizenship: An Analysis of Ya Es Hora ¡Ciudadania!* Washington, DC: National Council of La Raza, 2010.

Ramos Avalos, Jorge. "The Nameless Many," April 16, 2012. https://jorgeramos.com/en/the-nameless-many/.

Ramsden, Edmund. "Social Demography and Eugenics in the Interwar United States." *Population and Development Review* 29, no. 4 (2003): 547–93.

Reardon, Jenny. *Race to the Finish: Identity and Governance in an Age of Genomics.* Princeton, NJ: Princeton University Press, 2005.

Reed, Isaac A. *Interpretation and Social Knowledge: On the Use of Theory in the Human Sciences.* Chicago: University of Chicago Press, 2011.

Republican National Committee. *The Growth and Opportunity Project.* Washington, DC: National Republican Committee, 2013.

Reyes, Raul A. "National Council of La Raza's Rebranding as UnidosUS Is Smart, Inclusive Move." *NBC News*, July 11, 2017. https://www.nbcnews.com/news/latino/opinion-national-council-la-raza-s-rebranding-unidosus-smart-inclusive-n781856.

Roberts, Dorothy. *Fatal Invention: How Science, Politics, and Big Business Re-Create Race in the Twenty-First Century.* New York: New Press, 2011.

Roberts, Sam. "New Figure for 2010 Census: $1.6 Billion under Budget." *New York Times*, August 11, 2010. https://www.nytimes.com/2010/08/11/us/politics/11census.html.

Rodriguez, Cassaundra. "Fueling White injury Ideology: Public Officials' Racial Discourse in Support of Arizona Senate Bill 1070." Sociology of Race and Ethnicity 4, no. 1 (2018): 83–97.

Rodriguez, Cindy Y. "Latino Vote Key to Obama's Re-Election." CNN, November 9, 2012. https://www.cnn.com/2012/11/09/politics/latino-vote-key-election/index.html.

Rodríguez, Clara E., Michael H. Miyawaki, and Grigoris Argeros. "Latino Racial Reporting in the US: To Be or Not to Be." *Sociology Compass* 7, no. 5 (2013): 390–403.

Rodríguez, Ilia. "Telling Stories of Latino Population Growth in the United States: Narratives of Inter-ethnic Conflict in the Mainstream, Latino and African-American Press." *Journalism* 8, no. 5 (2007): 573–590.

Rodríguez-Muñiz, Michael. "Cultivating Consent: Nonstate Leaders and the Orchestration of State Legibility." *American Journal of Sociology* 123, no. 2 (2017): 385–425.

———. "Towards a Political Sociology of Demography." In *The New Handbook of Political Sociology: States, Parties, Movements, Citizenship and Globalization*, edited by Thomas Janoski, Cedric de Leon, Joya Misra and Isaac Martin, 384–406. Cambridge: Cambridge University Press, 2020.

Rosa, Jonathan. *Looking Like a Language, Sounding Like a Race: Raciolinguistic Ideologies and the Learning of Latinidad.* Oxford: Oxford University Press, 2019.

———. "Racializing Language, Regimenting Latinas/Os: Chronotope, Social Tense, and American Raciolinguistic Futures." *Language & Communication* 46 (January 2016): 106–17.

Rosa, Jonathan, and Vanessa Díaz. "Raciontologies: Rethinking Anthropological Accounts of Institutional Racism and Enactments of White Supremacy in the United States." *American Anthropologist* 122, no. 1 (2020): 120–32.

Rosa, Jonathan, and Nelson Flores. "Unsettling Race and Language: Toward a Raciolinguistic Perspective." *Language in Society* 46, no. 5 (2017): 621–47.

Rose, Nikolas. "Governing by Numbers: Figuring out Democracy." *Accounting Organizations and Society* 16, no. 7 (1991): 673–92.

Rose-Greenland, Fiona. "The Parthenon Marbles as Icons of Nationalism in Nineteenth-Century Britain." *Nations and Nationalism* 19, no. 4 (2013): 654–73.

Rosental, Claude. "Toward a Sociology of Public Demonstrations." *Sociological Theory* 31, no. 4 (2013): 343–65.

Ross, Janell. "Latino Voters 2012: Sleeping Giant Unlikely to Turn Population Growth into Power in November." *Huffington Post*, September 8, 2012. https://www.huffpost.com/entry/latino-voter-2012-population-power_n_1866131.

Rove, Karl. "More White Votes Alone Won't Save the GOP." *Wall Street Journal*, June 26, 2013. https://www.wsj.com/articles/SB10001424127887323873904578569480696746650.

Rowan, Helen. *The Mexican American*. Washington, DC: U.S. Commission on Civil Rights, 1968.

———. "A Minority Nobody Knows." *Atlantic Monthly*, June 1967, 47–52.

Rowland, Nicholas J., and Matthew J. Spaniol. "The Future Multiple." *Foresight* 17, no. 6 (2015): 556–73.

Rumbaut, Rubén. "The Making of a People." In *Hispanics and the Future of America*, edited by Marta Tienda and Faith Mitchell, 16–65. Washington, DC: National Research Council, 2006.

Russell, George. "It's Your Turn in the Sun." *TIME*, October 16, 1978.

Saavedra, Guadalupe. "On Powerlessness." *Agenda: A Journal of Hispanic Issue* (Summer 1976).

Sáenz, Rogelio, Cecilia Menjívar, and San Juanita Edilia Garcia. "Arizona's SB 1070: Setting Conditions for Violations of Human Rights Here and Beyond." In *Sociology and Human Rights: A Bill of Rights in the Twenty-First Century*, edited by Judith Blau and Mark Frezzo, 155–78. Thousand Oaks, CA: Pine Forge Press, 2012.

Saenz, Thomas A. "Rust Belt to Brown Belt: Attention to 2020 Election Should Change Trump Policies." *Huffington Post*, November 17, 2016. https://www.huffpost.com/entry/rust-belt-to-brown-belt_b_13021478.

———. "Trump Brown-Out: Senate Also Bears Responsibility for Ensuring Inclusive Cabinet." *Huffington Post*, February 1, 2017. https://www.huffpost.com/entry/trump-brown-out-senate-also-bears-responsibility_b_58929ba9e4b08ab684ca7b30.

Saito, Hiro. "Reiterated Commemoration: Hiroshima as National Trauma." *Sociological Theory* 24, no. 4 (2006): 353–76.

Salinas, Maria Elena, and Liz Balmaseda. *Yo Soy La Hija De Mi Padre (I Am My Father's Daughter)*. New York: HarperCollins, 2006.

Samora, Julian, ed. *La Raza: Forgotten Americans*. Notre Dame: University of Notre Dame Press, 1966.

Sanburn, Josh. "U.S. Steps Closer to a Future Where Minorities Are the Majority." *TIME*, June 25, 2015. https://time.com/3934092/us-population-diversity-census/.

Sánchez Barba, Héctor E. "Latinos Delivered, Now It Is Your Turn Mr. President." *Huffington Post*, November 16, 2012. https://www.huffpost.com/entry/obama-immigration-reform_b_2132431.

———. "NHLA's Latino Leaders Chart Bold Strategy to Advance Community Interests." *Huffington Post*, September 4, 2015. https://www.huffpost.com/entry/nhlas-latino-leaders-char_b_8085282.

Sanchez, Gabriel, and Matt A. Barreto. "In Record Numbers, Latinos Voted Overwhelmingly against Trump. We Did the Research." *Washington Post*, November 11, 2016. https://www.washingtonpost.com/news/monkey-cage/wp/2016/11/11/in-record-numbers-latinos-voted-overwhelmingly-against-trump-we-did-the-research/.

Sánchez, Héctor E., Andrea L. Delgado, and Rosa G. Saavedra. *Latino Workers in the United States*. Washington, DC: Labor Council for Latin American Advancement, 2011.

Santa Ana, Otto. *Brown Tide Rising: Metaphors of Latinos in Contemporary American Public Discourse*. Austin: University of Texas Press, 2002.

Sarlin, Benjy. "RNC Memo Cites Demographics, Bush, Sandy in Romney Loss." *TPM*, November 15, 2012. https://talkingpointsmemo.com/election2012/rnc-memo-cites-demographics-bush-sandy-in-romney-loss.

Sasser, Jade S. *On Infertile Ground: Population Control and Women's Rights in the Era of Climate Change*. New York: NYU Press, 2018.

Saulny, Susan. "Census Data Presents Rise in Multiracial Population of Youths." *New York Times*, 2011. https://www.nytimes.com/2011/03/25/us/25race.html.

Scherer, Michael. "Yo Decido: Why Latinos Will Pick the Next President." *TIME*, March 5, 2012.

Schor, Paul. *Counting Americans: How the US Census Classified the Nation*. Oxford: Oxford University Press, 2017.

Schultz, Susanne. "Demographic Futurity: How Statistical Assumption Politics Shape Immigration Policy Rationales in Germany." *Environment and Planning: Society and Space* 37, no. 4 (2019): 644–62.

———. "Reproducing the Nation: The New German Population Policy and the Concept of Demographization." *Distinktion: Scandinavian Journal of Social Theory* 16, no. 3 (2015): 337–61.

Schütz, Alfred. "Tiresias, or Our Knowledge of Future Events." *Social Research* 26, no. 1 (1959): 71–89.

Schweber, Libby. *Disciplining Statistics: Demography and Vital Statistics in France and England, 1830–1885*. Durham, NC: Duke University Press, 2006.

Scott, David. *Conscripts of Modernity: The Tragedy of Colonial Enlightenment*. Durham, NC: Duke University Press, 2004.

———. *Refashioning Futures: Criticism after Postcoloniality*. Princeton, NJ: Princeton University Press, 1999.

Scott, James C. *Seeing Like a State: How Certain Schemes to Improve the Human Condition Have Failed*. New Haven, CT: Yale University Press, 1998.

Seamster, Louise, and Victor Ray. "Against Teleology in the Study of Race: Toward the Abolition of the Progress Paradigm." *Sociological Theory* 36, no. 4 (2018): 315–42.

Selkirk, Kaethe, Cynthia Selin, and Ulrike Felt. "A Festival of Futures: Recognizing and Reckoning Temporal Complexity in Foresight." *Handbook of Anticipation* (2018): 1–23.

Seltzer, William, and Margo Anderson. "The Dark Side of Numbers: The Role of Population Data Systems in Human Rights Abuses." *Social Research* 68, no. 2 (2001): 481–513.

Shapin, Steven, and Simon Schaffer. *Leviathan and the Air-Pump: Hobbes, Boyle, and the Experimental Life*. Princeton, NJ: Princeton University Press, 2011.

Shear, Michael, and Julia Preston. "Deportation Policy Shift Is Signaled by Obama." *New York Times*, March 14, 2014. https://www.nytimes.com/2014/03/15/us/politics/deportation-policy-shift-is-signaled-by-obama.html.

Silber Mohamed, Heather. *The New Americans? Immigration, Protest, and the Politics of Latino Identity*. Lawrence: University Press of Kansas, 2017.

Silver, Patricia. *Sunbelt Diaspora: Race, Class, and Latino Politics in Puerto Rican Orlando*. Austin: University of Texas Press, 2020.

Simon, Patrick. "The Choice of Ignorance: The Debate on Ethnic and Racial Statistics in France." *French Politics, Culture & Society* 26, no. 1 (2008): 7–31.

Sink, Justin. "Obama Rebukes Deportation Criticism." *The Hill*, March 6, 2014. https://thehill.com/blogs/blog-briefing-room/200106-obama-rebukes-deportation-criticism.

Skrentny, John David. *The Minority Rights Revolution*. Cambridge, MA: Belknap Press of Harvard University Press, 2002.

Sohoni, Deenesh. "Restrictionist Discourse by the Numbers: The Framing of the Demographic Impacts of Immigration." *Social Problems* 64, no. 4 (2017): 476–96.

———. "Unsuitable Suitors: Anti-Miscegenation Laws, Naturalization Laws, and the Construction of Asian Identities." *Law & Society Review* 41, no. 3 (2007): 587–618.

Solinger, Rickie. "Bleeding across Time: First Principles of US Population Policy." In *Reproductive States: Global Perspectives on the Invention and Implementation of Population Policy*, edited by Rickie Solinger and Mie Nakachi, 63–97. Oxford: Oxford University Press, 2016.

St. George, Donna, and Brady Dennis. "Growing Share of Hispanic Voters Helped Push Obama to Victory." *Washington Post*, November 7, 2012. https://www.washingtonpost.com/politics /decision2012/growing-share-of-hispanic-voters-helped-push-obama-to-victory/2012/11/07 /b4087d0a-28ff-11e2-b4e0-346287b7e56c_story.html.

Stableford, Dylan. "Time Magazine Apologizes for Putting Non-Latino on 'Yo Decido' Cover." *Yahoo News*, February 24, 2012. https://news.yahoo.com/blogs/cutline/time-magazine -apologizes-putting-non-latino-yo-decido-170537015.html.

Stark, David, and Verena Paravel. "PowerPoint in Public: Digital Technologies and the New Morphology of Demonstration." *Theory, Culture and Society* 25, no. 5 (2008): 30–55.

Starr, Paul. "Social Categories and Claims in the Liberal State." *Social Research* 59, no. 2 (1992): 263–95.

Stavans, Ilan. "George Zimmerman, Hispanics, and the Messy Nature of American Identity." *Daily Beast*, April 6, 2012. https://www.thedailybeast.com/george-zimmerman-hispanics-and-the -messy-nature-of-american-identity.

Steinhauser, Jennifer. "Speaker 'Confident' of Deal with White House on Immigration." *New York Times*, November 8, 2012. https://www.nytimes.com/2012/11/09/us/politics/boehner -confident-of-deal-with-white-house-on-immigration.html.

Stelter, Brian. "U.S. Census Uses Telenovela to Reach Hispanics." *New York Times*, September 22, 2009. https://www.nytimes.com/2009/09/23/business/23telemundo.html.

Stengel, Richard. "America's New Decisionmakers." *TIME*, March 5, 2012.

Stern, Alexandra Minna. *Proud Boys and the White Ethnostate: How the Alt-Right Is Warping the American Imagination*. Boston: Beacon Press, 2019.

Steyn, Mark. "It's the Demography, Stupid." *Wall Street Journal*, January 4, 2006. https://www .wsj.com/articles/SB122531242161281449.

Stigler, Stephen M. *The History of Statistics: The Measurement of Uncertainty before 1900*. Cambridge, MA: Harvard University Press, 1986.

Stoddard, Lothrop. *The Rising Tide of Color against White World-Supremacy*. New York: Scribner, 2011.

Suarez, Ray. "Hispanics and National Politics: How Latinos Are Transforming the Electoral Map." *Foreign Affairs*, November 15, 2012. https://www.foreignaffairs.com/articles/2012-11 -15/hispanics-and-national-politics.

Suro, Roberto. "Here's What Happened with the Latino Vote." *New York Times*, November 9, 2016. https://www.nytimes.com/interactive/projects/cp/opinion/election-night-2016/heres-what -happened-with-the-latino-vote.

———. "The Power of the Latino Vote: Instant History, Media Narratives, and Policy Frameworks." In *Hidden Lives and Human Rights in the United States: Understanding the Controversies and Tragedies of Undocumented Immigration*, edited by Lois Ann Lorentzen, 205–23. Santa Barbara, CA: Praeger, 2014.

Tanton, John. "Witan Memo III." October 10, 1986. https://www.splcenter.org/fighting-hate /intelligence-report/2015/witan-memo-iii.

Tavernise, Sabrina. "Whites Account for under Half of Births in U.S." *New York Times*, May 17, 2012. https://www.nytimes.com/2012/05/17/us/whites-account-for-under-half-of-births-in-us.html.

———. "Fewer Births than Deaths among Whites in Majority of U.S. States." *New York Times*, June 20, 2018. https://www.nytimes.com/2018/06/20/us/white-minority-population.html.

———. "Why the Announcement of a Looming White Minority Makes Demographers Nervous." *New York Times*, November 22, 2018. https://www.nytimes.com/2018/11/22/us/white-americans-minority-population.html.

Tavory, Iddo, and Nina Eliasoph. "Coordinating Futures: Toward a Theory of Anticipation." *American Journal of Sociology* 118, no. 4 (2013): 908–42.

Taylor, Paul, Ana Gonzalez-Barrera, Jeffrey S. Passel, and Mark Hugo Lopez. *An Awakened Giant: The Hispanic Electorate Is Likely to Double by 2030*. Washington, DC: Pew Research Center, 2012.

Taylor, Paul, Mark Hugo Lopez, Jessica Martínez, and Gabriel Velasco. *When Labels Don't Fit: Hispanics and Their Views of Identity*. Washington, DC: Pew Research Center, 2012.

Teitelbaum, Michael S. "The Media Marketplace for Garbled Demography." *Population and Development Review* 30, no. 2 (2004): 317–27.

———. "Political Demography: Powerful Trends Under-Attended by Demographic Science." *Population Studies* 69, no. sup1 (2015): S87–S95.

Telles, Edward E. "Latinos, Race, and the U.S. Census." *Annals of the American Academy of Political and Social Science* 677, no. 1 (2018): 153–64.

Thompson, Debra. "Critical Race Temporality: Two Dimensions of Racial Time." Paper presented to Social Science and History Association, 2019.

———. "An Exoneration of Black Rage." *South Atlantic Quarterly* 116, no. 3 (2017): 457–81.

———. *The Schematic State: Race, Transnationalism, and the Politics of the Census*. Cambridge: Cambridge University Press, 2016.

Thompson, E. P. "Time, Work-Discipline, and Industrial Capitalism." *Past and Present* 38 (1967): 56–97.

Thornton, J. Mills. *Politics and Power in a Slave Society: Alabama, 1800–1860*. Baton Rouge: Louisiana State University Press, [1978] 2014.

Tichenor, Daniel J. *Dividing Lines: The Politics of Immigration Control in America*. Princeton, NJ: Princeton University Press, 2002.

Time Labs. "Find Out If Your State Is America's Past or Future." *TIME*, July 13, 2015. https://labs.time.com/story/census-demographic-projections-interactive/.

Timmerman, Kenneth R. "Trump Awakens the Sleeping Giant of America." *The Hill*, July 22, 2016. https://thehill.com/blogs/pundits-blog/presidential-campaign/288903-trump-awakens-the-sleeping-giant-of-america.

Tobar, Héctor. "How Latinos Are Shaping America's Future." *National Geographic*, July 2018, 86–103.

Trende, Sean. "The Case of the Missing White Voters." *RealClearPolitics*, November 8, 2012. https://www.realclearpolitics.com/articles/2012/11/08/the_case_of_the_missing_white_voters_116106-2.html.

———. "The Case of the Missing White Voters, Revisited." *Real Clear Politics*, 2013. https://www.realclearpolitics.com/articles/2013/06/21/the_case_of_the_missing_white_voters_revisited_118893.html.

Tufte, Edward R. *The Visual Display of Quantitative Information*. Cheshire, PA: Graphics Press, 2001.

Tuomi, Ilkka. "Chronotopes of Foresight: Models of Time-Space in Probabilistic, Possibilistic and Constructivist Futures." *Futures & Foresight Science* 1, no. 2 (June 2019): 1–15.

UnidosUS. "Trump's Plea for Unity in State of the Union Rings Hollow." News release, January 30, 2018.

Urla, Jacqueline. "Cultural Politics in an Age of Statistics: Numbers, Nations, and the Making of Basque Identity." *American Ethnologist* 20, no. 4 (1993): 818–43.

U.S. Census Bureau. "Census Bureau Announces Award of 2010 Census Communications Contract." News release, September 6, 2007.

———. "Census Bureau Launches 'Children Count Too' Awareness Campaign Featuring Nickelodeon's Dora the Explorer." News release, March 9, 2010.

———. "Census Information Centers." Washington, DC: Department of Commerce, 2020.

———. *Complete Count Committee Guide.* Washington, DC: Department of Commerce, 2008.

———. "U.S. Census Bureau Director Launches 'Indian Country Counts' 2010 Census Campaign at NCAI." News release, October 6, 2009.

———. "Most Children Younger than Age 1 Are Minorities, Census Bureau Reports." News release, May 17, 2012.

———. *2010 Census Integrated Communications Campaign Plan.* Washington, DC: Department of Commerce, 2008.

U.S. Commission on Civil Rights. *Counting the Forgotten: The 1970 Census Count of Persons of Spanish Speaking Background in the United States.* Washington, DC: Government Printing Office, 1974.

U.S. News & World Report. "Hispanics Push for Bigger Role in Washington," May 22, 1978.

Valdes, Gustavo. "Latino Officials See Big Hispanic Vote in 2012." CNN, June 23, 2011. http://www.cnn.com/2011/US/06/23/naleo.conference/index.html.

Valle, Ariana J. "Race and the Empire-State: Puerto Ricans' Unequal US Citizenship." *Sociology of Race and Ethnicity* 5, no. 1 (2019): 26–40.

Varela, Julio Ricardo. "LULAC President Says He Won't Resign over Trump Immigration Letter and Vows to Keep Fighting." *Latino USA*, February 1, 2018. https://www.latinousa.org/2018/02/01/lulac-president-says-wont-resign-trump-immigration-letter-vows-keep-fighting/.

———. "More Than 200 Entertainers, Activists and Leaders Sign Letter of Support for Latino Community after El Paso Shooting and Mississippi Ice Raids." *Latino USA*, August 16, 2019. https://www.latinousa.org/2019/08/16/queridafamilialetter/.

Vargas, Arturo. "Election 2012 and the Future of Latino Politics." *Huffington Post*, November 29, 2012. https://www.huffpost.com/entry/latinos-election-2012_b_2206867.

———. "Labels Aside, Latinos Share Common Values." Pew Hispanic Center, June 4, 2012.

———. "This Is the New Face of America." *Huffington Post*, March 25, 2011. https://www.huffpost.com/entry/this-is-the-new-face-of-america_b_840668.

Vélez-Vélez, Roberto. "All Puerto Rico with Vieques: Mobilizing Support through Social Skills and Field Dynamics." *Social Movement Studies* 14, no. 5 (2015): 539–56.

———. "Sixty Years before the Homicide: The Vieques Movement and Trauma Resolution." *American Journal of Cultural Sociology* 4, no. 1 (2016): 46–67.

Vespa, Jonathan, David M. Armstrong, and Lauren Medina. *Demographic Turning Points for the United States: Population Projections for 2020 to 2060 Population Estimates and Projections.* Washington, DC: U.S. Census Bureau, 2020.

Viatori, Maximilian. "Rift, Rupture and the Temporal Politics of Race in Ecuador: Whiteness and the Narration of Neoliberal Futures during and after the Cenepa War." *History and Anthropology* 26, no. 2 (2015): 187–205.

Vithayathil, Trina. "Counting Caste: Censuses, Politics, and Castelessness in India." *Politics & Society* 46, no. 4 (2018): 455–84.

Voices. "It's the Demography, Stupid." November 7, 2012. https://www.opensocietyfoundations.org/voices/it-s-demography-stupid.

Von Schnitzler, Antina. *Democracy's Infrastructure: Techno-Politics and Protest after Apartheid.* Princeton, NJ: Princeton University Press, 2016.

Voss, Kim, and Irene Bloemraad. *Rallying for Immigrant Rights: The Fight for Inclusion in 21st Century America.* Berkeley: University of California Press, 2011.

Waidzunas, Tom. "Young, Gay, and Suicidal: Dynamic Nominalism and the Process of Defining a Social Problem with Statistics." *Science, Technology & Human Values* 37, no. 2 (2012): 199–225.

Walker, Jack L. *Mobilizing Interest Groups in America: Patrons, Professions, and Social Movements.* Ann Arbor: University of Michigan Press, 1991.

Walker, Edward T., John D. McCarthy, and Frank Baumgartner. "Replacing Members with Managers? Mutualism among Membership and Nonmembership Advocacy Organizations in the United States." *American Journal of Sociology* 116, no. 4 (2011): 1284–1337.

Wang, Hansi Lo. "How the 2020 Census Citizenship Question Ended Up in Court." NPR, November 4, 2018. https://www.npr.org/2018/11/04/661932989/how-the-2020-census-citizenship-question-ended-up-in-court.

———. "How Trump Officials Cut the 2020 Census Short Amid the Pandemic." NPR, September 18, 2020. https://www.npr.org/2020/09/18/911960963/how-trump-officials-cut-the-2020-census-short-amid-the-pandemic.

———. "More than 2 Dozen States, Cities Sue to Block Census Citizenship Question." NPR, April 3, 2018. https://www.npr.org/2018/04/03/599159295/17-states-7-cities-sue-to-remove-2020-census-citizenship-question.

———. "Supreme Court Permits Trump Administration to End Census Counting Early." NPR, October 14, 2020. https://www.npr.org/2020/10/14/923565228/supreme-court-permits-trump-administration-to-end-census-counting-early.

———. "2020 Census to Keep Racial, Ethnic Categories Used in 2010." NPR, January 26, 2018. https://www.npr.org/2018/01/26/580865378/census-request-suggests-no-race-ethnicity-data-changes-in-2020-experts-say.

Weaver, Christopher. "Conceptual Census Super Bowl Ad: Bargain or Boondoggle?" NPR, February 8, 2010. https://www.npr.org/sections/health-shots/2010/02/super_bowl_ad_hypes_us_census.html.

Weiner, Myron. "Political Demography: An Inquiry into the Political Consequences of Population Change." In *Rapid Population Growth: Consequences and Policy Implications*, edited by Office of the Foreign Secretary National Academy of Sciences, 567–617. Baltimore: Johns Hopkins University Press, 1971.

Weiner, Myron, and Michael S. Teitelbaum. *Political Demography, Demographic Engineering.* New York: Berghahn Books, 2001.

Westoff, Charles. "The Commission on Population Growth and the American Future: Its Origins, Operations, and Aftermath." *Population Index* 39, no. 4 (1973): 491–507.

Wetherell, Margaret. *Affect and Emotion: A New Social Science Understanding.* London: SAGE Publications, 2012.

Wheaton, Sarah, and Steven Shepard. "Latino Groups Argue Exit Polls Were Too Generous to Trump." *Politico*, November 11, 2016. https://www.politico.com/story/2016/11/latino-groups-exit-polls-donald-trump-231268.

Whyte, Michael. "Episodic Fieldwork, Updating, and Sociability." *Social Analysis* 57, no. 1 (2013): 110–21.

Wines, Michael. "Deceased G.O.P. Strategist's Hard Drives Reveal New Details on the Census Citizenship Question." *New York Times*, May 30, 2019.

Wolfe, Patrick. *Traces of History: Elementary Structures of Race.* London: Verso Books, 2016.

Wong, Tom K. *The Politics of Immigration: Partisanship, Demographic Change, and American National Identity.* Oxford: Oxford University Press, 2017.

Woodward, Kathleen. *Statistical Panic: Cultural Politics and Poetics of the Emotions.* Durham, NC: Duke University Press, 2008.

Yackley, Joseph. "A Republican Post-Mortem: It's Demography, Stupid!" *Huffington Post*, November 11, 2012. https://www.huffingtonpost.co.uk/joseph-yackley/us-election-mitt-romney-gop-republican_b_2110744.html.

Young, Eric. "Faith Groups Mobilized to Raise Census Awareness with Jesus Story." *Christian Post Reporter*, December 16, 2009. https://test.christianpost.com/news/faith-groups-mobilized-to-raise-census-awareness.html

Yukich, Grace. "Constructing the Model Immigrant: Movement Strategy and Immigrant Deservingness in the New Sanctuary Movement." *Social Problems* 60, no. 3 (2013): 302–20.

Yzaguirre, Raúl. "The Decade for Hispanics." *Agenda: A Journal of Hispanic Issue* 10, no. 1 (January/February 1980): 2.

———. "Mexamerica." *Washington Post*, April 5 1978, letter to the editor.

Zarrugh, Amina. "Racialized Political Shock: Arab American Racial Formation and the Impact of Political Events." *Ethnic and Racial Studies* 39, no. 15 (2016): 2722–39.

Zeleny, Jeff, and Jim Rutenberg. "Divided U.S. Gives Obama More Time." *New York Times*, November 6, 2012. https://www.nytimes.com/2012/11/07/us/politics/obama-romney-presidential-election-2012.html.

Zepeda-Millán, Chris. *Latino Mass Mobilization: Immigration, Racialization, and Activism*. Cambridge: Cambridge University Press, 2017.

Zerubavel, Eviatar. "Lumping and Splitting: Notes on Classification." *Sociological Forum* 11, no. 3 (1996): 421–33.

Zuberi, Tukufu. *Thicker than Blood: How Racial Statistics Lie*. Minneapolis: University of Minnesota Press, 2001.

Zubrzycki, Geneviève. *Beheading the Saint: Nationalism, Religion, and Secularism in Quebec*. Chicago: University of Chicago Press, 2016.

Zubrzycki, Geneviève. *National Matters: Materiality, Culture, and Nationalism*. Stanford, CA: Stanford University Press, 2017.

INDEX

Note: page numbers followed by "f" and "n" or "nn" refer to figures and endnote(s), respectively.

A NOTE ON THE TYPE

This book has been composed in Adobe Text and Gotham.
Adobe Text, designed by Robert Slimbach for Adobe,
bridges the gap between fifteenth- and sixteenth-century
calligraphic and eighteenth-century Modern styles.
Gotham, inspired by New York street signs, was designed
by Tobias Frere-Jones for Hoefler & Co.